# The Shell Country Book

# THE SHELL
# COUNTRY BOOK

*by Geoffrey Grigson*

*with contributions by*
*John Mason, Ernest Neal*
*and W. J. Weston*

PHOENIX HOUSE LTD
LONDON

© Geoffrey Grigson 1962

Designed and produced by George Rainbird Ltd
2 Hyde Park Place, London w2
for
Phoenix House Ltd
10–13 Bedford Street, Strand, London wc2
Printed by the Aldine Press, Letchworth, Herts

First edition June 1962
Second edition September 1962

# Contents

## PART ONE: Man

CONTENTS

8

# PART THREE: Birds, Beasts, Insects and others

# About Birds     173

# PART FOUR: Flowers, Fruits, Foods

# PART FIVE: Man again

# COLOUR PLATES

A key to the plates will be found at the end of the book, on page 339.

13

14

*The endpapers of this book are from an
engraving by Thomas Bewick.*

Of Albion's glorious isle the wonders whilst I write,
The sundry varying soils, the pleasures infinite
(Where heat kills not the cold, nor cold expels the heat,
The calms too mildly small, nor winds too roughly great,
Nor night doth hinder day, nor day the night doth wrong,
The summer not too short, the winter not too long)
What help shall I invoke to aid my Muse the while?
    Thou Genius of the place (this most renownèd isle). . .
Go thou before me still thy circling shores about,
And in this wand'ring maze help to conduct me out:
Direct my course so right, as with thy hand to show
Which way thy forests range, which way thy rivers flow;
Wise Genius, by thy help that so I may descry
How thy fair mountains stand, and how thy valleys lie. . .

                                        Michael Drayton

# PART ONE

## *Man*

# Round the Village

THE VILLAGE itself – in England – is likely to have been founded by the English settlers, illiterate and barbarian, who cleared the heavy oak woods and utilized the strong rich soils of the valleys, changing the look of England far more drastically than the British had done before them. In some counties the village may be as old as the sixth century, even the fifth century, from 450 to 500.

The nucleus would have been a farmstead (where there was a spring or good water supply), which gathered more dwellings around itself, the inhabitants farming the 'open fields' as a community and pasturing their pigs and other animals on the 'common'. A look at the *Concise Oxford Dictionary of English Place-Names* will reveal the meaning of the ancient English name of the village.

OPEN FIELDS. Fields and their shape record ancient and less ancient history, and a map marking field boundaries (e.g. the ordnance survey maps of 2½ inches to the mile) will reveal very different patterns, including quite a few of the old open fields, each of hundreds of acres, which were particularly the rule in the Midlands. These great fields (two or three to a village, to allow for fallowing, i.e. for resting a field so that it regained its fertility) were frequently identified in name after the village they belonged to – 'Yatesbury Field', 'Wootton Fields', etc. These names may survive, and may be included on the map, even though the fields were enclosed a hundred or more years ago, and divided up with hedges, and allotted to different farms.

Now and again the several owners of one of these ancient open fields will have been too lazy to plant hedges, or distinguish their portions by more than a wire fence. When that happens, the open field remains, to all appearance, like a fossil out of the remote past of England – a field on the giant scale which gives an idea of the wide naked England of our ancestors, who were accustomed to a landscape not unlike that of northern France at the present time – hedgeless, boundless to the horizon, full of poppies and brilliant blue cornflowers, with here and there a wood.

The open fields were cultivated in strips, or 'selions', or 'lands', or 'acres', each one long and narrow to give a good run to the plough, each a quarter of an acre to an acre in size. These selions were grouped in furlongs. A farmer (and the lord of the manor) would have selions here and selions there in different furlongs. These furlongs or selion-groups made the open fields into a vast patchwork. The parallel selions of one furlong might go at any angle to the parallel selions of the next furlong, according to soil and contours and natural obstacles. This pattern of the ancient selion-groups can be traced even now in the pattern of the parallel ridges and furrows which often cross old meadows.

THE END OF THE OPEN FIELDS. It is a mistake to think that all enclosure occurred in the late eighteenth century and early nineteenth century. Sometimes working the open fields in the ancient communal fashion was abandoned at a much earlier date. Whole furlongs would be enclosed between hedges, producing smaller fields (as we use the word) with wavy ends and right-angled corners, or hedges might be put around individual selions producing an odd row of small narrow fields.

Wholesale break-up of the great fields quickened in the last decades of the eighteenth century, in a zeal for more profitable and less piece-meal cultivation of the land. Enclosure was achieved at first by a private Act of Parliament, then by local consent without an Act, and last of all by commissioners who made enclosure awards. The result was a revolution in way of life and in landscape.

The typical enclosure field, or subdivision of the old open field of our English ancestors, is rectangular and more or less regular, a neat job of the surveyor's craft. In spite of their thorny and elmy hedgerows such fields have made rather for an unatmospheric monotony of land-scape.

The farmers of the open fields had their farmsteads actually in the village, from which they went out to work every day, and from which the herd boys drove their beasts out to common. When enclosures came, a new farmstead was often built on the farmer's share of the old common land. But this was not always possible, and even today several farmsteads may still be grouped in the village, as they were a thousand years ago.

INTAKE FIELDS AND FARMS. Such enclosures are not the whole story of our farm landscape. From early times there were farmsteads away from villages and the open fields – isolated farms (especially in hilly country, and country once heavily wooded, or marshy country) which grew up as the farmers won more and more acreage from the surrounding waste of one kind and another. This tends to produce – particularly in the stony hilly districts – irregular intakes, irregular enclosures, added piecemeal. In the west and south-west such fields are surrounded, not by thorn hedges but by great sheltering, flowery, scrub-topped hedge-banks of earth and stones. Farms with such fields grew in much the same way as little farms had grown up in the Iron Age, or even the Bronze Age. Hedges of small Bronze Age or Iron Age closes – or what is left of them – can be seen here and there, for instance on the Wessex downs (earth hedges) and on the Isles of Scilly (granite hedges).

NAMES OF FIELDS. Fields have their names no less than towns or villages (see *Names of Places*, page 95). Names of intake fields, still spoken by the modern farmer and his men, may go back hundreds of years, may be Old English, Old Norse, Cornish or Welsh. Even closes cut up from the open fields sometimes preserve the name by which a furlong or even a selion was known – such as Goldfurlong, the furlong where corn marigolds insisted on growing, or Bandland, the 'land' or strip or selion on which it was usual to plant beans.

COMMONS have been called antiquities 'as old as English society' – 'the most ancient institution we now possess, older by far than Parliament, older even than the manor within whose organization and control they subsequently fell' (W. G. Hoskins). The common belonged to the same agricultural scheme of life as the open field, on which our ancestors – our English ancestors – of the sixth or seventh century were already raising their crops of corn. It was necessary land, on which men of the village (or the village grown into a town) and then of the manor grazed their cattle, their horses, their sheep, their geese, and on which their pigs rooted and picked up acorns, in common. Commoner's rights included the gathering of firewood, peat, bracken, nuts, etc., as well as grazing, so that the common was something of a 'General Store'.

The open fields of a village were generally the best land, the common was often land less worth cultivating. It might be open woodland, where the animals in the glades ate their way around oaks and patches of scrub – whitethroat scrub – and edgings of bluebells. It might be moorland or wild muscular hillside flaming with gorse, or with broom, as in Wales, or Cornwall, or Devon, or Cumberland; or sandy heath, as in Dorset, Hampshire, or Surrey; or marshland, as in the Fens. When enclosures came, millions of acres of common land were lost between 1700 and 1845 and transformed into farm land, either because the commoners did not in fact own their common (rights of common might have been allowed at some time by the lord of the manor over part of his own property) or were unable to prove their ownership. Today about a million and a half acres of common are left in England and Wales; and it was proposed in 1958 by the Royal Commission on Common Land that all of it should be open to the public as of right.

THE MANOR-HOUSE is still likely to be the chief house in the village, though all other traces of the old manorial organization and its courts and dues, etc., have disappeared. As the Anglo-Saxon centuries went by, the landholding system of manors under manorial 'lords' imposed itself on the community of the English countrymen, the lord owning some of the land in the manor (which was not called a manor, from the Old French *manoir*, a mansion, until after the Conquest), exercising various rights and enjoying various services from the people now under his thumb in their differing degrees of freedom and servitude.

Sometimes the manor and the parish lands around the village coincided. Sometimes there might be several manors in the parish, or the manors might overlap into neighbouring parishes. But the village, the local centre of life and farming, was the natural place for a lord's mansion, that manor-house which so often remains.

In some villages the manor-house is still known as the Hall, i.e. it is known by what was the English villager's word for the new *manoir* or mansion of the Norman lord, his halled mansion rising above their own one-roomed hovels. (A hall was the main part of any considerable house in the Middle Ages, the main community room for living, eating, even sleeping, to which other rooms were added. This predominance of the hall survives in the large dining hall of a medieval college as at Oxford or Cambridge.)

As well as a manor-house in the village, there may be a 'Manor Farm' alongside. Or the manor-house may have vanished, leaving only the Manor Farm. This was the lord's own property in the manor, worked by him, or by his men, for his direct livelihood.

THE CHURCH (see pages 30–51) may still have a few Saxon stones or Saxon stone-work in its structure, and may even be on the site of a pagan shrine (since the English settlers of the fifth and sixth centuries were not converted to Christianity until the seventh century). It may have been founded and built by an English landowner or lord of the manor before the Conquest, or built – or rebuilt – by a Norman lord after the Conquest. Often a part of the church, or side chapel, belonged (and may still belong) to the manor-house family, containing their dead, their memorials, their private pews – and even a comfortable fireplace built in during the eighteenth or nineteenth centuries.

Lords of the manor often continued to look on the church (and the parson as well) as their own private property, even including the church inside the privacy of their parks or gardens, a proceeding explained on pages 81–82.

THE PARSONAGE. Often from very early times the lord of the manor was the patron of the living of the parish priest, owning the 'advowson' or right of nominating a new priest. But once the priest becomes vicar or rector (for the difference, see page 103), the living, and the parsonage alongside the church, become the parson's own freehold, with all perquisites.

'The Old Rectory', 'The Old Vicarage', is now a common designation on the parsonage gate. In the eighteenth and nineteenth centuries mean little parsonages were often rebuilt on a scale suitable to clergy allied to the manor-house families or to clergy rich by holding several livings at once, residing in one parish and leaving others to be administered by poor curates; their new rectories or vicarages had nurseries, wine-cellars, stables, and large gardens. Modern clergy, on small fixed incomes, cannot afford the compulsory upkeep of these large parsonages, which are also made redundant by uniting benefices, so that a single parson serves several parishes. More and more parsonages are thus sold to retired generals, ambassadors, businessmen, and others who like a niche in what is left of the old country feudalism.

THE TITHE BARN. The traditional way of affording the parson his livelihood was to pay him tithe – i.e. a tenth of the produce of the land in the parish he served (though the parson generally had – and may still have – his own glebe or farm land as well). In time it became more convenient, for parson and parishioner, to substitute a cash payment for the tenth sheaf, the tenth piglet, and so on; and tithes are now centrally collected and doled out to the parsons – and are being gradually extinguished.

In earlier centuries the parson needed a barn for his tenth, though a still existing tithe barn will often have been built by a monastery which took the greater share of the tithes by becoming owner of the rectory (page 102).

THE PUB. Church, manor-house, parsonage and pub are often grouped in a village quartet. This is a grouping to be expected, but sometimes the public house or village inn alongside the church succeeds a medieval church house in which the 'Whitsun Ales' were celebrated, and in which the ale for these village feasts was brewed by the church wardens (the National Trust owns such a church house, built about 1500, at Widecombe-in-the-Moor in Devonshire). After the Reformation, Puritan Justices of the Peace did their best to suppress such jollifications. In Devonshire in 1595 the Quarter Sessions forbade church ales on the Sabbath as tending to 'the dishonour of Almighty God, increase of bastardy and of dissolute life, and very many other mischiefs and inconveniences'.

THE COTTAGES AND FARMHOUSES in a village are often thought to be much older than they are. Before the sixteenth century most peasants lived in one-roomed hovels, windowless and without chimneys, with an open central hearth. These hovels were built of mud and straw (cob), or wattle and daub, or turf, and roofed with thatch, turf, or shingles made from oak timber – little improvement after hundreds of years on Saxon one-roomed cottages, which were flimsy affairs partly dug into the ground.

The older half-timbered cottages or farmhouses are likely to have been built in the last twenty or thirty years of the sixteenth century. The older stone cottages and farmhouses (as in the Cotswolds) are likely to date from the seventeenth and eighteenth centuries. Cottages were seldom built in rows until the end of the eighteenth century, when enclosures were under way.

CRUCKS. Something to spot in villages is the rare cottage with its roof supported on crucks, i.e. on pairs of curving timbers joined so as to support the roof-ridge, and footed low on the walls, each pair cut, as a rule, from the same curved tree trunk, and then joined blade to blade in reverse. Crucks (not to be found in East Anglia or south-east England) were a rather primitive constructional method common in the Middle Ages and surviving well into the seventeenth century in some areas. They were used for barns and for small originally one-storeyed and often one-roomed dwellings. Often the crucks show in the end wall.

UPPING STOCKS. Another village item to notice – outside farmhouses, generally placed so that they can be reached from the house without crossing the dungy or muddy extents of the yard – are the few stone steps of an upping stock, still useful for mounting a horse, and essential in the days when a farmer's womenfolk rode pillion to market, etc., behind one of the men.

YEW TREES. There are yew trees – and very old ones – in many country churchyards. But it is not so commonly noticed that yews are also very frequent (in some districts) alongside cottages and farm-houses. It is difficult to be sure why they were planted in either situa-tion – or rather to be sure about the origin of the habit. Certainly it was not to provide wood for bows (made from the trunk timber of yew trees, and not from the branches). Yew foliage was cut as 'palm' for Palm Sunday, and yews undoubtedly gave protection from prevailing south-westerly rain and gales. But it is possible that the habit of plant-ing yews by churches and houses may have survived from a long for-gotten veneration for the yew as a strong, evergreen, enduring tree, a tree to be worshipped, with its own inherent power to protect.

THE WESLEYAN OR METHODIST CHAPEL, a plain affair of the eighteenth and nineteenth centuries, now often closed or converted into dwelling-house or garage, was a sign of the weakening power of the church and the manor-house, the parson and the squire. Notice that the chapel often occupies a scrap of waste, a corner where some dissenting villager or farmer perhaps owned a 'herb garden' –

i.e. a vegetable garden – which he was prepared to give up for his beliefs.

ROUNDHOUSES, or Blind Houses, or Cages, circular village lock-ups sturdily built in stone, are a relic of the duties and activities of the petty constable, the parish factotum superseded when modern police forces were established in the eighteen-forties. The constable kept the king's peace within the parish bounds, carrying a staff painted with the royal arms as a symbol of his authority. He could arrest a malefactor or anyone who committed a breach of the peace, and secure him in the roundhouse (or in the stocks, another relic of his authority) until it was possible to bring him in front of the Justices of the Peace. In Wiltshire villages, where a number of finely built eighteenth-century lock-ups of this kind can be seen, they are commonly known as 'blind houses' – not because they were temporary lodgings of the drunk, but because they were eyeless – they had no windows. Trouble was always to be expected at markets. Thus at Steeple Ashton, which was a market village, the blind house appropriately stands right alongside the market cross.

The old manorial organization will have left several more relics around the village. By the manor-house itself, or on the Manor Farm, there may be a dovecot; somewhere near the village there may still be a pound; and on the nearest convenient hill or by the nearest convenient stream there may be a windmill or water-mill.

DOVECOTS. Only the lord of the manor might have a dovecot. But he did not erect a tall stone dovecot or dove-house for the pleasure of seeing pigeons in flight. It was strictly practical and part of the business of keeping alive – as practical as his stew (Old French *estui*) or fishpond, his park for impaling deer (page 81), or his rabbit warren, ensuring a supply of fresh meat in the shape of squabs or young pigeons which could be lifted from the stone nesting-compartments (wood pigeons, our modern source of pigeon pie, were not easily taken before the invention of shotguns). This manorial perquisite caused envy and irritation; the pigeons might not be killed and did not confine themselves to the lord of the manor's own crops. The great medieval dovecot of the Knights Hospitaller (page 109) alongside the church at Garway, in Herefordshire, which now belongs to the National Trust, has nesting-boxes for 600 birds. The dovecot among the monastic buildings of Penmon, in Anglesey (built about 1600), has a thousand nests. Now and then a convenient cave or fissure was walled across and fitted with nesting-boxes, a dovecot on the cheap, such as the Culver Hole in one of the limestone cliffs of the Gower, near Port Eynon, in South Wales.

MILLS – water-mills, invented in the eastern Mediterranean in the first century B.C. – were already turning in England before the Conquest. Many new ones were built in the twelfth and thirteenth centuries as more land came under the plough, overshot or undershot according to the type of stream. Windmills (a later invention of the Arabs) also reached England towards the end of the twelfth century, and the dusty miller rapidly became one of the regular targets of country satire – 'hair grows in the palm of an honest miller' – a character rich among the poor, lusty, sly, and good with women. He certainly had the opportunity of cheating when he ground the farmer's grain, and he enjoyed a monopoly in each manor, each village; an enforced monopoly, since the mill was another perquisite of the manorial lords, who made 'grinding at the lord's mill' a condition in leases, and took steps to be sure that querns, or rotary hand-mills (from which the water-mill had developed) were not used on the quiet – though they were, for producing flour and also the malt required for brewing ale.

Windmill sites often leave two indicators behind them, the name 'Windmill Hill' on the map, and the small mound (occasionally a barrow was chosen) on which the mill was set. Windmills are either 'post-mills', fixed on a post so that the whole mill can be revolved and turned into the wind, or 'tower-mills', on which only the cap, carrying the sails, needs to be turned.

Often the site of an overshot water-mill, off one of the smaller, hillier streams, can be traced by the leat which conveyed the water from the stream along the side of the valley to the breast of the wheel; by the millpond, which stored water against drought, and by the pit in which the exterior wheel revolved. On Mainland, Orkney, the Ministry of Works now safeguards an example of the most primitive kind of water-mill, an adaptation of the rotary quern to water-power in such a way that the millstone is revolved by a small horizontal instead of a vertical wheel.

In cloth districts, such as Devon, Cornwall, Gloucestershire, water-mills were also used in the countryside to operate stamps for felling or tucking cloth ('tucking mills').

POUNDS. 'Impounding' this or that is a verbal legacy from the pound as an item of village life. In the pound, an enclosure with high walls (now usually in ruins) from which there was sometimes access to a spring or stream, the pinder of the manor impounded stray animals, which were much more frequent before enclosures hedged and fenced and shut in the English countryside.

> I have xii oxen, and they be ffayre and whight,
> And they go a-grasyng down by the dyke.
> With hay, with howe, with hay!
> Sawyste not thou myn oxen, thou lytyll pretty boy
> (Fifteenth century)

The owner of the strayed impounded oxen, pigs, etc., redeemed his animals by payment.

LOST VILLAGES – mostly in eastern England and the Midlands – have a new literature of their own and have become a new object of research and excavation. But the lost usually leaves a trace on the surface, and such village sites can be exciting to examine and explore. Some were destroyed in the twelfth century by Cistercian monks (page 104) making solitudes for themselves around their new abbeys. Others dwindled and then vanished for two chief causes – poor soil and the Black Death. The English settlers had not always chosen or cleared a good site for a village; villages were not always on fertile or easy land. They clung on as weak – and weakening – communities, dwindling away all the more quickly when the Black Death came in the fourteenth century, after which landlords often cleared out the few villagers who were left, and turned the village lands into great sheep walks. Many flourishing villages were destroyed for the same reason.

M. W. Beresford's *Lost Villages of England* (1954) reveals what to look for, and where. Sometimes – but seldom – a scrap of the medieval church still breaks the turf. Humpy ground in a waste corner may resolve itself, as you look, into an untidy plan of cottage sites, with little crofts or enclosures along sunken scraps of green lane which were the streets of the village. There may be a windmill tump on a hill (page 27), the turf round the humpy ground may swell into the ridge and furrow strips of the furlongs (page 20) of the old open fields. Nettles (which flourish on nitrogen from the decay of man's organic rubbish, and are often indicators of old habitation) may rise high on the lost village site in the summer.

ANCIENT VILLAGES. Quite a number of prehistoric villages or hamlets of a very different kind can be seen, which are more than names on a map, or slight mounds in the turf, or sites which have been excavated and reinterred. They are more or less remote, on waste ground, and in districts where the builder had plenty of loose stone to hand for their walls. Such villages include:

*Skara Brae*, by the edge of the sea on the Mainland of Orkney, discovered in 1866 by the shifting of sand dunes which had as suddenly overwhelmed the village upwards of 4,000 years before. The stone huts, with stone beds, belonged to limpet-eating people with herds of cattle and sheep, who buried their dead in chambered tombs under barrows (such as Maes Howe, page 58).

*Jarlshof*, overlooking the West Voe, in Shetland, a site continuously occupied for thousands of years, with late Bronze Age huts, a late Iron Age broch (page 70), round houses of the second and third centuries, a Viking settlement with rectangular houses, a medieval farmstead, and a seventeenth-century Laird's House.

*Chysauster*, in Cornwall, above Penzance, giving a great panorama of Mounts Bay and St Michael's Mount – the grass-grown huts and street of a farming, tin-smelting community of the second century B.C. to the third century A.D.

*Tre'r Ceiri*, the 'Homestead of the Giants', on an abrupt moorland hill rising to nearly 1,600 feet above Caernarvon Bay, where Caernarvonshire begins to narrow into the Lleyn Peninsula, a dramatic untidy hill-top 'fort' of terraced stone ramparts and stone huts, occupied during the Roman centuries.

*Din Lligwy*, at Penrhos-Lligwy in Anglesey, a little hamlet in a dell of trees of rectangular and also round limestone huts, in a half-acre space enclosed by a limestone wall, belonging to the fourth century.

One thing is immediately noticeable about the more ancient of these barbarian settlements: that their builders just set to and built, having chosen their site, without measurement or angle or straight line (except in as far as the stone they used, as at Skara Brae, had a more or less straight cleavage). Their huts and settlements tend to be more or less oval or circular: the huts, so to say, are the most natural-artificial surround of human bodies; the defensive wall – where there is one –

29

just loops itself around the huts. Right angles and straight lines came with civilization, from Rome – as in the Roman villas, camps and forts. There is a right-angled touch of Rome in the Viking houses of Jarlshof or the Welsh houses of Din Lligwy, or in the huts, rectangular instead of round, of the Anglo-Saxon settlers.

# Saints in the Church

Old churches were built and furnished when men thought more than we do in symbols and tokens. Where we might display a text in a dull way and dull lettering, the builders of these medieval churches, from the eleventh to the early sixteenth century, would suggest much the same thing, some virtue or some vice, some special item of belief, by depicting or carving the token which stood for it. Or the token might stand for God in various aspects, for the Virgin Mary and other saints, or for the devil.

The saints are a key to understanding the why and wherefore of old churches. Saints were revered in the Middle Ages (and are still revered by Roman Catholics) as intermediaries between man on earth and God in heaven. In a church dedicated to a saint, before an altar inside the church dedicated to some other saint, men invoked these inter-mediaries, and so obtained their help and persuaded them to pray to God on their behalf. Saints therefore do much to explain the archi-tecture and special features, subsidiary altars, side chapels, etc., of a medieval church. For one thing the church was the repository of relics of the saints. A saint's body, head, arm, leg, finger, a hair from his head, or the merest fragment of his bones, spread an ameliorating in-fectious sanctity around itself. The saint was already in heaven: to be buried near his relics, outside in the churchyard, or if possible still nearer to them inside the church, helped to secure a similar place in heaven for the deceased.

At the Reformation architectural or structural shrines could be broken up, reliquaries emptied and stripped of jewels and melted down, and relics thrown away. But it was not possible to erase every symbolic likeness of a saint involved in the structure of the church. Windows, costly to renew, were not always broken, wall paintings were more easily plastered over than scraped away, and it was hard work to cut away carvings in stone, on walls, on the tower, on the sides of a font, or to do much more than knock off a face or an inscription.

So the saints often remain, and can often be recognized by their traditional attributes or their special attitudes, speaking an international language of help, comfort, insurance against ills, and instruction.

Here are some of their attributes (other than such familiar ones as the lily of the Virgin, the keys of St Peter, the cross saltire of St Andrew, and the tokens of the four Evangelists, mentioned below on page 40).

## Attributes of some women saints

BAG (*i.e. a purse on strings*), BASKET, AND PITCHER. St Zita of Lucca, Virgin, who died in 1278, a serving-maid and the patroness of serving-maids. St Zita may carry a pitcher or a basket, but if the basket is filled with fruit and flowers, it will be St Dorothea, Virgin and Martyr. A certain Theophilus mocked her before her martyrdom in 311, and asked her to send him fruit and flowers from Paradise; which she did, sending him a basket of apples and roses. St Dorothea was patroness of gardeners.

BEDSTEAD. St Faith, Virgin and Martyr, of Agen, roasted on a metal bedstead, and then decapitated.

BREASTS – *either severed, or held in pincers, or pierced with a sword*. St Agatha of Sicily, Virgin and Martyr, of the third century, tortured and burnt for refusing the advances of the Roman governor of Sicily. Invoked against fire and lightning.

COW (*which she may be milking*). St Bridget, or Bride, who was born in Connacht on the first day of spring at sunrise. She fed on the milk of a special cow, and as mother of flocks and herds she made cows increase their milk and butter.

DRAGON. St Margaret of Antioch, Virgin and Martyr, a favourite saint invoked by women in childbirth. According to her legend, she was swallowed by a dragon: she made the sign of the cross, which swelled and split the dragon, a difficult delivery which caused her to pray in her martyrdom that God should help any woman who called on her, and that the child should be delivered safely. Margaret is pictured emerging from the dragon or thrusting a cross into it, or leading the dragon on a chain. She was one of the Fourteen Holy Helpers – the most helpful of the saints in heaven.

GIRL-CHILD, *with halo and book*. The girl-child is the Virgin; the saint

31

beside her will be St Anne, her apocryphal mother, teaching her to read.

PINCERS, *with or without a tooth.* St Apollonia, Virgin and Martyr of Alexandria, in the third century. Before she was burned alive all her teeth were broken in, for which reason she was invoked against toothache.

PORTATIVE ORGAN. This is played by St Cecilia, patroness of music and musicians (sometimes she plays a viol, a lute, or a harp). This Roman virgin and martyr of the second or third century had been married, after which she revealed to her husband that her body was guarded by an angel, to whom she had pledged herself. Organs were played at her wedding. She was beheaded in her bath after miraculously surviving an attempt to suffocate her by overheating the bathroom. Before the sixteenth century her emblem is not a musical instrument, but a wreath of roses and lilies, an angel having brought roses picked in heaven to her bridal chamber.

TOWER. Saint Barbara, Virgin and Martyr, carries the tower in which she was shut up by her father. She had three windows – to symbolize the Trinity – cut in her bath-house instead of two, and was beheaded by her father, who was afterwards struck by lightning. Three windows are shown in her tower. She was the tutelary saint of gunsmiths, armourers, artillery men, miners, invoked also against fire and thunderbolts, flood, and sudden death (since she prayed that the sins of those who remembered her passion should be forgiven). Another of the Fourteen Holy Helpers.

TRUE CROSS. St Helen, or Helena, mother of the Christian Emperor Constantine, holds or leans on a cross, i.e. the True Cross which she discovered in Jerusalem. English legend made her the daughter of King Cole.

WHEEL WITH SPIKES. St Catherine of Alexandria, Virgin and Martyr, and learned princess of the third century, was bound on her Catherine Wheel by order of the Emperor Maxentius. The wheel broke when she touched it, but she was beaten and beheaded. Catherine was the special saint of young girls, nuns, scholars and wheelwrights, one more of the Fourteen Auxiliaries, or most helpful saints in heaven.

## Attributes of some men saints

ARROWS *or Arrow piercing the body.* If the saint is young, naked, more or less, and without a crown, and if his body is transfixed by many arrows, he will be St Sebastian, Martyr, of the third century, a victim of Diocletian, who recovered from the arrows of Mauretanian archers only to be clubbed to death. He gave protection against the plague.

If the saint is crowned, he will be St Edmund, Martyr and King of the East Angles, frequent in East Anglian churches. He was shot to death in 870 by the Danes against an oak tree at Hoxne, in Suffolk, and was interred at Bury St Edmunds. St Edmund may hold a single arrow; he may have a wolf with him, since the Danes cut off his head, and it was guarded by a grey wolf.

AUGER. St Leger, or Leodegarius, of Autun, Bishop and Martyr, carries the auger with which his eyes were bored out, after the siege of Autun in 675 by the Duke of Champagne, or the iron with which the sockets were cauterized.

BASKET WITH LOAVES. St Philip the Apostle carries such a basket because of his answer to Christ before the miracle of the loaves and fishes (John vi, 5–7).

BEEHIVE. Carried by St Ambrose, Bishop and Doctor of the Church, because bees swarmed on his mouth when he was a child, and then flew up towards heaven.

BOAR, OR PIG. This will attend St Antony of Egypt, Abbot and Hermit and first Christian monk, who was so much tempted in the Egyptian desert, where he had a wild boar for company. Others would have killed and eaten the pig – but not St Antony, who subdued the deadly sin of gluttony. The pig may wear a bell. Pigs belonging to the brethren of the hospital Order of St Antony in London (Threadneedle Street) and other cities in Europe, were privileged to wander and feed in the streets, and were distinguished by a bell. Our ancestors invoked him against St Antony's Fire, which was the name given to the common disease of erysipelas and to the painful gangrene of ergotism which came from eating flour contaminated with ergot.

BOWELS ON A WINDLASS. These accompany, or emerge from, St Erasmus, or Elmo, of Campania, Bishop and Martyr, of the fourth century, whose bowels were wound out of him by the Emperor Maximian's torturers. As one of the Fourteen Holy Helpers, he was invoked by the seasick, and those with upset stomachs.

BOYS – THREE BOYS – IN A TUB. St Nicholas – i.e. Santa Claus – fourth-century Bishop and Confessor of Myra in Asia Minor, protector of children, sailors, merchants, travellers, virgins, bakers and thieves, is shown with three boys sitting up in a pickling tub. They had been killed and pickled during a famine, and offered to St Nicholas as food. He brought the remains to life. St Nicholas may also be shown with three golden balls or three bags, in reference to the dowries he secretly threw in through a window to save three poor girls from becoming prostitutes. He was the patron of pawnbrokers.

CHRIST-CHILD ON SHOULDER. Invariably carried by St Christopher, Martyr, of Lycia, who was roasted and beheaded. According to legend, he was the reformed ogre or giant Offerus, or Reprobus, who helped travellers across a dangerous ford and one night was surprised by the immense and increasing weight of a child, who revealed himself in mid-river to be Christ: Christopher was carrying the weight of the sins of the world. He is usually painted on the north wall of churches so that he could be seen at a glance from the south door; the sight of St Christopher gave a day's protection from all harm. He was invoked by gardeners (since his staff budded when thrust in the ground – so he was good for cuttings), by sailors, bookbinders, ferrymen and fishermen, and against the plague, lightning, epilepsy. One of the Fourteen Holy Helpers.

COMB OF IRON TEETH. Carried by St Blaise, Bishop and Martyr, of Sebaste in Armenia, beheaded in 316, after his flesh had been torn with wool combs, for which reason he was patron of wool-combers and the cloth trade. He may carry a lighted taper. On the way to prison he miraculously drew a fish-bone from a child's throat, after which the child's mother brought him food and a taper to lighten his darkness. Blaise declared that a yearly offering of a taper in his memory would relieve all sufferers from a bad throat. He, too, was numbered among the Fourteen Holy Helpers.

CRIPPLE *or beggar kneeling at a saint's feet.* This will indicate one of the most popular of saints, St Martin of Tours, Bishop, protector of vintners, conviviality, drinking and ex-drunkards. He was a Roman soldier (fourth century) who at the gates of Amiens divided his cloak with a sword and gave half to a beggar, who reappeared to him in his dreams as Christ.

CROWNED HEAD. A bishop carrying a crowned head represents St Cuthbert of Lindisfarne or Holy Island, carrying the head of St Oswald, King of Northumberland, who was beheaded by heathen Penda, King of Mercia, in 642. The actual head – or rather the skull – lies with the bones of St Cuthbert in that saint's great cathedral church

34

at Durham. It had been preserved as a relic on Holy Island, and when the monks left the island in 875 in fear of the Danes, taking St Cuthbert's body with them, the skull was placed in St Cuthbert's coffin.

CUP OR CHALICE *with a snake or small dragon coiling out.* Carried by St John the Evangelist, according to the legend that when a priest of Diana dared him to drink from a chalice of poison, he made the sign of the cross over the cup, which at once drew out the poison – i.e. the devil – in the shape of a dragon or snake.

DRAGON UNDER FOOT. As everyone knows, a knight in armour with a cross on a banner, trampling on a dragon and thrusting a spear into it, is St George (another of the Fourteen Holy Helpers). A feathered angel with a sword trampling a dragon (see *Michael Churches,* below) is St Michael the Archangel, Prince of Heaven.

GRIDIRON. A saint with a large gridiron will generally be St Lawrence, Deacon and Martyr, done to death in 258 by a Roman prefect on a gridiron on a slow fire; his roasting made him give out a sweet smell of holiness. Exeter Cathedral had coals from the fire among its relics. St Lawrence's feast is 10 August, about the middle of the period of the shooting stars known as the Perseids or St Lawrence's Tears (page 165).

St Vincent of Saragossa, Deacon and Martyr, is also pictured with a gridiron, on which he was tortured at Valencia in 304. He was a patron of vintners, sailors and brickmakers.

HIND. A saint in an abbot's robe with a crosier and a hind will be St Giles, who lived as a hermit in the forests of the south of France, about the seventh century. There he was fed by the milk of a hind. An arrow shot at the hind caused a lameness in the saint, of which he refused to be cured. He was therefore the guardian of cripples, beggars and blacksmiths, among the Fourteen Holy Helpers.

HORSESHOE. Emblem carried by St Eloy, or Eligius, Bishop of Noyon, and Apostle of the Belgians, who died in 660. He began life as a goldsmith, and was the saint invoked by smiths – blacksmiths as well as goldsmiths. According to his legend he cut off a horse's leg, shoed it, and replaced it on the horse. He is sometimes shown with the leg.

LILY. Often carried in one hand by St Dominic, founder of the Dominicans or Black Friars (page 108).

LION. Often accompanies St Jerome, most learned Doctor of the Church, who writes and wears a Cardinal's hat, and perhaps has an inkhorn – according to the legend that he pulled a thorn from a lion's foot, the lion staying with him, tame and grateful.

MANACLES. St Leonard of Noblac, Deacon and Confessor, and hermit of the sixth century, holds a set of irons or chains in token of the prisoners he persuaded King Clovis to set free. He was the tutelary saint of all the possessed, of prisoners and captives, pregnant women, people possessed of evil spirits or in the grip of disease – all who needed to be unchained.

SCALES. The winged and feathered St Michael (see *Michael Churches*, pages 49–51) holds a sword in one hand, and in the other, frequently, a set of scales on which he weighs the souls of the dead.

SCALLOP SHELL. St James the Greater, Apostle, wears a scallop shell on his pilgrim's hat. The shell was the badge adopted in the twelfth century by pilgrims to his great shrine and supposed burial place at Santiago de Compostela in Spain. St James often wears a pilgrim's gown, staff, bottle, and scrip or bag –

> Give me my scallop shell of quiet,
> My staff of faith to walk upon,
> My scrip of joy, immortal diet,
> My bottle of salvation,
> My gown of glory, hope's true gage,
> And thus I'll take my pilgrimage.
>
> Sir Walter Ralegh

SORE OPEN ON THIGH. A saint pointing to an open sore on his thigh will be St Roch, who died in 1327, a Frenchman born with a red cross on his chest, who ministered in Italy to those sick of the plague, curing many of them, and himself recovering from an attack. His infection caused him to be expelled from Piacenza. He lived in a wood outside the city, where a hound fed him and where he healed beasts as he healed men. St Roch was invoked more than any other saint in the great epidemics of plague.

STAG *with a cross between its antlers*. St Hubert of Liège, Bishop, who died in 727, was turned from a nobleman's life of hunting when he went out with his hounds one Good Friday and encountered a noble stag bearing a crucifix between its antlers. A voice told him that if he did not give himself to God he would soon go down into hell. So St Hubert was revered by huntsmen and was invoked by sufferers from hydrophobia – from the bite of mad dogs.

A saint with stag and crucifix may be the Roman martyr Eustachius or St Eustace, who had also changed his life after meeting such a quarry; he, yet another of the Fourteen Holy Helpers, was invoked in situations of special difficulty.

# Animals in the Church

Here as well are some of the animals to look for in a medieval church, real or imaginary, tokens of good or evil, virtue or vice, God or man. Often the discovery of a Salamander with a knot in its tail, or a Hart eating a snake, or some such enigmatic creature, will be the reward of exploring a church which has otherwise lost all of its ancient character and smells sourly of stale air and furniture polish. Most of the creatures will be carved – on fonts, over doorways, on capitals, corbels, or tombs, on bosses, or screens or bench-ends or misericords (which are the carved projections under oaken choir-seats which fold back), inside and outside. Some will be painted (for instance, a Mermaid often combs her hair and holds up a mirror in the dangerous waters around the feet of St Christopher, in wall-paintings). Some are to be found in stained glass windows. Some will be fabulous, some will be animals which exist and play a fabulous part.

## CREATURES OF FABLE

DRAGONS, first of all, with wings, long sinuous tails and four feet ending in claws, stand for Satan, evil, sin. Archangels and angels, saints (such as St George or St Margaret of Antioch) and saintly persons, may stand on a dragon, a knight on his tomb may rest his feet on a dragon. 'Thou shalt tread upon the lion and adder: the young lion and the dragon shalt thou trample under feet', says Psalm 91. Or St Michael the archangel may thrust at a dragon, the medieval carver or artist having in mind The Revelation of St John the Divine: 'And there was war in heaven: Michael and his angels fought against the dragon; and the dragon fought and his angels, And prevailed not; neither was their place found any more in heaven. And the great dragon was cast out, that old serpent, called the Devil, and Satan.'

In the family of dragons there were other kinds, evil and good, which were frequently represented. Sometimes you encounter –

THE AMPHISBAENA, which like other creatures was borrowed from the half-fabulous natural history of Greece and Rome. Greek for a 'both ways' creature, the Amphisbaena is a snake or serpent with wings and a head at each end, so that he can move backwards or forwards, a Mr Facing Both Ways, Satan who deceived us.

THE SALAMANDER, another Greek animal, is a dragon with wings and two legs, who can be recognized by the way he ties his tail into a knot. He lives in flame, so was a good creature, not an evil one, since good men, likewise, can continue to live among the flames of temptation.

Asps and Basilisks (Greek again) were mentioned in the Vulgate, the Latin Bible used by everyone before the Reformation. When Psalm 91 in the Authorized Version says 'Thou shalt tread upon the lion and adder', the Latin of the Vulgate said 'Thou shalt tread upon the asp and the basilisk'.

THE ASP, then, in churches is a snake with wings who puts one ear to the ground, and stuffs the end of its tail into the other ear. The asp is 'the deaf adder that stoppeth her ear; Which will not hearken to the voice of charmers, charming never so wisely' (Psalm 58), the man who will not hear or believe.

THE BASILISK, a creature which ruled like a king in the empty desert of Libya and could kill without biting by the glance of its eye, can be recognized as a tailed and winged serpent with a cock's head and (usually) two clawed feet. He is malignant evil.

So much for dragons. Fabulous creatures include as well, the Griffin, the Unicorn and the Phoenix.

THE GRIFFIN is to be recognized by his combination of eagle and lion. He is lion behind, eagle in front, with a hooked beak. Greek by origin, the Griffin in churches is a good animal, doubly royal, as if he combined the lion's strength and the eagle's keen-sightedness (since eagles, by legend, can look the sun straight in the eye).

THE PHOENIX. We still know this wonderful bird. There is never more than one in the world, who re-makes himself by fire on a nest of spices; thus the new Phoenix is born of the cinders of the old one. A bird of Christ's Resurrection.

THE UNICORN. We still know him as well. The Unicorn is ivory white: no animal more pure. He is strong and cannot be taken by ordinary means. Yet he lays his head and horn in tameness on a virgin's lap. So in that situation in a church carving or painting the Unicorn is Christ, who entered into the Virgin's womb and became man: he symbolizes the Incarnation. The Unicorn's horn ('But my horn shalt thou exalt like the horn of an unicorn' – Psalm 92) was specially holy, symbolizing the Cross.

Some fabulous creatures in the zoology of our churches are partly human. These are mostly bad. But not, to begin with:

THE CENTAUR, half man, half horse, often aiming his bow and arrow, as in the Greek fables in which he originated. He is Christ in combination with the vengeance of the Lord upon those who betrayed him. ('For it is written, Vengeance is mine; I will repay, saith the Lord.' Romans xii, 19.) This Centaur, or Sagittarius (archer), will sometimes be seen on a Norman font.

THE BLEMYA is a frequently carved outlandish human, with no head, and with eyes, or eyes and mouth, in his chest or his belly. Is he the deadly sin of Gluttony? By Greek and Roman account the Blemyae were a people of Ethiopia. In Shakespeare's play they are Othello's

> . . . men whose heads
> Do grow beneath their shoulders . . .

THE SCIAPOD also comes out of Africa. He sits with a single wide foot, a 'shadow foot' shading his head like a parasol. Perhaps a figure of Sloth (though on their single foot the Sciapodes were supposed to travel with great speed through the deserts of Libya).

THE MERMAID. No doubt about the Mermaid, the sea-dwelling fish-woman, who entices men to destruction by her beauty and her sweet singing. Seals may have suggested the Mermaid, but she took on the characteristics of the Sirens of antiquity, goddesses of death and love, half women, half birds – instead of half fish – who lured seafarers ashore to their destruction.

THE WODEWOSE, common in churches, is the Wild Man, shaggy with hairs, living in the forest, and a token perhaps, of the soul of man in its original innocence. Sometimes the Wodewose fights evil in the shape of a lion.

## CREATURES OF FACT

In church carvings and so on, the creatures of fact, the ones which really do exist, are often no less creatures which acted in fable. Some derive from the Bible, some derive from antiquity, and the part they each played in ancient fables could be turned into a Christian token without much difficulty.

Of these tokens some remain familiar, and we understand what they mean without hesitation. For instance, we know the *Agnus Dei*, the Lamb of God carrying a bannered cross of victory, who is Christ (John i, 29). We know the Fish which is also Christ, and the Dove, which is the Holy Ghost who descended on Christ, the Gospels say, in the form of a dove when he was baptized. We know the tokens of the four Evangelists – St Mark's, which is the Winged Lion (very familiar as the symbol of Venice); St Luke's, which is the Calf with wings; St Matthew's, which is the Winged Man, or angel; and St John's, which is the Eagle with wings outspread – the eagle of the modern lectern. These are the Four Beasts of The Revelation of St John the Divine iv, 6–7: 'And before the throne there was a sea of glass like unto crystal: and in the midst of the throne, and round about the throne, were four beasts full of eyes before and behind. And the first beast was like a lion, and the second beast like a calf, and the third beast had a face as a man, and the fourth beast was like a flying eagle.'

Other animals we do not interpret at a glance.

THE LION (without wings) may be Evil which is fought against, or is trodden underfoot, like the Dragon (see above). Also the Lion may be vigilance, or virtue in conflict with the Dragon; or courage and strength.

THE ELEPHANT, very oddly shaped out of ignorance, and shown with a howdah on his back in the form of a castle, is the warrior animal who fights or falls upon the Dragon of evil (the Elephant and Castle, as an inn name, derives from this medieval notion of the elephant with a howdah). Elephants also stood for the Fall of Man, since it was believed that the Elephant had no bones and fell when the hunter sawed through the tree against which it rested.

THE APE, sometimes trodden underfoot like the Lion or the Dragon, is Fraud.

THE FOX, sometimes carrying away a goose as in the folksong, is Deceit, another Devil's animal, or the Devil as deceiver.

THE WOLF, is the Devil as sly murderer and thief. A representation in church of a dog-like animal which licks or bites its foot is the wolf Satan approaching with privy paw the sheepfold of the followers of Christ (cf. The Gospel of St John x, 12). He licks his paws, according to legend, to make his approach more silent; should his paw make a noise, the Wolf reproves it with a bite.

THE WHALE, or the huge open-mouthed, saw-toothed fish which suggests a whale, is by origin at any rate Aspido Chelone, the Sea-Tortoise, who by legend swallows the small unwary fishes, and also plunges to the bottom with sailors who land on his back, which looks like an island. So it stands, again, for the Devil.

THE ANTELOPE catches his saw-edged horns in foliage or branches, and betokens mankind caught in the tangle of sin.

THE TIGRESS looks at herself in a mirror, a token of the pursuit of goodness interrupted by the blandishments of this world.

THE PANTHER, on the contrary, stands for Christ's resurrection from the dead. It was believed that the Panther slept for three days, and then scared Dragons away by the exceeding sweetness of his breath.

THE CAMEL, kneeling down to receive its load, is another symbol of Christ, taking on himself, and taking away, the sin of the world (John i, 29).

THE HART attacks and eats a snake, so reminding the spectator of the forty-second psalm, 'As the hart panteth after the waterbrooks, so panteth my soul after thee, O God.' It was the breath of snakes or of dragons which made the hart so dry, in medieval belief, so pantingly in need of water.

As for the birds in church other than the Dove and St John's Eagle with the outstretched wings and the fabulous Phoenix, one of the commonest is –

THE PELICAN, bending its head down and round and pecking at its breast, from which drops of blood fall to feed its clustered young ones. The story in the Middle Ages was that the Pelican killed its young, and then gave them life again, after three days, by means of its own blood. So the Pelican of Pity tokened Christ in the sacrament of the Lord's Supper, and also the Redemption of fallen man through the Passion of Christ – 'For thou wast slain, and hast redeemed us to God by thy blood' (Revelation v, 9).

THE CRANE (a bird still to be seen wild in the England of the Middle Ages) holds a stone in its claw, and is then a symbol of Christian watchfulness. While all the other Cranes in the flock slept, so the story went, one Crane kept watch, holding a stone as a precaution. If it fell asleep, the stone would drop and wake it up again.

THE PEACOCK is the proud bird which symbolized immortality (that is why peacocks with their splendid tails were often painted, as well, above the stable in the great Nativity pictures by Italian artists of the fifteenth century).

THE SWAN is sometimes carved – looking more goose-like than graceful, it is true – as a virtuous bird which sings before it dies, at the prospect of felicity to come.

THE OWL mobbed by other birds was often carved as a token of evil in the unaccustomed light of day, or as a token of the Jews who preferred the dark hours of ignorance to the light of the Christian revelation. Here too the BAT should be mentioned, carved as a creature of twilight and the Devil.

THE COCK, the weathercock high on the tower or the spire, must not be forgotten, though we tend to take him for granted. Often he is an admirable piece of ancient metal-work. He tells more than the direction of the wind. Having crowed when St Peter denied Christ, and as herald of day after darkness, he signified watch and pray and was the symbol of wakefulness against sin.

# Plants in the Church

There are plants to be found and recognized in churches, but they did not excite the carvers so much as the animals, real and fabulous, except for a short while in the second half of the thirteenth century, when men began to look at nature with affection and wonder under the influence of St Francis and his Franciscan friars. Even then the plants did not mean so much as the animals. Authorities say that most of the leaves and flowers carved in churches lack a special significance as symbols. All the same, some of the plants which the thirteenth-century carvers very beautifully represented, were certainly ones with a magical or quite respectably supernatural reputation. So there were four possible reasons for carving them. First, the carvers looked with delight at the leaves, flowers and tendrils of nature, and liked to represent them. Secondly, the plants with a reputation for power would be the ones most familiar to them. Thirdly, they may also have thought that plants known to be powerful against evil would have kept evil spirits (which seemed very real) out of the church. Perhaps all three reasons were combined. Also it does happen that several of these plants of power have a habit of growth and a cut or divided leaf shape particularly suited to carving and to decorative effect.

Earlier on, and later, the carving of plants was more conventional. In Norman times, on the side of a font, perhaps, or on the tympanum over the doorway into the church, men often carved in a conventional way a tree of no recognizable kind symbolizing the Tree of Life, from the Book of Genesis and from The Revelation of St John the Divine, and elsewhere in the Bible ('To him that overcometh will I give to eat of the tree of life, which is in the midst of the paradise of God.' Revelation ii, 7) – very appropriate to the moment of christening when a child entered the Christian community, or the moment, simply, of walking into church. Also because Christ said, 'I am the vine, ye are the branches: He that abideth in me, and I in him, the same bringeth forth much fruit' (John xv, 5), and because of the Last Supper, in which Christ took the cup and gave it to his followers, the Vine with its grapes in heavy bunches is frequently carved, early and late, conventionally and according to nature (vineyards were common in medieval England, so the thirteenth-century carver could study vine leaves and stems and tendrils and grapes at first hand).

The Lily and the Rose also occur – especially the Rose. They are both emblems of the Virgin Mary. Long before Christianity, roses had been sacred to the goddesses of love, to Venus in Italy, to Aphrodite in Greece. The carvers thought of the Song of Solomon, 'I am the rose of Sharon, and the lily of the valleys. As the lily among thorns, so is my love among the daughters' (Song of Solomon, ii, 1–2). Though we now mean other flowers by the Rose of Sharon and Lily of the Valley, the rose of the Song of Solomon was taken to be one of the wild roses or the familiar scented, yellow-centred red rose, the *Rosa gallica* of medieval gardens, and by 'lily of the valleys' they understood the white heavily scented Madonna Lily we still grow. In the art of our medieval churches this Madonna Lily, token of the Virgin's chastity and purity, does not only grow out of the pot in scenes of the Annunciation, when the Angel Gabriel announced to Mary: 'Behold, thou shalt conceive in thy womb, and bring forth a son, and shalt call his name JESUS' (Luke i, 31). Christ in paintings on the wall or in carving is sometimes crucified on a branched Madonna lily, instead of the usual cross.

What other plants observed from nature did the thirteenth-century or early fourteenth-century stone-masons set upon capitals and arches and shrines and fonts and tombs and canopies and bosses in the roof, and elsewhere? In exploring churches at home and abroad (particularly in Normandy), it is worth looking to see and keeping a record. Here are some of them:

OAK LEAVES AND ACORNS. The Oak was a sacred tree (sacred to Zeus, Jupiter, Thor, Thunor) long before Christianity. Its leaves and acorns were believed in the Middle Ages to ward off evil spirits.

HAWTHORN LEAVES, FLOWERS AND FRUIT. Very common. Hawthorn was the chief May Day plant in England and Normandy, powerful against evil of every kind.

MAPLE LEAVES. The leaves make an excellent sculptural pattern. The Maple was often thought of as a kind of oak, and was perhaps credited with the same powers.

HOLLY LEAVES AND BERRIES. Holly again was thought of as a protective plant (which was the origin of our use of holly at Christmas).

IVY LEAVES AND BERRIES.
HONEYSUCKLE LEAVES, FLOWERS, BERRIES, TWINING STEMS.
MUGWORT LEAVES, which have an intricate flowing sculptural form.
BUTTERCUP LEAVES AND FLOWERS.
CREEPING CINQUEFOIL.
BRYONY LEAVES AND TENDRILS.

All these have had a reputation of power. Bryony with its huge roots was the English substitute for the powerful Mandrake. The Creeping Cinquefoil, the 'five-fingered' plant from the shape of the leaves, had power against witches and evil, European herbalists came

to call it *Potentilla*, or the Little Powerful One. Buttercups were used to make protective garlands on May Day; and few plants have had a more universal reputation for power than the Mugwort of summer and autumn roadsides.

Among other plants which were carved were:

WILD HOP.
YELLOW WATER LILY.
MULBERRY.

Sometimes the leafy branches of the Oak, or the Hawthorn or the Maple are carved growing from the mouth of a frowning Jack in the Green, or Green Man (Plate 3), who was the sacrificial victim of May Day ceremonies, and was perhaps allowed into churches from quite early times (he is to be seen in Romanesque churches, at home and abroad, in a more conventional shape) as a symbol of the Resurrection.

The plants in churches are often carved high up – for instance, on the bosses in the roof (a favourite place for Green Men). So field glasses may be necessary in searching for them and identifying them.


# Church Monuments

Every monument in a church is also a monument of the Christianity, the common beliefs, and the art of its period – and perhaps of a local school of craftsmen.

Thirty years ago the admired monuments were brasses, tomb chests and effigies of the Middle Ages, Renaissance monuments of Tudor times, and Elizabethan and Jacobean monuments often with coloured figures, or half-figures, and kneeling children. Baroque monuments of the end of the seventeenth century and beginning of the eighteenth century (the earlier ones populated by cherubim with golden wings and pink cheeks), huge baroque-cum-classical monuments and rococo monuments of the eighteenth century, immense allegories from floor to ceiling in nave or chancel, and neo-classical sentimental composi-tions in white marble belonging to later decades of the eighteenth century and the beginning of the nineteenth century – all of these were much disliked, especially by vicars and rectors.

This was unfair, though it is understandable. The eminent dead on such monuments, and in their inscriptions, are very self-satisfied, and more conscious of living than dying, of their virtues and social rank than their sins. But this in itself is historical and fascinating like any-thing else from the past; and since in the eighteenth century they designed with a wonderful sophistication, balance and coolness, their church monuments, which exist by the thousand, deserve to be looked at no less than their mansions, now supported by public half-crowns, their landscape gardens, temples, grottoes, and lakes by 'Capability' Brown, their paintings and their furniture. The contrast between age and age and between the different concepts of death, life and religion which may be all crowded together in a single church, is the great inexhaustible pleasure of the exploration of churches.

MEDIEVAL TOMBS AND BRASSES. The dead of these memorials are *dead*: whatever their garments, their arms and armour, their insignia, and in spite of the lion or the hound at their feet, they lie in the church with hands together in prayer and eyes up to heaven, in the attitude of the dead tidied up for burial. Inscriptions (most of them in sacer-dotal Latin) are plain and brief. They have been sinners. They have no straight path to heaven. Angels kneel around them. Figures of saints around the monument are an invitation to intercede with these helpers on behalf of the dead, however grand or powerful (or wicked) they have been in life. Emblems (such as the Instruments of the Passion – spear, scourges, ladder, pincers and hammer, pestle and mortar for pounding the myrrh, etc. – or the Five Wounds of Christ, or the Trinity group of God the Father holding Christ crucified between his knees, with the Dove overhead) indicate the emotions of unquestioned belief. Medieval tombs, though, now seem plainer and more stern than they actually were, since their original colouring has worn off.

46

Towards the end of the Middle Ages, effigies (especially of priests) emphasize the charnel horrors of death. Halfway between corpse and skeleton, and crawling with toads and worms, they emphasize the contrast between miserable mortality – the Dance of Death – and desired immortality.

MONUMENTS OF THE LATER SIXTEENTH CENTURY AND THE SEVEN-TEENTH CENTURY. The new Protestant memorials avoid the once deeply felt symbols of the Catholic centuries. Allegorical emblems, less direct, less emotional, less real on two levels, now abound – particularly emblems of mortality, including skulls, crossed bones, hour-glass, scythe. The kneeling children of the dead man and his wife (or wives – since there may be one on each side of him) supplant kneeling angels. Figures of the Virtues supplant patron saints. The dead still lie on their backs, still have their hands together in prayer, but they are more realistic, are portraits. Often they begin to prop themselves up, or following Italian example, the dead may be upright busts on the wall (Shakespeare, in Stratford-on-Avon church, c. 1616–23). Much pomp and colour, much worldliness, much expenditure. John Webster's grim play *The Duchess of Malfi* (c. 1612–14), talks of fashions in tomb-making:

> Princes' images on their tombs
> Do not lie, as they were wont, seeming to pray
> Up to heaven: but with their hands under their cheeks
> (As if they died of the toothache) – they are not carved
> With their eyes fix'd upon the stars; but as
> Their minds were wholly bent upon the world,
> The selfsame way they seem to turn their faces.

Inscriptions (in English) lengthen, and celebrate virtue, wealth, marriage, descent and descendants, and position.

But this was a time of pride, strength and delicacy in verbal expression, as well as pride in wealth and show. At any rate, every monument of the sixteenth and seventeenth centuries from Cornwall to the Border and from East Anglia to Wales, grand and expensive or more or less humble and provincial in design, is worth examining, since it may be redeemed by a quite remarkable poem on the dead man or on death and heaven or by phrases such as the ones which the poet Fulke Greville, Lord Brooke (murdered in 1628) wrote for his own tomb in the chapter-house of St Mary's, Warwick:

> Fvlke Grevill, servant to Qveene Elizabeth

Conceller to King Iames and frend to Sir
Philip Sidney. Trophaeum peccati. (Monument of a sinner)

MONUMENTS OF THE LATER SEVENTEENTH AND THE EIGHTEENTH
CENTURY. Fulke Greville's inscription marks a half-way stage between
an underlying medieval humility and an eighteenth-century bland-
ness, between intimations of a personal god and ideas of a more abstract deity. Allegory continues on the monuments, the emblems
including obelisks (eternity), funeral lamps with gilded flames (resurrection) and cherubim (immortal bliss) with wings or like cupids,
with arms and legs and a body, sometimes displaying a grief which
belongs rather to the manor-house than to heaven:

> With wringing Hands the little Cherubs moan,
> And Fun'ral Lamps appear to blaze in stone.
> John Dart, *Westmonasterium*, 1723.

Monuments neatly framed between columns straight, or twisted like
barley-sugar, give way to elaborate dynamic tableaux. Allegory extends through the whole composition in marble involving many classical properties, urn (emblematic container of ashes), sarcophagus
(emblematic coffin, on ornamental feet), pyramid (eternity), etc., and
personifications of Eloquence, Justice, and so on. Flowers, personifications in female form, cupid-cherubim, angels with trumpets take to
the sky and the white marble clouds in baroque movement, and
statues of the dead are all the more animated:

> Next a less pious Posture they provide,
> On Cushions lolling, stretch'd with careless Pride.
> John Dart

They also stand, and strike attitudes, and join in the allegorical fun.
Polished inscriptions in prose, carefully balanced and antithetical, relate the great offices they have held, their moral virtues, their indul-
gence (and firmness) towards their families or the poor, their liberality
to tenants, their 'affable condescension' to neighbours not so high in
the scale of society. The dead all seem to have left a happy, well-regulated life by a side door, for a happy, well-regulated eternal life, which
is their due, in company of a well-regulated and polite deity, who is
very little in evidence in the detail of the monument.

Towards the end of the eighteenth century monumental composi-
tions become simpler and more sentimental in a neo-classical style
derived from Greece. The personifications return from the sky to the
ground or the marble slab and join parents mourning and drooping

over children, or sons and daughters mourning over parents. Or they bend – Faith, Hope, Charity, etc. – over urns or sarcophagi; and the emblems include marble willows, dying flowers and broken columns, although the figures or busts or medallion portraits of the departed may still present firm and admirable likenesses. This neo-classic church sculpture, frequently contrasting white marble against black, was an advance from the bland balance and common sense of the eighteenth century towards those 'romantic' feelings which we generally prefer in the novels and poems of the time.

Many of the learned emblems migrate to the headstones of the poor outside in the churchyard, or to the memorials of yeomen in the nave, in either case the work of local craftsmen rather than London or big city designers. Thus the Cherub-Turtles (as the poet Christopher Smart called them), emblems of eternal bliss, were still being carved and coloured in the nineteenth century (for instance, in Welsh churches, Plate 1).

A careful look round the borders and ledges of a monument from the late seventeenth century to the early decades of the nineteenth century will usually discover the sculptor's name. After which follows the pleasure of turning him up in Rupert Gunnis' *Dictionary of British Sculptors 1660–1851* published in 1953, a book necessary to the pursuit of monuments. Other books to consult are: H. Macklin, *The Brasses of England*; F. H. Crossley, *English Church Monuments*; Katharine Esdaile, *English Monumental Sculpture Since the Renaissance* and *English Church Monuments 1510–1840*.

Note: after visiting one of the great houses now turned into half-crown museums, a free visit to the church is always worthwhile in search of the monuments and effigies of those who built the house, or lived in it, the good, wise, proud, foolish, corrupt, and hypocritical.

# Michael Churches

Why are St Michael's churches – there are hundreds of them all over the country – usually on the top of hills?

St Michael is the archangel, the captain of the heavenly host. 'And there was war in heaven: Michael and his angels fought against the dragon; and the dragon fought and his angels, And prevailed not; neither was their place found any more in heaven. And the great dragon was cast out, that old serpent, called the Devil, and Satan, which deceiveth the whole world: he was cast out into the earth, and his angels were cast out with him. And I heard a loud voice saying in heaven, Now is come salvation, and strength, and the kingdom of our God, and the power of his Christ' (Revelation xii, 7–10). So in the Middle Ages men thought of St Michael as an instrument of salvation. With the Lord he would come down from heaven on the last day (1 Thessalonians iv, 16) and then – like Osiris in Egyptian mythology – he would weigh the souls of the dead. In the meantime this flaming winged feathered being, who floated between heaven and earth, occasionally lit upon summits and intervened in the affairs of men. In the first century he struck a rock with his sword at Colossae, in Asia Minor. At the end of the fourth century he appeared on Monte Gargano in Italy. In the sixth century he flashed on to Adrian's Mole, above the Tiber, at Rome; in the eighth century he showed himself to St Aubert and told him to build a church on Mont St Michel in Normandy.

Hill-top dedications do more than echo these supposed appearances. In fact a church of this *caeli satrapa* or Prince of Heaven crowning our English or Welsh hill has links with the Christianity of Coptic anchorites or monks in the deserts of Upper Egypt in the fourth century. The Egyptians had thought of their god Osiris as 'the light of the sun which vanishes in the shadows every evening to reappear more brilliantly at dawn'; Egyptian monks gave Osiris-like qualities to this archangel, who was also weigher of souls, and built chapels to him on the roof of their monasteries where they would catch the first rays at sunrise.

Coptic Christianity much influenced the practices of British Christianity in the Dark Ages, which probably explains the abundance of Michael churches and chapels on the hills of Cornwall, the West of England and Wales. Veneration of St Michael continued after the Norman Conquest into the Middle Ages, and dedications went on apace. Sometimes in an English church St Michael will have a loft chapel raised up towards the sky in the old Coptic manner. Christchurch Priory in Hampshire, for example, has a St Michael's Loft, a large chamber, in which there seems to have been an altar, above the fourteenth-century Lady Chapel.

Many hill-perched churches or chapels of St Michael have disappeared or are now in ruins. In Wales (which still has many hill-churches at places named Llanvihangel, i.e. Michael's church) only two stones among the grass and whortleberries are left of a St Michael's chapel on the very top of isolated Skirrid Fawr, in Monmouthshire. In Cornwall there were Michael's chapels on the windy summits of Rough Tor and Rame Head. In Somerset and Devon St Michael's ruined churches still rise above the grand isolation of Glastonbury Tor, where a carving shows him weighing the souls, and Brent Tor. The most wonderful of the Michael's mounts of the British Isles belongs to Ireland – the island-rock of Skellig Michael off the Kerry coast, where nearly 700 feet above the Atlantic the saint has a little medieval church surrounded by the more ancient beehive huts or cells of a Celtic monastery.

St Michael is recognizable in churches by his sword, his wings, his feathered legs and arms, and the devil in the shape of a dragon under his feet; or by the scales he holds in one hand, sometimes with a naked soul in one pan and a devil in the other.

Medieval churches or chapels dedicated to St Catherine (see page 32) are also frequently on hill-tops, since St Catherine's body was supposed to have been transported by angels to the top of Mount Sinai and to have been discovered there in the ninth century.

Some books to consult on saints, symbols, birds, plants, etc., in churches: R. L. P. Milburn, *Saints and Their Emblems in English Churches*; M. D. Anderson, *Animal Carvings in British Churches* and *The Imagery of British Churches*; Nikolaus Pevsner, *The Leaves of Southwell*.

# Barrows of the Dead

When the Funerall pyre was out, and the last valediction over, men took a lasting adieu of their interred Friends, little expecting the curiosity of future ages should comment upon their ashes.

Sir Thomas Browne

## ROUND BARROWS

Though the Bronze Age inhabitants of Britain were not quite the first and were not the last to build round barrows over the dead, most barrows of that shape in the countryside are theirs; and though thousands have been destroyed, it has been calculated that upwards of 20,000 round barrows remain, from the Isles of Scilly to the Orkneys, from East Anglia to Ireland, some high and full on bare heath or moorland or chalk downs or wolds, some ploughed and harrowed and rain-washed almost to the ground.

The basic rule was one barrow for one person – no doubt an important person or an importantly related person in clan or tribe. The barrow might be raised over a body (or skeleton) or over ashes. Body-burial, or skeleton-burial, was the practice of the first of the Bronze Age settlers who crossed the Channel about 1800 B.C., nearly 4,000 years ago; it was never completely given up, although cremation became the general custom. The body or skeleton, the ashes or charred bits and pieces, were placed in a pit, or a 'box' of stone slabs, with a stone lid. Sometimes in the earlier centuries, a body was enclosed in a coffin carved out of a log of oak (which was the commonest tree of the period, and perhaps sacred as in historic centuries). Ashes and charred oddments of a body were usually placed under a large wide-mouthed earthenware vessel, or urn, turned upside down. Then the mound was piled up, of soil or stones according to the situation.

A round barrow, in volume like a bowl the wrong way up, is the shape you would expect. No one likes digging, or makes a pit larger than it need be. So first of all the uncremated bodies or skeletons were buried not usually at full length, but on one side, with head forward, arms bent and knees bent up towards the chin and heels tucked up behind, in pits to match, which were more or less rectangular. Urn and ashes were fitted into a pit to match, which was more or less circular. If you are going to cover such a round pit or rectangular pit, or a rectangular stone box, you will go round and round throwing up earth or small stones till you end up with a heap more or less circular (like a bonfire heap in the garden). Excavators have found evidence that barrow builders collected earth in baskets, which they tipped over the grave. But no one wants to carry earth too far, and frequently the barrow builders appear to have traced a circle the right distance away around the grave, after which they dug up the required amount of soil round the circumference, heaping it inwards. This would leave a ditch round the barrow, and such ditches can often be seen, after 3,000 years or more.

After a while the more sophisticated barrow builders came to like their shapes geometrically exact, and not approximate. A circle had to be a true circle, and they liked an exact symmetry of curve and swell. This is true of Wessex – the chalk country of Wiltshire, Hampshire, Berkshire, Dorset, which was the richest centre of active life in England through the round barrow centuries. In Wessex, early on, they varied the pattern of their round barrows in several ways, preferring one shape or another for men or for women. Some Wessex barrows are inverted bowls with a surrounding ditch and then a raised bank round the outside of the ditch. Other large barrows were built with a flat circular space around the barrow, between the barrow and the ditch. Archaeologically this flat space is called a 'berm', a word of French origin which was used in the terminology of fortification for a ledge between a ditch and a rampart. Under a Wessex 'bell-barrow' of this kind with a berm and a ditch it seems that men were usually interred. Much smaller barrows surrounded by a wide berm, then a ditch, and then a bank, known as 'disc-barrows', were heaped over the ashes of women. Women's ashes were also covered by 'saucer-barrows', of inverted saucer shape, with no berm, but with a ditch and a bank. And now and again in Wessex you find near other barrows what is called a 'pond-barrow', though it is no barrow at all, but a round shallow concavity, a saucer the right way up, something like a very shallow empty dewpond, surrounded by a bank. Though burials took place in these pond-barrows, they are considered to have been enclosures in which the dead bodies were left to rot or dry before they were cremated or buried, and then safeguarded under a proper barrow of one shape or another.

Outside Wessex the rule is bowl-barrows with or without a ditch.

Under their mounds the dead were provided (not very generously, since there is no great point in being too generous to the dead) with requirements for a ghostly continuation of life – meat or grain, liquor in mugs, stone battle-axes and bronze knife-daggers, amulets and ornaments, and sometimes a dog for hunting or herding.

Thinking of these round barrow building peoples of more than a thousand years from about 1800 B.C., we have to visualize men and women who lived by keeping cattle and pigs (as well as sheep and goats), by fishing, trapping, and hunting (especially red deer, which were then common over Britain), by growing barley, and collecting wild fruit, such as blackberries, and wild food plants. In religion they perhaps paid their chief respect to a mother-goddess who looked after the fertility of crops and herds – and wives. Their better weapons and tools were made of bronze, more and more used as the centuries went by, their more powerful and richer men wore ornaments of amber and jet and Irish gold (the known amount of gold recovered from barrows is not very great, though it includes a wonderful tippet of beaten gold found in a barrow in North Wales, gold ornaments from barrows near Stonehenge, and a gold cup from a barrow on the Cornish moors near the Cheesewring, found in 1818, and lost to archaeology for a while, when George IV used it as a shaving mug. The tippet and the mug are in the British Museum). They had not by any means abandoned the use of stone, flint in particular, which was still chipped into tools and

53

knives, especially into the neatest of barbed arrowheads. They tanned leather, they wove cloth (from nettle fibre), and they made coarse pottery without a wheel. In art, they were considerable masters of abstract design – or at any rate geometric patterns.

Often (not only in Wessex) these Bronze Age round barrows are grouped – or aligned – in 'barrow cemeteries', as if each such cemetery or cluster or alignment had belonged to a chieftain's family. Each family of the kind may have lived in a large round house of wooden or stone uprights, thatched or turfed, near the barrow cluster. In fact, it has lately been suggested that 'henges' – i.e. circles of bank and ditch enclosing holes in which wooden posts were set or in which there are circles of upright stones – may be remains, not of temples, but of such round houses of chieftains and their families and retainers. Sometimes flint flakes and scrapers and broken arrowheads are ploughed up around the barrow clusters.

So there is the picture, in the clear light of a climate dryer and warmer than our own – a wide grassy landscape (even where today there may be moor and bog and cotton-grass), a round house, a graveyard of tall barrows, and much coming and going, dogs barking, a travelling bronze-smith arriving, herds of cattle and flocks of sheep in the distance, herd boys driving the pigs or the goats farther afield into the scrub or the open woodland, the goats leaving behind them (as goat herds do in the Mediterranean countries) a scent on the air. Or perhaps smoke ascending from the oak branches of a funeral pyre on a space up by the barrow cemetery, where a new barrow would soon be raised against the skyline.

A death demanding such a funeral fire and such an addition to the barrow cemetery may have occasioned grimness as well as sadness, since evidence has been recovered suggesting that the dead man was sometimes accorded the benefit of company in his new shadowy life – i.e. that others were killed, burned, and buried with him, to continue in his service.

That picture of ancient living and dying can be finely imagined by anyone who visits the barrow cluster and alignment in the middle of Salisbury Plain, at the point where the road from Amesbury, Andover and London, A 303, intersects A 360, running north from Salisbury. Here on the turf, by a trackway, there are barrows with ditches and berms, bell-barrows, bowl-barrows, disc-barrows, saucer-barrows, a perfect pond-barrow, in all twenty-six barrows, and from an earlier age (see below) a long barrow as well. On a bright day, with larks overhead and lapwings flying to and fro, and wide horizons of Salisbury

Plain all around, it seems a quiet infinitely agreeable place to have lived. Bronze daggers, amber beads, and two of the red-coloured incisors of a beaver (beavers existed in Wales, if not in England, as late as the twelfth century) have been found in these barrows. Looking north one can see barrows belonging to other groups, or alignments, shadow-marked on slight rises or ridges across the Plain. Barrows were deliberately placed in positions which made them visible and prominent in this way against the sky or the land – usually on the 'false crests' of a slope or a hill, not on the actually highest point or line where they might be invisible from below. Obviously Bronze Age people liked to remember their dead – or at least the important dead who merited all the hard work of raising a barrow.

Notice (1) that the top of a round barrow is often flattened or dimpled, which may be due to the collapse of a grave pit inside, or the collapse of the small wooden death-house which was sometimes built over the remains; (2) that often a barrow will have been planted with trees by eighteenth-century or nineteenth-century improvers of landscape – pleasantly for us, but not for archaeologists. The trees grow very well, rooting into the heaped up surface soil which forms most of the barrow; (3) that very low, weathered and worn barrows, like other earthworks, show up best in the horizon light of early morning or evening.

## LONG BARROWS AND CHAMBERED BARROWS

Long barrows are grander, and pompous, and more ancient (generally) than the round barrows of the bronze-using chieftains. For one thing many of them are chambered, and remotely connected with ancient stone tombs in the Mediterranean: it is possible to go inside some of these chambered barrows, to walk, or crawl, or crouch one's way into the actual chambers of the dead.

55

About 3000 B.C., or some centuries earlier, settlers had reached Britain, with cattle, sheep, goats, pigs and dogs, and established themselves on warm, dry country (especially chalk and limestone), where they could graze their animals, and clear plots of ground each spring to grow wheat or barley. For protection they built 'causewayed camps' (page 61, below) on the tops of hills, probably around their huts and hovels. They knew little or nothing of metal, making weapons and edged tools out of flint and other hard stones, and sinking flint mines here and there into the chalk after flint of the best quality (two of these mines, at Grimes' Graves in Norfolk, have been opened and are now kept open as ancient monuments). Stone and flint axes were in demand for clearing scrub and woodland.

These people buried their dead – their important dead – when enough corpses or skeletons had accumulated, under the thick end of long barrows made of earth. The counties where most of these long grass-grown earthen barrows are to be found, include Dorset (especially in Cranborne Chase), Wiltshire (the long barrow mentioned above at the Winterbourne Stoke crossroads, on Salisbury Plain, is such a barrow), Hampshire and Sussex. The people who built them also spread northeast to Yorkshire and Lincolnshire, and left other, though smaller, groups of long barrows on the dry Lincolnshire wolds and the dry bold chalk lands of eastern Yorkshire (for instance, at Rudstone, a parish full of peculiarities, where there are two long barrows side by side, a huge standing stone alongside the church, and a Roman pavement, on which cavorts a brightly coloured, witch-like Venus).

Often these earthen long barrows are very big and very impressive, like long boats turned upside down on a hill-slope, sunken more at one end than the other. The Wiltshire long barrow at the Winterbourne Stoke crossroads is 240 feet long, the Pimperne Long Barrow beside the main road A 354 in Dorset nearly half as long again.

The men who built the earthen long barrows had originated in northern France. Making longer sea voyages, to begin with, from Brittany and the French Atlantic coast, other peoples came to Land's End, and so up the coasts of Wales, Ireland, the Isle of Man and Scotland. Contemporaries of the earthen long barrow builders, they lived in much the same style (though they sunk no shafts after flint, and had no causewayed camps). For their dead – again dead chieftains and their families – they contrived tombs like caverns, with stone chambers and passages, which were then heaped over with barrows either long, or oval, or more or less round.

In the course of so many centuries the earth or small stones they heaped up have frequently worn away, leaving the massive walls and roof of stone slabs. The older antiquaries associated these naked mysterious structures with the 'Ancient Britons' and with Druids and mistletoe and sacrifice, and gave them the Celtic, or Cornish, name 'dolmen'. Irish people, as plausibly but more poetically, thought of them as the bed of the magic love of Diarmuid and Grania.

With local differences of shape and size these chamber tombs, which are much commoner than the unchambered long barrows of earth, exist in the Isles of Scilly and in Cornwall, around and at the back of the Severn Estuary, in Wales (especially Pembrokeshire and Anglesey), along the Irish coast and across the north of Ireland, in the Isle of Man and on Arran, in the Hebrides, the Orkneys and Caithness, and round the Moray Firth – along the sea-routes. There is a little group of chamber tombs in Kent round the Medway, not far again from the sea; and there are round barrows with stone chambers on the limestone in Derbyshire.

The most famous and some of the most perfect and easily accessible of these stony chambers of the dead are the ones in Gloucestershire, Somerset, Dorset and Wiltshire and Berkshire, where their builders, coming in from the Severn Estuary, met (and mingled with?) the builders of the earthen unchambered long barrows and of the causewayed camps.

There is a main difference between these two kinds of long barrow. An unchambered barrow was raised over a multiple burial, and that was that. It was done with, and new burials called for a new barrow. A chambered barrow (often covering a 'nave' of great slabs, with 'transepts' or side chambers) could be opened again and again for family burials, and used over a long stretch of time.

My own choice of chamber tombs to visit – all ones which can be entered – would include:

West Kennet Long Barrow, near Avebury (recently excavated, and its chambers and courtyard restored).

Belas Knap, at Charlton Abbas, on the Cotswolds.

Hetty Pegler's Tump, at Uley, on high ground above the Severn, another of the Gloucestershire or Cotswold barrows.

Stoney Littleton Long Barrow, in Somerset.

Bryn Celli Ddu, in the parish of Llanddaniel-Fab, in Anglesey, a round barrow with passage and chamber and a phallic pillar, in a splendid situation of corn fields looking across the Menai Straits to the mountains of North Wales.

New Grange, on the Boyne, in Co. Meath. The mightiest of chamber tombs, with a carved stone at the entrance.

Maes Howe, at Stenness, on the Mainland of Orkney.

## OTHER BARROWS

To return to round barrows without chambers, the habit of building them did not die out with the various peoples of the Bronze Age. It is true that later on (after 1000 B.C.) other immigrants came, and founded larger farming communities, and buried their more numerous dead (after burning them) in cemeteries more like our own. The burnt scraps were collected into an urn (usually), and the urns were simply placed in holes in the ground, where they have remained – as Sir Thomas Browne wrote of his Walsingham urns in Norfolk (though they were Anglo-Saxon, and not from such a Late Bronze Age cremation-cemetery) – 'scarce below the roots of some vegetables.' All the same, there do exist Late Bronze Age barrows. And along with Iron Age cemeteries, Roman cemeteries and Anglo-Saxon cemeteries, there also exist some barrows of Celtic chieftains, some Roman barrows (sometimes above ashes in a glass urn), as well as Anglo-Saxon and Viking barrows.

A few of the Anglo-Saxon round barrows are still called by the names of the great men who were buried under them. On the edge of the Berkshire Downs, in East Hendred parish, Cwichelm, King of the West Saxons, who died in 593, is buried in the barrow called Cuckhamsley ('Cwichelm's *hlāw*', or barrow) or Scutchamer Knob. A hole in this barrow suggests that it was rifled for treasure. Not far away in Buckinghamshire there still exists the large round barrow or *hlāw* of the chieftain Taeppa, in the old churchyard of the place we continue to call Taplow. The barrow is empty now, since Taeppa's grave treasures (in the British Museum) and Taeppa's skeleton were removed by excavators in 1883.

Everyone knows of the richest of all barrow finds – of the Suffolk ship burial recovered in 1938–9 under one of the Sutton Hoo barrows, at Sutton, on the river Deben, a few miles up from the sea. The barrow over those treasures was raised about 655–60. Less than a hundred years later, an Anglo-Saxon poet wrote his epic poem of *Beowulf*, giving us a near and rare look at the burning of a great man's body and the fashioning of his barrow.

This description in *Beowulf* may fit the sentiments of two and a half thousand years of the raising of round barrows over the remains of a chieftain or a member of a chieftain's family, and give some feeling of the solemnity of ancient rituals.

King Beowulf at last is dying, after his attack on the dragon (who had guarded treasure, in the manner of dragons, in another barrow). He says –

> Tell the famed fighters
> To raise on the headland
> A bright barrow over me
> After my burning.
> High upon Hronesness
> It shall recall me.
> Sailors shall call it,
> In their distant boats driving
> Over the dark seas,
> Beowulf's Barrow.

His people obey him:

> Then the Geats set ready
> A firm fire-pile for Beowulf,
> And hung it with helmets,
> Shields, and bright corselets
> (As Beowulf had bid them),
> And mourned as they laid there
> The lord whom they loved.
> And they roused on the headland
> The fiercest of fires,
> The smoke of the wood
> Rising dark from the glow,
> Flames crackling, men keening,
> Till down died the draught,
> And the body was gone,
> Heated through to the heart.

They sang laments, an old woman with her hair bound sang a dirge for Beowulf, the smoke vanished in the sky:

> Then they built up a barrow
> On the edge of the headland
> A high one and wide one
> Far sailors could see,
> And in ten days they finished
> Their great fighter's beacon.

> They had walled round his ashes
> As the wisest advised them,
> They had laid in the barrow
> The rings and adornments –

the gold, says the poem, from the barrow-hoard of the dragon. Last
of all –

> Men brave in fighting,
> Twelve sons of chieftains
> Rode round the barrow
> Telling their sorrow,
> Lamenting their great king,
> Praising their hero,
> Reciting his actions. . . .

Barrow-building came to an end with Christianity.

Observe, by the way, how the terms for barrow differ in different
areas. Most of them are words originally meaning no more than a hill
or a mound. 'Barrow' itself is the south country and south-west country
derivative of the Old English *beorg*, a hill; which is applied to burial
mounds in several other forms – 'bury', 'burrow', 'borough', and (in
Sussex especially) 'burgh'.

An Englishman before the Conquest would have known it was a
burial mound you were talking about, if you said *hlāew* (the word used
in *Beowulf*). This is the time-honoured English term for a barrow (also
meaning mound or hill), surviving as 'law' in Northumberland,
and as 'low' in many counties, especially Derbyshire, the Midlands
and the South. An ancient Dane or a Norwegian, on the other hand,
would have spoken about burial under a *haugr*, another hill word for
a burial mound now surviving from East Anglia to the Orkneys as
'howe' ('how', 'houe', 'haw', etc.) as in the famous Maes Howe in
Orkney.

Some other barrow words are 'cop', 'knap', 'knoll' or 'knowe',
'ball' (a round hill) and 'tump', all of them hill or hillock terms; 'butt'
in Hampshire, which meant a mound (from the French) before coming to mean a special kind of mound for practising archery. Also
'toot' or 'tout', which meant a look-out place.

In Cornwall and Wales 'carn', or 'cairn' in Ireland, means a barrow
of small stones. *Bryn*, a hill or mound, is another Welsh barrow term,
as in Bryn Celli Ddu, the Barrow of the Black Wood.

# Hill-forts

Most 'rings', 'rounds', 'buries', 'castles', etc. – i.e. hill-forts encircling the tops of hills, or on high ground – belong to a fairly recent time, the last two and a half centuries B.C. and the half century or so A.D. up to the invasion and conquest by the Romans.

There is an exception. A very few 'causewayed camps' in the south of England, most of them in the chalk country, were built between two and three thousand years earlier by the herding and land-scratching people who sank the first flint mines, began the clearance of the English countryside, and heaped up the earthen long barrows (page 55). These are camps surrounded by a bank and ditch or several banks and ditches, through both of which there are a number of irregularly spaced 'causeways' to the hill and the grazing grounds outside. Not many of these very ancient earthworks have resisted the rain and frost and surface changes of so many thousand years. The banks and ditches are often worn very low, and are best discernible in the evening light. 'Causewayed camps', elaborate in their rough plan, seem to have been places in which cattle were periodically rounded up, and penned, and sub-penned, so to say (rather as in a cattle-market), and slaughtered.

Knap Hill, in Wiltshire (just where the by-road from Marlborough to Alton Barnes drops into the Vale of Pewsey) is surrounded by one of these camps, still quite clearly defined on a long-shadowed evening. On one side of the camp a chambered long barrow (page 54), known to the Anglo-Saxons as Woden's Barrow, and to us as Adam's Grave, is visible against the sky. Just below and alongside the camp is the site of a Romano-British farmstead, where the moles throw up Roman nails and red sherds of pottery, and at the back the ancient grazing grounds still have their cattle.

Fewer than twenty 'causewayed camps' are known, compared with a great number of the familiar hill-forts, their ramparts still high, their ditches still deep and full of shadow. These forts were called into being by fighting and raiding in a disturbed era. The country had filled up. British peoples making tools and weapons of iron, which was new to Britain, had been arriving since about 500 B.C. At first they had lived in round wooden farmhouses inside a circle of ditch and rampart and wooden stockade, each farm having about fifteen acres of small fields for grain and a wide spread of grazing grounds.

More immigrants meant competition and raiding and cattle-thieving and slave-taking – and defence, i.e. more permanent and effective

61

ditches and ramparts around a farmstead, in place of a stockade; and these new conditions meant taking to the hill-tops. The slopes helped defence, and the hill-top gave a wide surrounding view, a chance of detecting marauders before they were at the gate.

A more or less simple hill-fort of a few acres enclosed by a single rampart and a single ditch will probably have belonged to the second or third century B.C. If it was attacked, well and good: it was stronger than a stockade farmhouse. If it was not attacked, the new rampart made it a more sheltered and permanent stockyard, easier to maintain.

Conditions grew more dangerous and chaotic and pressures increased in the first century B.C. Old hill-forts were adapted and strengthened. Some were made and abandoned, or half made and never finished, because danger had passed. Some were resorted to only in times of danger. Others were permanently inhabited. Small, large, very large, farmstead forts, village forts, town forts, were built with multiple ramparts and ditches around the contour of a hill; behind the width of ditches and ramparts the inhabitants and their cattle were out of range of arrows and particularly of sling-stones. Since hill-tops are windy and wet places (the climate of Britain was no longer the dry and genial one of the second millenium B.C.) the thatched wooden huts, or thatched huts of wood on stone footings in the stony districts, were clustered along the rim of the interior space, where the inner rampart gave the most shelter.

Grain from the small irregular fields outside (the bounds of which are often visible in the evening) was dried and stored in silos dug into the ground, round pits wider at the bottom than the top. Seed grain for the next sowing was stored above ground in small stilted granaries, in pots. Flour and meal were ground (by the women) in small revolving hand-mills, or rotary querns, which have been found in hill-fort excavations. Iron was smelted in some of the forts, and smiths were at work. There were looms in each hut, as in a modern cabin in the west of Ireland.

Some of the greater hill-forts were stormed, in time to come, by Roman legionaries; and most of the hill-forts were abandoned after the Roman conquest, in an era of peace and order and government which had no use for feuds and independent or private fortresses. The inhabitants of some of the large hill-forts transferred, or were transferred, from hill-top squalor, windy discomfort and inconvenience, to walled Roman-patterned towns at a lower level – for instance, from Bigbury to Canterbury, Maiden Castle to Dorchester, the Trundle (where a 'causewayed camp' preceded the hill-fort) to Chichester.

Some of the commoner names for hill-forts of one kind and another have been mentioned. The English settlers recognized them as fortified places, and gave many of them names containing *byrig* (dative of *burh* or *burg*, a fort), which has changed to 'bury'. In Cornish and Welsh a fort was *caer*, giving such names as Carwen, the White Fort, in Cornwall; or Caer Caradoc, Caradoc's Fort, in Shropshire, for a celebrated hill-fort along and around a narrow lofty hill above the trunk road between Ludlow and Shrewsbury.

Roman forts such as were built for soldiers operating against the North or against the inhabitants of Wales, were quite different – as different as a ruthlessly straight, carefully surveyed Roman road from the windings of a ridgeway or ancient track, or as the lines and right angles of a Roman town or Roman villa (farm estate buildings) from the untidy curlicue lay-out of a British village or a British farmstead. Roman forts are rectangles or squares of bank which runs straight from rounded corner to corner. The large British hill-fort suggests a horde, the Roman fort, which avoided hill-tops for wide spacious high situations, suggests drill on a parade ground. If the fort was in frequent use at exactly the right strategic centre, the banks of turf or clay might be rebuilt in stone.

## FOGOUS, OR WEEMS, OR SOUTERRAINS

In Ireland there was never a need for enormous high-perched hill-forts of the English kind. The Irish kept to the earlier habit of building combinations of ditch and rampart around a farmstead. Some 20,000 of these raths, as they are called, survive, many or most of them built in the first seven or eight centuries A.D. Smaller men had smaller and simpler raths of a single bank and ditch, chieftains had triple ringed forts, stronger and grander. Such a fort would descend in hereditary succession, as a famous Irish poem bears witness, a poem of the eighth century about the rath at Rathangan in Co. Kildare:

> The fort by the oak trees there
>    Was Bruidgi's, was Cathal's,
>    Was Aed's and Ailill's,
>    Cuilini's, and Conaing's,
>      And Mael Duin's.
> The fort in turn outlives
> Each of these kings renowned,
> Whose hosts sleep in the ground.

Early or late, these Irish raths often have a souterrain, a long, underground, chambered passage, roofed and walled with stone. Explore a souterrain by candlelight, and you see a mysterious building much as it was fashioned and left in ancient times; for which reason souterrains should be more famous than they are.

The making of souterrains (like the making of chambered barrows long before) spread from the Atlantic coasts of France to Brittany, from Brittany to the Land's End of Cornwall (where a souterrain is called a fogou, from the Cornish word for a cave), then to Ireland, and Scotland (where they are 'weems', from the Gaelic for a cave, or 'Pict's Houses'); spreading even to Denmark.

The best Cornish fogou, at Halligye, in the Lizard peninsula, opens in the garden of one of the cottages of a small isolated hamlet which succeeds a fortified Iron Age settlement or farmstead, of which the fogou was a part. There are others which can be visited in Ireland (e.g. at Ballintemple, near Garvagh, and Ballywoolen, near Castlerock, both in Co. Derry) and in Scotland.

Prosaically a souterrain is a cellar, a storage place; but there are elements of plan and structure, such as low lintels across the passage or trip stones protruding from the floor, which suggest secrecy, and the concealment of valuables, as if the souterrain had been safe or hidden fireproof strongroom as well as cellar. The *Landnáma-bók*, the Book of the Settlements and Generations in Iceland, written down early in the twelfth century, tells how Lief the Icelander acquired the name of Sword-Lief, how he went raiding in Ireland, and 'found a great earthhouse there': he entered, 'and it was dark inside till light shone from a weapon which a man was holding. This man Lief slew, and took the sword and much other riches. After this he was called Sword-Lief.'

See Evelyn Clark's *Cornish Fogous*, 1961, which deals with Irish and Scottish souterrains as well.

# Dykes or Pales

Earth is plentiful, valuable, and worthless. It can be heaped up into barrows, camps, hill-forts, etc., and when such 'earthworks' are not required any longer, nobody can be bothered to shift the stuff. So earthworks of all kinds are apt to survive, when far younger, solider walls of useful and valuable stone are apt to vanish.

Britain has an abundance of ancient earth-built dykes – 'dyke' originating in the Old English word meaning ditch, and in the names

ER·I·FODYN
ING·MEN
DDA·YN·WNO
1635

In Memory of

1 Monmouthshire landscape, with bust of Landor, tombstone
cherub, and Redstart

2   (*left*) A Wiltshire White Horse (Cherhill, 1780)
3   'Green Man', resurrection symbol from medieval church

4  The Long Man of Wilmington, chalk-cut giant, from a symbolic landscape of Sussex

5 Urns from Bronze Age barrows (with the Great Cross of
Conbeline, eighth to twelfth centuries, Glamorganshire)

6   Limekiln, and standing stone of Dark Age chieftain Corbelanus, in idealized Cardiganshire landscape

7　Church and vapour trails, Suffolk, county of rare Avocets and of tumulus which covered the Sutton Hoo ship burial

8  (*left*) Birds in winter
9  Curlew on the wing, and Swallow

10  Birds and bats, summer dawn

11   Sea birds, including Cormorant and Gannet

12  (*left*) Yellow Wagtail and Cuckoo
13  Sky creatures, including Kestrel

14 (*left*) Turtle Dove, alighting on sheaf of oats
15 Moorhens and chicks, Fallow Deer, Jackdaws

16   Thrushes in winter, with Long-tailed Field Mouse

of these old earthworks coming to mean the whole complex, both the ditch or trench and the rampart, both the space which is left, and that which is heaped up from the space. Rampart and trench are inevitable aspects of each other, but each contributes to the purpose of a dyke or ditch.

The purpose was composite. The Romans called such a sophisticated dyke as Hadrian's Wall a *limes*, the word which gives us 'limit': dykes delimited, which is one use; dykes kept out (and kept in), which is another use. The first dykes in Britain were built seven centuries or so before the Roman Conquest, and the last were made in the Middle Ages. Large or small, long or short, lines or enclosures, they are expressions of property sense, or 'what we have we hold': they are cruder and bulkier equivalents of the modern fence, which is strengthened by law-abidingness (and perhaps with barbed wire and a notice saying 'Keep Out' or 'Trespassers Will be Prosecuted') instead of by depth of ditch, and tons of earth and a palisade.

1 Dykes on the chalk uplands of Wiltshire, Dorset, Hampshire, Berkshire, are mostly the remains of earthworks which enclosed ranches or grazing-grounds of the centuries from about 800 B.C., the emphasis as much on Keep In as Keep Out; though the great earth ramparts – such as the double rampart of Grim's Ditch, on the chalk of Wiltshire, Dorset and Hampshire, near Salisbury – would also have effectively hindered the quick processes of cattle thieving. Grim's Ditch enclosed sixteen square miles of grazing.

Dykes across the Wolds in East Yorkshire, towards Flamborough Head, were no doubt boundaries of much the same kind and date. Five square smooth miles of Flamborough Head itself are cut off in this way by the Dane's Dyke, more than two and a half miles from sea to sea. (This may be 'Dane's Dyke' because in due time it protected a Danish settlement. Flamborough means the *burg* or fort of Fleinn. This Dane would have been taking advantage of fortifications made perhaps many more than a thousand years before he took over.)

2 Not so long before the Romans conquered Britain, the Belgae crossed from the Continent, and established towns. The approaches to their towns at Colchester, St Albans and Wheathampstead, to settlement, meadow ground and plough ground, were cut across by short lengths of dyke – very wide deep trenches with only shallow ramparts.

Other dyke systems were built before the Romans came, including dykes closing gaps between forest and forest in front of Chichester and the wide grazing grounds of Selsey Bill; and a dyke system, another

Grim's Ditch, near Blenheim in Oxfordshire, stretching between two rivers.

3 When the English began to invade and settle after the breakdown of Roman Britain in the fourth century, they did not come as a homogeneous force, and there was soon boundary trouble between the various kingdoms. So earth trenches and ramparts were required once more.

Wansdyke (properly Wansditch), sixty miles of high rampart and deep trench, with breaks, across Somerset and Wiltshire, used to be thought a British defensive boundary of the fifth to the seventh century, against the English. It has now been differently explained. A potent cause of dyke building seems to have been the rise of the Mercians, the forceful men of the *mearc*, the march, the boundary, or boundary district (the Marches), who carved a kingdom out of the unexploited oak forests of the Midland counties. Their neighbours needed to contain them, lock them out, protect themselves and their cattle. Wansdyke is now interpreted as a barrier raised in the seventh century by the West Saxons, the men of Wessex, across the run of the old Fosse Way of the Romans, to keep Mercian war parties out of Somerset, the rich grazing country into which the Wessex men drove their flocks and herds every summer as 'summer settlers' (Somerset is still a county of grass and milk).

The East Angles had trouble with the Mercians. At some time in the same century they appear to have raised the short, huge Cambridgeshire dykes, including Fleam Ditch and Devil's Ditch, across the chalk passage between impenetrable fen and impenetrable forest, i.e. across the Icknield Way, which was the corridor route giving access to Norfolk and Suffolk from the south-west. Battle burials have been found along the Cambridgeshire dykes. At one point on Bran Ditch the skeletons of nearly fifty soldiers were unearthed. They had been captured, then beheaded.

Other short dykes close a gap, and a route, in this typical way, often across a ridge or a valley.

Contrariwise Offa's Dyke, very similar in construction and more than 120 miles long, from the Dee to the Severn (though once more with breaks where natural obstacles made earthworks unnecessary) was built later, about 785, by the Mercians, under their king Offa, to prevent the British raiding from Wales into their Midland farms.

Dyke building spread down to Cornwall, up to Scotland, and over to Ireland, where the great Black Pig's Dyke travels across country, like Offa's Dyke or Wansdyke, seventy-five miles from Castleblaney in Monaghan to Bundoran on the Donegal coast, nearly cutting Ireland in two (there are breaks again where the dyke was unnecessary, e.g. when it comes to a lake).

It would have been no easy business for raiders to drive back cattle or sheep across a Black Pig's Dyke, a Wansdyke, an Offa's Dyke, indeed any other such dyke, short or long, whether topped with a palisade or not, in the days when the ramparts were at their full height and the trenches were still uniformly deep, steep and unsilted. Quite a short delay could have been fatal. For that reason, though watch might be kept, there was no need to string soldiers along one of the major dykes. Things to notice are not only that breaks in a dyke or a sudden ending of a dyke may be explained by thick forest or bog or fen which has long ago disappeared, but that the trench (west along Offa's Dyke, north along Wansdyke, etc.) will always be on the side away from the territory of those who made the dyke, on the side from which incursions were to be feared. Also that the mystery and great labour of dyke-building has been confidently ascribed, as the names show, to giants, and the Devil, and the Danes, and to the great god Woden (Wansdyke was Woden's Dyke – *wodnes dic* – see page 119), generally called Grim. The English forgot that many Grim's Ditches had been the work of their own ancestors.

Dykes were also raised, imposingly, around Anglo-Saxon estates; and in the Middle Ages, earth still being a useful, plentiful and free substance, ditch and trench combinations continued to be set around parks and woods. In the fifteenth century a dyke, the Pale Ditch, was built across the country to delimit and protect the English Pale, the chief settlement area of the English – or Anglo-Normans – in Ireland.

# Motte and Bailey

The last, but least recognized, of the great earth shifters or earthworkers were the Normans after their invasion of 1066.

On the Bayeux Tapestry the Normans are shown raising a castle at Hastings, in immediate consolidation of their victory: they are hurriedly and busily spading up earth and stones in what the Normans called a 'motte', or tall mound, on top of which they placed a wooden tower. At the bottom, flanking the motte, they would have added a courtyard, a 'bailey', or space enclosed (*bailler*, to enclose) by ramparts, a ditch and a palisade.

This was the pattern of a quickly built effective instrument for the subjugation of the English, who had cared little for castle-building, had not studied this new castle technique, and were defenceless. When one of the new lords of England took possession of estates in a still dangerous and discontented countryside, up went a motte-and-bailey – even a chain of such forts – at the dominating points, such as the side of a road over a pass, or beside a ford or on a high key position looking out across a vale; and the people they forced to do the spade-work were the English. Such forts were hard to tackle with short-range weapons and without siege equipment.

Here and there, later on, a motte-and-bailey castle would be re-fashioned grandly and hugely in stone; but in England and Wales alone there are upwards of 900 castle mounds which were never capped by anything more than a wooden keep. Not all of these belong to the phases of invasion and settlement. Others went up (especially in the Midlands) during the troubled years of Stephen's reign (1135–54), when the nobles, according to the *Anglo-Saxon Chronicle*, 'cruelly oppressed the wretched men of the land with castle-work', filling the new castles 'with devils and evil men'. The areas of the thickest con-centration of castle mounds – Pembrokeshire and Carmarthenshire, and the whole length of the Marches, along the ancient boundary of Offa's Dyke – tell an obvious story. Gloucestershire, Herefordshire, Montgomeryshire, Radnorshire, Shropshire, Denbighshire, Flint and Cheshire are motte counties to a degree; and in Wales motte-building was quickly adopted by the Welsh against the intruders.

How are mottes to be recognized? They do not always have a name. On a map they may be marked only as Earthworks. Even now the (usually) circular mound is likely to be tall (perhaps twenty or thirty feet, or higher still), steep, and flat across the top. There will probably be a trench around it (i.e. a moat, which is the same word by origin as motte: moat or motte having been applied, like 'dyke' – page 64 – to the double complex of trench and mount). This moat or trench would have been filled with water if there happened to be a convenient supply.

The adjoining bailey, on one side, as likely as not will be roughly oval. It may have disappeared. Or you may be able to trace the sur-rounding inner rampart (which was topped with a palisade of split logs), the trench, which joined the trench around the motte, and the smaller outer rampart, and the gap in these bailey ramparts where a bridge or causeway was set across the trench.

The castle owner lodged himself and his family in the wooden tower, which rose up twelve feet or so on the motte (above another palisade surrounding the flat summit). In the bailey lived the men at arms, in rectangular buildings of wood including a hall and stables and storerooms. Often the turf outline of these buildings is visible. Sometimes there are pits, in which grow nettles well nourished by the nitrogen from old organic rubbish. The motte may cover an acre or two acres of ground. Along the Marches 'tump' is a common word for a motte; across the border the Welsh use the word *tomen*.

In 1169, under Henry II, the Anglo-Normans began the invasion of Ireland, and again set up wooden motte-and-bailey forts. There are also Scottish mottes of this late time (in Scotland a motte is a 'mote').

One thing which can be seen in these castles of the individual invaders and overlords is the start of that extraordinarily complete division of interest and culture and status between a squirearchy (Norman) and the peasantry (English), which continues, so far as squirearchy or peasantry still exist; in Ireland the pattern was repeated even more severely and divisively. The castle tump is perhaps the foundation of English snobbery.

Note: for a spectacle of continuity and contrast, visit if you can Tomen-y-Mur, the Tomen of the Walls, in Merioneth, on a high platform, with blue mountains at a distance, above A 487 from Dolgelly to Ffestiniog. Here is a Roman fort, complete with a small soldiers' amphitheatre, built in campaigns against North Wales under Frontinus or Agricola; at one corner stands a grass-green *tomen* or motte, built, so it is thought, by William Rufus when he drove against North Wales in 1096 and 1097, and used again by the English in 1114. Alongside is a now deserted farmstead. Below, fully visible from the flat summit of the *tomen*, crouches the atomic power-station of Trawsfynydd.

## OTHER FORTIFICATIONS

Many more structures remain to speak of disturbance, robbery, death, defence and invasion or threat of invasion – not only hillforts and the great Forts of the Saxon Shore which the Romans built against Anglo-Saxon raiders in the fourth century (the best of these to visit are Porchester Castle in Hampshire, Pevensey Castle in Sussex), not only the grandiose castles which succeeded motte-and-bailey, not only Tudor coastal forts built against France and Spain and the Martello towers of the south coast, built against Napoleon, but others from the brochs of the Iron Age to the innumerable concrete pill-boxes built against Hitler, which are now up to their slits or tops in hogweed and bushes.

BROCHS (from the Old Norse word *borg*, meaning a stronghold or fort) are fortified farmsteads or farm hamlets with a round tower, found in northern Scotland, especially in Orkney and Shetland. The tower (only the Broch of Mousa in Shetland now has a tower rising to something like the full height) stood forty or fifty feet above a walled courtyard, in which there were small more or less circular dwellings. Often the brochs are on the shore, by a small sheltered natural harbour.

The broch people flourishing from about 200 B.C. to 100 A.D. were Celtic and seem to have originated on the Atlantic coast of France and to have been related to fort-builders in western Cornwall at the other end of the British Isles. They farmed – growing barley, keeping cattle, sheep, pigs, etc. – they fished, and evidently fought, developing these strong, defensive, hollow-walled forts, the top of which (reached by steps through the hollow of the walls) gave a long warning view over sea or land. The Broch of Mousa is the classic example among several hundred sites. In the Orkneys there are still some fourteen feet of tower to the Midhowe Broch (one of three in a group) on Rousay, a broch set between two narrow creeks. The Broch of Gurness, on Mainland above the strait dividing Mainland and Rousay, has a considerable height of tower, and has also been excavated, cleared, and preserved.

CRANNOGS. In the shallow lakes in Ireland and in the Scottish highlands crannogs are artificial islands or house sites made by heaping stones and earth on a timber foundation (*crannag* is the Gaelic for 'timber structure'). Defensive crannogs were fashioned about 850–1050, in the insecure era of Viking raids, although some crannogs go back another 2,000 years or so. Island Machugh Castle, Co. Tyrone, was built in Tudor times on a crannog in Lough Catherine intermittently or continuously occupied since the nucleus of the crannog was made in neolithic times.

MOATED SITES, square or rectangular instead of roundish or oval like the earlier crannogs, are common in some of the English counties. Desolate behind their screen of blackthorns and beyond their now bridgeless moats of black water and dead leaves, these were homestead sites of the twelfth to fourteenth centuries, an inversion of the crannog principle, their builders creating, so to say, the lake instead of the island. Anyone who has puzzled himself about crossing such a moat will realize that it would have given real security against sudden entry or attack, so long as the householders had drawn in their wooden bridge, or drawn it up.

ROUND TOWERS, in Ireland, slender and tall, with entrances above ground level and tiny window openings and conical summits, were another response to raids by the Norsemen. These repositories and refuges (sometimes attached to one of the small monasteries) of the Irish were a speciality of the years 850 to 1050, or thereabouts; difficult for raiders in a hurry to break into or set on fire.

PELE OR PEEL TOWERS. These peculiar sturdy little oblong towers in Northumberland, Cumberland, and also Westmorland were mostly built during the troubles with Scotland in the fourteenth century. A pele is a palisaded area. Inside the stockade of earth and stakes the tower with three storeys was a house built upwards instead of hori- zontally – upwards for defence against marauding Scotsmen or the sudden influx of war.

A typical pele tower of the Middle Ages will begin with a vaulted ground floor chamber, which was the buttery or service room of the house. A stone staircase (sometimes there was only a ladder which the householders could draw up behind them) goes to the hall, or main living and sleeping room on the first floor, above which was the par- lour used for sleeping by the master and mistress of the house. Pele towers were no longer required when the Union of the Crowns of England and Scotland in 1603 brought peace to the border, and more comfortable houses were built alongside (in Westmorland, farther away from the dangers of the border, the pele towers had often been built as an appendix to a hall on the ground level). All the same a good many pele towers continued in use. Parsons, in particular, could not always find the money for new vicarages or rectories. The rector of the moorland parish of Elsdon in Northumberland, south-west of Rothbury, described in the seventeen-sixties how he lived in his rectory pele tower of the fourteenth century (still to be seen) – cows on the ground floor, the curate and his wife and the maid sleeping in the first floor kitchen, and himself sleeping in the parlour between two feather mattresses, 'to keep me from being frozen to death, for, as we keep open house, the winds enter from every quarter, and are apt to creep into bed to one.' He wore three night-caps, fortified his throat with a pair of stockings, and hung his greatcoat on his own back for want of a wardrobe. Round the very fine ruined pele tower at Edlingham in

Northumberland (between Rothbury and Alnwick) there are still remains of the stone fence or wall which replaced the older palisade.

BOW OR CANNON. When you are going round a medieval castle, look for one tell-tale item ominously introducing our world of the hydrogen bomb. In the walls, in the towers, are there small slit openings? Or by any chance small openings combining a slit and a round hole, like a large keyhole upside down? Or small stone-framed circular holes, without a slit?

Through the arrow-slits, the small slit openings, the crossbow was discharged. Then by the last decades of the fourteenth century large cannon were brought against castles, on ship if the castle stood by the water, or on land. Castle defenders replied with small calibre falcons and falconets, etc., which they fired through an adapted arrow-slit, or gun-port, a slit with a gun hole having a diameter up to ten inches. By mid-fifteenth century this gun-port had become simply a round hole without a slit. By the end of the fifteenth century gun-ports became rectangular. (See B. H. St J. O'Neil's *Castles and Cannon*, 1960.)

# A Miscellany of Things

STANDING STONES, standing solitary on field or moorland, are apt to find their way on to the map, and to demand explanation. Better, or safer, at any rate, always to start with the prosy explanations. One such explanation is provided by cow hair caught in the rough edges of the stone: quite sizeable stones have been set up, in pastures, for cattle to scratch against – not so much out of kindness as from a desire that the cattle should rub against something they cannot push down or destroy.

A large stone is the time-honoured durable to use if you want something or someone to be remembered. So a standing stone may have been set up as a boundary mark. Or it may be a gravestone or memorial stone of the Dark Ages which was never inscribed.

If it was not for the rough inscription in Latin saying that Corbelanus was buried there, how could one ever interpret the rough dumpy stone which juts up (Plate 6) in a Cardiganshire cornfield above the sea at Penbryn? He was a chieftain, and in the early Christian centuries such men were often buried by roads or tracks or on their own ground, 'a custom not yet displaced by the Christian desire to lie in a churchyard' – or in a church – 'in close contact with the relics of the saint, and so ensure a place in Heaven' (C. A. Ralegh Radford).

A standing stone may be the last remnant of a burial chamber inside a barrow (page 55) which has long disappeared. It *may* also have been an idol or a revered fertility symbol. St Samson of Dol in the sixth century was crossing east Cornwall (still independent, and a long way from the English invaders and settlers), in the neighbourhood of Bodmin: he encountered Britons giving wild homage to a stone idol, 'an abominable image, on a hill-top', whereupon he destroyed the image, which was perhaps no more than a large standing stone, and set a cross on another standing stone nearby. The enormous yet slim and very tall Rudstone in the churchyard at lonely Rudstone in east Yorkshire, must have been something dragged there and erected for veneration on a low hill-top. Afterwards it was christianized into a 'Rood Stone' – a stone of the Cross – and a church was built alongside.

An old name for a standing stone may do no more than indicate that five hundred or fifteen hundred years ago people invented a reason to explain its presence. How could the stone which gives its name to Taston (near Spelsbury, Oxfordshire) have come there, English settlers asked themselves, unless it had been thrown down by their god Thunor (Thunor's Stone – see page 120)?

STONE CIRCLES, in common thought, still glow in a mystic light of druids and sacrifice and the ancient Britons, and Welsh bards at an eisteddfod (wearing robes which were designed by an Anglo-German Victorian R.A., Sir Hubert von Herkomer). It cannot definitely be said that any existing stone (or earth) circle, neolithic or Early Bronze Age, of any size, or any combination of a circle (or circles) of standing stones with a circular mound of earth, or any circle revealed by air photography, had anything to do with religion; and the assumption that Avebury, for instance, or Stonehenge, was the centre of a religious observance (long before the Druids of the Iron Age and the Roman era) unquestionably owes much to the old romantic theorizing. It may be true; but it may also be true that they are only the remnants of the circular stockades and round houses of a line of extra important chieftains.

Religious or secular, it is possible to think of Stonehenge as a very large roofed round house inside its enclosure, and of Avebury as a pair of roofed round houses with stone uprights inside a great circular ditch and a great stockade of stone posts, with an infilling between the posts which has long disappeared.

In the same way – which makes sense instead of mystery – other stone circles according to circumference may also be uprights of larger or smaller stockades, or uprights of larger or smaller round houses. Where long free stones were not available, chieftains' round houses and stockades were made of timber.

Small round houses or round huts, Bronze Age and Iron Age, which never had high walls, have left 'hut circles' of low stones behind them, averaging twenty feet or so in diameter. These are common on Dartmoor, in settlement groups. In stony country there are also low stone circles which were once retaining kerbs around Bronze Age barrows heaped up with small stones instead of soil.

Long alignments of standing stones can also be explained as prehistoric hedges or boundaries which have lost the infilling there used to be between stone and stone.

ROMAN VILLAS, or their sites, are marked on the 1-inch maps. But when we make a pilgrimage and look at mounds and lines and rectangles in the turf, at scraps of mortared walling, an excavated well, at a pavement or two under a modern tin roof, and at remains of central heating and baths, it is not so easy to put two and two together.

Villas were neither villas, as we use the word, nor 'Roman', although they were romanized: they were the larger farmsteads or estate headquarters of the Roman centuries, belonging, not to Romans from Italy or some other part of the Empire who had settled in Britain, but to the well-to-do aristocratic Britons who had a foot both in town and country, and had come to adopt Roman ways, rebuilding and elaborating their farmsteads on a more or less Roman plan.

Like manor-houses in centuries to come, the villas varied in size, wealth, importance and sophistication. A prosperous villa at the end of the third century or in the fourth century obeyed rule and setsquare, a half-timbered house on footings of stone or concrete, tiled, and centrally heated. Floors were tessellated, and there was glass in the windows. The walls were plastered and painted. Round the courtyard or walled farmyard there were quarters for the farm servants (sometimes they were slaves), and barns, stables, stone threshing-floors, workshops, and perhaps a dovecot. On the wide estate wheat was grown; and cattle, pigs, sheep, goats, horses and dogs were among the farm animals. The owner and his family might be well educated, brought up on Virgil and Horace, worshipping Roman gods and goddesses who were depicted in the mosaic pavements, and drinking wine imported, then as now, from Italy or Spain (though some villas had their own vineyards and made their own wine). But there would

74

have been every gradation between educated and uneducated, sophis-
ticate and provincial, as in our own manor-house society. The villas
were happily situated for shelter and sunshine on the sides of valleys
looking east or south. As the towns disintegrated at the end of the
Roman rule in Britain, so did the villas. It is thought that the English
settlers found them deserted and in ruins.

ROADS AND TRACKS. The animal's way and the unthinking,
unplanning or casual human's way from one point to another, even if
there are no obstacles, is not a straight line. Habitually, though,
animal or man-animal will go from A to B by much the same route;
which becomes a path. Such a path becomes a track, if many of them
use it. And eventually man's track becomes a road. So a winding –
always a winding – 'modern', hard-surfaced road, even a considerable
main road, as often as not follows or conceals in itself some ancient
pathway or trackway.

Having business to transact (since even 4,000 years ago there were
'factories' where flint or stone axes were made), early man also had his
long distance tracks or trade routes. Since he avoided overgrown valleys, and forest and thorn scrub, these were very often ridgeways – on
high ground, where the going was safer, drier, and easier (and where
most of the settlements were located). Ridgeways are the oldest roads,
and they are lonely; they do not join up existing settlements, though
along their winding route the map may reveal neolithic or Bronze
Age remains or Iron Age hill-forts.

Valley roads, with even more twist on account of the terrain, which
join farm to farm and village to village, are likely to be Anglo-Saxon in
origin, or medieval, the original paths of those who preferred the
valleys and cleared the denser forests. Often an ancient ridgeway up
above will be roughly paralleled down below for a few miles by a far
twistier road or lane joining up Anglo-Saxon settlements which have
never been deserted.

ROMAN ROADS. Most Roman roads – most of the easily recognizable ones, at any rate – are through roads in straight stretches of
considerable length –

> This Roman Road runs straight and bare
> As a pale parting line in hair

– part of a system of governmental roads carefully surveyed, ditched,
and surfaced, and as direct as possible.

A well-preserved piece of Roman road will show an *agger* or raised ribbon, with a ditch on either side, and a narrower stony road surface on top of the *agger*. Originally the *agger* of an important road may have been several feet high and perhaps fifteen yards across. The road along this *agger* was made of large irregular lumps of stone bonded with gravel or smaller stones of some kind. A key road might be upwards of thirty feet wide on a forty-five or fifty foot *agger*. Roads half as wide are much commoner; and originally the road surface would have been quite steeply cambered, much like one of the military roads of France.

It is a mistake to think of Roman roads as paved with flat slabs of stone. When an ancient Englishman called a Roman road a 'stræt', as in Watling Street, or Ermine Street, he was using a word borrowed from the Latin *strata* or *strata via* meaning a way which was levelled, covered or surfaced, i.e. a way metalled with irregular bits of stone compacted into a smooth surface. Later on, after the Norman Conquest, Roman roads were often called 'causeys' because of the *agger*, causey or *caucie* in Old French meaning a raised way. Fosse Way, the Anglo-Saxon name for the great Roman road from Lincoln down to the Devonshire coast, is another reminder of the structure of Roman roads, referring to the fosse or ditch on either side.

Notice if you drive for some way along a stretch of Roman road which is still in use (e.g. the Fosse Way) that it will directly link few villages or farms, and be nearly as lonely (except for traffic) as a pre-historic ridgeway. Anglo-Saxon settlers avoided the Roman 'streets', which would have laid them open to surprise and rapidity of attack.

Wheeled traffic used the Roman roads, as rut marks show in the compacted metalling (for instance, in a piece of road kept exposed at Blackpool Bridge in the Forest of Dean, near Blakeney). After the Roman period wheels were uncommon on most of the roads until the seventeenth and eighteenth centuries. In some of the hillier western counties pack-horses were still the rule even into the nineteenth century.

WAYSIDE CROSSES. Stone crosses by the roadside were often put up in the Middle Ages along the way to church and churchyard at points where it was customary for the bearers to rest a coffin, during which time prayers would be said. The rector of Camborne in Cornwall willed money in 1427 for a series of such crosses along the road to his church.

TOLL-HOUSES or TURNPIKE COTTAGES. Turnpike cottages, sometimes very pleasant little pieces of eighteenth-century architecture, occasionally displaying a board or slab detailing the tolls which had to be paid, still exist by the hundred. They are relics of the first modern revolution in the upkeep of roads. In the century of the Tudors roads were scarcely more than tracks. In 1555 an effort was made to improve them by an Act of Parliament ordaining that every parish had to keep its own roads, its own section of the highways, in proper repair, the parishioners contributing 'statute labour', either direct or indirect. It was a system which gave poor returns. If the road was good enough for the slow affairs of the parish, that was that: why should the parishioners care about through travellers in a hurry – or in the mud?

Wheeled traffic was increasing, so there was a call for harder, wider roads with fewer sloughs of despond; and in the latter years of the seventeenth century the parish system began to be supplemented by the work of Turnpike Trusts. Bad sections of highway were taken over by these local committees, ditched, and surfaced, and kept in repair; and the work, or most of it, was financed by tolls which users had to pay (other roads were still the responsibility of the parish), or by putting the lease of the tolls up to auction. Hence the turnpike cottages at the beginning and end of each turnpiked stretch or where other roads came into such a stretch. Across the road there was a gate or turnpike (a word which first meant a spiked barrier against attack), and on the toll-collector's cottage wall a board detailed the tolls which had to be paid for carriages, waggons, carts, horses, animals on the hoof, etc. Most toll-gates and tolls were abolished by 1895, seven years after the establishment of the county councils, which in the end took over the duty of good maintenance.

GREEN LANES and ENCLOSURE ROADS. 'Green lanes' are older roads 'unadopted' into the road system. They may be pre-historic ridgeways or trackways, they may be disused lengths of Roman road, and often they were routes used, before the railway age, by drovers driving pigs or cattle to the great markets and towns.

In the seventeenth century the standard width for a cart way into market towns was eight feet, or nearly twice the width of a cart. But before the time of modern hard surfaces roads of every kind were inclined to diverge – to wriggle – this way and that where there was room, so that traffic could avoid mud and ruts and pot holes. Green lanes spread in this way. This need of width was also recognized when open fields of the old manorial system (page 19) were enclosed, and when in consequence new parish roads were made or old roads adapted and straightened. Enclosure roads of this kind are straight, as a rule, and usually forty feet wide from hedge to hedge or ditch to ditch, with a metalled track down the middle and wide grass verges on either side.

When road-making improved and the hard-surfaced road was confined within unvarying limits, the once necessary wide green verges of roads were often enclosed, legally or illegally. Squatters took possession or built a cottage, or a strip was added to an adjoining field. Sometimes a line of elms along a field marks the old line of the green verge.

FORDS. Even now by no means all the streams are bridged at the point where a road crosses them, and there are fords to be discovered and enjoyed not only on by-roads in Wales and other mountainy districts, but even in such low-lying country as Norfolk.

Fords deepened and flooded, fords were defended, at fords armies or raiding parties were held up, at fords men were killed or drowned, in summer the fords are low and make a pleasant sound. So they are frequently in evidence in early poetry – at any rate early Welsh and Irish poetry. 'Every gleaming furrow is a full river', says an Irish winter poem of the tenth century –

> And every ford is a full lake.

A Welsh winter poem (twelfth century) says

> Mountain snow, there are fish in the ford

– which there are not when the ford is low in summer; and a Welsh summer poem of the twelfth century declares

> Delightful is the top of the broom, a trysting-place for lovers,
> Very yellow are the clustering branches;
> The ford is shallow

– i.e. all is well.

The ancient names we still use for hundreds of towns and villages end in -ford, though the river or stream may have been bridged centuries ago. Often the shallow fording stretch can be detected above or below the bridge, together with the approaches. Welsh ford names will often begin with *rhyd*, a ford; Cornish ford names with red- or res-. If you plot the names in almost any district, you will find the ancient names in -ford much commoner than the ancient names in -bridge. The names will often describe the length or depth or breadth of the ford, will identify it by its colour, by the name of someone who lived nearby, or by trees or flowers which grew there. In Wiltshire, Bulford is the ford which was marked by a fine show of *balut* or red campion, Clatford the ford where 'clotes' or yellow water-lilies grew.

BRIDGES. The simplest form of bridge is a tree cut down and trimmed and laid across from bank to bank. The bridge is improved if you give it one – or two – handrails, and if you level off the trunk. In Devon, Cornwall and Somerset such foot-bridges, often near a ford, are known as 'clams'. Perhaps it was a clam – across the little river Biss – which gave rise more than a thousand years ago to the name Trowbridge, the 'treow' or tree bridge, for the capital town of Wiltshire; in which county there is also, in one of the parishes, a Pantry Bridge, originally 'the bridge of the pine tree'. And there are many Stockbridges, from another word for tree trunk.

The narrow stone bridges alongside a ford (or alongside both a ford and a modern road bridge), often with a causey or raised approach on either side, were the pack-horse bridges, which kept the trade routes open in the months of flood. They were essential for the carriers' trains of pack-horses conveying goods of every kind. The stone clapper bridges or clappers of Dartmoor, Exmoor and Cornwall (from a Medieval Latin word *claperius*, a heap of stones) are such pack-horse bridges of a crude cyclopean kind, thrown across streams which could swell very quickly into dangerous torrents.

Rivers in England were bridged by the Romans in stone as well as timber. By the English before the Conquest they were sometimes bridged in stone, more often in timber (up and down England there are bridge places named from the words *thel brycg*, i.e. plank bridge – such as Thelbridge in Devon or Elbridge in Kent; in the areas where Norse was spoken there are bridge names from the Norseman's word for a plank, such as Felbrigg, in Norfolk). Stone bridges were built very abundantly in the Middle Ages, often as an act of piety. Travel was increasing and there were new towns, fairs and markets to go to, and new pilgrimage routes. Such medieval bridges (particularly of the fifteenth century) can be recognized by their pointed arches, and by the V-shaped extensions beyond the line of the parapet, which helped to break the force of the water and allowed space into which the foot-passenger could – and can still – squeeze himself from traffic.

FERRIES. There were rivers and estuaries which could not be bridged – some of which have been bridged for road traffic only in recent years. Ferries were the answer. Regularly maintained ferries were commonly established in the Middle Ages, when ferry rights were valued as property and a source of revenue, making at the same time a pleasant, and sometimes a dangerous, break in a long journey. At Saltash on the Tamar, where there is now a road bridge as well as a railway bridge, the clanking steam ferry on chains, joining Devon and Cornwall, descended from a medieval ferry, the rights in which were at one time granted by the Black Prince to a retainer who had lost an eye in the fighting at Poitiers.

The ferryman's trade now brings too small a return on the minor foot-passenger ferries, which are rapidly disappearing after an existence of six hundred or eight hundred years. For instance, minor ferries across the Severn and across estuary rivers in South Wales have been abandoned since the Second World War, though they are still marked on the ordnance survey maps.

FORESTS. Reading *Grimm's Fairy Tales* has given us a wrong idea of English forests – a Black Forest idea, which can best be realized abroad or deep inside the twentieth-century conifer forests established by the Forestry Commission. To begin with, the forests were extents of primeval woodland on soil, such as clay or gravel, too poor or too difficult to be worth clearing and cultivating. But they were worth preserving for game – for deer and wild boar – and in the Middle Ages, before and after the Conquest, they survived as royal hunting grounds or chases, 'the secret retreats of kings and their chiefest delights'. Their character as remnants of primeval landscape was modified (partly by rights of common, which were respected); and such 'forest' was partly wooded, with deciduous trees, especially oak, and partly open with sunny glades among the dark foliage (though a 'forest' might also be moorland, with no trees at all).

The deer hunted in the forest were the king's game. Forest and game were strictly protected by forest laws and local forest courts, and were administered by wardens, and more directly by the foresters they employed, who lived a lonely greenwood life directed against the poacher's art.

In a forest area, finally cleared perhaps in the seventeenth century and transformed into rather poor farmland, it is still possible to discover many traces of the old order. The area may still be called a forest, and it is a mark of the antiquity of forests that forest names are sometimes British, such as Savernake or Bradon. Berkshire is the shire of the old pre-English forest of Bearrne, the hilly district. Forest words or forest terms will still dot the map. There may be names with -leigh (from *lēah*, a clearing), or lawn (from *launde*, a glade, or a pasture in the woods), or -shaw (from *sceaga*, a copse), or -hurst (from *hyrst*, a wooded hill), or purlieu, for a strip once on the edge of the forest (from a legal word for perambulating the forest boundaries so as to define them), or names to do with the pampered and protected deer, such as Lipgate or Lypiatt, i.e. a leapgate, a fenced gap or gate which deer could leap, though it kept out other animals. Here and there ancient oaks nearly old enough to have given shelter to medieval huntsmen survive in a copse or a corner. There may be farms named this or that 'lodge', where there once stood lodges built for the temporary entertainment of royal or privileged hunting parties.

In an old forest area most of the existing cottages, farmhouses, etc., are likely to be modern and rather nondescript and mean. If there is a church, it will probably be Victorian. If there is a village, it may have the rather flimsy look of an encampment, instead of the settled comfortable look of a village with rich farms and a past of more than a thousand years.

PARKS may be as old as the thirteenth century, or as recent as the middle or later years of the eighteenth century when noblemen and rich country gentlemen surrounded their new classical mansions with a wide serenity of carefully designed landscape.

The older parks attached to castle or mansion were more than an adornment or a luxury. Their owners needed fresh meat in the winter months, obtained a royal licence, and enclosed a park (often from one of the ancient forests) in which they kept deer both for sport and venison. These older deer parks were surrounded (page 67) with banks of earth topped with palings too high for the deer to leap. Later deer parks of the era when the herd of deer grazing around ancient oaks or in glades of bracken was not so much a necessity as a pleasant sight and a pleasant sign of wealth and position, are often recognizable by now gapped and intermittently tumbled walls of unusual height.

Why is a parish church so often to be found inside a park as if it were the private chapel of the great house, which is now open for half-a-crown? Usually as a consequence of eighteenth-century dictation and grandeur. Manor-house, church, and village are generally more or less of a unit. In the eighteenth century an out-of-date Jacobean or Tudor manor-house was often grandly rebuilt, and the owner wanted privacy and an enlarged or new landscaped park around the house. The owner liked to include God, and exclude the villagers. So the church often came inside the park boundary or the garden boundary, in the new design. Now and again if the boundary could not be conveniently re-drawn so as to exclude the village, the village was calmly destroyed and the villagers were rehoused out of sight (which was done at Milton Abbas in Dorset). Or the church might be destroyed and rebuilt to match. At Stourhead in Wiltshire (where the eighteenth-century landscape garden belongs to the National Trust) the village was re-designed and trees were planted so as to bring the medieval church into the garden picture. At Croome d'Abitot in Worcestershire, be-tween Worcester and Tewkesbury, the Earl of Coventry in the seven-teen-fifties gave himself a new house and a new park: he then pulled down the medieval church and built a new Georgian Gothic church at the right scenic point on the edge of his new park, which was land-scaped for him by 'Capability' Brown (1716–83), the master of the natural 'improvement' of park and landscape (see page 324).

A landscape park designed by Brown or one of his followers is likely to have several special features. Immediately around the mansion there may be a ha-ha, a combination of ditch and sunken wall, of French origin, so devised that from the house the garden seems joined to nature, i.e. seems not to be divided from the park, or seems to merge into the park, as the park beyond merges into the countryside.

Beyond the ha-ha, in the middle distance, there will be clumps of trees, then a winding, dammed-up artificial river (as at Croome Court, Croome d'Abitot) or a winding artificial lake. The ends of the lake or 'river' will be concealed by trees or by a real or a mock bridge. Beyond this winding water, winding belts of trees will be broken here and there for a long prospect, or vista.

When a nobleman asked 'Capability' Brown to work for him in Ireland, Brown replied that he 'had not finished England'. Certainly landscape parks by Brown or made under Brown's influence did create much of the modern look of England. When Brown died, Horace Wal-pole said that the dryads ought to wear black gloves in mourning for this second husband of Lady Nature.

PROSPECT TOWERS or OBSERVATORIES. Landscape gardening, combined with grottoes, artificial caves, classical temples,

'Chinese' rock-work, the damming of valleys to form ornamental lakes and waterfalls, the provision of ha-has, or invisible sunken fences, which preserved an illusion of natural unity, while dividing the ground immediately in front of a mansion from the surrounding park or landscape, and the establishment of 'eye-catchers' (perhaps in the shape of a pseudo-Gothic ruin) so as to draw the eye to the telling point in a vista – these were all part of a movement among the more cultured rich men of the eighteenth century to 'improve' a nature which was newly discovered and enjoyed. We inherit the results, not only in so wonderful and admirable an eighteenth-century landscape garden as Stourhead, in Wiltshire (now restored, and preserved, by the National Trust), but in the eighteenth- and early nineteenth-century extension of landscape design (with clumps of trees, pine trees exactly placed for effect, and so on) outside the garden or the park and across the whole estate. This led to extensive tree-planting around villages, houses and farmsteads, and changed the look of England from a seventeenth-century meanness and nakedness.

Prospect towers or 'observatories', usually medieval in design, were a part of this extraordinary movement. On his pseudo-medieval Brislee Tower (1781) above the woods of Alnwick Park, in Northumberland, the Duke of Northumberland set an inscription in Latin which epitomizes these feelings for nature, vista, and improvement:

Look round!
All these things I planned.
Mine are all the dispositions
And the design.
Also I planted many of these trees
With my own hand.

Still admired, but no longer cared for, and often falling to ruin, these prospect towers have often lost the internal floors and the upstairs room in which the ladies and gentlemen of the big house took their tea and read such poems as Thomson's *Seasons* or Dyer's *Grongar Hill*, before enjoying from the observatory itself, i.e. from the top stage, evening prospects across a vale to distant horizons.

Such towers were memorials as well, piously commemorating public service. Henry Hoare, in 1772, finished off the Stourhead gardens by building a hill-top prospect tower commemorating King Alfred. The triangular tower set up above the Tywi Vale and Grongar Hill and the ruins of Dryslwyn Castle, near Llanarthney in Carmarthenshire, commemorated Nelson (with tablets inscribed to him in English, Welsh and Latin). Here on the first floor there was a sumptuous banqueting room with Gothic panelling and fittings of fine silk, below the central tower, which was the actual 'observatory'.

OBELISKS and COLUMNS and other hill-top monuments belonging mainly to the eighteenth- and early nineteenth-century era of moral and libertarian self-confidence were also part of the movement to improve spectators by improving landscape. Whether the monument commemorates a man or a battle, it will be carefully sited in the landscape, a focusing point from miles around, and the inscription will indicate moral sentiments of liberty, service and patriotism. Thus the obelisk on the field of Naseby (Northamptonshire), erected by the Lord and Lady of the Manor of Naseby in 1823, first remarks that the Royalist defeat there on 14 June, 1645, 'led to the subversion of the throne, the altar and the constitution', but then adds that it left 'a useful lesson to British kings never to exceed the bounds of their just prerogative, and to British subjects never to swerve from the allegiance due to their legitimate monarch.'

WHITE HORSES. All of these intaglio figures cut through the turf into the white chalk of hill slopes – all the ones which exist – are modern, with the single exception of the White Horse across the scarp of the Berkshire Downs above Uffington. This was probably cut in the first century B.C. by the British. It is a figure in the non-representational tradition of Celtic art. There is a hill-fort of the second century B.C. alongside the horse, which may have been a cult figure or a tribal emblem.

The Uffington Horse much appealed to antiquaries in the eighteenth century, and in 1778 another horse was cut into the escarpment of Salisbury Plain (visible from the railway near Westbury, in Wiltshire) in the realistic manner of a horse by Stubbs, the great horse-specializing artist of the time. At least nine other horses were then cut in Wiltshire in the course of a hundred years, in the same realistic tradition, as well as a few in other chalk counties. (Plate 2.)

Two other hill-horses, both destroyed, have a claim to antiquity. At Westbury an elongated creature certainly preceded the horse cut in 1778. The other, destroyed before the end of the eighteenth century, was a red horse instead of a white one, cut into the limestone of the Edgehill escarpment above the Warwickshire village of Tysoe. Like the Uffington Horse, this Red Horse of Tysoe may have been another

cult figure or a tribal emblem, Tysoe (see page 120) meaning the spur
or hill of the war-god Tiw. The first record of the Tysoe Horse goes
back to 1607.

Books to consult are W. C. Plenderleath, *The White Horses of the
West of England* (1885), and Maurice Marples, *White Horses and Other
Hill Figures* (1949).

HILL GIANTS. The Long Man of Wilmington (Plate 4) whose
tall outlines are cut down to the chalk of the South Downs above
Wilmington village in Sussex, and the huge club-brandishing, ithy-
phallic Cerne Giant, outlined in chalk above Cerne Abbas in Dorset,
are both presumably ancient. The Cerne Giant might have been the
obscene jest of a ribald free-thinking eighteenth-century nobleman
making fun of antiquaries, though it is now a little shakily interpreted
as a Romano-British cult figure of Hercules of the second century. It
was not recorded until 1764. The Long Man was not recorded until
1779, whereas records of the Uffington Horse go back to the twelfth
century. However, a turf-cut figure of the giant Gogmagog existed on
the slope of Plymouth Hoe as early as 1486, and was later given the
company of a giant comrade. Another Gogmagog existed on a slope
near Cambridge, about 1600. The Whiteleaf Cross, a Latin cross on a
triangular base cut into a chalk slope of the Chilterns looking over the
Vale of Aylesbury near the Icknield Way, was recorded first in 1742,
and may have been a wayside cross of the Middle Ages. See the book
by Maurice Marples, mentioned under WHITE HORSES.

CUP-AND-RING MARKS. In the British Isles there are no
painted caves, no rock sculptures of the Old Stone Age, and there is
not much in the way of elaborate or exciting rock carving from the
later prehistoric centuries. Most worth seeing are the boulders on the
wide Northumberland moors below the Cheviots, and in sight (many
of them) of the North Sea, carved mysteriously with cup-and-ring
designs, usually dated *c.* 1600–1000 B.C. There are such markings on
stones elsewhere, in the south of Scotland, in England, Wales, and
Ireland, especially on stones forming part of Bronze Age or Neolithic
barrows, but Northumberland has the best concentration, beginning
not far south of the border with the great roadside boulder lying like a
whale in the heather above the waterfall glen of Roughtinglinn, north
of Wooler. There are good clear carvings to be seen on the brow of
Dod Law, above the Till on one side and the village of Doddington on
the other, a few miles south-east of Roughtinglinn; on Weeton Moor,

just to the east of Wooler; at Old Bewick, to the south-east again, a little east of a great hill- or cliff-fort; and then a good many miles farther south near the Lordenshaw hill-fort, on the wide moors immediately south of Rothbury. The carved rocks humping out of turf, heather, or bracken are not always easy to locate. Some of the ones carefully and cheerfully described in guide-books have been removed; but when at last one comes to the right rock out of all the surrounding rocks, all the possible rocks, there is no mistaking the deep cups and the incised concentric circles round them and the incised lines striking out from the cup across the circles. What are they? Why were they carved? Impossible to say. Possibly they were debased images or symbols or indications of a goddess of fertility or life – of life in death, a cult derived from the Near East (see O. G. S. Crawford, *The Eye Goddess*, 1957).

HOLY WELLS are relics of an ancient delight in the ceaseless welling up of springs, a delight in clear sparkling water which is about as old as mankind.

A *wella*, *wielle* or *waella* in Old English meant primarily a spring, water on the move, not stagnant and stale and dirty but at its liveliest and purest. Since water was necessary for life, since springs or wells continued to flow though everything else dried up, continued cold and refreshing in the sultriest weather (or contrariwise, since water from a thermal spring as at Bath or Buxton continued to be warm when there was snow and frost), such wells in their spontaneity seemed to have life and power. Qualities find a name: the well was identified with a minor deity, a nymph, a goddess of fertility, a god or goddess of healing, to whom offerings were made in order to earn this deity's goodwill. Near Cerrawburgh on the line of Hadrian's Wall coins were thrown into a holy well or spring which was sacred to the Romano-British goddess Coventina. The custom of leaving offerings of flowers at a well, as well as coins or bits of metal or rags, also survives from very ancient practice. The Roman poet Horace celebrating the Bandusian spring in one of the most famous of the world's poems, says that the spring, 'more sparkling than glass', deserves offerings of sweet pure wine and flowers. Properly persuaded with offerings, the well (or its being) may cure diseases, induce fertility, provide glimpses of the future, grant wishes and bring good fortune.

Christian authorities frequently denounced and forbad well-worship, but since the delight in springs is so strong and so basic, missionaries had to change pagan into Christian. Like St Samson christianizing a menhir or standing stone in Cornwall (page 73), it is recorded that St Columba, or Colum Cille, in Scotland changed a well which the Picts worshipped into a holy well. Wells, in fact, which had belonged to a goddess such as Coventina had to be associated with favourite saints, and were still resorted to – as they are resorted to even now – for the old purposes.

Just as veneration of wells outlived this change from paganism to Christianity, so the christianized saint's well outlived the Reformation; after which many sacred curative wells were secularized into spas, doctors attempting to rationalize the irrational by solemnly analysing the waters and ascribing pseudo-scientific effects to them because of their chemical impurities. This in turn caused doctors and others with a good business sense to develop entirely new, entirely secular spas, exploiting even the scummy sulphureous springs which smelt of bad eggs and seemed anything but 'pure'. Most of these seventeenth-century and eighteenth-century spas have had a short life. The more successful spas were the ones which developed out of a very long magical or religious past. Thus the hot springs at Bath had been sacred to Sulis, a Romano-British counterpart to Minerva, and the warm springs at Buxton had been the Aquae Arnemetiae of the Romans, and later had been associated with St Anne, and frequented by the lame and the sick and the barren whose crutches, shirts and shifts hung round her spring and her chapel. At the Reformation St Anne's baths and wells at Buxton were locked and sealed on the orders of Thomas Cromwell, Henry VIII's vicar-general. But the habit was too strong, and Buxton's future as a pseudo-scientific spa was grander than its past as a place of holy waters. This St Anne, mother of the Virgin, was a favourite patroness of holy wells, chiefly perhaps as an encourager of fertility, since her own barrenness had been divinely corrected, according to one of the apocryphal gospels. In Wales the water of a St Anne's well (at Llanfihangel, in Glamorganshire) flowed out through the stone breasts of a figure of this saint.

Holy wells (the corresponding word for such a well is *ffynnon* in Wales, *tobar* in Scotland and in Ireland) were associated with innumerable holy men and women, English, British and Irish as well as those common to medieval Christendom. Probably more wells belong to the Virgin than anyone else – including the various Ladywells in England, and in Wales the holy wells called Ffynnon Fair or 'Mary's Well'. It should be mentioned, by the way, that the marked frequency of holy wells in Cornwall, Wales, and Ireland (where they number as many as 3,000) is due rather to conservatism and isolation than to a specially Celtic veneration for springs. They were certainly as common among the English.

Often the wells were roofed with small stone buildings (some charming medieval examples include St Melor's Well at Linkinhorne and Dupath Well in St Dominick parish, both in East Cornwall, both of the fifteenth century, and St Agnes' Well at Cothelstone, near Taunton), and they were frequently made to flow into a stone bath or tank, so that the diseased could immerse themselves or thoroughly splash themselves in the holy water. St Antony's Well, near Micheldean in Gloucestershire, has such a stone pool, in which people bathed against erysipelas (St Antony's Fire) and other skin diseases which could be alleviated through St Antony's kind intercession. Such diseases were particularly common in the Middle Ages.

A chapel dedicated to the saint was frequently built alongside the well for prayer, and as a repository for offerings (quite a number of wells are in churchyards); and in the chapel or the well building there might be relics of the saint to help in the cure. In Pembrokeshire, till the First World War, at Ffynnon Deilo (Teilo's Well), in Llandilo, under the south slopes of the Precelly mountains, water was drunk out of the brain pan (now lost) of St Teilo's skull, or what was thought to have been his skull. One very common practice in England and in Wales has been to continue to use water from the holy well for church baptisms. May was a special month for visiting wells and seeking relief in the waters, especially on the first three Sundays or three Thursdays in the month.

Some English well names conceal the oldest beliefs and practices. At Elwell in Dorset you can visit the Wishing Well – the Old English *hæl* well, which meant the well of good fortune or the well of healing. At Fritwell village, north of Oxford there may once have been a wishing well, a well of *freht* or divination. Here and there, there are springs called Bridewell or Bridwell, i.e. fertility wells once visited by brides after marriage (though in Wales and Scotland a 'Bride Well' may be a well dedicated to St Bride or Bridget). Holy wells in Wales seem to have been much visited for the sake of fertility, the suppliants drinking the water of the well sweetened with sugar; Catholic King James II and his second queen visited one of the most celebrated of all pilgrimage wells, St Winefrid's Well, at Holywell, in Flintshire, on 29 August, 1686, in order to procure a son by influence of the saint. (The best book on holy wells in general – as well as in Wales – is *The Holy Wells of Wales* by Francis Jones, 1954.)

GOSPEL OAKS endure more as names than as trees. Either way, they will be found on parish boundaries, and were taken as convenient enduring marks of the exact boundary line – also as convenient stopping-places during the processional beating of the bounds in Rogation week, led by the lord of the manor and the parson, who blessed the crops and the land. Before the Reformation crosses were carried, crosses were traced on the ground, and the gospels were said or sung 'to the corn', under the Gospel Oak. Perhaps there was some survival of tree worship in this respect for the oak tree. After the Reformation the ceremonies weakened, and were gradually abandoned.

DENEHOLES and MARLPITS. Deneholes in Kent, Essex, Hampshire, Sussex and elsewhere, have been accounted for in many odd ways. If you dig a shaft into the ground and then dig outwards from the foot of the shaft, you are obviously digging for something; and since deneholes go down into the chalk (often through a considerable cap of clay and top soil), and since chalk was used – and is still used – for 'marking' fields which require lime, obviously that something was chalk. A denehole is a chalk mine. Pliny wrote that in Britain they sank shafts for chalk, which was spread on the fields. Nearly 2,000 years later Sussex people (according to O. G. S. Crawford, writing in 1953) remembered denehole diggers going round with a donkey and a windlass – much as specialists went round making dewponds. So a denehole may be British and ancient (as old as Roman Britain, or older still), or modern. Most deneholes collapse, and leave a tell-tale depression in the ground. They may be seventy to a hundred feet deep, and they were often notched down the shaft with footholds. Along downland escarpments, it was easier to dig into the slope for chalk-marl. There are miles of such downland marlpits in Wiltshire and elsewhere – shapeless conglomerations of grass-grown pits and mounds, often with a cart-track leading away from them.

LIMEKILNS. The most extraordinary limekilns are the tall cyclopean ones of golden-yellow sandstone at Beadnell Harbour, in Northumberland, preserved by the National Trust. They belong – and so do many limekilns around the countryside – to the late eighteenth century. Lime was 'burned' for making lime mortar, which was increasingly required for building in stone during, and after, the seventeenth century, and for lime-washing the outside of houses. Lime was also the first artificial fertilizer. The agricultural improvers of the eighteenth century promoted its use as a sweetener of acid soil, in

89

preference to sea-sand which had a much lower content of lime, or chalk dug from marlpits and deneholes. Then came the Napoleonic wars. More food was needed, more corn land was ploughed, and greater supplies of lime were imperative. So in the last years of the eighteenth century and in the first decades of the nineteenth, thousands of country limekilns were built from Cornwall to Scotland, from Northumberland to Wales and Ireland. It was more important that they should be nearer the farm than the quarry. From cliff or estuarine quarries broken limestone was cheaply and easily transported by sea, and kilns were apt to be sited on accessible beaches, at lonelier harbours (the grey fumes from a burning kiln are unpleasant), or as far as possible up tidal rivers.

The heavy structure of limekilns gives them a medieval look, especially when a kiln has more than one 'body' or crucible. The arches gave access to the kindling hole at the bottom of the bodies, which were charged first with dry kindling wood and then alternately with layers of soft coal and layers of limestone. Where possible the kiln was built into a hillside, which could easily be cut away to form the necessary ramp up to the platform around the bodies. Coal and stone were carted or barrowed up to the platform from the sea-barges; when the body cooled the lime was heaped on to the platform and taken off to the farms by cart or pack-horse. (Plate 6.)

The poet John Clare was a limeburner's labourer in 1817 and 1818, tending kilns day and night – often by himself – in the limestone country near Stamford. On an upturned lime scuttle he sat down and wrote the prospectus for his first book of poems. This was at Ryhall, in Rutland.

RED HILLS are among the least known but by no means least exciting of prehistoric antiquities. They are to be found along the shallow coasts of the North Sea, especially in Essex, in the shape of slightly raised platforms of red earth, near the winding traces of tidal creeks; which were saltings of the pre-Roman era. Fires were made heating earthenware troughs or saggers upraised on constructions of earthenware bars. Salt water from the creek was poured into the sagger, and overflowed on to the bars. The water evaporated, the salt crystallized and was scraped off when the saggers and the bars had cooled down. These bars and troughs had a short life. They broke up, and gradually raised the site to a 'red hill', still to be detected after more than 2,000 years. Essex farmers are glad of a red hill on their land, since the red soil is uncommonly fertile, giving splendid crops of kale and potatoes. For the explorer the red hills also have one particular advantage: they give him something he can take away. The plough every year turns up vitrified lumps of briquetage, red or green, and as intriguing as some strange geological specimen.

CAVES. There is no warrant for thinking that caves were necessarily the first 'houses' of mankind in Britain or anywhere else. For one thing there are not enough caves to go round, and the best caves are confined to districts of limestone or sandstone, for another thing hut sites and tent-pits of the Old Stone Age have been discovered. All the same, men at most times, from very ancient to more or less modern, have never been averse to occupying a convenient cave. Sandstone caves in particular can be enlarged and improved, and actually made (in England the most remarkable semi-artificial cave or cliff dwelling is a hermitage-cum-chapel of the fourteenth and fifteenth centuries at Warkworth, in Northumberland, pecked into the golden sandstone above the river Coquet). Shallow caves or cave shelters were often preferred to deep caves – particularly when they opened on a wide, clear prospect.

In several counties limestone caves were intermittently occupied by palaeolithic hunting parties some 20,000 years ago. Of these, one of the most exquisitely sited is the shallow little hall of King Arthur's Cave, high up above the Wye, in Herefordshire, in a limestone brow. A convenient cave was likely to be occupied on and off for centuries or millennia. King Arthur's Cave still gave shelter to pottery-using neolithic people many thousands of years later; and caves were occupied in the Bronze Age, the Iron Age, the Roman era, the Dark Ages, the Middle Ages, and more recently still. A number of caves in the Mendips, in Scotland and in Ireland, are known to have been used as forges by Iron Age smiths.

For caves, caving and cave archaeology, county by county, the best – indeed the only comprehensive – book is *British Caving* (1953), by members of the Cave Research Group. But there is also a guide to *all* the considerable caves in Britain – *Britain Underground*, by N. Thornber, A. H. and R. D. Stride and J. O. Myers, published in 1953 by the Dalesman Publishing Company and the Blandford Press.

SWEAT HOUSES. A speciality of the Irish, and not uncommon (though no longer used) in the Irish countryside. They are small half-egg-shaped stone huts with low doorways under a wide lintel, in which people (in damp Atlantic Ireland) sweated out their rheumatism in the summer months. Just as the cottage cloam oven was preheated with faggots burned inside before the loaves were inserted, so the sweat house was heated for two days or so with a fire which quickly burned down to a pile of hot ashes. The ashes were swept out, the hot floor was insulated with rushes, and a party of the naked inserted themselves, and sat round on turf seats. When they were sufficiently salmon-red and sweating, they emerged and soused themselves with cold water from a brook. The whereabouts of good examples in Co. Tyrone and Co. Derry are given in *Ancient Monuments in Northern Ireland Not in State Charge* (Stationery Office, Belfast, 1952).

MAZES, MISMAZES, TROY TOWNS. There are not many of these left, and at least two good ones have been destroyed within the last thirty years – the mazes at Comberton in Cambridgeshire and on Boughton Green in Northamptonshire. The turf maze was an amenity or institution of town or village life, usually on the green, the common, the fairground, by a holy well to which pilgrims came for healing (there was a mismaze once on Tadmarton Heath in North Oxfordshire, where there is a holy well), or wherever the traditional place for games and celebrations might be. There 'treading the maze' – i.e. balancing one's intricate, narrow, frequently reversed way, competitively (?), to the central point – was one of the regular entertainments.

This rather simple fun was probably introduced (or reintroduced) into Great Britain in the Middle Ages, after the Conquest. It seems to be very ancient, and to be descended from a maze game played in the fields by Roman children, which later on was transformed into what the Romans called the *Lusus Troiae*, or the Game of Troy, a mock fight played by troupes of boys, one younger, one older, and partly on horse-back, at shows staged by emperors. Aeneas was supposed to have brought the game from Troy, and Virgil describes it in the *Aeneid*.

Usually round, the mismaze or Troy Town was cut in the turf so as to leave little raised balks or ridges on either side of the track. The game may have had a ritual origin, and may have had some connection with the Cretan labyrinth. In France in the Middle Ages mazes similar in pattern to the English turf mazes were laid down in tiles on church floors – there are such mazes in the cathedrals of Bayeux and Chartres – apparently adopting the Troy Town as a symbol of the winding way of life which led at last to Jerusalem, the name given to the centre of the maze, to the happy everlasting home of the virtuous.

But country people treading a mismaze at fair time hardly had any such idea in their heads.

The classic quotation for mismazes is Titania complaining to Oberon in *A Midsummer Night's Dream* that

> The nine men's morris is fill'd up with mud,
> And the quaint mazes in the wanton green
> For lack of tread are undistinguishable

– which Shakespeare wrote at a time when clergy and magistrates were still trying to suppress the revels and the church ales and the 'wanton May games', which may have involved treading the maze. Probably a great many mazes were destroyed under the Commonwealth, and 'mismaze' or Troy or Troy Town now survives frequently in place-names where there is neither trace nor recollection of a maze. In the seventeenth century the turf maze of the village green and the common was elevated into a toy of the formal garden, a real puzzle of varied design, a teasing labyrinth with high hedges of hornbeam or evergreen.

Mazes to visit are the mismaze at Breamore, in Hampshire, south of Salisbury, the maze on the common at the back of the castle ruins at Saffron Walden in Essex, the maze at Troy Farm, Somerton, north of Oxford, the pebble maze at Troy Town on the island of Agnes, in the Isles of Scilly, the mazes on the green at Hilton in Huntingdonshire, made (or remade?), according to the obelisk at the centre, in 1660, and at Wing in Rutland, and the maze at Alkborough in Lincolnshire known as Julian's Bower (possibly from Iulus, who plays the Game of Troy in the *Aeneid*). Much serious information about mazes is collected in *Mazes and Labyrinths* by W. H. Matthews (1922).

DEWPONDS – do *not* fill themselves up with dew. They are simply round saucer-like artificial ponds designed for sheep on the dry chalk uplands particularly of Sussex and Wiltshire, and they fill themselves with rain water. Since they are built on the porous chalk they have to be leak-proof, and are generally lined with clay under a protective layer of flint. The large sloping area around the central area of storage acts as a collecting margin, or funnel. 'Dewpond' is a word of nineteenth-century origin and the concept that these ponds regularly fill up with dew is a nineteenth-century whimsy. See A. J. Pugsley's *Dewponds in Fable and Fact* (1939).

CANALS began to carry their barges across the may-tree watersheds of England in the last decades of the eighteenth century, as an instrument of the improved technology of the era. After a brief heyday they were killed in the decades after 1830 by that quicker, more flexible and more efficient instrument of the new technology, the railway.

Through earlier centuries a vast amount of the traffic of this country went by sailing-boat along the coasts and up tidal estuaries and rivers rather than along muddy tracks and bad roads. Canals extended that sea and river traffic, and the development was precisely the one to be expected, after the introduction of the lock (invented in Italy) and the use of locks to improve navigation of the rivers in the sixteenth, seventeenth and eighteenth centuries.

The first canal in England was actually the Car Dyke which the Romans built (primarily as a drain?) between the rivers Witham and Nene. In Devonshire a short canal was opened in 1566, to bring ships from the Exe estuary to Exeter. In 1761 the Duke of Bridgewater opened the canal by which the coal barges brought coal from Worsley to Manchester, and canals soon proliferated.

Some of the things to look for on the course of moribund or abandoned canals are: old wharfs, public and private, and side-cuts (timber yards and coal yards often continue on their canal sites, though the canal has long been dry); canal basins or harbours; reservoirs, for keeping up the water-level; locks, and locks in series (such as the twenty-nine locks on the Kennet and Avon Canal at Devizes, opened in 1810); side-ponds alongside locks, for the conservation of water; inclined planes, which joined different levels in hilly terrain, the barges ascending or descending on iron railways; embankments, cuttings and aqueducts (such as the famous Chirk Aqueduct – painted in a celebrated water colour by Cotman – which carries the Ellesmere Canal across the Vale of Chirk, in Denbighshire); tunnels, through which the barges were legged by men lying on their backs and thrusting against the roof; 'turnover' bridges, which carry the towpath when it changes from one side of a canal to the other; and the often charming design of lock-keepers' cottages (for instance, along the Gloucester and Berkeley Canal, opened in 1827; or the round tower cottages along the Thames and Severn Canal, opened in 1789, one of the wider canals, on which sailing barges were used).

Note, too, the rope cuts gouged into the stonework of bridges or tunnel entrances.

# Names of Places

Names of places are odd things, not to be trifled with, and often meaning something they do not appear to mean. English has greatly changed since the ancient days of Anglo-Saxon settlement, when most of our place-names were bestowed. That is one source of the enigma of names. Another is that in modern or recent speech we have often changed a name to our own idea of its significance, or to something which sounds normal in modern speech (much as a scientific plant-name may acquire a new English form, Gallant Soldiers for Galinsoga, Sally-my-handsome for Mesembryanthemum). Several names which were quite different to begin with, and so have different original meanings, may all have acquired the same modern form. There are many places called Hinton. Some of them mean high farm, some monk's farm. An Ashton usually means ash-tree farm, but there are Ashtons corrupted from ancient names in which the Ash- was originally a man's name such as Aeschere. Yet another Aeschere's tun remains Asserton. This might suggest to you that another place named Asserby also had to do with a man named Aeschere. But you would be wrong: Asserby was a farm which belonged to a Dane named Asford.

Very confusing. And on top of it all there are Cornish, Welsh and Gaelic names which overlap into English districts. There are very ancient British names which have survived (especially for rivers). Perhaps some of the names which puzzle the philologist survive from a language older than Celtic, a language used by Bronze Age or Neolithic invaders four thousand or five thousand years ago. Invasion succeeding invasion, the settlers from Norway and Denmark left Scandinavian names in midland and northern and eastern counties, and the Vikings left them round the coast far to the south, on bays, islands, headlands. French names (and Latin ones too) were added by the Normans, who often gave a French look to a name they found in use, or translated such a name into a French (or Latin) equivalent.

To discover the real significance of the names around the countryside, to be sure of what a place-name means, there is only one thing to do, which is to turn to the work of modern scholars, who instead of guessing have searched for the earliest and least altered forms of each name before hazarding an interpretation.

For many counties there will be a volume or volumes in the series published for the English Place-Name Society. The chief names of

England – but only England – towns, villages, rivers, lakes, mountains, hills, headlands, etc., are interpreted in Eilert Ekwall's *Concise Oxford Dictionary of English Place-Names*, and in spite of a prosy title few country books excite the mind as much as A. H. Smith's *English Place-Name Elements* (1956). The scholarship in these books replaces romantic guessing. John Aubrey 300 years ago was quite certain that Slaughterford in Wiltshire was a ford where the Danes had been slaughtered in a battle. He was even more certain and more delighted when he found that the uncommon plant called Danewort, or Dwarf Elder, which was supposed to grow in many places where the ground had been soaked with the blood of slaughtered Danes, actually grew in the village. But he was quite wrong, since the ancient English called the crossing of the stream the 'ford where the blackthorn or sloe-thorn grows' – *slahthorn-ford*. Beware. In the next county of Gloucestershire there is another Slaughterford, and it has nothing to do with sloes or slaughter: it is the ford of the *slohtre*, or muddy place.

All the same, as one walks, reads a map, drives round in a car, reads the signposts, one can keep in mind (with caution) a few probabilities and possibilities.

*-chester*, *-caster*, or *-cester*. A name with that ending will have been given by our English ancestors to a place with fortifications, and especially to a Roman town; *ceaster* having been an ancient borrowing from the Latin collective plural *castra*, which originally meant a fort or encampment.

*Street*. A name containing street, or beginning with *street*, *streat*, *strat*, is likely to be on a Roman road, which was a *via strata*, a paved way.

*-ton*. Many thousands of places have a name ending in *-ton*. Most often it means a farm or a manor. What it does not mean is a town in our

modern sense, though -*ton* and 'town' derive from the same Old English word, which was *tūn*. People still talk of 'churchtown' when they mean the village or hamlet around a church, and the folk-song about the fox taking the goose from the farm says in the refrain that 'the fox is gone out of the town O'.

-*ham* at the end of a name may mean a meadow, and it may mean a village or a homestead (from the word which gives us 'home'). -*hampton* is 'home farm'.

-*borough*, -*burgh*, -*bury*, -*berry* may indicate several things. It may come from *burgh*, as we have seen, a fortified place, a camp, a hill-fort, also a fortified house, then a fortified manor, or a town (last of all a borough as we understand it). It may come from *beorg*, which means a hill, either a natural one or a small hill, a mound made by human hands, a burial mound, changing to our word barrow. So side by side in Wiltshire you have Silbury and Avebury, in which '-bury' means a different thing. Silbury, the largest prehistoric barrow or artificial mound in England, seems to have been called by the English the *sele beorg*, the barrow of the willow trees, while Avebury, where the circular ditch and mound of the ancient 'temple' suggested a fortified camp, was called the *burh* belonging to the Englishman Afa. In Marlborough, not far from Silbury, 'borough' does not mean a town but the huge mound or *beorg* (now in the grounds of Marlborough College) where the *meargealla*, or marsh marigold, grew.

-*cot*, -*cott*, -*cote*, i.e. a cottage, or a shelter.

-*wick*, or -*wich*, is likely to mean a group of buildings, frequently a dairy farm, though a -*wick* on the coast may be Scandinavian and not English, from the Old Norse *vik* for a creek or a bay.

-*worth*, -*worthy* (particularly in Devon and Somerset), -*wardine* (particularly in Shropshire and Herefordshire, as in Bredwardine) come from related Old English words, which mean a small enclosure made around a dwelling house.

*Stock* or *Stoke*, at the beginning or at the end of names, does not usually mean much more than place, though *stoc* in Old English often came to mean a holy place connected with a church, a saint, or a monastery. Tavistock in Devon is the holy place by the river Tavy, where an abbey was founded about 980.

-*stow*, especially with a saint's name in front of it, is likely to indicate a holy place where there was a church. Morwenstow in North Cornwall, the home of the poet R. S. Hawker, is the Stow of St Morwenna;

Wistanstow in Shropshire the stow of St Wigstan or Wystan, the saint after whom the poet Wystan Hugh Auden is named. 'Stow' in this sense arose as a special limitation of the meaning, often found in place-names, of a place where people congregated.

*-port* does not always signify a port or harbour, even if the place is on the sea. Frequently it meant a town with the right to hold a market (a town with walls and a town gate, *porta* in Latin).

*-lake* and *-well* are two water words or water endings with an older meaning, 'lake' usually from a word meaning a stream, not lake in our sense, 'well' from a word meaning to well up or well out, i.e. a spring, and not a well dug deep into the ground. *-bourne*, another water word, is from *burna*, which continues in Northumberland and across the Border as 'burn'. A 'winterbourne' is a stream which flows only in the winter, a common name for villages along a winterbourne in the porous chalk country of Dorset or Wiltshire.

*-den* may mean valley (though in the counties of the Weald a *-den* name may refer to a *denn*, which meant a place in the woods where animals were grazed). *-combe* especially in Dorset, Cornwall, Somerset, Devon, around Dartmoor and Exmoor also means valley, a word borrowed by the English from the British (*cwm* in Wales).

*-don* may mean hill. As 'down' – for instance in South Downs – it comes to mean open smooth hilly country.

So far these have been all English names or parts of names. Move into counties where Danes or Norwegians settled, and from Scandinavian languages different word-combinations appear on the map, on the signposts (much as different plants will appear – foxgloves, rowans, etc. – when we move from areas with plenty of lime into acid areas). Valleys are no longer *-den* or *-combe*, but *-gill* and *-dale*, a large hill or small mountain becomes a *-fell*, a *-beck* becomes commoner than a *-brook*. There are names in *-by* meaning farm or village, in *-thorpe* meaning a hamlet in contrast to the larger village alongside, a minor farm-stead settled from a larger one. A fall on a stream becomes a *foss* or a *force*, a small lake is now a *tarn*. Move into West Devon or cross the Tamar into East Cornwall or move along the Marches, and at once there will be a sprinkling of names derived a thousand or more years ago from the language of the British. *Lan-* in front of a saint's name in Cornwall, *Llan-* in Herefordshire or Shropshire (Cornish *lan*, Welsh *llan*, a church) serves for English *-stow* behind a saint's name. *Tre-* for a farmstead begins a name, in place of -*ton* at the end of a name. Names begin with *Ty*- or *Chy*- for a house, with *Bod*- or *Bos*- for a dwelling place. Prehistoric hill-forts or places named after them do not always end in the English *bury*, but will often start with *Car*-, the Cornish equivalent.

## PROPERTY NAMES

All such words are possible or likely clues to part of the meaning of a good many place-names. There are names which may also tell you, with tolerable certainty and immediacy, something about the historic ownership of a particular village, manor, farm, etc. Place-name scholars talk of nature-names (Snowdon, snow hill; Thames, dark river; Liverpool, muddy pool), and also habitation-names, and folk-names, which indicate original settlers (Exeter, *ceaster* or Roman town by the river Exe. Nottingham, the *hām*, the village or homestead which was settled by the Snottings, the followers of the Englishman named Snot). Nottingham could be called a collective property-name. Later a particular property, or particular manor (there existed manors – though the word was not used – before the Normans came) will be known by the name of the individual who comes to own it. The Englishman Beorhtric comes to own a farm, a *tūn*, which is thereupon known to his neighbours as 'Beorhtric's tun', Ubba comes to own the farm which is called 'Ubba's tun'. The way these property-names – like other names – are pronounced and spelt changes as the centuries go by. Ubba and Beorhtric forgotten, their farms become Upton and Brixton, and to decipher such pre-Conquest names one has to go to the books. But at least we can learn at a glance something about a good many property-names as they were modified after the Norman Conquest.

When the Normans took possession of England there was revolution in ownership. The old English owners were killed or went into exile (some even as far as Byzantium, where they joined the Imperial Guard), or remained as dispossessed nobodies. Often the English name of a property now belonging to a Norman acquired the supplement of the Norman's own name, which is still tacked on, in a still familiar guise. This was all the more likely to happen if the English name was rather a common one. For example Easton is a common name – the eastward *tūn* or farm. So is Wootton – the woodland *tūn* or farm. After the Conquest, various Eastons in the single county of Wiltshire were distinguished before long as:

99

Easton Bassett, belonging to the Bassetts
Easton Grey, belonging to the family of Graisz or de Gray
Easton Percy, belonging to a Piers
The various Woottons in the same and in next-door counties became:
Wootton Bassett, belonging again to the Bassetts
Wootton Fitzpaine
Wootton Glanville
Wootton Rivers
Wootton Courtney
– according to owner.

This is the process, extended through nearly all of England, which explains names so attractive and so odd to ourselves as, for example, Lydiard Tregoze, Kingston Bagpuize, Layer Marney, Radford Semele, four which like many others not only unite a pre-Conquest name with the name of a post-Conquest owner, but unite as well the name of a place in England with the name of a place in Normandy. Radford Semele (in Warwickshire) is the place by a reddish-looking ford which became the property of a de Simily, a Norman who came from Semilly, in Normandy. Layer Marney (in Essex) is that village named after the Layer stream – one of several – which was acquired by a de Marinni, from Marigny in Normandy. Kingston Bagpuize (in Berkshire) is the king's *tūn* or royal farm which in due season passed to a Norman named de Bachepuz, from Bacquepuis. Lydiard Tregoze combines Lydiard (a name the English had taken over from the British) with the name of the Tresgoz family, its post-Conquest owners, who originated in La Manche at Troisgots.

Sometimes ownership will be indicated in another way. A manor may have belonged to the king – and will have been distinguished simply as *King's So and So* or *So and So Regis* – 'of the King'. It may have belonged to one of the great dukes, and have had *Ducis* – 'of the duke' tacked on to the end, like Collingbourne Ducis, which belonged to the Duke of Lancaster. Land also went to great spiritual lords, to a bishop an endowment of his see, to abbeys and priories in England, old or new. Ottery in Devonshire (which was to be the birth-place of the poet Coleridge) went to the cathedral church of St Mary in Rouen, and so for all future time became Ottery St Mary. One of the Winterbornes in Dorset was given to an abbey at Caen: Caen was corrupted to Came, and this Winterborne (where the poet William Barnes was rector) is still Winterborne Came. 'Bishop' in a place-name will be obvious and tell-tale; though part of the name, instead, may be the Latin 'Episcopi' – 'of the Bishop'.

## MONKS AND NUNS AND PLACES

The organized religious life of monks and nuns and others was immensely extended after the Norman seizure of England. Monks and nuns in their pious retirement could pray for your soul, so that you could be certain – or less doubtful – about its safe passage over Whinny Muir and across the Bridge of Dread into happiness; and they might undertake to continue those prayers for ever if, as a great landowner, you founded and endowed a monastery for them; or even if you made smaller grants or bequests of property to a monastery already founded. Existing from the era when the monks of St Benedict's Order came with Augustine to Canterbury in 597 (or even from Celtic times), and continuing until they were suppressed between 1536 and 1540, it is not surprising that abbeys, priories, and the like should have left names behind from end to end of the country, names which persist though every stone of the abbey buildings may have disappeared and though there may scarcely be a wrinkle or a green ridge in a meadow to show where they stood.

These monastic names are obvious as a rule, and collecting them, as a special deposit of the name-fossils of history, can teach one a great deal about the organization of the countryside in the Middle Ages. A monk, a *monachos* in Greek, is someone on his own, a member of a community set apart from ordinary life, and though monks or nuns might tend the poor and the sick and give hospitality to travellers, and might open part of their churches to public worship, their monasteries might also be set far apart from the rest of mankind. This was specially true of some of the orders, less true of others. Often, though, dwellings would collect outside the precincts of a monastery, and a town would develop, and the place apart would find itself in the centre of things. This is what happened, for instance, at Malmesbury, in Wiltshire. First of all, in a long continuity, an Irish monk or hermit, Maildulf, chose a dry rocky spur above the forest and between two streams, as a retreat where he could live and meditate in company with a few other hermits or monks, founding with them a small British monastery. The English arrived. The small British monastery (probably with other dwellings around it by this time) became an English abbey of Benedictine monks. The Normans arrived in their turn. The abbey – with a town around it – continued and grew more rich and powerful, building a great church with a high spire where Maildulf and his monks had lived in huts around a small wooden church; and was at last suppressed and despoiled, leaving only fragmentary ruins, and the town which now continues on its own; but keeps also the very ancient name of Malmesbury – one of the unobvious religious names, since Malmesbury was once *Maldulfes burgh*, the fortified place of the holy man Maildulf – since even holy men needed protection. So one thinks of Malmesbury as a town monastery. Other monastic communities, anxious to live up to the monk's vow of individual poverty and to avoid the temptations and distractions of a town life, would establish their convents deep in the countryside or even in wilderness.

To look at names scattered from Scotland to Cornwall makes additional sense of some of the famous and less famous ruins which are left here and there. The ruins are few, the names are many. In England and Wales there still existed more than 800 abbeys and priories when suppression and dissolution overtook them in the sixteenth century. The names they have left are of all kinds, their own names now distinguishing the places where they stood, the names of properties they owned near or far, miles or even counties away, names of manors, farms, mills, fields, bridges, woods.

In the name of a village the word Abbot, Abbess, Prior, Canon, Nun, like the name Bishop, may indicate one particular kind of property and one particular process which has marked English life: it may indicate that a religious house had become owner not only of the principal manor, but of the church and the priest's benefice or living, along with the right to appoint him, as well as all the perquisites of the living – the glebe or farmlands of the priest, and the tithes (the tenth part of their yearly produce, the tenth of their hay crop and their corn harvest, every tenth chicken, lamb, piglet, and so on, which those who farmed in the parish had to pay over to the priest, to the parson, for his keep).

Before coming to the monastic names, this is the point for explaining the difference, first, between an abbey and a priory, second, between a rector and a vicar. The difference between an abbey and a priory was one of rank, but not always of size. The abbeys were independent houses ruled by an abbot, i.e. the 'father', or an abbess, consisting of not less than twelve monks or nuns. The priory, a convent under a prior or prioress, sometimes began in a small way as a dependency of one of the abbeys. A dependency it might remain, directly controlled by the abbey, or it might grow and become independent. Other priories were independent from the start, and were often considerable. The Cistercians had only abbeys. Some religious orders – for instance, the Dominican and Carmelite friars – had only priories. The English cathedral monasteries were called priories, but they had the rank of abbeys.

As for rector and vicar, the parson was a rector – i.e. ruler – and his benefice was a rectory, if he controlled all of it himself. He was a vicar – i.e. a representative – if he carried on his cure of souls in a parish on behalf of an abbey or priory, a bishopric or a cathedral priory, which had acquired the benefice and so become itself the ruler or rector. The religious house, having power to appoint or remove the vicar, would allow him for his keep only part – and a smaller part – of the tithes. When at last the religious houses were dissolved, their rectorial rights in a parish were treated like any other kind of monastic property which was granted or sold by the Crown. In this way a parish might acquire a lay rector, i.e. the farmers in the parish now found that they had to pay the greater part of their tithe every year to some layman near or far, while the lesser part still went to the parson, who still remained a vicar.

To return to the name-fossils which remain from the vast religious organization of the medieval countryside, here according to the different kinds of religious house, the different orders of monk, nun, canon, friar, etc., are examples of the kind of place-name to notice and look for.

The Benedictines, or Black Monks (because of the habits they wore), followers of the rule of St Benedict, were the great parent order of the monastic life in the Middle Ages. They reached England several centuries before the Conquest, with St Augustine of Canterbury, in 597. The Black Monks were particularly the monks of the towns and the cities. Westminster Abbey, for instance, was Benedictine, and their abbeys included Glastonbury, Malmesbury, Shrewsbury, Bury St Edmunds, Gloucester, Tavistock, and Battle Abbey, which the Conqueror founded so that the monks could pray for the souls of those who had fallen in the Battle of Hastings. The cathedral priories – which included Canterbury, Ely, Durham, Winchester, Rochester and Norwich – were Benedictine. Included later among the Black Monks were the Cluniac monks, a reformed order who took their name and origin from the great abbey of Cluny in France. Kings, queens and great lords founded, endowed, and enriched Benedictine houses, which scattered many names over the country, as the number of their manors and benefices, and so on, increased.

Some names which relate to the Black Monks:

*Abbotsbury*, Dorset, where some buildings still remain of the abbey, which was founded about 1044. The name means 'the [fortified] manor of the Abbot'.

*Cerne Abbas*, Dorset: the village called Cerne which belonged to the abbot (*abbas* in Latin). Here the Black Monk monastery was founded in 987.

*Astley Abbots*, Shropshire: the Astley which belonged to the Abbot (of Shrewsbury).

*Monk Bretton*, West Riding: the Bretton where [Cluniac] monks established their priory, in the twelfth century.

*Monkton Deverill*, Wiltshire: the Deverill – one of several Wiltshire villages of the same name – distinguished by having a tun or manor of the monks (the Black Monks of Glastonbury, who had owned this manor since Anglo-Saxon times).

The Cistercians, or White Monks, came to England after the Conquest, in 1128. The object of their order was to live a religious life of reformed purity and loneliness. Their founder, St Bernard, of the Abbey of Cîteaux, or in Latin *Cistercium* (after which they were called Cistercians), near Dijon, enjoined them to labour with their hands in solitude. Instead of being town monks as the Benedictines so often were, they removed themselves from the neighbourhood of men and settled (with a wonderful eye for serenity and shelter) in distant undeveloped valleys – particularly in Yorkshire and the north, and in Wales – where they could turn the level floor of the valley into rich hay and farm land, while pasturing their sheep on the surrounding moors and hills. Most of their abbeys were founded within twenty-four years, between 1128 and 1152. Possessions or parts of domain far away from the monastery they would administer from separate 'granges', farmsteads served by lay brothers. All their abbeys were dedicated to the Virgin Mary. Several of them were given French names or names in a French form by the French-speaking monks who founded them. Above all monks the Cistercians modified and changed Welsh and English scenery – not always for the better, since their thousands upon thousands of sheep slowly destroyed the aboriginal woodland of the hills. Building their convents and churches in a style deliberately matching the purity and austerity of the rule of St Bernard, they were the monks of some of our most beautiful monastic ruins, including Fountains and Rievaulx in the wildernesses of North Yorkshire, Tintern, Beaulieu in Hampshire, and Melrose in Roxburghshire.

Some names relating to White Monks:

*Abbey Dore*, Herefordshire: the abbey (founded 1147) by the river Dore.

*Beaulieu*, Hampshire: the Abbey of St Mary de Bello Loco, or Beautiful Place, in French *Beau Lieu*.

*Buckland Monachorum*, Devonshire: Buckland of the [Cistercian] monks, whose abbey here was founded in 1278.

*Dieulacres*, Staffordshire: the abbey (founded in the twelfth century) named in Old French *Dieu l'acreisse*, God grant it increase.

*Rievaulx*, North Riding: the abbey in Ryedale, a name translated to the French *Rievaulx* by the monks from the great abbey of Clairvaux (*Clara Vallis*, bright valley), who were the founders in 1131, as Jervaulx is French for Uredale.

*Monkgarth Pool*, Cumberland: 'Pool of the monks' fishery' (*garth* usually means enclosure) belonging to the White Monks of Calder Abbey.

*Vaudey*, Lincolnshire: abbey founded in the twelfth century. A French form of *Vallis Dei*, the Valley of God.

*Strata Florida*, Cardiganshire: the monks' Latin for Ystrad fflur, Valley of the flowers, for the valley among the wildernesses of the Cardiganshire hills, where the abbey was founded in 1164. A name wonderfully evocative of the Cistercians.

*Fountains Fell*, West Riding, on the moors above Malham, because it was included in sheep walks belonging to Fountains Abbey.

Names containing the word 'grange', usually of a farm which was once a Cistercian grange, are frequent. For example Grange, in Borrowdale, in the Lake District – once a grange which belonged to Furness Abbey.

Nuns were no less familiar in medieval England than monks, and were also distinguished in common speech by the colour of their habits. Counterpart to the Black Monks were the Black Ladies, the Benedictine nuns, whose convents large or small were often founded long before the Conquest. Their properties were scattered over the country and have left many names behind which are obvious in meaning. The greatest convent of the Black Nuns was the hill-top abbey of Shaftesbury in Dorset, founded about 888. This was the largest nunnery in the British Isles, and though nothing is left of it now except foundations and a few carved stones in a garden, the nuns' church was surmounted by a cloud-piercing spire loftier than the spire of Salisbury

Cathedral. The great abbey of Wilton, in Wiltshire (founded in the ninth century) also belonged to these once familiar Black Ladies.

Often a nun was called a minchen, a word which was the feminine of monk, and which frequently occurs in minor place-names.

Some names relating to the Black Ladies:

*Abbotston*, in Dorset, originally Abbedeston or Abbesstone, i.e. the *tūn* of the abbess, a manor belonging to the Wilton nuns.

*Brewood Black Ladies*, Staffordshire, where a priory of the Black Ladies was founded about 1189.

*Maiden Winterbourne* (more commonly Maddington), Wiltshire, i.e. Nun Winterbourne (or the Maiden *tūn*, or manor) belonging to the Black Ladies of Amesbury Priory.

*Godstow*, Oxfordshire. 'God's assembly place' or 'God's church', from the abbey founded about 1133.

*Nunburnholme*, East Riding, a priory of nuns founded there in the twelfth century.

*Mynsion Lands*, in Pelynt, Cornwall: a property which belonged to the nuns of Wilton Abbey.

Cistercian nuns, White Ladies in contrast to the Black Ladies, and counterpart to the Cistercian monks of sequestered valleys, were also familiar in the England of the Middle Ages, though like the Cistercian abbeys, their houses did not come into being before the twelfth century. These were the nuns, for example, of the priories of:

*Nun Appleton*, in the West Riding.

*Nun Thorpe*, in the North Riding.

*Nun Cotham*, in Lincolnshire.

*Aston White Ladies*, Worcestershire – a property of the White Ladies or Cistercian nuns of Whistones Priory, in Worcester.

The orders of monks and nuns already mentioned were the largest and the most important (though not the only ones) in medieval Britain. The men and women of God living in communities according to rule also included Canons and Canonesses, whose convents proliferated before the end of the twelfth century. The Canons differed from monks in being all of them in canonical orders, i.e. they were all priests. They included – to name the two most important orders – the Augustinian or Austin Canons, who followed the Rule of St Augustine in small groups, housing themselves in a great many small priories, and the less

numerous Premonstratensian Canons (founded by St Norbert at Pré-
monstré in France). The Premonstratensians still maintained thirty
abbeys at the Dissolution, compared with about 170 Augustinian
houses.

According to the habits they wore, these again were commonly known
as Black Canons (Augustinian) and White Canons (Premonstratensian). The name 'Black Ladies' was applied to Augustinian Canonesses
as well as to Benedictine nuns, and 'White Ladies' to Premonstratensian Canonesses as well as to Cistercian nuns.

Canons and Canonesses have peppered the countryside with names,
for instance:

*Beauchief Abbey*, Derbyshire, Premonstratensian, founded 1173–6,
i.e. the abbey occupying a *Bellum Caput*, or *beau chef*, a beautiful head
or spur of land.

*Blanchland*, Northumberland, i.e. the *Alba Landa*, the White Glade or
Lawn, where the Premonstratensian or White Canons built their
priory in 1165. Farther down the Tyne the village at Bywell has
two churches, the White Church, which belonged to these White
Canons of Blanchland, and the Black Church, which was the property of the Benedictine or Black Monks of Durham Cathedral.

*Dean Prior*, in Devonshire (where Herrick wrote so many of his
poems) – since it belonged to the Augustinian Canons of Plympton
Priory.

*Canons Ashby*, Northamptonshire – where the Austin Canons set up
a priory about 1147.

*Canonsleigh*, Devonshire, site of a priory of Austin Canons, founded
about 1161.

*Brewood White Ladies*, Shropshire – otherwise Boscobel Priory,
founded about 1199 by the Premonstratensian or White Canonesses.

*Minchin Buckland*, or *Buckland Sororum*, in Somerset, i.e. Nuns' Buckland, or Buckland of the Sisters. First a priory of the Sisters of St
John of Jerusalem, then of Augustinian Canonesses.

'Canon' in the name of a place may also refer to the secular canons
of a cathedral chapter – for instance, Canon Pyon in Herefordshire,
which belonged to the secular canons of Hereford Cathedral, or Whit-
church Canonicorum, in Dorset – Whitechurch of the Canons, i.e. the
Canons of Wells Cathedral and Salisbury Cathedral.

## FRIARS, TEMPLARS, HOSPITALLERS

Names which contain the word 'friar' may not be due to the Mendicant Friars of one kind and another, who brought new zest, piety and humility into Christian life from the beginning of the thirteenth century, by moving among the people outside the cloister. A 'friar' is a *frère*, a *frater*, a brother; a monk is a 'brother', as a nun is a 'sister'; and members of quite different religious orders, including the Templars and Hospitallers, were also *fratres* and were often called 'friars'. So a 'friar' name *may* refer to monks or friars, the Templars or Hospitallers. The Mendicant Friars – Dominicans (Black Friars), Franciscans (Grey Friars), Carmelite Friars (White Friars) and Austin Friars, to name the chief orders, set up their usually modest houses for the most part in cities and towns, where the names of streets, etc., recall their existence.

'Temple' this or that, or the name 'Temple' by itself, often in a lonely part of the country, always indicates one special fact: that property was owned there by the Knights Templar, that famous order of Soldiers of God which the Dominican and Franciscan friars detested and helped to bring down in disgrace at the beginning of the fourteenth century. The Templars, or Poor Knights of Christ and the Temple of Solomon, were founded early in the twelfth century after the First Crusade, and were pledged to protect the holy places of Palestine and the pilgrims who flocked to them from all the countries of Europe. Divided into ranks, wearing their beards long, and vowed to poverty as well as the strictest chastity and self-denial, the Brothers could nevertheless acquire property as an order. On their manors they would establish here and there a small 'preceptory', housing a few of the brethren, who supervised the farming, kept an eye on the scattered properties, and collected the rents and revenues. The preceptory, like the grange of a Cistercian monastery, might have its own chapel, and this might be round in form, in special homage to the Holy Sepulchre in Jerusalem, which lay at the heart of their existence – such as the round churches at the Temple in London (their English headquarters), at Northampton, and at Laon, north-east of Paris. After the loss of the Holy Land and the end of the Crusades, the great power of the Templars and the great wealth they had amassed after nearly two centuries excited jealousy. They were accused – falsely, it seems – of heresy and black magic in their very secret meetings at dawn, of spitting on the cross, child murder, devil worship, intercourse with demons, and homosexuality; and the order was finally suppressed everywhere in

1312, and deprived of all its possessions. In France trial of the Templars ended in many executions by burning. In England (where all the Templars had been arrested in 1308) they were treated less severely, though the Master died in prison in the Tower. 'Temple' on the map may betoken a preceptory, or a *camera* (a smaller kind of estate centre or estate office), or else some isolated manor.

Some Templar names:

*Temple Bruer*, in Lincolnshire, near Sleaford, after a preceptory of which the tower is left, though nothing remains of the round church which is known to have been built here.

*Temple Combe*, Somerset, after a preceptory of which there are still a few ruins.

*Temple*, on the Cornish moors, after a preceptory.

*Temple Guiting*, Gloucestershire, a lonely Cotswold village, site of a preceptory.

*Temple Farm*, near Rockley, Wiltshire, the site of a preceptory in a valley deep in the Marlborough Downs.

*Temple Hirst*, West Riding (preceptory).

*Templeton*: there are Templetons (*tūn*, or manor, of the Templars) in Pembrokeshire, Berkshire and Devonshire, the last a high lonely parish with no village, between Exmoor and Dartmoor.

The Crusades brought into being three great orders of Soldiers of God – Templars, Teutonic Knights, and Hospitallers. While the Holy Land remained in Christian possession the Hospitallers – the Order of the Friars of the Hospitals of Jerusalem, or of the Hospital of St John of Jerusalem – looked after the welfare of the pilgrims to Jerusalem, maintaining hospices for them, and nursing the sick. They continued as a hospital order, wealthy and important in France, England, etc., controlling their estates from small 'commanderies', which often sheltered pilgrims and wayfarers. When their ancient rivals, the Templars, were suppressed, the Hospitallers were granted much of their property and many of their preceptories. Like the Templars, they built a number of round tomb-like churches in homage to the Holy Sepulchre, of which there are two in England, the church of the Holy Sepulchre at Cambridge, and the church of their patron saint, St John the Baptist, at Little Maplestead, in Essex.

Hospitaller place-names (less common than Templar names) include:

*Kemeys Commander*, in Monmouthshire. Site of a small commandery, which had been a *camera* of the Templars.

*Fryerning*, in Essex, once *Ginge Hospitalis*, the place named Ginge or Ing where the knights had a hospital – 'Ing of the Friars', i.e. of the *fratres* or brothers of the order.

*Mayne Ospitalis* or Fryer Mayne, in Dorset, near Broadmayne. Once a commandery.

*Godsfield*, near New Alresford, Hampshire. A commandery founded about 1170, of which the chapel (fourteenth century) is standing.

*Yspytty Ifan*, North Wales, on the border between Denbighshire and Caernarvonshire. Site of a *hospitium* (*yspytty*) founded in the twelfth century. The church has the Hospitallers' St John for patron saint.

'Spital' is a frequent countryside name for a place where there once stood one of the many other hospitals or hospices piously founded in the Middle Ages for the sick and the old and for poor travellers. Some were dependencies of a convent, and were maintained by nuns or monks, others might belong to a special order, such as the brothers of St Lazarus of Jerusalem, also a military-religious order founded in Jerusalem after the First Crusade, which cared for lepers, and had taken Lazarus, since he was believed to have been a leper, for its patron saint. Our way of addressing a nurse as 'sister' derives from this religious control of medieval hospitals.

Some hospital names:

*Burton Lazars*, Leicestershire, i.e. Burton of St Lazarus, from its hospital for lazars or lepers, founded early in the twelfth century, and run by the brothers of the Order of St Lazarus.

*Maiden Bradley*, Wiltshire, i.e. Bradley of the Maidens, the poor women lepers for whom a hospital was founded there in the twelfth century.

*Spittal*, near Tweedmouth, Northumberland, where there was a lazar-house in the thirteenth century.

*Spital on the Peak*, Derbyshire, near Castleton. A hospital for the aged poor founded in the fourteenth century.

*Spital in the Street*, north of Lincoln, on the side of Ermine Street, a hospital for the poor, founded in 1396.

*Yspytty Ystwyth*, Cardiganshire. A grange (also used as a hospice) on the Ystwyth, which belonged to the Cistercian abbey of Strata Florida, nearby.

# Names of Rivers

Someone takes out a boat on the Severn or the Thames. Someone else asks where he has gone, and the reply is more likely to be 'down to the river' than 'down to the Thames' or 'down to the Severn'. It may even be 'down to the water'.

This is worth remembering, since the name by which a river is still known will often have meant originally no more than 'river', or 'water', or 'stream', without qualification. It is a little disappointing, but it does not imply that our remote ancestors were necessarily much duller-witted than ourselves.

Some names are bestowed, some, without being bestowed, grow out of the use and then disuse of common words. 'Water' in English might be used easily or carelessly for a lake, a river, a ford, a tidal estuary; but to distinguish, for example, one lake, one 'water' from its neighbours, a qualification was required. So in the Lake District lakes were distinguished by their owners or their position. Derwentwater was the 'water' or lake on the river Derwent, Ullswater the 'water' or lake which belonged to Ulf. A word, by itself, on its own, equivalent to 'stream', 'water', 'river', might continue as a name, when the word had dropped out of common speech. *Burna* was the Old English for stream, *fleot* the Old English for a river-like inlet of the sea. For a particular stream, a particular inlet, *burna* or *fleot* might continue as a name when the words were no longer in general use, and had changed in pronunciation. *Burna* (see page 98) might continue as 'the Bourne', *fleot* as 'the Fleet' – which is still the name, to give one example, for the long ribbon of salt water behind the Chesil Bank on the coast of Dorset.

Much the same thing could happen in a different way. New invading and settling Englishmen would hear some words which were already names and some which were not. They might point to one river and learn that it was the Dart, or the Tamar, or the Dove, as we now call them, British names which signified 'oak-tree river', 'dark river', and 'black river'. They might point to another river, and the British reply would be *avon* – 'river' (*afon* is still the Welsh for river). Knowing no British, they would take this word *avon* for a name, and it would stick – as indeed it has stuck, a little confusingly, alone and unqualified, to half a dozen Avons in several counties.

Indeed the names of most of our larger rivers are British, and not English. The invaders took them over from the people they dispossessed, from the language ancestral to Cornish and to modern Welsh, which had been spoken for centuries. In Australia river-names used by the black-fellows and in America river-names used by the Indians were to be taken over in exactly the same way.

Our three greatest rivers, Trent, Severn and Thames, are all British, Trent and Severn of unknown significance (though the Trent, which is liable to overflow, has been explained as the 'over-runner', the 'spreader', or 'trespasser'), Thames probably meaning the 'dark one'. Thames, though, is one of a company. As well as the Tamar, dark in its deep valley dividing Cornwall from Devon, Oxfordshire's Thame, the various Tames and Temes, and Tavistock's Tavy in Devonshire, all come from the same word and have the same meaning of 'dark one' or 'dark river'.

## OTHER BRITISH NAMES

The Exe rising on Exmoor and running down to Exeter, the Usk in South Wales in its long vale, which so delighted the poets Vaughan and Dyer, the rivers Esk of Cumberland and Yorkshire, and the Axe pouring out of Wookey Hole below the Mendips, are all from a British word *isca*, meaning water (which gives us also that special water we name whisky – in Gaelic *uisge beatha*, or 'water of life').

The Wye, dividing England and South Wales and slipping into the Severn estuary, the Wey in Surrey and Dorset's Wey coming to the sea at Weymouth all originate in the same British term which may have meant 'flowing water'. Another British word for water in movement gave rise to the several Fromes of western England. The lazy Ouse of the Midlands, the Fens and King's Lynn, seems to come (like the Ouse of Yorkshire) from a word amounting to no more than 'water'.

The Darenth, which Samuel Palmer painted at Shoreham in Kent, and the various Derwents of the North are all identical with the Dart, running and scurrying from Dartmoor, and all are forms of a British name which signified '(river of) the oak-trees' (*derw* in modern Welsh means oaks collectively). Another tree name is the Fowey in East Cornwall, meaning in Cornish '(river of) the beech-trees', which still grow here and there along its banks, rather unexpectedly.

Generally it was movement, force, stillness, slowness, speed, crookedness, light or dark or mere wateriness which 'named' a river for our British ancestors. Just as the Dove of Derbyshire's Dovedale, small yet spectacular between the shadowed limestone walls of its canyon, is the 'black one' (*du* is the modern Welsh for black), so the Lugg, rising in brown Radnorshire, and crossing Shropshire and Herefordshire to its junction with the Wye, is the 'bright one'. The Aire, welling out of the limestone under the tall amphitheatre of Malham Cove in the West Riding, is the 'strong one', a river-name held to be identical with the Isère, and Germany's Isar –

> On Linden, when the sun was low,
> All bloodless lay the untrodden snow,
> And dark as winter was the flow
> Of Iser, rolling rapidly.

The Wharfe in the West Riding is the 'twister', the 'winding one'. The Tweed is the 'powerful one', which is appropriate for its quick descent to the North Sea. The contrast of the quick Tweed and the slow Till, its tributary, wriggling or snaking slowly across the flattish lands between the Cheviots and the sea, is well expressed in the folk poem:

> Says Tweed to Till
> 'What gars ye rin sae still?'
> Says Till to Tweed
> 'Though ye rin with speed
> And I rin slaw,
> For a man that ye droon
> I droon twa.'

Till means no more than 'flowing one'. The Tyne means much the same. The Tees, which churns down from the fells and over Cauldron

Snout and High Force, is the 'boiling', 'bubbling', 'seething' one. The Kentish Medway was named the 'flowing water' (as in Wye and Wey) which looked like mead, the honey drink, perhaps from the yellow reflections along its smooth surface.

A very few British river-names indicate something more fascinating – that some rivers in the British Isles, as elsewhere, were held in respect as gods or goddesses. One was the Dee, another the Brent, now flowing through the most undivine suburban regions of Middlesex into the Thames. The Dee, along with other Dees in Scotland and Ireland, was the *Deva*, i.e. the goddess (*duwies* in today's Welsh); and the goddess was a goddess of war. In the Middle Ages people living near the Dee believed that the river changed its fords every month: when the current flowed towards the Welsh bank, the Welsh would have a fortunate year; when it flowed towards the English bank, good fortune would be with the English. The Brent was the mother-goddess Brigantia, goddess of abundance, increase, and prosperity – i.e. the Brigit who became that favourite saint of Ireland and Celtic Scotland, St Brigid, whose crosses made of rush are still placed on St Brigid's Eve under the thatch of Irish cabins, above beds, and doors, and cow-stalls, to bring good fortune to the family and the cattle and the young calves.

## ENGLISH RIVER-NAMES

Of course there are also English and Scandinavian river-names. In the north there are names, in particular ending in -a, from the word *á* which the Norsemen used for river – the name Greta, for example, which belongs to several rivers. The meaning is 'river of stones'. This most exactly fits the two limestone Gretas of the west and the east of Yorkshire, the Greta below and between the mountains of Ingleborough and Whernside which goes in and out of limestone caves and over polished limestone surfaces, and the more celebrated Greta which slides down over limestones and through a small limestone gorge to join the Tees. 'River Greta near its fall into the Tees – shootings of water threads down the slope of the huge green stone' (the poet Coleridge in 1799).

In the south, many river-names mostly ending in -ea, -ey, -ye or -y derive from the Old English *eā*, for river – for instance the Waveney of East Anglia, which was the *eā* of the shaking bog or fen, or the clean little Ampney Brook in Wiltshire and Gloucestershire, which runs into the Thames, and was the *eā* which belonged to Amma the Englishman, or rather where Amma lived. Sometimes *eā* survives as a name by itself, changing to the Yeo in Devon, or the Eye in Leicestershire. The river-name Rea or Rye will most often be a contraction of the Old English words meaning 'at the *eā*', 'at the river'.

There are English-named rivers called for their speed, their strength, their sloth. The Lynn of Lynton and Lynmouth in North Devon, earns its name from the occasionally destructive speed and energy with which it tears down from Exmoor. The Old English was *Llynn*, a torrent. Stour, name of various slow but forceful and sullen streams, is English, meaning 'powerful one'. Now and again a river is named for its animals. Otters are responsible for the Otter in Devon and Somerset, a name shortened from the Old English for 'otter stream', 'otter *eā*'; also for Northumberland's Otterburn.

The European Beaver (nearly extinct in our islands by the end of the twelfth century) has left its name as a memorial, but only on a few streams, as if it was already becoming rare when the English arrived. The Beverley Brook in Richmond Park, in Surrey, was a 'beaver stream'. There must have been beavers, too, in a little stream in North Wiltshire, on the banks of which a farm is still called Beaversbrook (see also page 206).

Many names of rivers, like other topographical names, are a warning against the obvious conclusion. Long ago the river Mole in Surrey was supposed to have been so named because the stream burrows like a mole and disappears into soak-aways along its porous chalky bed. It was really named from the town of Molesey, just as the Cam (properly the Granta) derived from Cambridge (instead of Cambridge from Cam), Cambridge being a corruption of the ancient name which meant Granta Bridge. Granta, in turn, was a British name for muddy river. (River names have their special book, Eilert Ekwall's *English River-Names*, 1928.)

# Hill Names

Here and there the English, though one would expect them to be less intrigued by hills than by rivers (which have to be crossed, whereas hills do not have to be climbed) took over an old British name for a hill or a range of hills. A trouble with British names is that they cannot always be interpreted. The Chilterns in Buckinghamshire and the Cheviot in Northumberland and the Cannock of Staffordshire's Cannock Chase are British names (probably) which are indecipherable in that way. The Mendips, the Malvern Hills, the Quantocks are British. So are various hills beginning in *pen* and *bre*.

*The Mendips.* Mendip contains the word to be seen so many times on the map of North Wales, *mynydd*, a mountain, though otherwise the meaning is obscure. The same word is concealed in Longmynd, name for that long crumpled hill squashed upwards in Shropshire by the birth-pressure of the Welsh mountains – the long *mynydd*, long mountain. Minehead in Somerset is also from *mynydd*, because of the hills, more than a thousand feet high above the town.

*The Malverns*, another ridge longer than it is wide, stand up so prominently, turn so blue above the flat lands of the Severn, that they were bound to have a name, which newcomers were bound to ask. The name conceals two other words familiar on Welsh maps – *moel* (anciently *mel*), which means bald, and *bryn*, a hill. Malvern was the hill which was bald. Bald its archaic rocks remain in the wind, with scarcely a tree.

*The Quantocks.* Like 'Kent' – the county of Kent, and Derbyshire's Kinder Scout – the name has been derived from a British word which meant edge or rim (remember how many English-named hills are called something 'edge'). 'Edge' for the Quantocks will make good sense to anyone who has walked along their top above Alfoxden and Nether Stowey. Coleridge on the Quantocks:

> Friends, whom I never more may meet again,
> On springy heath, along the hill-top edge,
> Wander in gladness . . .

The edge makes a view-platform above the sea:

> Now my friends emerge
> Beneath the wide wide Heaven – and view again
> The many-steepled tract magnificent
> Of hilly fields and meadows, and the sea,
> With some fair bark, perhaps, whose sails light up
> The slip of smooth clear blue betwixt two isles
> Of purple shadow.

Could the same word, part for the whole, have been applied first to the long edge or rim of the North Downs, and have then been extended to the Kent stretching out underneath?

A good many hill names in what is now England begin with *pen*, which is both Cornish and Welsh for height, hill, top, or top end –

among them Lancashire's Pendle Hill, which is a case of triplication, or repeated tautology. To Pen the English added 'hill', and the name became Pendle, absorbing 'hill' into itself unrecognizably, so that 'hill' was added again.

*Penyghent*, that fine mountain in miniature of the West Riding, means hill of the plain (though its neighbours, Whernside, i.e. quern hillside, where quern stones and millstones were quarried from millstone grit, and Ingleborough, Ingold's fort, the ramparts of which remain on the flat summit, are both named in English). Penyard in Herefordshire, high above Ross-on-Wye, is Welsh for high hill.

*Bre* names, remaining obstinately behind like islands among the sea of English, perpetuate another Cornish and Welsh term for hill – they include Worcestershire's insulated Bredon (a duplication, *bre*, plus the Old English *dūn* for 'hill'), Somerset's Brean Down, upholding an Iron Age fort above the Bristol Channel (though not Somerset's Brendon Hills, in which the *bren* is 'brown', from the autumn colour of the bracken), and Buckinghamshire's Brill – *bre* plus 'hill' – which 'commands a most extensive and richly varied prospect, comprehending a panoramic view of nine counties'. This is Brill of the folk-rhyme, declaring that

> At Brill on the Hill
> The wind blows shrill.

Dunkery in Somerset may be another British name, meaning stone fort.

English-named hills involve other words and endings than -ton or -don (see page 98) or -bury or -borough, which may mean either hill (*beorg*) or fort (*burh*, *bury*) from those Iron Age hill-forts which are so common.

*Hōh*, which meant a ridge, often along the sea, is a hill-word surviving in 'hoe' and 'heugh' and many place-names – in Plymouth Hoe, the Heugh and Hugh Town of the Isles of Scilly, in North Devon's Martinhoe and Trentishoe, cliff-perched above the Bristol Channel.

*Tor*, chiefly to be found in Devon and East Cornwall and the special mark of holidays and days out on Dartmoor, is English (unexpectedly), implying a hill breaking out in rocks or crags. Miners from Dartmoor and Cornwall are supposed to have taken the word to Derbyshire and the Peak during the Middle Ages. Yes Tor: eagle tor, Haytor: ivied tor, Mam Tor: breast tor.

*Low*, so common a word for hill round the Peak, is also English (*hlāw*), and like the *beorg*, which becomes 'bury', 'borough', etc., is often used for a barrow.

*Bank*, which the English borrowed from the Danes, is a hill word still used in dialect, for instance in Herefordshire and in Shakespeare's Warwickshire. When Shakespeare wrote 'I know a bank where the wild thyme blows', it was a rise of hill which he had in mind, something far loftier than the 'bank' of ordinary modern speech.

Northward begin the hills called by Scandinavian terms, notably 'howe' from *haugr* (also used of barrows) and 'fell'. The 'Scout' of Kinder Scout was a Scandinavian word for upthrusting or overhanging rock, which was added to the old British name. The same word, or an allied one, is likely in lofty Skiddaw, the howe of the rock, or crag. Scafell, England's highest mountain, is a Norse equivalent, more or less, to the Malvern of the British – the fell with a bald head.

## WELSH HILLS AND MOUNTAINS

Westward of Offa's Dyke the Welsh hill-names abound in full population –

| | |
|---|---|
| *bron*, | breast, round hill |
| *bryn*, | small hill |
| *cadair*, | chair |
| *carnedd*, | cairn |
| *carreg*, | rock |
| *cefn*, | ridge, back |
| *clogwyn*, | cliff, precipice |
| *crib*, | crest |
| *glyder*, | heap |

| | |
|---|---|
| *maen*, | stone |
| *moel*, | bald (hill) |
| *mynydd*, | mountain |
| *pen*, | summit |
| *ysgol*, | ladder |

– and so on. Englishmen should remember that the mountain they call 'Snowdon', the snow hill, is properly, piously, and respectfully called Eryri, which may mean the height of the eagles (*eryr* is eagle), or more likely and less poetically the shingles (*yr eryr*), i.e. the tiles, the roof.

# Names and Gods and Demons

Our English or Anglo-Saxon forebears invading across the North Sea in the fifth and sixth centuries brought their gods, their myths and their demons with them. They settled to a pagan agricultural squalor, set up temples in clearings and glades, and worshipped for a while in their own tough and rough way, before the coming of Christianity.

Quite a few names of places and objects recall their Germanic religion, in particular their gods, chief of whom were Woden, Thunor, Frig (Woden's wife), and Tiw or Tig, the gods of Wednesday, Thursday, Friday, and Tuesday, and the malignant and unpleasant population of demons whom they imagined in the dark corners, the waste places, the black, stagnant pools, etc., of the countryside.

## NAMES OF GODS

*Woden*. The god of gods, credited with great wisdom and magic power. Not surprisingly our ancestors ascribed to him remarkable works which seemed more than human in their scale. Woden's special places – where he must have been worshipped – include the now unlovely industrial centres, both in Staffordshire, of Wednesfield (Woden's field or open space) and Wednesbury (Woden's *burh* or fortified place); also Woodnesborough, near Sandwich in Kent, which means Woden's hill or mound. The medieval church at Woodnesborough actually stands alongside this Woden's hill, where there was no doubt a temple to Woden in the days before St Augustine (who reached Canterbury in 597).

*Wansdyke* (i.e. Woden's dyke), the long defensive boundary of ditch and rampart striding across the Marlborough Downs in Wiltshire, is

Woden's principal monument (see page 66). At one point near Wansdyke, a long barrow stands on the edge of the chalk hills above the Vale of Pewsey. This was anciently known as *Wodnesbeorge*, i.e. Woden's barrow, another of his magic works (it is now Adam's Grave).

As 'Grim', i.e. the masked one, Woden was also supposed to have built the various dykes commonly given the name Grim's Ditch (page 65).

*Frig*, Woden's wife, the Venus of our ancestors, is commemorated in fewer place-names. She may have been worshipped at two places in Hampshire – Frobury (Frig's fortified place), a farm outside Kingsclere, and Froyle (Frig's hill), near Alton; also at Fretherne, on the tidal waters of the Severn in Gloucestershire, a name meaning Frig's thorn-tree. (The Whitethorn or May, which is a plant of sex and fertility, may have been sacred to Frig, much as in later centuries it was sacred to the Virgin Mary.)

*Thunor*, the Thursday god, the rumbling of whose chariot wheels sounded in the thunder, is remembered in names of several places, chiefly in counties around London, and often on more or less high ground, as befits a sky god. He had temples in Essex at suburban Thundersley, near Southend, and at lonely Thunderley (where there was a church), not far from Saffron Walden; in Surrey, near Hindhead, at Thursley, an old iron-mining and iron-smelting parish, where the church is dedicated to St Michael, the patron of hill-churches. These three names mean Thunor's glade. He may also have had a temple at Thundridge (Thunor's ridge), near Ware in Hertfordshire, and his stone, his monolith, remains at Taston (i.e. Thunor's stone) in the Oxfordshire parish of Spelsbury.

*Tiw*, or Tig, the Tuesday god, and a god of war, preserves memory of his worship most excitingly in the Warwickshire villages of Lower, Middle and Upper Tysoe – Tig's *hōh*, i.e. the 600-foot spur, ridge, or escarpment which cuts through a stratum of reddish ironstone on the face of which there existed until 1798 the Red Horse of Tysoe. This figure of a horse *may* have been cut as an Anglo-Saxon offering to Tig or Tiw; who is also commemorated in the names Tuesley (Tiw's glade) in the Hindhead neighbourhood in Surrey, and Twiscombe (Tiw's valley or combe) in Devonshire, near Whitestone.

The various Scandinavian settlers arrived when Christianity was in the ascendant and when the old Germanic religions were on the wane, so their related deities (Odin, Thor, Tyr, Frigg) are little represented in our place-names. Roseberry Topping, the name of the fine shapely sandstone hill on the very edge of the North Yorkshire moors, unexpectedly contains the transformed name of Odin or Óthinn. Topping (hill-top) was added to an earlier 'Othenesberg' (Óthinn's hill), which was corrupted to Roseberry. Odin was also Grímr to the Scandinavians (as Woden was Grim to the English). So the Danish settlers of Norfolk, puzzled by the strange depressions on the Breckland heath which in fact were all that was visible of ancient neolithic flint-mines, called them the 'graves of Grímr' – nowadays Grimes' Graves, or in the proper Norfolk speech, Grimmer's Graves.

## NAMES OF DEMONS

A place where a god is given a temple is a place which is frequented, and which may quite probably develop into a village or a town. A place where men expect to encounter a demon will be quite different. The demons our ancestors believed in were man-sized, and dwarf-sized, and dangerous, always up to such unpleasant acts as shooting disease and death in their direction. So they were imagined in unfrequented places, which were to be avoided; and for that reason their names are still to be found for the most part out in the fields, in waste ground, in corners, nooks, dells, caves, pools, ponds, thickets, among rocks, on hills and on barrows. In many counties such places are named after:

1 The *pūca*, later called puck or pook. This demon would live in a Pookpit, a Pookmead or Pookcroft, a Pooklake (i.e. stream), a Pookmarsh. In Sussex a path (*stīg*) on which a puck had the habit of walking, gave rise to the name Puckstye. In the same county Pookhill (*Puck of Pook's Hill*) was named not after a puck's hill, but a puck's *healh*, or corner.

2 The demon called by the Anglo-Saxons a *sceocca* or *scucca*, who has left names beginning (as we now spell them) with Shuck, Shack, Shock, on hills, barrows, streams, etc.

3 The sizeable man-eating blood-drinking demon called a *thyrs* in Anglo-Saxon districts and a *thurs* in the Scandinavian districts, ancestral to the goblin who is still called a Hobthrush or Hobthrust. *Thyrs* and *thurs* have bequeathed their names to limestone corners and limestone caves in which a *thurs* would live like Homer's Polyphemus (for instance, in the Peak district – Thor's Cave, Thirst House Cave – and in the West Riding), to barrows (e.g. Hob Hurst's House, on Beeley

Moor in the Peak, Obtrusch Rogue or Obtrush Rook, on Rudland Moor in North Yorkshire), to woods and valleys, to a ford (Thursford, from a ford on the Stiffkey, in the north of Norfolk), and to lakes and ponds. Grendel, the savage demon of giant strength in the eighth-century poem *Beowulf* was a *thyrs*, living under the black surface of a lake. A *thyrs* must also have lived under the now ornamental lake in the park at Tusmore (*thyrsmere*), in Oxfordshire, north of Bicester.

## DRAGONS AND TREASURES

Our ancestors told stories about dragons or 'worms' which guarded treasure, especially the treasure buried with a chieftain inside a barrow, and flew about at night emitting flames (as in *Beowulf* once more). Such a dragon or fire-drake (*draca* in Old English) was responsible for more than one Drakelow (i.e. dragon's barrow), including the Drakelow near the Trent, south of Burton-on-Trent, and for Drake North, in the Hampshire downland parish of Damerham, near Fordingbridge, which was *drakenhorde*, i.e. dragon's hoard, a thousand years ago. A treasure barrow stands high up on the Derbyshire limestone near Monyash at Hurdlow (i.e. hoard barrow). There may have been another one at Hordle (i.e. hoard hill) near Lymington in Hampshire.

# PART TWO

## *The Sky*

# About the Stars

Out on the lawn I lie in bed,
Vega conspicuous overhead
In the windless nights of June
                              W. H. Auden

We know the stars are not immutable, or eternal, we know that they do not move around the earth in courses grandly regular and uniform, we know that they do not govern our affairs. But astronomical knowledge is not the same as emotional reaction; and most of us react to the stars on a brilliant night as if they were as immutable or eternal as they seem, and as our ancestors believed them to be. Yet most of us feel a little guilty about stars and constellations, not being quite sure which is which.

So here is a respectable minimum of knowledge of names and whereabouts, less for the star-gazer than the star-noticer; beginning with stars visible all the year round, and stars visible in the nights of summer. The summer skies are not so dark, the stars are not so brilliant. Orion the Great Hunter and Sirius (the brightest star of the sky) are nowhere to be seen, but at least the puzzling out of the constellations can begin in June or July without shivers.

It will be noticed, as we go round the sky, that if the star groups or constellations are mostly called by Greek or Latinized Greek names, the stars themselves have Arabic names or names in an Arabic form. This needs explanation. Most star names have come down to us from the Greek, some through Latin, a greater number through Arabic. The star knowledge of the Greeks was collected and enlarged in his writings by the last of the great astronomers of antiquity, Claudius Ptolomaeus (whom we know as Ptolemy), an Alexandrian of the second century (c. 100–170), who observed his stars and planets and celestial phenomena in the clear skies of Egypt. Science declined in the early Christian centuries; and through the Dark Ages and the early Middle Ages the scientific study of the heavens was continued only by the Arabs (who had conquered Alexandria and Egypt) – in Baghdad especially, and in Cairo and Damascus, then in Spain in the twelfth century. The Arabs knew what Ptolemy had written. They knew his *Megale Syntaxis* or Great System of Astronomy, also called the *Megiste Syntaxis*, or Greatest System, which included his catalogue of the constellations and the stars visible to the naked eye. Keeping the Greek title in Arabic disguise, Arab astronomers translated the *Megiste Syntaxis* as the *Almagest*, giving Arabic equivalents for the most part for the Greek star names. When astronomy was at last revived in Europe, we first of all knew Ptolemy's writings by translations of the Arabic *Almagest* into Latin. So we took over the star names in Arabic forms, many of which we have never abandoned.

That is the explanation, in the pages which follow, of Dubhe and Altair and Fomalhaut, of Algol, Alpheratz, Aldebaran and so many others – so many names with simple enough meanings, yet with a spangled look and sound which add extra mystery to the mysterious. In star literature the chief stars are now generally identified not by their old names but – in each constellation – by letters of the Greek alphabet. If these star pages of the *Country Book* whet your appetite, you will need, sooner or later, a star atlas and other star books. So the constellation letters have been added after the star names. (One necessary inexpensive star weapon to acquire is *Philip's Planisphere, showing the Principal Stars Visible for Every Hour of the Year.*)

## THE CIRCUMPOLAR STARS

The Circumpolar Stars are the ones visible all the year in our latitude. The first clues in the dome overhead (a dome it really seems, if you look and think about it) are the Great Bear and Polaris, or the Pole Star. Fix these two – always there in the north – and the rest of the naked-eye stars can be fitted gradually into place and identified.

### *The Great Bear, or Ursa Major, and the Little Bear, or Ursa Minor, and Polaris*

In America they use another name for the Great Bear – the Dipper. Think of it for a moment straddling the northern sky as a dipper, i.e. as a ladle or basin with a handle, for dipping water out of a cauldron. The two stars which form the side of the basin farthest from the three stars of the handle are the Pointers. Draw a line through them, extend it, and you come, not direct, but close to the rather lonely Stella Polaris, which the Arab astronomers called Alruccabah, pole of the heavenly sphere, index of the sky, indicator (though not exactly so) of the North. Not very bright, this Pole Star, but obvious, and in fact the brightest star of our second constellation, which is the Little Bear, or Little Dipper.

The Great Bear (always looked upon in this guise as a she-bear) has many other names. Besides the Dipper, it is the Plough, the Wain, and Charles' Wain. The Plough and Waggon names were Greek. As well as Megale Arktos or the Great She-Bear, the Greeks called this constellation Amaxa, which meant both wain (or waggon), and plough. Certainly it is like a plough of the old-fashioned kind, with handles, drawn by oxen or horses, though rather less like a modern waggon. The Charles the wain belongs to in English tradition is not Charles I, as many people think, but Charlemagne – Charlemayne's Wayne, the name going back to Anglo-Saxon times, to *Carles Wægn*. It was also another vehicle in Greek, a *pheretron* (*na'sh* in Arabic), a bier on which the dead were carried. The dead in the more ancient beliefs of Egypt went to this sky neighbourhood around the Pole Star, where the stars were always visible all night and all the year round and were therefore eternal, and were called 'those that know no destruction', or 'no tiredness'.

The names for the Great Bear are still not exhausted. The Romans called it not only Ursa Major, but Helice, the Twisting One, since it twists around the Pole Star. Egyptian names also included the Haunch and the Bull's Thigh. The Chinese identify the four stars of the body with K'uei-hsing, the God of Examinations. They also call them the Northern Bushel (K'uei-hsing carries a bushel-measure to measure the ability of the examinees).

Bear names, though, are the most widespread and probably the most ancient of all. At first consideration, the Great Bear does not much resemble a bear. The three 'handle stars' are commonly thought of as the she-bear's tail; but bears have so little of a tail that we may believe a different theory – that the Great Bear was named many thousands of years ago (perhaps in the Ice Age) as a divine animal roughly resembling a bear the other way round, i.e. a bear (coincidentally a Polar Bear?) with its neck stretched out. So the tail in the sky would become a neck; and this constellation would be like one of those Polar Bears, with head and neck exaggerated, and legs pointing inwards, which Eskimos carve out of walrus ivory.

Since the Great Bear is really the Emperor of the constellations, as well to know the names of her seven stars from snout or handle end to the Pointers – all of them Arabic. First comes Benetnasch (Chief of the Daughters of the Bier), also called Alkaid (The Governor). Then Mizar (The Veil or Cloak) – you should also be able to see the star Alcor (The Weak One) on Mizar's back – and then Alioth (Tail of a Fat Sheep). These are the three snout, handle or tail stars, from left to right – i.e. the Ursa Major stars $\eta$, $\zeta$, $\epsilon$. In the body: first (after Alioth), Megrez (The Root), then Phecda; and last the two Pointers, Merak (The Stomach) and Dubhe (*Al dubhu*, The Bear) – in the same order the Ursa Major stars $\delta$, $\gamma$, $\beta$, $\alpha$.

The Little Bear, far less conspicuous than the Great Bear (especially in the summer sky) has more or less the same figuration in miniature, and in reverse. It is the little she-bear, the great she-bear's cub. First body, then neck, if you think of it as another but smaller Polar Bear; in which case Polaris, its bright star (the star $\alpha$), would be situated in the snout. The first two 'body' stars of the Little Bear are the Guardians of the Pole, the brighter one ($\beta$) is Kochab (Arabic, the Star). The Greeks, and the Romans after them, also called the Little Bear Cynosure (*Kunosoura*), or Dog's Tail.

What seems to us to be the sphere of heaven and of the stars surrounding the Earth, also seems to us to revolve round the Earth, on the axis of the two celestial poles. The Pole Star marks the northern pin of this revolution. In reality Earth, by its own rotation of day and night, makes it appear to the earthly watcher of the skies that the stars are wheeling round the Pole from east to west, are 'rising' in the east and travelling to 'set' in the west, exactly like the sun or the moon (except the circumpolar ones, which travel round the Pole and the Pole Star without vanishing). But since the Earth also circles around the Sun (as well as rotating each period of day and night on its own axis), and takes a year to do so, our view of the stars also changes through the year. So we observe, for example, 'summer stars' and 'winter stars'; though Polaris and its neighbours are visible all the year round, we see the Pleiades and Orion, for example, only in the winter, and have our best view of Lyra and Aquila in the summer.

## Cassiopeia

After the Great Bear and the Little Bear, the easiest of the circumpolar constellations to determine is Cassiopeia, which you may like to think of by its Arabic name of the Kneeling Camel, or by its Eskimo name,

which is the Stone Lamp – two ideas which fit its shape more immediately than the idea of a mythical queen of Ethiopia (Cassiopeia) sitting in her chair. In summer, Cassiopeia is a slightly squashed W, in
autumn and winter, as you look up into the sky, a slightly squashed
M. That is enough to identify it, on the far side of Polaris from the
Great Bear.

## *Draco, or the Dragon*

At first the pattern of this very long and winding constellation takes a
little distinguishing. It winds – at first a line of single stars, rather
dim – between the Great Bear and the Little Bear, then wriggles towards Polaris, and curves round again to conclude in the Dragon's
Head, a small quadrilateral of stars. A devilish constellation, said Gerard
Manley Hopkins – thinking of Revelations xii – 'And there appeared
another wonder in heaven; and behold a great red dragon, having
seven heads and ten horns, and seven crowns upon his heads. And his
tail drew the third part of the stars of heaven' – wreathing around the
Pole as the Devil also wreathed around the Tree of Life.

The signposts are now established, visible always, all clear nights, all
clear hours through the year. But from now on, in describing summer
and winter stars, the assumption is that the star-watching or star-
noticing will not be at eccentric hours – only in the first hours after
dark (or between summer dark and midnight).

# THE SUMMER STARS

You can now add to your circumpolar identifications first of all those
groupings which are only seen, or are most prominent, during the
summer. And rather than going backwards and forwards, from darkness into indoor light to read, you can place on a table in the garden
this book and a candle inside a jam jar, and get to work.

Polaris you know. Now turn your back more or less to Polaris; or
rather stand with your left shoulder to Polaris, so that you can sweep
the sky by turning your head between left shoulder and right.

## *Cygnus, or the Swan*

We must start with the Swan (more or less overhead from August to
October). Cygnus appears as a cross in the sky, with four stars and a

star of intersection. A line through the third and fifth stars of Cassiopeia cuts into Cygnus, if you extend it, below the star of intersection.

Cross or Swan – at any rate it is not altogether unlike a swan flying across the summer sky (though it was also known to the ancient astronomers as Vultur Volans, the Flying Vulture). The longest arm of the cross is the stretch of the swan's neck, to the star Albireo (rather faint), which is the swan's head ($\beta$). The wings spread at right angles, more shortly, from the star of intersection ($\gamma$), which is called Sadar (Arabic for Breast); and the tail star, brightest of the constellation ($\alpha$), is Deneb – rather green (from the Arabic name meaning the Tail of the Hen).

## Lyra, or the Lyre, with Vega

Next Vega, and Vega's constellation, which is the lyre on which Orpheus played, or to which Orpheus sang, and so charmed the rocks and winds and waterfalls and birds and wild beasts, such is the power of poetry and music. After the Thracian women tore him to bits, Apollo (who had given him the lyre) and the Muses asked that the lyre should be placed among the stars. Vega, though, comes from an Arabic name, which means the Falling Vulture.

Vega ($\alpha$ of the Lyre) is the Summer Star of all stars, the second brightest in northern latitudes; white, or white with a tinge of blue – very conspicuous and decidedly overhead. But that does not fix Vega at a single glance into the confused order of the sky. The Swan is a clue. Vega shines within an extension of the angle of those two arms of the cross of the Swan which are farthest away from Cassiopeia. Or join Deneb, the tail star and brightest of the cross-stars of the Swan, to the loftier of the wing or cross-stars. You are now halfway to Vega. Continue (curving a little to the right) as far again and a little farther, and there is Vega – once discovered, never forgotten.

There are other names for Vega and other stories about so notice-able a star. The Chinese identify it with Chih-nii, the Heavenly Spin-ster, who spins seamless clouds and other garments for her father, Lao-t' ien-yeh, Father-Heaven or the August Personage of Jade. The Welsh call it Telyn Arthur, Arthur's Harp.

There is another good way of being sure of Vega and the Lyre (which is otherwise not much of a sky feature, though it has two other bright stars, $\gamma$ and $\beta$, Sulaphat and Sheliak) – but this involves finding another bird in the sky, the Eagle.

## Aquila, or the Eagle

The Eagle can be seen from early summer to autumn, just in the eastern, then in the southern sky, and the south-western sky. The con-stellation (on the map rather than in the sky) has another bird shape: head – not very bright – wings and tail. The tail is distinct and spread: three stars, close together in a straight line. The middle one is the large, brilliant Altair – *el-nasr-el-tair*, the Eagle that flies. This is $\alpha$ in the constellation. Of the other two, the brighter star ($\gamma$) is Tarazed, the fainter is Alshain ($\beta$), Arabic for the Falcon. These three, always easy to pick out of the sky, point direct to Vega, overhead.

## Delphinus, or the Dolphin, or Job's Coffin

This small packed constellation is now very easy to find, though its stars are dim – a humped or crushed circlet of stars to the left, or north-east, of Altair and his two other tail stars in the Eagle, not un-like the formal representation of a dolphin curving from the water. The Greek myth makes this the kindly Dolphin, which saved the poet Arion, by swimming him ashore on his back, when sailors would have murdered him, or the dolphin (see page 222), who ran messages for Poseidon the sea-god.

## Sagittarius, or the Archer

The indications of Sagittarius are not at all the obvious body, limbs or weapon of an archer in the sky; they are two four-sided shapes side by side, so distinct that you feel compelled to ask their name. They hang low down towards the southern horizon, below that straight line of the Eagle's tail, Tarazed, Altair and Alshain.

The visual concept of the sky is that hollow globe or sphere with the spectator's Earth as centre. Inside this sphere we look upward to the zenith, to the highest point above our heads, in our half of the sphere. Projecting the plane of the equator of the Earth, we imagine a celestial equator dividing the hollow, visual sphere of the sky into the hemispheres.

The two quadrilaterals of Sagittarius are actually below this equatorial line, south towards the dark rim of Earth.

## Scorpio, or the Scorpion, with Antares

As much as we see of Scorpio, the Scorpion at which the Archer shoots his arrow, also lies below the equator of the sky, away to the west of the Archer – a twisting string of considerable stars, of which three towards the western end stand in close line across the sky rather like the three stars in the Eagle's tail. Midmost of the three, the splendour of the constellation, is red or orange-red Antares, or Cor Scorpii ($\alpha$ Scorpii), Heart of the Scorpion, at which Sagittarius the Archer is shooting his arrow (Antares – in Greek 'anti Ares' – the [red] rival of Ares, or Mars, the red planet and the god of war).

Gerard Manley Hopkins noticed this summer star when he was holidaying in the Alps, on 22 July, 1868: 'Above the Breithorn, Antares sparkled like a bright crab-apple tingling in the wind.'

## Piscis Australis, or the Southern Fish, with Fomalhaut

Fomalhaut, a red brilliant, is all that we, in our latitudes, can see of the constellation of Piscis Australis, or the Southern Fish. A low horizon is required for a view of Fomalhaut ($\alpha$ of the constellation) which rises into fullest view in the last days of August and the first days of September, far down in the south, roughly SSW. of Cassiopeia, and SSE. of Cygnus. Fomalhaut is another Arabic name – Mouth of the Fish.

The Summer Stars indicated so far are ones which have been visible mainly with your left shoulder towards Polaris. Reverse yourself; *right* shoulder to Polaris, so that you look towards the west, and can regard the sky by looking round from right shoulder, north, to left shoulder, in the south.

## *Bootes, with Arcturus*

The first two stars of the snout of the Great Bear (or the handle of the Dipper, or the Plough), Benetnasch and Mizar, $\eta$ and $3$, point in a line to large Bootes – to the upper end of his kite or diamond (four stars in a kite or diamond figure). Bootes is the Greek for Ploughman, the driver of the oxen which draw the plough.

The triangular top of the kite is clear enough in the sky, culminating in the star named Nekkar ($\beta$), Arabic for the Digger and stemming from Mizar ($\epsilon$), Arabic for the Veil. Then outstanding in the tail of the kite is the yellow surprise of the first magnitude star Arcturus ($a$). Arktouros in Greek means the Bear-Guard, the star which keeps watch on the Great Bear – or really the name of the whole constellation, which was also called by the Greeks Arktophulax, the Bear-Keeper. In the Middle Ages we knew Arcturus also as Arturis, i.e. King Arthur. This was to fit in with the Great Bear as Charles' Wain, since Arthur was associated with great Charlemagne as one of the Nine Worthies. Bootes was also thought of as the huntsman of the Great Bear.

This is a spring as well as summer constellation.

## *Canes Venatici, or the Hounds, with Cor Caroli*

It is pleasant to know in the sky one star – though not a very bright one – named after an English king. If Charles' Wain does not belong to Charles I, but to Charlemagne, Charles I does have a star in the same district of the sky. Below the handle stars of the Dipper, the Wain, the Plough, or the Great Bear, three small stars form a triangle, apex downwards. Dim in the summer sky, these are the Canes Venatici, the Hounds, constellated and named in the seventeenth century by the German astronomer Hevelius, who thought of these stars as the hounds of Bootes. English astronomers of the Restoration wanted to name the whole constellation after the beheaded king, but only Cor Caroli, the Heart of Charles, has persisted as the name for the star at the apex ($a$).

## Corona Borealis, or the Northern Crown

No difficulty. Next and close to the kite of Bootes – on the far side from the Great Bear – eyesight by itself entirely detects the cup rather than the crown shape of Corona Borealis, though the stars are not very bright ($a$, the brightest of the seven stars which form the cup, is Alphecca, the Bright One, or Gemma). The Arabs called Corona Borealis the Broken Plate, thinking of it as flat with a piece out. The Greeks thought of it as the marriage crown or wreath which Dionysos placed on the young head of his wife Ariadne – the wreath of jewels and of gold which Dionysos had been given by Aphrodite, the goddess of love.

The British called it Caer Arianrod, the Camp or Hill-fort (its shape is not unlike the shape of a hill-fort of the Iron Age) of the British goddess Arianrod, who was one of the Children of Don.

Like Bootes, the Northern Crown is on view in spring as well as summer.

## Virgo, or the Virgin, with Spica

Spica, or the Ear of Corn ($a$), a clean white star of the first magnitude, is the surest indicator of Virgo, which has an erratic, zigzagging shape, low in the western sky, as a summer constellation (in spring look for Virgo in the south). A line joining the two stars of the kite of Bootes, on the side of the Northern Crown, to yellow Arcturus, and then continued, comes very close to Spica.

Virgo was a constellation which indicated harvest-time in the Mediterranean. The Egyptians made it the constellation of Isis. In their mythology this Earth-Mother, escaping from the evil Set, who murdered her husband Osiris, dropped her sheaf of corn, the grains of which formed the Milky Way. Above this Isis-Virgo in the sky is that Great Bear, which the Egyptians also called the Thigh of Set, that demon of the gods.

Spica, the Ear of Corn, is not the only harvest star in Virgo. The brightish star ($\epsilon$) nearest to the Great Bear is Vindemiatrix or Vindemitor, which in Latin means the Grape-Gatherer.

# THE AUTUMN STARS

## Pegasus, or the Winged Horse

A good many summer constellations, their position shifted so that they look unfamiliar (for instance, Aquila, Cygnus, Lyra), are still to be seen in autumn; but this is notably the time for recognizing the great box of Pegasus, which now lifts itself grandly above the eastern horizon, in that area, eastward of Cassiopeia and Cygnus, which has seemed so pallid and tantalizingly empty during the summer nights.

Pegasus was the horse with wings. Poseidon, the god of the sea, took the shape of a stallion and coupled with Medusa, one of the three Gorgons. Perseus now cut off Medusa's head, and from her neck and her blood a horse was born – this winged horse who became sky messenger of Zeus.

Actually the top left-hand star of the box or square, as it rises in the autumn, is borrowed from the neighbouring constellation of Andromeda ($\alpha$ in Andromeda). Its name from the Arabic is Alpheratz, shortened from an Arabic name meaning the Navel of the Horse. The top right-hand star of the box ($\beta$ in Pegasus) is Scheat, Arabic for Good Fortune. The bottom left-hand star ($\gamma$) is Algenib, the Flank or Side; and the bottom right-hand star ($\alpha$) is Markab, the Saddle.

From Markab, the constellation of Pegasus continues to a small triangle of three stars – small in comparison with the great box filled with the darkness of air.

## Andromeda, with the Great Andromeda Nebula

Andromeda – not the most stirring of constellations – is best seen in the autumn, south-east of the sprawling W of Cassiopeia, and is best located by recognizing first of all the Great Square of Pegasus – since Andromeda begins (as we have just seen) with the star Alpheratz ($\alpha$ Andromedae), which is also the top left-hand corner of the box. From Alpheratz, Andromeda curves into two star lines, the upper line (ending near Cassiopeia) rather faint, the lower one strong. In the strong line first comes Sirrah ($\delta$), followed by Mirach or Mizar ($\beta$), and Almac (The Badger); and from this Badger ($\gamma$), the strong line continues to one of the two brightest stars of Perseus ($\alpha$ in Perseus) named Mirfac or Algenib (a star name already encountered in Pegasus).

The first clue to the Great Nebula (the only spiral nebula you can see without telescope or binoculars) is the star Mirach ($\beta$). From Mirach, two fainter stars ($\mu$ and $\nu$) stand at right angles to the strong line. Just beyond the second of them comes the spiral nebula, a small pallid blur in the darkness hardly suggesting its true nature as a great galaxy or system of stars immensely distant.

Round and including Andromeda, we have a family party in the sky. Andromeda, saved from the sea-monster by Perseus (next door), was daughter of Cassiopeia (above).

Perseus will come under the Winter Stars, on page 143. For Aquila, or the Eagle, also an autumn constellation, see under the Summer Stars, on page 131.

# THE WINTER STARS

Identification of the Summer Stars, in the paler sky between sunset and midnight, began from Polaris and the Great Bear and the circumpolar stars. In winter, especially when there is no moonlight, each sparkling star and constellation is more distinct, in a more thorough night. Star-noticing can begin earlier; and like the moon, stars look their best and brightest as they rise, and before they are aloofly suspended in mid-heaven.

Orion is the great indicator in the winter sky, a constellation as familiar as Ursa Major, or even more familiar. Polaris and the Bear and the rest of the circumpolar congregation are still there towards the north, though the constellations swing around the pole into unfamiliar positions.

To begin with, look around the sky at about seven o'clock in late December, in the days of Christmas when early night has a most benign quality.

Find the Pole Star, Polaris, by the Pointers of the Plough or the Great Bear or the Dipper or Charles' Wain (down at a less familiar angle near the earth); and first of all turn your back to the eastern horizon and contemplate the western sky, and see what has happened to some of the autumn and summer constellations. They have not all vanished. Cygnus, the Swan, is now decidedly the great cross in the sky, foot pointing to earth, arms left and right. Below to the left, within the extended angle of the stem of the cross and the left arm, shines – still – the bright Altair, with his two companions, in a line. Below to the right, within the extended angle of the stem of the cross and its right arm, summer's Vega, once so prominent in the zenith, hangs even nearer the earth, and will very shortly have disappeared. Higher, and more towards the south, the great autumn square of Pegasus is still aloft.

Now turn your back to Cygnus, to the west. Leftwards again, the Great Bear slopes into heaven. Resplendent stars stretch along the horizon, till you come to that triangle of magnificence, enclosing what most people think of as Orion, in fact enclosing the belt and dagger of this giant of the sky. Winter –

And the sprawling Bear
Growled deep in the sky;
And Orion's hair
Streamed sparkling by:
But the North sighed low:
'*Snow, snow, more snow!*'

## *Orion, with Betelgeuse and Rigel, and the Stars of the Belt*

The many stars of Orion can be traced into a man-shape, though Orion was giant rather than man – a giant hunter born of the earth, which was inseminated for the purpose with a bull's hide full of the seed of Zeus, Hermes and Poseidon. In the sky, as on earth, this lustful greedy hunter, who threatened to hunt all the animals to extinction, pursues Pleione and her daughters (the Pleiades), is followed by his hounds (Canis Major, Canis Minor), and strides above the hare (the constellation of Lepus) which he delighted to hunt. And ahead of him, he threatens the bull (Taurus). Long before he was Orion of the Greeks, this star giant glittering in the black sky was the powerful and angry Ninurta, hunter and god of war and fierce enemy of wickedness among the ancient Mesopotamians. But he was also Osiris to the Egyptians, the god of resurrection and goodness.

To the eye, as he climbs above the horizon, this Orion or Ninurta or Osiris is first of all the three stars of his belt encircling a very narrow waist, and the three lamp-like stars of the huge triangle which encloses the belt. The names confuse two myths about this constellation – the myth of the hunter, and an Arabic myth which made the constellation into a Bride, the Djanza, killed by her husband's too powerful and zestful embrace. Of the stars which form the triangle, two are the giant's left and right shoulders. His left shoulder is the reddish or orange Betelgeuse ($\alpha$), from the Arabic for the Djanza's shoulder; the star – not so brilliant as Betelgeuse – which marks the right shoulder ($\gamma$) is the Latin-named Bellatrix, the Warrior (-Star). The third of the lamp-like stars of the triangle ($\beta$), brightest in the constellation and one of the five brightest stars in the sky – is Rigel. This comes from the Arabic word meaning the Foot; though Rigel is rather one of Orion's knees, since his legs are held to continue to two fainter stars which belong to the not so very noticeable constellation of Lepus, the Hare. The other knee-star of Orion ($\kappa$), also adds confusion, since its name is Saiph, or Sword, shortened from the Arabic name which means Sword of the Giant – whereas we think of Orion's dagger as the small stars hanging from his belt between his legs, and passing through the Great Orion Nebula (which can be seen without binoculars on a dark night, a diffuse nebula of clouds of gas, not a galaxy of stars).

Last of all, Orion's Belt, sloping with such precision across the sky. From left to right the names of the three stars of the belt ($\zeta$, $\epsilon$, and $\delta$) are Alnitak, Alnilam and Mintak. Alnitak and Mintak simply mean the Belt; Alnilam (or Alnitam), in the middle, means, with a proper touch of poetry, the String of Pearls – rather a name for the girdle worn by the Bride than for the belt worn by Orion.

If you follow Orion's Belt up the sky from the moment when Mintak, then Alnilam, then Alnitak, appear above the black and solid horizon until the whole constellation swings to its height in the southern sky, you will understand another belief about these three stars – that they represented the Three Kings, Caspar, Melchior and Balthasar, riding on their December journey from the eastern horizon to Bethlehem.

For a time in France Orion was re-named Napoleon – in Napoleon's heyday as the great hunter and war god of Europe.

## Lepus, or the Hare

Not a very sparkling or proud assembly, but immediately ascertainable below Orion, who liked the hunting of the hare. Low in the sky, the stars of the Hare can be seen like a swastika (with its arms from right to left instead of left to right) radiating around the central and brightest star Arneb (Arabic for Hare), which is also Orion's left or easterly foot. But it you look at Lepus a little differently, it seems wide enough to be the chair or seat of the giant huntsman above, which was how the Arabs thought of it.

Now for the resplendence of the stars (particularly grand in the early evening) between Orion and the Great Bear, low at first along the eastern prospect. Round about seven p.m., between Orion and the Bear, the inescapable constellation will be Gemini, with Auriga higher above. Then later in the night, Orion and Gemini will have swung round and upwards; and Orion's hounds of Canis Major as well as Canis Minor will have joined a spectacle which includes in Orion itself and eastward of Orion no fewer than six of the major coruscations among all the stars.

138

## Gemini, or the Twins, with Castor and Pollux

Gemini rises, a long rectangle more or less, between Orion and the
Great Bear. Orion recognized, there can hardly be any doubt about
Gemini, since between Orion – or more exactly between Betelgeuse
and Bellatrix on the southern side, and the Great Bear to the north –
the only three bright stars are the three beauties of Gemini – Alhena,
first ($\gamma$); then Castor and Pollux, the actual twins ($\alpha$ and $\beta$), hanging
clear and bold above each other; Castor white, Pollux, below, dark
yellow or orange. To make sure, look for two strong stars in a straight
line with Betelgeuse, more or less in the direction of the Great Bear.
The first from Betelgeuse (across the Milky Way) will be Alhena,
bottom right-hand corner star of the long box of Gemini, the second
will be Pollux, of the first magnitude, bottom left-hand star of the box.

Another method: draw a line across the body of the Great Bear from
Megrez to Merak, the lower of the two Pointers, and its extension will
come close to Castor and Pollux. Or better still, the extension of a line
between the second and third of the handle stars of the Bear – between
Mizar and Alioth ($\zeta$ and $\epsilon$) – comes direct to Castor and Pollux.

Castor and Pollux have been called the hunters of the Kangaroo
(i.e. of Capella) by Australian aborigines, the Two Antelopes by the
Bushmen of South Africa, the Two Kids by the Egyptians, and the
Two Peacocks by the Arabs. For the Greeks, the two stars became their
most famous pair of mythical twins, Kastor and Polydeukes (Castor
and Pollux), sons hatched from the egg engendered by that union of
Zeus as a swan with Leda.

## Auriga, or the Charioteer, with Capella

When Castor and Pollux have risen, these twins make the whereabouts
of Auriga, or at any rate of its principal star Capella, very obvious in
the higher heaven. Extend a line through Castor and Pollux, diverge
slightly to the right: there, first, is the second brightest star in Auriga
($\beta$), which is named Menkalinan, the Shoulder of the Holder of the
Reins – i.e. of the charioteer; then comes the yellow clarity of Capella
($\alpha$), of the first magnitude – second brightest of the winter stars, high
enough to be visible all the year round, and in the winter months in
the zenith, overhead, as counterpart to Vega in the summer zenith.

The charioteer, in Greek myth, is Erichthonios, son of Hephaistos
(Vulcan to the Romans), by Athene, or by his accidental impregna-
tion of Gaia; he was legendary king of Athens, and he invented the
chariot with four horses. Auriga's three principal stars, Capella,

Menkalinan and a third (θ) of slightly less magnitude than Menkalinan, appear as a boldly evident triangle. But Capella means a She-goat; and if two stars are borrowed from the adjoining constellation of Taurus, the shape of Auriga also resembles the end of a shepherd's or goatherd's crook. Two stars from Taurus – Aldebaran and El Nath – form the top of the staff, then the crook curves round to Capella itself, and farther round to a little triangle of dimly visible stars which are the Kids. But Capella is a she-goat, and the two small stars nearby are the Kids.

## Taurus, or the Bull, with Aldebaran

Forgetting, for a moment, the stars and constellations on the Castor and Pollux side of frosty Orion, Auriga is the proper introduction to Taurus, or the Bull. Above great Orion's head (as he rises higher in the sky) we have, on the side of the Great Bear, Gemini with Castor and Pollux; towards the Pole Star, Auriga with Capella; and now on the other side, opposite Gemini, we have Taurus, or the Bull.

The stars of Auriga curve around, as we have seen, from Capella like the curved end of a crook, the straight staff of which begins with El Nath in Taurus (β) and continues with the great star of the constellation, Aldebaran (α), red and prominent, tingling in the sky with its neighbours of the triangle of Orion. Most people, however little they know of the stars, are familiar with the Pleiades, grouped together in the winter sky (and regarded anciently as part of the constellation of Taurus): Aldebaran, Oculus Tauri (The Bull's Eye), the red eye of the Bull, shines between Orion and the Pleiades.

In western languages Aldebaran both looks and sounds a wonderful name, as if it contained in itself all the glitter of the winter sky – but it is Arabic for no more than The Follower, the star which follows the Pleiades across the sky from east to west.

## *Canis Major, or the Greater Dog, with Sirius*

Sirius they watched above where armies fell.

A line continued through the great stars of the pearly belt of Orion (on the opposite side to Taurus and Aldebaran) comes to Canis Major, the first of the two groups of hounds on their master's heel. But the chief star, Sirius or the Dog (α), brightest star in either hemisphere, twinkling in splendour above the black horizon, is so prominent, so different from any other star, that directional aids to Canis Major are really not required.

Sirius, from the Greek, means the Scorching (Star), and when Sirius rose in conjunction with the sun, the hottest weather of the year began for the Greeks. But for us Sirius is the scorching object in the cold winter sky.

Far more important, to the eye, than the constellation it belongs to (or you might say, than the constellation which belongs to it), Sirius is so bright that like Venus (though Venus is much brighter) it can even cast a shadow. The colour of this great twinkling star offers a puzzle. The ancients called Sirius a red star. Field-glasses will show its modern colour as a cold crystalline blue, and Sirius is thought to have changed its colour. But to the eye, Sirius will often seem to be twinkling in spangles of blue (or emerald-blue) and red – most of all, when Sirius is rising and is still fairly low in the winter heaven; as it appeared to Tennyson, when he described the three sons of the king in the fifth part of *The Princess*. The light made them glance

> Like those three stars of the airy Giant's zone,
> That glitter burnish'd by the frosty dark,

and their helmets shone

> as the fiery Sirius alters hue,
> And bickers into red and emerald.

(For the twinkling of the stars see page 147.)

The bright star alongside Sirius is Murzim (β), the Herald, which rises just before Sirius itself.

In watching Sirius against the black solidity of a hill or a yew tree, remember also that this great star was worshipped by the Egyptians as a minor goddess, Sopdet (called Sothis by the Greeks). In the summer the first morning rising of Sirius, or Sopdet, after conjunction with the sun had made the star invisible, warned them that the Nile would soon flood; so with this heliacal rising of Sirius the Egyptian year began.

Sirius for the Egyptians was also the star of Isis, mother-goddess, goddess of the crops, wife of the good Osiris (who was Orion, nearby), shining not only to announce the fertile flooding of the Nile, but to guide the travellers she protected, especially on their sea journeys.

## Canis Minor, or the Lesser Dog, with Procyon

Sirius has another herald, the yellow star Procyon, of the first magnitude ($a$ in Canis Minor), which collects to itself a constellation of small stars situated eastward of Orion, and divided by the Milky Way from Sirius and Canis Major. Procyon (a Greek name meaning Before the Hound) also rises before Sirius; and follows Orion as another of his hounds. Procyon, and to the west, red Betelgeuse in Orion, and the bickering Sirius below form between them the most gorgeous of the triangles of the night, with Sirius as the southern apex.

## The Pleiades, or the Seven Sisters, or the Virgils

The Greek poetess Sappho wrote about the Pleiades and love and herself more than 2,500 years ago:

> The Moon has set,
> The Seven Stars have set as well:
> It is the middle of the night,
> The hours go by
> And by myself I lie.

Looking at this famous group of stars in the night, westward of Orion, no one need think of them as part of the constellation of Taurus, in which they have been included since the time of the ancient Greek astronomers. They float by themselves; and though in the group there are many more stars than seven, most of us on clear nights can distinguish six stars without the aid of field-glasses – and more than six if we look at the Pleiades sideways and not direct. (This is because a frontal image falls on the cones of the retina, in the 'yellow spot', which are sensitive to colour, but less sensitive to low illumination than the rod-like cells of 'night vision' in other parts of the retina). The Greeks had a story that seven Pleiades could be seen until the Trojan War, when one of them made off, like a comet, towards the North Star – and vanished.

In Greek myth the Pleiades were most desirable young goddesses, daughters of Pleione and Atlas, who carried heaven on his back. Wild

Orion chased them across Boeotia, and chases them still across the sky. They were likened as well – this is probably the origin of the name Pleiades – to a flight of wild doves. The Romans also named them the Virgiliae, the Spring Stars (we see them, in our latitude, in early spring as well as in winter).

Australian aborigines see the Pleiades as a flight of cockatoos, some of the jungle Indians of Bolivia call them the Little Parrots. Tennyson's description is better than most:

> Many a night I saw the Pleiads, rising thro' the mellow shade,
> Glitter like a swarm of fireflies tangled in a silver braid.

## Perseus, with Mirfac and Algol

Perseus is a late summer and autumn as well as a winter constellation, to be found by following the bolder of the two lines of stars which constitute Andromeda (constellation of that daughter of Queen Cassiopeia whom Perseus had rescued); or else by following the Milky Way from Cassiopeia. Most of Perseus overlaps the Milky Way, between Cassiopeia and the star Capella; but it is a constellation of rather confused and muddling shape.

The bolder line of Andromeda continues direct to the bright star Mirfac or Algenib in Perseus ($a$), inside the Milky Way. The celebrated star Algol ($\beta$) – which varies in the intensity of its light – is outside the Milky Way.

When Perseus killed the Gorgon named Medusa, he sliced off Medusa's head – that object of extreme horror which turned all those who saw it to stone. The Greeks called Algol and its immediate neighbours by the name Gorgoneion, the Gorgon's Head, which they imagined Perseus to be holding in his left hand. This name the Arab astronomers translated to Ras-el-gol, Head of the Ghoul, or Demon, which gives our name Algol for the single star – a star which was looked upon as the most baleful in heaven.

# THE SPRING STARS

Aquila, Corona Borealis and Virgo are three of the spring constellations which last into summer; they have been described under the Summer Stars. One major prominent constellation climbs from winter to spring up from the eastern sky with a bold position across the southern sky in March and April. This is –

## Leo, or the Lion, with Regulus

In December the Lion's head pushes up over the edge of Earth. At this time the head looks less a head than a hook or sickle – it is often called the Sickle – handle downwards, the handle beginning with white Regulus, the most prominent star in the constellation (α). Then as he climbs into the sky, the sickle resolves itself into the outline of the head and chest of a lion couchant – like the sphinx at Gizeh. The Sphinx, who is Hormakhis or Hor-in-akhet, the sun-god Horus on the Horizon, may in fact be the constellation of the Lion. The star Regulus is also Cor Leonis, the Lion's Heart; and at full stretch the Lion's body extends across the sky to the obvious star Denebola (β), or the Tail (from the Arabic name meaning the Tail of the Lion). Regulus is the only star of the first magnitude in Leo. If some of the other stars in Leo's outline were as bright, this constellation would have the magnificence of Orion or the Great Bear.

To be sure of Leo, extend a line from Megrez and Phecda, the two left-hand stars of the body of the Great Bear, and it will come straight to the Sickle or the Lion's Head.

A reminder – remember, if you need to join up your sky at less familiar hours when the shapes and relations are confusing at first sight, that the Great Bear, or the Plough, and Cassiopeia swing around on opposite sides of the Pole Star. For instance, at half past one on Christmas night (not an unlikely time for a glance at the stars) the Great Bear, or Plough, to the north-east will be with handle to the ground; whereas Cassiopeia, to the west, will be not an M or a W to your view, but will be standing upright like a capital Greek Sigma. Either constellation, once recognized, will start to bring the unfamiliar looking population of the stars back to familiarity, will set in place the lion's head of Leo, Andromeda, Auriga, Perseus and so on.

# THE BRIGHTEST STARS IN OUR LATITUDES

Here is a check list of the fourteen brightest stars – numbered in order of brightness – which can be seen in our latitudes. All of them have been mentioned in the pages about the Circumpolar Stars, and the Stars of Summer, Autumn, Winter and Spring. Have you identified them all?

1 Sirius, in Canis Major (page 141)
2 Vega, in Lyra (page 130)
3 Arcturus, in Bootes (page 133)
4 Capella, in Auriga (page 139)
5 Rigel, in Orion (page 137)
6 Procyon, in Canis Minor (page 142)
7 Betelgeuse, in Orion (page 137)
8 Altair, in Aquila (page 131)
9 Aldebaran, in Taurus (page 140)
10 Spica, in Virgo (page 134)
11 Antares, in Scorpio (page 132)
12 Deneb, in Cygnus (page 130)
13 Fomalhaut, in Piscis Australis (page 132)
14 Regulus, in Leo (page 144)

Of these fourteen, the Winter Stars are:

Sirius
Capella (also to be seen in spring and summer)
Rigel
Procyon
Betelgeuse
Aldebaran
Regulus (also to be seen in spring and early summer)

And the Summer Stars:

Vega
Arcturus (also to be seen in spring)
Altair (also to be seen in spring and winter)
Spica (also to be seen in spring)
Antares
Deneb (also to be seen in autumn and early winter)
Fomalhaut

# THE MILKY WAY

Here are some things worth recollecting at the sight of this mist of stars in the night sky.

Seeming to wander or flow around the sky, this star system, to which our own Sun belongs, has been thought of variously as a way, a path, a road, a river. The Greek astronomers spoke of the Milky Way as a milky circle around the star sphere. Greek myth explained this soft milky suffusion among the stars as the result of Hera's suckling of her divine offspring. Drops of her escaping milk made the milky circle in heaven, and also grew into lilies when they fell on the Earth. (Hera was consort of Zeus, who in turn was god of the sky and of all things.)

The Egyptians conceived of the Milky Way in a more agricultural manner. When Isis, the Earth-Mother, fled from Set, she dropped her sheaf of corn, and the grains of wheat became the Milky Way, marking the path of her escape (see page 142).

Like earlier religions, Christianity had its own way of regarding the Milky Way. In medieval Europe, when pilgrimage was a favourite pastime, the Milky Way was held to be a divine marking-out in the sky of the pilgrim routes. A favourite pilgrimage took travellers from every country, England included, to the shrine of the apostle St James, in Compostela, in the north-west corner of Spain. According to Spanish legend, the body of the saint had been shipped by his disciples to Spain, which he had tried to convert to Christianity, and had been buried at Santiago (i.e. St James) de Compostela, where pious men rediscovered it in the ninth century. So the Milky Way was the Way of St James, or the Via di Santiago. Spaniards still remember that. They look at the Milky Way, and declare that even the stars are on pilgrimage to Santiago de Compostela, where the Milky Way is supposed to end. We have called the Milky Way the Walsingham Way, since it marked the pilgrimage way to the great shrine of the Virgin Mary at Walsingham in Norfolk.

More commonly our name for the Milky Way was Watling Street, since the long Roman road which came from Wroxeter to London (down Edgware Road) and continued from London to Canterbury, was also the pilgrimage road to the shrine of St Thomas à Becket. Pilgrimages to Rome caused the Italians to name the Milky Way the Strada di Roma.

Christianity also made the Milky Way the way into Heaven – as imagined with great magnificence in Milton's *Paradise Lost*, where the

Creator travels by the Milky Way at the end of the sixth day of creation:

> He through Heav'n,
> That open'd wide her blazing portals, led
> To God's Eternal house direct the way,
> A broad and ample road, whose dust in gold
> And pavement stars, as stars to thee appear,
> Seen in the Galaxy, that Milky way
> Which nightly as a circling zone thou seest
> Powder'd with stars.

## THE STARS REFLECTED

Sometimes look at the stars reflected – the constellations reversed – on the sea (on rare occasions, perhaps in a sheltered bay, when it is still enough), on a lake, on a pond, even a puddle. Gerard Manley Hopkins, who found the stars wonderful at all times, made a note in his summer diary in 1864, on mirrored stars – 'Reflection of stars in water. – Pointed golden drops. Gold tails.' Thomas Hardy, another star poet, made this winter note after a walk in the winter of his eightieth year (1920):

> *January 19.* Coming back from Talbothays by West Stafford Cross I saw Orion upside-down in a pool of water under an oak.

## TWINKLING

The brighter stars twinkle – for the most part when they are low down in the sky, and best of all in winter, and when the weather is slightly windy, and damp – say, in those benign days which so often occur before Christmas. Sirius notably twinkles, or scintillates, as he rises into such a wintry sky, he seems to be alive, to change colour between red and emerald (see page 141). The Pleiades twinkle, especially as they rise. So do the stars of the 'triangle' of Orion, or the stars of Orion's belt, as they edge and climb into the sky.

The twinkling is caused by a wavering in the air – by air waves (such as those we see rising off a hot road or a hot tin roof in the summer) which curve the rays of light. The colours appear to chop and change because rays of differently coloured light, according to colour, reach the eye some direct, some reflected (see M. Minnaert's *Light and Colour in the Open Air*). The phenomena, though, are more important than the explanation, since twinkling is one of the beauties of the night.

Everyone knows that stars twinkle, and planets do not. But this is not quite true. Jupiter in the night does not twinkle, nor does Mars, nor does Saturn. Mercury, though, may twinkle: so may Venus, when she hangs very low in the sky.

Twinkling with or without changes in colour is not, of course, the same thing as seeing stars rather as we conventionally draw or cut out a 'star'. Gerard Manley Hopkins made this note in his diary in August, 1864:

> The sky minted with gold sequins
> Stars like gold tufts
> golden bees
> golden rowels
> Sky peak'd with tiny flames.
> Stars like tiny-spoked wheels of fire.

Seeing stars in that way, as Hopkins described them, is due to imperfection of our eyes, especially if we are short-sighted. There is a story about the astronomer Sir William Herschel and the new more powerful telescopes he made at the end of the eighteenth century, when everyone still thought of stars as 'tiny-spoked wheels of fire'. Henry Cavendish the chemist and physicist sat next to him at dinner, then turned and gravely asked him, 'Is it true, Dr Herschel, that you see the stars round?'

'Round as a button.'

Cavendish said nothing more to Herschel till the end of dinner. Then he turned to him again, and asked, 'Round as a button?'

'Round as a button', Herschel said again; and that was that.

# THE NIGHT SKY THROUGH FIELD-GLASSES

The night sky was explored, and filled by ancient belief with divinities great and small, and with names, during long centuries when the astronomer had nothing to observe with except his own eyes.

Our own eyes are all we require still to grasp the identity and shape of the major constellations, to admire the New Moon, or Sirius in the winter sky, or Venus as the Morning or Evening Star. But field-glasses even of a modest power (say of ten multiplications) are worth using at night on special occasions or to reveal special beauties, once we know our way around. They are worth turning, of course, on to the Moon in its phases or eclipses, or on to comets. But they are best used on a spectacle of several objects which all appear together inside the field of vision – for instance, on a conjunction of planets with each other or of a planet with the moon, or on the occultation of a planet by the moon, in those moments when the planet disappears behind the moon or reappears. Field-glasses should be turned on to pairs of stars (for instance on to Mizar and its 'rider' Alcor in the handle of the Plough), on to the Pleiades, whose faint fireflies they will change at once into seven, eight, nine, and more, definite stars, like a small Plough or Wain with a stump of a handle, or on to the faint constellation of Cancer, or the Crab, (between Leo and Gemini, in the winter sky), for a clear view of that cluster of stars called the Praesepe, the Manger, (also called the Hive of Bees), at which the four surrounding stars called the Aselli, the Little Asses or Ass' Colts, are feeding.

Field-glasses can show some of the moons of Jupiter (though even the strongest glasses will not reveal the rings of Saturn), and they give an enchanting beauty of definition to the Milky Way.

Before 'perspective cylinders' or 'Dutch trunks', i.e. telescopes, were invented in Holland about 1608, astronomers had only a few tricks to help their vision – looking with the side of the retina, for example (see page 142), at fainter star groups, sitting in the dark for three-quarters of an hour or so before star-gazing, or observing the stars from a dark room through only a tiny opening, so as to shut out most of the sky brightness. The first telescope Galileo made (in 1609) multiplied nine times. In 1609 he saw the mountains of the Moon in a telescope multiplying twenty times. In 1610 he saw Jupiter's moons in a telescope multiplying thirty times. The first Englishman to have a clear telescopic view of the Moon was Sir William Lower, who at Traventy in Pembrokeshire in July, 1609 looked at the full moon through his 'cylinder', and wrote that 'In the full she appeares like a tart that my cooke made me last weeke; here a vaine of bright stuffe, there of darke, and so confusedlie all over.'

# The Planets

Home by starlight and Jupiter, stumbling down steep dark lanes.

Gerard Manley Hopkins

The Heav'ns and all the Constellations rung,
The Planets in their stations list'ning stood.

John Milton

Planets are wanderers in the sky – they are what the Greeks called
*planetes asteres*, wandering stars, which makes detection and identification of the planets visible to the eye one of the chief of natural pleasures,
or of sky pleasures. The 'wanderings' are regular and calculable, yet
seem to be haphazard. The stars are fixed, the planets come and go
and intrude, as it seems, among the familiar constellations. So the five
planets clearly visible from Earth without field-glasses or telescope –
Mercury, Venus, Mars, Jupiter, Saturn – and the Sun and the Moon,
were identified, from civilization to civilization, with some of the principal gods. A day of the week was assigned to each of them (the Sun of
Sunday and the Moon of Monday were also regarded as planets), and
their comings and goings, risings and settings, conjunctions, occultations and eclipses, were held to affect the destinies of man on earth.

The planets are to be seen above the horizon between east and west,
in their orbital journeys around the Sun, the true star of our planetary
system whose light they reflect with such brilliance. Each planet swims
along the zodiac, which is the imaginary band or belt of sky space
traced around the sphere of the stars on either side of the ecliptic; in
turn the ecliptic is the path dividing the zodiac which the Sun appears
to take round the Earth. Along the zodiac, which is eighteen degrees
wide (i.e. a little less than twice the sky distance between the top stars
of the body of the Great Bear, that is, between Megrez and Dubhe, δ
and α, which are ten degrees apart) are located the famous but not all
very conspicuous or brilliant constellations which gave their names to
the twelve signs or equal divisions of the zodiac, or 'circle of creatures'
as the name meant in Greek.

These are:

Aries or the Ram
Taurus or the Bull (page 140)
Gemini or the Twins (page 139)
Cancer or the Crab (page 149)
Leo or the Lion (page 144)
Virgo or the Virgin (page 134)
Libra or the Scales
Scorpio or the Scorpion (page 132)
Sagittarius or the Archer (page 131)
Capricornus or the Goat
Aquarius or the Water-carrier
Pisces or the Fishes

To discover where and when a planet is visible you need to know the whereabouts in the sky of these zodiacal constellations, and you need an almanac (such as *Whitaker's Almanack* or the *Nautical Almanac*); also a Star Atlas, and a Planisphere, which is an adjustable star atlas (neither is expensive or difficult to obtain). Month by month the almanac will say that a particular planet is too near the sun for observation, or that it is a morning star or an evening star – that Jupiter, for example, 'is now a morning star *in Libra*, rising shortly before sunrise' or that 'Mars, *in Cancer*, is an evening star from sunset till midnight'. The position may be given more precisely, it can be plotted on the star map in advance; and the planet detective will know where to look, and will quickly recognize a bright intruder into the familiar pattern of a constellation along the zodiac (the line of the ecliptic, which bisects the zodiac, will be marked on the star map or the planisphere).

The almanac will also give warning of other events or phenomena – of the conjunctions, when planets come into each other's company (Venus with Mars, Mars with Saturn, and so on) or come near the moon; of the occultations, when a planet is hidden by the Moon, disappearing behind the Moon and reappearing.

Mercury, the smallest of the family, and Venus, the most brilliant, are both nearer than our own planet to the Sun, and are only seen as morning and evening stars in the east or the west, before sunrise and after sunset. Mars, Jupiter and Saturn, further out from the Sun than our planet, appear in their tracks to advance, retreat, halt and move again. They have a wider range of visibility along the zodiac and need more careful plotting among the constellations. (Of the other planets, Neptune demands field-glasses, Pluto is invisible without a major telescope, and Uranus can only just be detected by the unassisted eye.)

# BRIGHTNESS OF THE PLANETS – AND THEIR STEADINESS

The brightness of the planets as we see them in the sky of course varies. Think of the Pole Star which is not so very bright, then of Sirius in the winter sky (page 141), the brightest of all the 'fixed' stars, and about nineteen-and-a-half times as bright as the Pole Star. By comparison:

Saturn at its brightest is about two-and-a-half times less bright than Sirius; at its dimmest, very much less bright – indeed only about two-and-a-half times as bright as the Pole Star.

Mercury at its brightest is rather less bright than Sirius; at its dimmest, very much less bright, also about two-and-a-half times as bright as the Pole Star.

Jupiter at its brightest is about two-and-a-half times brighter than Sirius; at its dimmest, rather less bright than Sirius, yet still about nineteen times as bright as the Pole Star.

Mars when brightest is more than two-and-a-half times as bright as Sirius; yet when dimmest is about sixteen times less bright than Sirius, and not very much brighter than the Pole Star.

Venus, most brilliant object in heaven after the Moon and the Sun, shows at her brightest about eight times as bright as Sirius. When dimmest she is still five-and-a-half or six times as bright as that brightest of stars, and more than ninety-seven times as bright as the Pole Star.

Twinkling, as a criterion distinguishing planets from stars, has already been discussed (page 147). Though Venus and Mercury may twinkle, Venus usually, and the other planets always, shine with a steady light. Degree of brightness apart, no one can mistake the fiercely blinking or twinkling Sirius for the steady shine of Jupiter or Mars.

## Saturn

Distant, and relatively dim among the brighter planets, though a giant second only in size to Jupiter. As a god of the Romans, he is the son of Earth and Sky (Uranus, the next planet away in space) and the father of Jupiter. As a god of the Greeks, he is the great Kronos, who ate all his new-born sons, Zeus excepted, in fear of usurpation. His day is Saturday, *Saturni dies*.

Like Mars and Jupiter, Saturn's appearances are not limited to the twilights of morning and evening. His rings cannot be detected without a telescope. Titan, though, the largest of his moons, can be seen with field-glasses – if they are strong enough. (The times will be given in the almanac.)

## Jupiter

Except for Venus, Jupiter and Mars in their courses are the most blazing of all the stars or planets. Jupiter indeed is the greatest of the planets in (actual) size. Travelling through the zodiac, he may be visible for hours on end, or indeed all through the night.

*Thursday, 17th December, 1801.* We heard waterfowl calling out by the lake side. Jupiter was very glorious above the Ambleside hills, and one large star hung over the coombe of the hills on the opposite side of Rydale water.

*Friday, 29th January, 1802.* Many stars were out, the clouds were moveless, in the sky soft purple, the lake of Rydale calm, Jupiter behind. Jupiter at least *we* call him, but William says we always call the largest star Jupiter.

> Dorothy Wordsworth, in her *Journal* (– and a warning to be sure of your planet – though Jupiter it must have been).

It is possible to see four of Jupiter's twelve moons with good field-glasses (see page 149), when they are in the right position.

Jupiter, or Jove, with whom this largest of the planets is identified, was the chief god of the Romans, and the Zeus of the Greeks – both of them the great gods of the sky. Jupiter's day is Thursday (the French *jeudi*, from *Jovis dies*, the day of Jove, but for us the day of the great sky-god Thor or Donar).

This planet, shining over Mesopotamia, was the great god Marduk.

## Mars

The red planet – so the planet of bloodshed, of the war god Mars of the Romans, Ares of the Greeks – one of the sons of Jupiter or Zeus, and the husband, by contrast – or the lover – of the planetary goddess of love, Venus, or Aphrodite. His day is *mardi* of the French (Mars and *dies*), our Tuesday, after the war-god of the Anglo Saxons, Tiw. These two – the red with the white, the fiery with the gentle – need to be seen in conjunction.

The red of Mars gives him away immediately. When he comes close to Earth, his neighbour in orbit around the Sun, nothing in the sky mixes such redness and such vividness. At such times, for instance, Mars is very much brighter than the red star Antares (the 'rival of Ares') in Scorpio, which – see page 132 – is the red eye of the Scorpion. He walks through the zodiac, sometimes an evening or morning star, sometimes high above the horizon, always unmistakable.

## Venus

The Evening Star and the Morning Star or Day Star. This was the star and goddess of love, Ishtar of the Mesopotamian cities, Aphrodite of the Greeks, and Venus of the Romans.

Aphrodite, lover of Ares (Mars), daughter of Ouranos (Uranus), was born in a peculiar way. Kronos (Saturn) castrated Ouranos, the sky god, whose members fell into the sea, engendering Aphrodite out of the foam. As the most lovely of the goddesses, she deserved to be imaged in this Star of Love, the most vivid of all the heavenly bodies after the Moon and the Sun.

For the Incas of Peru, Venus was Chasca, or the Long-haired Star (since we see it with rays), the star and god who created flowers.

Venus is covered perpetually with clouds, which reflect the Sun's light, and make the shining of Venus so strong, so dominant, in the green or pink emptiness above the horizon before sunrise, or the blue emptiness of the western sky after sunset.

*July 10, 1867.* At sunrise it was fog. Morning star and peach-coloured dawn.

Gerard Manley Hopkins

Either morning or evening Venus is even less mistakable than Mars; but weeks may go by during which she appears only in the morning, or does not appear at all. Then suddenly like a surprise we see her back again over the trees, over the darkening world, as the light of day seeps in colours out of the sky.

We still feel that she is the Star of Love, and certainly she gives the sky a wonderful blend of serenity and excitement, or excited suspense. In the morning, it is worth getting out of a warm bed to see her – especially in conjunction; and in her time the sight of Venus has drawn many people from warm beds upon a different account, since like the nightingale in *Romeo and Juliet*, she warned lovers before daylight that they must separate.

A poet's star – or planet – above all others. Coleridge among English poets felt the gleam of Venus all through his life, as joy and love. Unhappy as a schoolboy, he sat and watched it out on the leads at Christ's Hospital, he wrote (like William Blake) one of his first poems to the Evening Star, and said that he never saw the Evening Star setting behind the mountains without feeling that a hope had gone out of his soul, 'as if a love were gone, and a sad memory only remained'. He was a special student of conjunctions:

*Monday evening, July 9, 1804, about 8 o'clock.* The glorious evening star coasted the moon, and at length absolutely crested its upper tip . . . It was the most singular and at the same time beautiful sight

I ever beheld. Oh, that it could have appeared the same in England, at Grasmere!

(Coleridge saw this conjunction of Venus and the horned moon from Malta.)

Samuel Palmer painted and drew magic-seeming conjunctions of Venus and the crescent moon, which he felt to be on the moonlit borders of Heaven.

Another conjunction:

*Feb. 25, 1868, Shrove Tuesday.* Fine and very warm; at night the new moon almost on her back and Venus, very bright, a little to the left above – the old moon very visible.

*Feb. 26.* This evening they were as opposite, both very bright and the dark part of the moon remarkably clear and milky. – Fine and warm, with wind.

Gerard Manley Hopkins

When very bright, Venus (like Sirius. but even more so) will cast a shadow on the ground.

## Mercury

Finding Mercury is a business of exact timing: he is so close to the Sun. The almanac will say whether Mercury is visible, and if so, whether as an evening or a morning star. Low in the east or west or south-west, before sunrise or after sunset, he will not be visible for long, swallowed up very quickly in light or in darkness. In the evening, he will not be seen until the afterglow has faded sufficiently. Nimble, quick, elusive, this is the planet of the Roman god Mercury, the Greek god Hermes; the Messenger of the Gods, in either case, who was born in the twilight and was associated very closely with Venus or Aphrodite, the goddess of love, goddess of the nearest planet to himself. His day is the *Mercurii dies*, the French *mercredi*, our Wednesday, or day of the god Woden.

The patron of authors, small and seldom seen.

# The Sun and the Moon

Ruddy at first, yet ere a minute's told
Its burning red keeps glowing into gold,
And o'er the fenny level richly flows,

155

Till seeded dock in shade a giant grows.
John Clare

The honey-pale moon lay low on the sleepy hill. . . .
W. B. Yeats

# THE SUN

Quite natural that all over the world, the Sun should have been a god. He gives heat and light, is responsible for the visible beauty of the world; and is so strong – eleven thousand million times brighter in appearance on Earth than Sirius – that he cannot be looked in the eye, by a mortal.

Some of the gods who were the Sun, or had solar characteristics:

Egyptian: Ra, the creator; and Horus, the falcon-god and son of Isis.
Mesopotamian: Shamash, the god of justice.

My friend, who was ever so exalted
That he could climb to heaven
And everlastingly dwell with Shamash?
*The Epic of Gilgamesh*

Persian, Eastern Mediterranean and Roman: Mithra.
Greek: Helios; and Apollo, god, among much else, of poetry and the arts.
Japanese: the great goddess Amaterasu.
Aztec: Tezcatlipoca.
Peruvian: Inti, the chief of the gods.

The giant sunflowers we grow, flowers which are heliotropic, i.e. which follow the sun round during the day, each a golden disc with golden rays, were first celebrated by the Incas as the flowers of Inti, their sun-god. Peruvian priests wore a sunflower of real gold on their chests. (The heliotropic 'sun-flower' of Europe is the dandelion.) Christians have made the Sun a symbol of Christ, partly because it is the great luminary, and partly because the Sun had been identified with Mithra, the Unconquered Sun, in the religion which was rival to Christianity. Mithra, the Unconquered Sun, was now conquered by the Sun of Righteousness.

156

*Eclipses*

Eclipses of the Sun and Moon (of which the almanac gives a fair warning) were shroudings of the bright face of a god. The Greek idea in the word eclipse was that the Sun had abandoned his seat in the sky. Eclipses, when the day darkens to a strange twilight or the Moon changes from brightness to a sultry copper in Earth's shadow, were periods of evil and misfortune. John Milton, most astronomical of poets, knew why and how eclipses happened, but he felt and expressed that old notion that eclipses were times in which evil had licence. So he wrote that the ship in which his friend Edward King was drowned in a calm crossing of the Irish Sea, must have been built in an eclipse:

> It was that fatal and perfidious bark
> Built in th'eclipse, and rigged with curses dark
> That sunk so low that sacred head of thine

And Satan, new-arrived in hell, looked like the Sun among clouds or the Sun in total eclipse, an archangel ruined, but yet with some original brightness –

> As when the Sun new ris'n
> Looks through the horizontal misty air
> Shorn of his beams, or from behind the Moon
> In dim eclipse disastrous twilight sheds
> On half the nations, and with fear of change
> Perplexes monarchs. Dark'n'd so, yet shone
> Above them all th'Archangel.

The twilight of eclipse still seems disastrous – or at any rate disturbing, a disturbance of normal life.

We should not miss an eclipse, partial or total, since they cannot be seen so often in a lifetime. In England total eclipses of the Moon will next be visible in 1964 (25 June, 19 December); but we shall not see a total eclipse of the Sun until 11 August, 1999. (If you wish to test someone's general knowledge – or particular knowledge – ask him the meaning of a Saros. It is the term we borrowed from the Greeks and the Greeks borrowed from the Babylonians, for the period – about eighteen years and eighteen days – of the recurrence of similar eclipses.)

*The Rising Sun*

Churches are commonly orientated – built on an east-west line, with the altar and the sanctuary (and often the chief window) at the eastern end, facing the sunrise; Christians are commonly buried with their feet to the east. It is quite true that when Stonehenge was refashioned about 1650–1500 B.C., with a double circle of stones in the centre, the axis of the circle was aligned east and west, towards the Sun as it rose on 22 June, the longest day of the year.

But neither this nor the roundness of Stonehenge is any proof that it was a sun-temple, in the shape of the wheel of the Sun. It may have been; and the feeling that it was such a temple, which brings crowds to Stonehenge for the Solstice, is not really so ridiculous as archaeologists declare. Any delusion which gets people up for sunrise has its merits. Archaeologists point out that those who rebuilt Stonehenge may have required a way of determining a fixed point every year, from which they could calculate their calendar. But that would also have been a religious ceremony. If Stonehenge was used in that way, it would have been more than a prosaic solar compass.

## The Setting Sun

When the Sun goes down, colours spread both in the western sky above his descent and above the place of his disappearance, and opposite in the eastern sky. Can you describe the order in which the colours come and go, westward and eastward (they will be complicated, of course, by clouds)? Few of us could do so offhand, though it would not have been so difficult for Gerard Manley Hopkins, so often quoted in this book, who was among the most exact and passionate observers among all the poets, repeatedly describing and analysing sunsets in his journals. In the west, the sky first turns yellow, then green appears above the yellow as the Sun vanishes. After the orb has set, the colours above the horizon will be brown, orange above that, then yellow – at first. Later an arch, a rose of rose-pink, forms and spreads in the sky above the yellow and the orange or orange-red, the brown having disappeared. Later still violet, or purple or plum-purple (that is Hopkins' description) extends above the rose-pink; the yellow and the orange-red remain below. Hopkins described this stage, when the brilliant rose – 'the rosy field of sundown' – opens in the west and deepens to crimson, in the poem he called *A Vision of the Mermaids*. Under the plum-purple

> – the west had grown
> To an orb'd rose, which, by hot pantings blown
> Apart, betwixt ten thousand petall'd lips
> By interchange gasp'd splendour and eclipse.
> The zenith melted to a rose of air;

> The waves were rosy-lipp'd; the crimson glare
> Shower'd the cliffs and every fret and spire
> With garnet wreaths and blooms of rosy-budded fire.

The violet, the purple, becomes wonderfully strong at the expense of the rose, and spreads a clear twilight glow on everything. Then the sky begins to fade – to orange, then yellow, then green or greenish-blue – and the great colour show concludes.

Opposite the sun, in the east, the order of colours appearing above red will be orange, yellow, green, blue; changing, after the Sun has dipped and gone, to violet, surmounted by crimson, orange, yellow, green, and blue. Gradually these colours are lost in the rising shadow of the Earth.

## The Northern Lights, or the Merry Dancers

In the night sky, the Sun has two particular children (or three, if you count the reflected light of the moon). These two are the Northern Lights and the Zodiacal Shine.

> The Upper air burst into life!
> And a hundred fire-flags sheen,
> To and fro they hurried about!
> And to and fro, and in and out,
> The wan stars danced between.

I think Coleridge, a southerner, had never seen the Northern Lights, when he described them in those lines in the *Ancient Mariner*. A southerner needs luck to see them: there may be four or five displays visible in the year, but the southerner will always be indoors, at the theatre, or somewhere else. A lifetime may go by before he catches a glimpse of the Northern Lights. The remedy is to spend a year on the cliffs of Caithness.

The Sun emits electrified particles. The particles cause the gases in the upper atmosphere to glow, in the manner of a gas-filled neon lamp. Displays, though, greatly vary in pattern, grandeur, brilliance, and colour. The usual colour is white, or yellowish white. We are most likely to see patches of light, or diffusions of light, or arcs above the horizon, bisecting the sky, with rays towards the zenith. The rays *can* be red, or red and green, and these rays or streamers may seem to move and alter length. The sky below the arch will seem darker. Towards the Arctic, displays may exaggerate themselves into supreme

159

splendour, into crowns surrounded with rays, into sinuous curtains like a scroll, into great swaying hanging curtains shaped rather like a curtain of stalactite in a cave – stalactite curtains in the northern cave of night.

The poet George Crabbe, who suffered dreams under the influence of opium, like Coleridge and De Quincey, dreamt himself under the power of demons, who placed him actually in the Northern Lights:

> They placed me where those streamers play,
> Those nimble beams of brilliant light;
> It would the stoutest heart dismay,
> To see, to feel, that dreadful sight
> So swift, so pure, so cold, so bright,
> They pierced my frame with icy wound,
> And, all that half-year's polar night,
> Those dancing streamers wrapped me round.

Coleridge imagined his description of the Northern Lights from books. Crabbe probably saw them from his home on the Suffolk coast, Gerard Manley Hopkins saw them, and described them, several times. In Lancashire, in 1870, when (compare Coleridge, above) he saw stars *through* the Lights:

*Sept. 24* – First saw the Northern Lights. My eye was caught by beams of light and dark very like the crown of horny rays the sun makes behind a cloud. At first I thought of silvery cloud until I saw that these were more luminous and did not dim the clearness of the stars in the Bear. They rose slightly radiating thrown out from the earthline. Then I saw soft pulses of light one after another rise and pass upwards arched in shape but waveringly and with the arch broken. They seemed to float, not following the warp of the sphere as falling stars do but free though concentrical with it.

The lights appealed to him as a 'busy working of nature wholly independent of the earth and seeming to go on in a strain of time not reckoned by our reckoning of days and years'. Hopkins observed a more wonderful Aurora a month later, also from Lancashire, a little before seven in the evening (late evening is the usual time):

It gathered a little below the zenith, to the S.E. I think – a knot or crown, not a true circle, of dull blood-coloured horns and dropped long red beams down the sky on every side, each impaling its lot of

17 Badger and cubs, and Nightjar catching moth

18  (*left*) On the hunt: Stoat, and Sparrow-hawk picking up Yellow-hammer
19  Grey Squirrel

20  (*above*) Common Toad, eating a beetle
21  Buzzard, Roe Deer, and (right) a Red Deer doe

22   (*left*) Adder and young, in the Highlands (with Wild Cat, Short-eared Owl, and caterpillar of Emperor Moth)

23   Skulls and Antlers

24    Various snails

25  Various beetles

26 Butterflies, common and rare

27   Bees and wasps

28 (*above*) Sea Anemones
29 Blue-grey form of Opelet Anemone, with part of colony of
Plumose Anemone

30    Spring flowers, including Fritillaries and Pasque Flowers

31  More spring flowers

stars. An hour or so later its colour was gone, but there was still a pale crown in the same place.

He saw the Lights from Edinburgh in 1871 – 'beautiful but colourless, near the horizon in permanent birchbark downward streaks but shooting in streamers across the zenith and higher sky, like breath misting and then being cut off from very sensitive glass.'

Aurora Borealis – i.e. Northern Dawn – is a romantic-sounding scientific name for the Northern Lights, which was invented by one of the great astronomers of the seventeenth century. But the Northern Lights are not a dawn.

## *Zodiacal Shine*

Perhaps on some evening when you have been looking for Mercury as an evening star, or admiring Venus in the sky after sunset, you may see the Zodiacal Shine – after twilight and Venus have finally disappeared, and when there is no moon.

The Shine at any rate will be there. It is not a matter of chance like a display of the Northern Lights, and the only trouble is to detect it and recognize it; and to know where to look, and when it will be most apparent. As for the whereabouts, remember the zodiac, and the ecliptic (page 150) – because this Zodiacal Shine (which is nothing so spectacular as the Northern Lights) lies, or climbs, across the sky along the constellations of the zodiac, and keeps position with them more or less. The best time to look for its tall pearly light is in January, February and March, when the angle of the zodiac to the sky is fairly steep, on the darkest of nights. The next most favourable time to see it, if you care to get up that early, is in the early mornings, in the east, in September, October and November, sloping the other way, from east to south.

A fairly wide blunt-ended cone or triangle of light shows from the western horizon towards the Pleiades (the position in February), sloping below Andromeda and Pegasus; along its southern limit this cone of light is well defined, but along the north its light is dimmer, and less milky or pearly, and its boundaries are not so definite.

The Sun is responsible for the Zodiacal Shine, as it is for the Northern Lights. Only in this case the Shine is mainly due to a zone of cosmic dust which surrounds the Sun, and scatters or reflects the sunlight. The Zodiacal Shine glows also above the horizon in the east, from September to November, towards dawn – again along the zodiac.

32   Flowers of early summer, including Water Avens

# THE MOON

If the Sun is gold, and the master of the day, obviously the Moon is silver, and mistress of the night. As a goddess the Moon was often looked upon as the sister of the Sun.

Moon goddesses – or gods (since she is not always feminine) – include:

Egyptian: Thoth, the Moon-god with the head of an ibis. Khons, god of the crescent moon, of healing, and of casting out demons.

Mesopotamian: Sîn, the Moon-god, father of Shamash the Sun-god and of Ishtar the Evening Star and goddess of love; the god of Mt Sinai.

Greek: Phoebe, the Pure One. Selene, sister of Helios and Eos (the Dawn) and mother (by Zeus) of the Dew. Artemis, the virgin Huntress (Diana). Hecate, the goddess of the Underworld.

Peruvian: Mama Quilla, whose brother and husband is Inti, the Sun-god.

Indian: Varuna.

Chinese: Ch'ang-o.

Japanese: Tsuki-Yomi.

The idea of the Moon as 'queen and huntress, chaste and fair' is still strong. When the Russian *lunik* made its impact on the surface of the Moon in 1959, many of the comments in the newspapers suggested that the Russians had interfered with the Moon's aloof and ancient chastity.

The light of the Sun can burn. The light reflected by the Moon, quite harmless in fact, was imagined to be powerful and dangerous, since it was no less the light of a goddess or a god. In our language the Moon was originally masculine, the Sun feminine. It was dangerous to sleep in the moonlight; and a lunatic was one who suffered from a recurrent madness due to the changes or phases of the Moon. The Moon might be chaste, but she was not altogether innocent. As well as Artemis she was Hecate, Moon-goddess of the Underworld, of wizards, witches, ghosts, and spells.

## *The Moon in Her Phases*

A crescent moon is the Moon in the first stages of waxing or increasing (*luna crescens*), and not a waning moon; though from the crescent moon 'crescent' comes to mean the shape. When the Moon is waxing, the cusps, or horns, as you face her are to the left; when she is waning, the horns are to your right. The New Moon sets in the evening. So we see more of the new waxing Moon – most of us – than of the Old Moon as she wanes, when she rises later and later, each night.

Earth-shine or Earth-light is the faint lighting-up of the dark part of the moon's surface by light reflected from Earth – 'the Old Moon in the New Moon's arms' – as the moon is waxing.

Dorothy Wordsworth, in her *Journal*, March 1802:

> On Friday evening the moon hung over the northern side of the highest point of Silver How, like a gold ring snapped in two, and shaven off at the ends. Within this ring lay the circle of the round moon, as distinctly to be seen as even the enlightened moon is.

Coleridge in his poem *Dejection*:

> For lo! the New Moon, winter bright!
> And overspread with phantom light
> (With swimming phantom light o'erspread,
> But rimmed and circled with a silver thread)
> I see the Old Moon in her lap foretelling
> The coming on of rain and squally blast.

The silver stitching or rimming around the 'Old Moon' from the cusps of the New is an exquisite thing to see.

So is a conjunction of the New Moon with Venus or Jupiter (page 149), when the moonlight has not yet become strong enough to dim or to put out the lesser luminaries of the sky in her neighbourhood – an effect which Sappho described:

> The stars round the fair Moon
> Hide their glittering look from us
> When all-but full she silvers all the Earth.

Actually the brightest full moons are those in winter; and the full moon is some 383,306 times less bright than the Sun.

## Four Moons at the Full

In spring Easter is a full moon festival, celebrated on the first Sunday after the full moon which follows the vernal equinox – which is that time in the spring when the Sun crosses the celestial equator (page 132) at the point where the equator and the ecliptic (page 150) intersect.

The Harvest Moon is that splendid full moon of the autumn which hangs over newly reaped cornfields or harvesters still at work – as in the harvest paintings of Samuel Palmer – nearest the autumnal equi-nox (which is that second time in the year when the Sun crosses the equator at its intersection with the ecliptic). The orbit of the Moon is then almost parallel with the horizon, and every evening while the Harvest Moon lasts, it rises later by only a few minutes, instead of the usual fifty and a half minutes. Daylight merges into full moonlight, and the Moon hangs between the night and the day low above the horizon, enormous, as it appears, and yellow, or orange (since the violet and blue rays have been scattered from view by the dense atmosphere between ourselves and the Sun).

The Hunter's Moon is the next full moon after the Harvest Moon of September, about as splendid and as large. Curiously neither 'Harvest Moon' nor 'Hunter's Moon' are very old terms. They do not seem to have been used much before the eighteenth century.

The Honeymoon, the full moon rising large, and as sweet and yellow as honey, is ironically and metaphorically, in its original meaning, the full moon of love at the time of marriage (full moon was the phase propitious for a wedding), which wanes in the following weeks as the Moon wanes. So without the irony, the Honeymoon becomes the first month of marriage, and less exactly, the holiday beginning of married love.

## *The Moonglade*

One of the most beautiful of all lunar effects on earth is the track of reflected moonlight across a lake or the sea – the track in line between the Moon and the spectator. A word for this is Moonglade – which seems to have been invented by the American poet, James Russell Lowell, in the eighteen-sixties.

# Shooting Stars and Comets

## SHOOTING STARS

Comets have been held unlucky – at any rate to kings and princes. Meteors, falling stars or shooting stars, streaking across the sky and burning out in a very few seconds, were too transient and frequent to be threatening in that way, as a rule. The idea that shooting stars fore-tell wind out of the quarter they shoot from goes back more than two thousand two hundred years, to the writings of the Greek astronomical and weather poet, Aratos. Some people (in Ireland, for example) believe that meteors are souls on their way from dead bodies to hell; which probably has developed from the Roman belief that there was a star in heaven for each individual, and that when he dies, his star falls and disappears for ever. Many people wish when they see a shooting star; but all of the wish should be formulated before the star vanishes.

These oddments of the solar system – or some of them – seem to be the result of the dispersal of the heads of comets, as if the heads were meteors in loose association. Different meteor-streams have each their orbit around the Sun – orbits which may be intersected by Earth's orbit. When Earth encounters the stream, at this point of intersection, our gravitational pull captures some of the meteors, and the falling captives then write their lines of light across our atmosphere, tiny scraps of ore or rock burning out between seventy and thirty miles overhead.

So shooting stars may be thought of as a blend of regular and irregular, of the calculable and incalculable. It is rather like partridge shooting. The season comes round once a year, but each year the number of partridges in the shops may vary. Earth, according to time-table, crosses the orbit of a stream of meteors, but some times more and some times fewer meteors are captured, and then observed as shooting stars. A new stream may be encountered, an old stream may disappear.

Even so there is a measure of statistical regularity. Some streams produce, as a rule, so many shooting stars that an observer may count on seeing up to fifty or sixty an hour, during the phase of intensity. Other streams produce only a few. From some streams the shooting stars are bright and white, from others they are not so bright. From some they are very quick, from others relatively slow.

The showers have been named after the constellations *against* which they originate, i.e. the constellations really situated far away in the stellar background. The two heaviest showers are, in winter, the Geminids, from an area of sky with the constellation of Gemini or the Twins (page 139) in the background, and in summer, the Perseids, from an area with the constellation of Perseus (page 143) in the background.

The Perseids are quick in their fall, but rather faint. They occur between 1 August and 20 August, and fall most frequently, when one may see fifty to sixty an hour, about 12 August. 10 August is the Festival of St Lawrence, the martyr who was grilled to death at Rome on a gridiron. So these Perseids (which have been recognized for centuries) are called the Tears of St Lawrence.

The Geminids, of which one may also observe fifty to sixty an hour at their maximum around 12 and 13 December (they fall from 9 December – 14 December), are brighter and more rapid.

The Taurids, falling from the direction of Taurus or the Bull (page 140), and not far from the direction of Aldebaran, the Bull's Eye, occur from 26 October to 16 November, five or six an hour at their maximum about 7 November. By contrast they fall slowly.

The Lyrids, from the direction of Lyra or the Lyre (page 130), falling between 20 April and 22 April, about ten per hour at their maximum on 21 April, are another swarm known for centuries. Quick and white and making a long tail or streak across the sky, these Lyrids answer very well to the shooting stars which Virgil also mentioned in the *Georgics*, which he wrote about 40 B.C., as a prognostic of wind:

> Often again, a threat of winds, you see
> Stars quickly slide across the sky,
> Trailing at length upon the black of night
> White tails of fire.

# COMETS

A comet is something 'long-haired' (*kometes* in Greek) – a long-haired star. Halley's Comet, the most famous of the long-haired stars, one which Shakespeare must have seen in 1607 and which also appeared in 1066 before the Battle of Hastings, and was embroidered, star and tail and all, on the Bayeux Tapestry in which his courtiers give warning of the portent to King Harold, is due back again, on its orbit round the sun, in 1986.

Shakespeare began *Henry VI* with a Dead March and the lines:

> Hung be the heavens with black, yield day to night!
> Comets, importing change of times and states,
> Brandish your crystal tresses in the sky.

That comets disturbed mankind (and still do, though without cause) is not at all surprising. Everyone who saw the Comet Arend-Roland hanging in the northern sky in April 1957 or the Comet Mrkos in August in the same year, will realize how astonishing it is that a great luminous object should all of a sudden intrude in a familiar region of the sky, a bit like a white bull in a flower-garden.

The stars in earlier centuries seemed orderly and intelligent because they kept their positions relatively and appeared to wheel in regular, immutable procession around the sky. The planets and the Sun and the Moon were also calculable bodies, moving along the path of the zodiac. But a comet appeared from nowhere, shone or glared for some weeks, scorning a regular path in the zodiac, a regular return (so it appeared).

*July 13, 1874.* The comet – I have seen it at bedtime in the west, with head to the ground, white, a soft well-shaped tail, not big: I felt a certain awe and instress, a feeling of strangeness, flight (it hangs like a shuttlecock at the height, before it falls), and of threatening.
Gerard Manley Hopkins, on one of the notable comets of the nineteenth century.

The long gaseous hair, actually so thin that it does not hide a star, is harmless to Earth, if Earth has to pass through a comet's tail. Actually the long hair of a comet is pushed out of the head or nucleus by the pressure of the Sun's radiation – so that a comet is not always followed by its tail. When it is travelling away from the Sun, the tail precedes it, like the smoke of a ship travelling with the wind.

# The Look of Clouds

The shapes and formations of the clouds, each due to particular circumstances, were first analysed, classified, and given a set of names (since much elaborated) by the Quaker scientist Luke Howard, F.R.S., in 1803. This excited poets and painters, including John Constable, who looked at clouds all the more intensely, sketching them with a more thrilling effect.

Cloudage ranges from fog on the ground to delicate wisps six miles above us, and meteorologists nowadays have grouped the cloud population into families, High, Middle, Low, and Heap Clouds, into the two broad divisions of the Heap Clouds (which can be simultaneously low based and high topped) and the Sheet Clouds.

## High Clouds

Looking up from the ground you can see past low clouds and clouds of middle height, to the High Clouds, the sheets of which may be broken, divided, patterned. Constable painted low rain clouds, ragged and uneasy and dark in the sky, but he also liked the five- or six-mile high *cirrus* clouds (*cirrus* is the Latin for a lock or tuft of hair) – clouds of ice crystals, in which you can see no shadow, which curl or appear crispy, in threads, or fibres (Luke Howard's word); sometimes turning up at the ends like thin brushes, or fraying and making detached tufts ('Mare's Tails'), or folded feather plumes, all as if they had been drawn or painted in the sky in quick strokes, white pigment on blue.

'Mackerel Skies', in which the clouds are rather like fish scales, in waves or ripples, may belong to this High family of ice crystal clouds as *cirrocumulus*, a blend of cloudlets and cirrus wisps or threads or fibres, making a variety of mottled, speckled, scaly, wavy, rippled, banded skies or patches, aerial fleeces, aerial flocks of sheep – cloudage which turns a lofty pink at sunset.

The ice crystals of another form of cirrus, *cirrostratus*, high sheets or layers of cloud like a translucent skin, cause the halos or rings of light some distance out from sun and moon (at an angle or radius of 22 degrees). Long shapes of cirrostratus are called 'fishes', 'salmon', or 'Noah's Arks'.

## Middle Clouds

Samuel Palmer, painting in the eighteen-twenties, much liked small *altocumulus* clouds of the Middle family (between 6,500 and 20,000 feet), layers of rounded little water-drop clouds, which make a dappled or sheep-flock sky pattern: he liked to draw the full moon rising towards such clouds and lighting each one up from below, while the night sky shows between the chinks – one of the most wonderful of the phenomena of night. Some mackerel skies are really altocumulus, though the altocumulus cloudlets often look fatter and coarser, and more like herded sheep. Palmer's drawings reveal the shadowing which distinguishes altocumulus from the much loftier cirrocumulus. *Altostratus* clouds spread a gloomy, watery, streaky veil across the sky, which blurs the sun or moon, and never causes a halo in the manner of the icy cirrostratus.

## Low Clouds

Descending again, the family of Low clouds (from ground level up to about 6,500 feet) includes not only the long low bars of *stratus* (which catch sunset colours so vividly and then go dark), but *stratocumulus*, moving whitish grey and soft across the sky in low rolls of cotton wool, and various forms of ragged or shapeless and blowsy murky raincloud or *nimbus*. Constable often sketched the raincloud from which rain appears to hang down, the trailing rain meteorologists call *virga* (Latin for rod, or twig), which does not reach the ground.

## Heap Clouds

are the up-building, piling clouds (*cumulus*, Latin for heap or pile), formed by the rising of warm air bubbles which expand, cool, and condense their moisture into cloud.

*Cumulus* clouds, 'woolbags', 'cauliflowers', sail in white bulk in the blue summer sky. Above, they are rounded; underneath, they are flat or horizontal, as if sliced off with a sky-knife. They build up in the morning, then dissolve in the evening, after a serene life. They may be relatively small and serried, they may build and bulge and tower into gleaming rounded Himalayas of the sky. They may drop a shower.

But they may develop as well into rain-cumulus, *nimbocumulus* (*nimbus*, Latin originally for violent rain, then for a thunder-cloud), promising either heavy showers or thunder, lightning and downpour. Goethe wrote several cloud poems in excitement at the writings of Luke Howard, including one about the development of cumulus and thunder-cloud:

> And if the fit substance should be summoned
> Straight to the higher air
> High stands the cloud, piled up most splendidly
> In firm-built blazon of its might and strength;
> And, as you fear and well may live to see,
> The threat above makes tremors down below.

The signs distinguishing thunder-cloud from cumulus are (i) a blurred base, often with that 'virga' again, instead of the neat horizontal base of the cumulus, (ii) the dome in the sky losing its form and roundness, and fraying out into a form of cirrus – sometimes making a great ominous anvil shape of cirrus ice-crystals in the sky, as if thunderbolts were to be hammered out.

It pleased Goethe very much that the top of thunder-clouds should blow off into cirrus in this way:

> A heavenly light compulsion brings release,
> A pile unravels into flakes
> Tripping like tiny lambs, combed
> Lightly into clusters.
> So at last what lightly comes to being
> Down below, above flows
> Into the Father's lap and hand.

The solid gleaming summer domes of cumulus appealed also to

Samuel Palmer; he drew and painted such clouds with bars of stratus, as one sees them so often, floating horizontally across their flanks.

Remember the formula for estimating how far you are from a thunderstorm. Every five seconds of the time between flash and thunder indicates about one mile of distance.

## Vapour Trails

We have a modern cloud unknown to the cloud-classifiers, cloud-painters, cloud-poets, cloud-admirers of the past – the vapour trails or condensation trails of the high flying aeroplane, caused by the cooling of exhaust vapours by contact with cold air, which condenses the moisture they contain (Plate 7). Like other High clouds they catch the rosy light of sunset in a blue sky; and they may still be seen gleaming in the darker night sky, perhaps framing a full moon, beautiful things which were first painted by Paul Nash (who had a passion for seeing or imagining cloud flowers blossoming in the sky).

(C. J. P. Cave's *Clouds and Weather Phenomena* is the happiest brief handbook to clouds – and also sunsets, rays, halos, coronae, which are explained in more detail in M. Minnaert's *Light and Colour in the Open Air*. Many sky queries will be answered by reading *The Meteorological Glossary* published by the Stationery Office.)

# PART THREE

*Birds, Beasts, Insects
and Others*

# About Birds

For, lo, the winter is past,
The rain is over and gone;
The flowers appear on the earth;
The time of the singing of birds is come,
And the voice of the turtle is heard in our land.

Song of Solomon

## BRILLIANT BIRDS

There are some birds which everybody knows – Robin, Swan, Thrush, Rook, Blackbird; but there are others, not quite such every morning or every afternoon creatures, which suddenly flash themselves into notice by peculiar voice, peculiar flight, or a brilliant peculiarity of feathers. Some of these are the birds of poetry and legend. They excite our curiosity when we encounter them, so they are also birds to recognize. On the whole our birds in these islands are sombre. If you see one of the exceptions, with a startling touch of the Bird of Paradise, then according to when and where you see it, it is likely to be one of the following, arranged according to the colour which first strikes your eye.

### *First of all, if the Striking Colour is Blue*
### The Kingfisher

On streams, winter and summer, flashing by in determined flight; or you may surprise a Kingfisher, perched, intent and sharp-beaked, on a branch or a projecting root overhanging the stream. No bird in the British Isles is more tropical-seeming; blue-green above, chestnut below. A flash of blue – or sapphire, more exactly – is the impression a Kingfisher gives in flight. That is how Andrew Marvell saw the

Kingfisher three centuries ago, flying between night and day on streams near York:

> The viscous air, wheres'ere she fly,
> Follows and sucks her azure dye;
> The jellying stream compacts below,
> If it might fix her shadow so;
> The stupid fishes hang, as plain
> As flies in crystal overta'en;
> And men the silent scene assist,
> Charm'd with the sapphire-wingèd mist.

A keen wedge of a bird, short tail, longish bill, smaller than a thrush.

## The Jay

In woods, or near them. All times of the year. A Jay is often frightened up from the tangle at the edge of a wood, quickly disappearing into cover with a broken, sore-throated laugh or scream. As it vanishes, you notice the blue and black stripes or bars on each wing. The general impression is of a fairly large pinkish or greyish-pink bird, which may also give you time to notice the rather wide ruffled crest of black and white, and a white blob on the wings, and a white rump above a black tail. Gamekeepers and shooters inherit an ancient medieval dislike of 'the scorning jay', so they shoot jays, hang them on fences, and wear the blue-barred wing-feathers in their hats or buttonholes.

## *If the Striking Colour is Scarlet*
## Greater Spotted Woodpecker

Not so large as the Green Woodpecker (which also has scarlet, but is dealt with under Green Birds, below). The Greater Spotted Woodpecker is a black and white bird of the tree trunks with scarlet touches. Both the cock and the hen have scarlet behind the tail, but the cockbird is the one more brilliantly dressed, with scarlet as well at the back of his black and white head. The young are also scarlet-headed; and it is a fine, refreshing, unexpected sight to see a family party in the summer exploring a tree.

## Lesser Spotted Woodpecker

Smaller, sparrow-size; and also black and white, but in bars, and only the cock has a scarlet-topped head. The woodpeckers which drum so rapidly and noisily are these two, Lesser Spotted Woodpecker and Greater Spotted Woodpecker – not the Green Woodpecker. This drumming by the Spotted Woodpeckers made them into sacred birds in Italy; their drumming was prophetic, and could be interpreted. In fact Picus, the Woodpecker, had been changed from human shape into bird by the witch Circe, who loved him, but was not loved by him in return.

(There is scarlet also on the Goldfinch – but that comes under the birds whose striking colour is Gold, page 178.)

## *If the Striking Colour is Chestnut, a Quieter Red, or Pink*
## Redstart, or Firetail

The small bird, nearly robin-sized, with a red 'steort' (Anglo-Saxon) or tail. But red does not do: it is a fire tail, a tail – and a rump – of fire, of a surprising chestnut, which flashes and flickers magnificently. The cock has this splendid tail, a black throat, a line of white above his eyes, a slate-blue back and crown, and a chestnut breast. But redstarts are not to be seen everywhere. They are migrants, arriving in April and off again in September. They like old trees, walls, rocks, neglected orchards, pollard willows – the willowy fringes of the Cherwell above Oxford, for example, or country of rock and sycamore in Monmouthshire and along the Welsh Marches. (Plate 1.)

## The Bullfinch

Along hedges, in gardens, among fruit trees pecking the buds to bits. A bird, with a thick, bullish, seed-splitting beak, as brilliant and surprising (the cock-bird) as the Redstart. The effect is a flaming rose, set off by blue-grey and black and white. The cock has a black head,

superb rosy cheeks, and rosy front, blue-grey back, black tail, black wings. In autumn and winter bullfinches forage in parties through the bare hedges.

## The Hoopoe (*If you are lucky*)

You *might* see a Hoopoe on a lawn or in a meadow, where there are trees about; or you might hear one saying to itself gently – with infinite gentleness, and persistently – from an invisible perch inside the leaves, *poo, poo-poo*. If you do, it will be in the south, in May and early summer. No bird is more distinctive. Predominantly the Hoopoe is pink. It raises and lowers a pink crest edged with black, and its wings and tail are barred with black and white. Read the nightingale story, on page 199.

## The Crossbill

The Crossbill's beak *crosses*, like secateurs; and this queer bird uses its secateurs on conifer seeds. Behaving like a miniature parrot of the pine-woods, the Crossbill does nest in Britain, does flit around pine-woods in winter; but is not common. The cock is rosy pink, though dun on his wings and tail.

## The Stonechat

Stonechats should perhaps go under Black and White. A restless, flickering, slightly less than robin-sized creature, to be seen all the year round, balancing itself on spurs of gorse. The cock-bird is chestnut-breasted. If he faces you on his brown or green or golden spur of gorse, you see the chestnut. Sideways on, you see his black head and his white cheek. A 'chat' from the noise he makes: his voice is a chatting together or clicking together of stones – as if of smooth pebbles (page 195).

## *If the Striking Colour is Green*
## The Green Woodpecker

– or Yaffle, or Rainbird; about as typical a bird, when it allows a good view of itself (which it does not do very often), as a Kingfisher. Feathers of green, yellow, black and scarlet. The impression, though, is one of green or yellow, according to angle. If this woodpecker is flying away from you, you may notice the yellow rump; but sideways it is a green bird – green on the back and the wings; on its head it flaunts black and scarlet (the female lacks the scarlet). It will fly in loops, down, up, down, up – rather heavily from the grass where it has been feeding on ants, to the trees, where it hunts insects and grubs. The

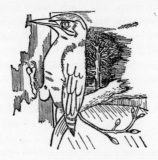

woodpeckers which drum are the Green Woodpecker's smaller relations, already described. This is the Woodpecker which laughs, or makes a mocking, far-carrying, yaffling noise, which was supposed to foretell rain.

Andrew Marvell on the Green Woodpecker:

> He walks still upright from the root,
> Meas'ring the timber with his foot;
> And all the way to keep it clean,
> Doth from the bark the wood-moths glean.
> He, with his beak, examines well
> Which fit to stand and which to fell.
>
> The good he numbers up, and hacks;
> As if he mark'd them with the axe.
> But where he, tinkling with his beak,
> Does find the hollow oak to speak,
> That for his building he designs,
> And through the tainted side he mines.

Marvell's name for the Green Woodpecker was 'Hewel', i.e. the hew hole. But since it has the bright colours of a parrot, the Green Woodpecker is also called Popinjay, as well as Hewel, Yaffle and Rainbird – 'popinjay' having come to us as a name for the parrot, by way of France, from an Arabic word *babbagha*.

## *If the Striking Colour is Gold, or Yellow*
## The Golden Oriole (*If you are lucky*)

In the southern counties, to which this excellent bird is an uncommon
visitor; and in the summer only. The cock has the purest golden-yellow
head and body, black wings, and black, partly golden-yellow-tipped
bill. Oriole is supposed to be from the Latin *aureolus*, golden. If so, it
is a pun, because 'oriole' is the sound which the Oriole makes, very
softly, liquidly, sweetly, from the deep leafage of trees in which the
Orioles hide, not often showing themselves. Or more exactly the Oriole
repeatedly murmurs its French name *loriot, loriot, loriot,* or its Provençal
name *auriou, auriou, auriou.* On holidays in France in May or June you
are likely to hear, rather than see, Golden Orioles, in, for example,
one of those small and tidy poplar plantations beside a stream. Eager
and imaginative people see a Golden Oriole in every Green Woodpecker; but there is no green to mar the aureole yellow – and the size
of the two birds is different. The Golden Oriole is not much larger
than a Thrush. The Green Woodpecker is some four inches longer.

## The Goldcrest

The smallest of English birds, plump creatures not much over three
inches long. Acrobatic and quick, fluttering and squeaking along in
hedge-row parties, and at once to be distinguished by the golden crest
– on the cock-bird – which is a real gold or orange and yellow, made
all the brighter by the black line between the gold and the olive-green
of this atomy's head, neck and body.

> Oct. 5. (1872) – A golden-crested wren had got into my room at
> night and circled round dazzled by the gaslight on the white ceil-
> ing; when caught even and put out it would come in again. Ruffling
> the crest, which is mounted over the crown and eyes like beetle-
> brows, I smoothed and fingered the little orange and yellow feathers
> which are hidden in it. Next morning many of these about the room
> and enclosed them in a letter to Cyril [his brother] on his wedding
> day.
>
> Gerard Manley Hopkins

## The Goldfinch, or Goldspink

> The king sent his lady on the sixth Yule day
> Three goldspinks, three starlings, a goose that was gray,
> Three plovers, three partridges, and a papingo-aye[1]

[1]Papingo-aye, i.e. popinjay, a parrot (see page 177).

And no wonder, because the Goldfinch is very brilliant on a close view. It has a chevron of gold set between black on each wing, conspicuous as it flies; and then the best and most expensive scarlet above and below its beak, emphasized by neighbouring areas of black and white. Italian painters of the Quattrocento liked to include goldfinches in their paintings. In life – say, as a party of goldfinches explores the white heads of a colony of thistles, or flutters through an orchard – their lyrical look is increased, to balance the gold, by a sibilant and silvery voice, a silver twitter of a song and a silver twittery call-note.

For the Grey Wagtail (which is not very grey) see page 197.

## SOME BLACK AND WHITE BIRDS (*not sea or shore birds*)

Birds, at any rate, with a black and white, or with a black or (in some special way) a white, effect. Here perhaps should be included the Stonechat, the Greater Spotted Woodpecker and the Lesser Spotted Woodpecker, which have been mentioned a few pages back.

### The Moorhen

Moorhens look black, except for a scarlet or red patch at the back of the bill (which is yellow), a white strip along each side, and white under their tails, which they cock into view. This is the big, almost domestic bird of home, village, or farm ponds, to be seen on road, lane, meadow, orchard, running back to its rushes or cover, in an obvious hurry, appearing almost to lean forward as it runs. Now and again Moorhens will come and feed with poultry. Especially delightful are the nestlings, small items of black down, seven, eight, or more in a family. (Plate 15).

A 'Moorhen', because this bird frequents not so much 'moors' in modern terminology as 'moors' or 'meres' in the older sense of marshy places with standing water, and small ponds, and rushes (among which, and of which, Moorhens make their nests as a rule).

### The Magpie

The name is a pleasant familiarity by origin – a pie (because in Latin it was *pica*, then *pie* in French) addressed as Mag, or Madge, short for Margaret – much as Beatrix Potter gave names to her birds and beasts (see page 198). Magpies are black and white in effect, though the black is really a metallic shimmer of blue and green. The very long, untidy, lopsiding black tail at once identifies this large bird of road-sides and thorn thickets, which has a black head, black and white wings, and white feathers on the sides and below. So the (Mag)pie gives us the words 'pied' and 'piebald'. Count your magpies –

> One for sorrow,
> Two for joy,
> Three for a wedding,
> Four for a boy.

Before and after the breeding season you may meet as many as seven or eight magpies in a party:

> One is sorrow,
> Two is mirth,
> Three is wedding,
> Four is birth,
> Five is silver,
> Six is gold,
> Seven is a secret
> Never to be told.

Any day, any journey, you are likely, they are now so common, to see more than one magpie before the journey is finished. I always cancel the sorrow if I see the second of the day's Margarets, not in company with the first, but an hour or even two or three hours later. There are deathlier versions – one for instance saying that Four is death, and that while Five is heaven, Six is hell, and Seven the devil himself; and there have been in custom a good many ways of countering the unlucky numbers. One is to make a cross with your thumbs, another is to lick your finger and make the sign of the cross on your shoe. Perhaps in a car it would serve to lick your finger and make the sign of the cross on the windscreen. Simpler (if a weakness in yourself): Lift your hat to the Magpie.

## The Lapwing, or Peewit or Plover

Also with a black and white effect, white below, black above and round the neck, although the black has a metallic green quality. This is the bird – protected against the gun – which flocks in the winter, stands and runs about in the fields, displaying its prettily curved crest (which will bend over in the wind), and showing a pale chestnut under its tail. Often to be seen from a car, in the roadside fields. Overhead in

flocks, lapwings fly like large snowflakes – clumsy-appearing (f)lap-
wings, though the name – *hleapwince* in Old English – comes more precisely from two words meaning to leap, and to totter, waver, or wink.
In nesting time especially, the Lapwing flaps and lunges around, and
screams or 'peewits' like an unoiled hinge. Even William Blake, who
had no great care for nature, noticed lapwings:

> O Lapwing, thou fliest around the heath,
> Nor sees the net that is spread beneath.
> Why dost thou not fly among the corn fields?
> They cannot spread nets where a harvest yields.

Gerard Manley Hopkins, an undergraduate at Oxford in 1864, was
more precise:

> Peewits wheeling and tumbling, just as they are said to do, as if with
> a broken wing. They pronounce *peewit* pretty distinctly, sometimes
> querulously, with a slight metallic tone like a bat's cry. Their wings
> are not pointed, to the eye, when flying, but broad, white and of a
> black or reddish purple apparently.

(Plover – a rain bird, a bird of wet and rainy places, from the Old
French *plovier*; rain in Latin is *pluvia*.)

## The Dipper, or Water Ouzel

A plump bird which you might suppose (though it is not a wren of
any kind) to be a large water-wren. In effect, a bird of black (really
greyish brown) plumage, with a white neck and white shirt-front.
With black tail cocked, the Dipper *dips*, and bobs, hardly ever still. It
lives along quick rocky streams, especially moorland ones. In the bank
or under bridges, sometimes in reach of the mist of a waterfall, dippers
build a domed, wren-like nest, chiefly of moss and leaves.

## The Ring Ouzel

Another bird which likes moorland and rock, though not a bird of the
streams. Resembles its relative the Blackbird (the Ouzel); but it has
no golden bill, and half round its neck is a ring, or rather a crescent, of
white feathers.

## The Wheatear

A summer bird of the moors, the downs, and rough hills, who arrives in the spring and goes again in September. An obvious bird, though it is not much larger than a Robin. White rather than black is the Wheatear's mark, though he has blackish wings, and black and white tail. In the Civil War century a Wheatear was still called, not so politely, a 'Wheatears', that is to say, a bird with a white arse. From rock to rock, stone to stone, a Wheatear(s) will fly off a few yards, let you approach, and fly off again, each time flashing its white rump.

## BIRDS ALONG THE COAST

Besides the gulls of one kind and another (commonest of all, the Herring Gull, on cliffs, in fishing harbours, inland following the tractor and the plough), a few particular birds insist upon being noticed, some birds of the sea or the cliffs, or the tidal zones. First –

## The Oystercatcher, or Sea-Pie

Large, quick-running, low-flying. Black and white, black above, white below, black-headed. In contrast, a longish orange-red bill, and longish red legs. The bird – party by party – of a thousand beaches. No one is about, the tide is turning, and the oystercatchers (who do not 'catch oysters') are in possession, on the margin of the foam, on the glistening sand. Bathers arrive, and the oystercatchers take to the wing, trilling loudly and ringingly as they fly to the nearest low sea-weedy rocks; where they perch and stand, bill into the wind, not a feather out of place. It could well be called the Summer Holiday Bird. (Plate 45.)

## The Terns

Here and there round the coasts, especially from an offshore boat, where there are sandy seas, you may see – and they are not to be mistaken – terns or sea-swallows. That second name is the clue. These are elegant, dainty birds, which might have been born of sea air or sea wind – more elegant in fact than any swallow. The ones most likely to be encountered are Arctic Tern, Common Tern and the much smaller Little Tern; and though they are not strictly and absolutely white, they give the impression of a white, at times, fluttering elegance; light on the air; long tapering wings, long narrow tails; searching, twisting, hovering; then chopping (rather than plunging or diving) on to the sea with the faintest splash. The harsh scrape-like little noises they utter almost set the teeth on edge. Close to, their black crowns are visible; and you may detect the scarlet beak which distinguishes the

Arctic Tern from the black-tipped blood-orange beaked Common Tern.

## The Gannet, or Solan Goose

Huge gannets, white birds, so far as the distant eye can tell, strong and deliberate on the wing, are often to be seen from cliff tops, near or far away from their Irish, Welsh or Scottish island gannetries. Suddenly from eighty or a hundred feet or even more above the blue sea, the Gannet drops, diving on to a fish, and throwing up a splash of white on the blue. Unmistakeable. (Plate 11).

## The Eider, or St Cuthbert's Chicken

A sea duck; and 'St Cuthbert's Chicken' because Eiders were much loved by St Cuthbert in the seventh century, when he was a hermit on the chief of the Farne Islands (where the eider still nest), off the low coasts of Northumberland. The eiders nest all around St Cuthbert's cell, and in the Middle Ages their tameness during the nesting season was ascribed to the holiness of St Cuthbert, who made his island into the first of bird sanctuaries. While he watched and prayed on Farne, wrote one of the Durham monks in the twelfth century, he had assured the eiders 'a continuity of peace and quiet, allowing no one to touch them, slaughter them, or molest them with any mischievous intent'.

'That ability to rear their young', wrote the monk, 'which had been afforded them in time past, he assured to them as a heritage for ever in glorious peace and watchful solitude. Indeed, when he lived a solitary life on the rock he so tamed the aforesaid winged and swimming creatures that they gave him unquestioning obedience. He prescribed for them where they should nest, and exactly when they should arrive and when they should leave. So they still arrive at fixed times, and in the hour of need and adversity have recourse to the familiar protection of the Blessed Cuthbert.'

The nesting eiders are still protected on the Farnes; which are a bird sanctuary.

Eiders are sometimes to be seen with the Scoters, sometimes in parties, large or small, off the rocky sandstone or basalt stretches of Northumberland. When you see them floating near the seaweed rocks, pair by pair, the drake is smartly black and white, the female drab and meek in brown. Eiders also fly in an unusual way, beating their wings as you would expect, but then gliding; much as one may pedal then freewheel on a bicycle.

## The Common Scoter

A sombre, black-billed, black-feathered sea duck which calmly rides the seas around the coast (especially in winter), where it feeds on mussels. Now and again a Scoter will be surprised on a lonely beach. He scuffles for the sea, unable to rise from the land.

## The Puffin, Sea-Parrot, or Tammie Norrie

Most likely to be seen off Scottish, western and Irish coasts at sea in flocks or rafts; a comic bird – as comic as the Dodo – perhaps owing its name to the puffed-up appearance of its head and large beak. The beak – this is odd – changes shape, or size rather, and colour. In summer the Puffin flaunts a beak divided into red and blue with yellow edgings. This beak seems to cover most of its face, like an underwater swimmer's mask, so a Scottish rhyme about puffins of the Bass Rock says

> Tammie Borrie o' the Bass
> Canna kiss a young lass.

Lundy, off the north coast of Devonshire, was so called by the Vikings because it was a nesting island of the *lundi*, as the Puffin was called in Old Norse.

## The Cormorant and the Shag

Cormorants and Shags fly low and powerfully above the sea, and perch on rocks, sometimes with their wings half spread, and swim and dive after fish self-confidently, coming up to the surface after a dive, and shaking or quickly turning their rather long-beaked heads from side to side.

Anciently they were confused, and were both known as Cormorant, a name we took from the French word, which is *cormoran*, and which the French took from the Latin *corvus marinus*, or sea-raven; though except for their black plumage no birds could look or act less like a raven. The Cormorant's reputation shared in the darkness of the character of ravens. The devil in older paintings is sometimes shown as a Cormorant perched on the Tree of Life in the Garden of Eden. Milton in *Paradise Lost* described how Satan made his way to the Garden, climbed the wall, and changed his shape:

> Thence up he flew, and on the Tree of Life,
> The middle tree and highest there that grew,
> Sat like a cormorant; yet not true life
> Thereby regain'd, but sat devising death
> To them that lived –

which was something Samuel Taylor Coleridge remembered, when, as a poet and author, he likened publishers to Cormorants on the Tree of Life.

Cormorants are larger than Shags, and have white cheeks. When they are breeding in spring, they have a white patch on either side between wing and tail, whereas Shags have no patches but do have the distinction of a crest, which gives them a slightly shaggy or ruffled look. (Plate 11.)

## The Raven

Not exclusively a bird of the coast; but ravens are commoner where high cliffs give them a secure nesting-place. The Raven looks like a Bird of Power. Catch sight of him on a wall of rock at the top of the cliff, and you see an all-black funereal bird; black, strong, thick beak, black legs. On the wing, you may hear him croak harshly, as if his voice were as black as his feathers.

> There were three ravens sat on a tree,
> Downe a downe, hay downe, hay downe.
> There were three ravens sat on a tree,
> With a downe.
> There were three ravens sat on a tree,
> They were as black as they might be . . .

And in that traditional poem they were about to eat the dead knight in the field. They are eaters of carrion – when it is to be had. The Greeks called the Raven a *korax*, which is the croak turned into a name; regarded him as a bird of Apollo, and foretold the future by the way he croaked and flew.

Ravens *croak*, rooks *caw*, jackdaws *chatter*.

# SWANS

Swans on English rivers are to our credit. Our birds are the Mute Swan, a species of the lands around the North Sea and the southern Baltic; and long ago, at least as far back as the Middle Ages, we entered into an arrangement with swans, and swans with us. We liked them (and, it is true, liked to eat them); and swans and men have for a long while lived on more or less amicable terms. We now eat them no more, and the relationship is firmer still; swans contemplate us without fear, on rivers and lakes, protected by the law, by their own beauty, and by a combined pressure of myth, legend, poetry, painting, madrigal, opera, and ballet. We have sacrificed our killing instinct to our sense of beauty – for once.

Some swan facts. The cob, or male bird, in the breeding season, can always be distinguished by one thing – the enlarged black knob on top of its bill.

The Mute Swan lives up to its name. It is mute (except for hissing when you come too near). It does not sing; 'swan' seems to have a root meaning of sounding or singing, but this was probably the sounding of the swan's wings in flight.

All the same, the swan of the Greeks which sang sweetly before it died, according to belief, was certainly our species; it was to be seen wild in Greece, but it was not an everyday bird, so on that account, by adding rarity to beauty, the Swan was all the more a proper bird to be sacred to Apollo particularly and to Venus (or for Zeus to enter into when he united himself to Leda, one of whose eggs hatched into the white Helen of Troy). Swans live in two worlds: the world of mind as well as the world of nature, a blend which helps to preserve them.

> The silver swan, who living had no note
> When death approach'd unlockt her silent throat.

The explanation of the swan singing before it dies is best given by Plato (himself a poet as well as a philosopher) in his record or version of some of the last words of Socrates. Socrates is in prison; he is to drink the hemlock and die. His friends round him are sad, and hesitate to ask him questions, but Socrates is calm and cheerful and he says, 'You do not seem to think that I can see as far ahead as a swan. You know that when swans feel the approach of death, they sing – and they sing sweeter and louder on that last day of their lives than they have ever sung before. Of course they are singing for joy, because they are going back to that god whom they serve; yet some people maintain quite wrongly that the swans sing out of sorrow because they have to die. That is only because such people are afraid of death themselves; they do not realize that birds never sing because they are hungry or cold. Distress does not make them sing; it does not make even nightingales or swallows sing, or hoopoes, though hoopoes are supposed to sing a lament. It is my view that swans sing, not because they are sad, but because they belong to Apollo: they are prophetic birds, they know what happiness they will have in the next world; so of course they sing; and on the day when they have to die, they are happier than ever they were. I am like the swans, I, also, belong to Apollo, and he has made me just as clear-sighted as the birds, in my opinion. So I am not at all upset because I have to leave this life.' – Plato, *Phaedo*.


# GARDEN BIRDS

What birds frequent a garden depends on the garden, its trees, its shrubs, the presence or absence of water, and a good many other factors. It will have its casual visitors, as well as its winter or summer residents. Everyone will know Thrush and Blackbird and Robin and Hedge Sparrow (at any rate the Hedge Sparrow's nest, with its sky-blue eggs), Chaffinch, and Wren with its cocked tail. Also the commoner tits –

the Blue Tit (a soft blue set off by yellow; blue crown above white cheeks, a blue tail, blue wings and a yellow underside) and the Great Tit (which is larger, more aggressive; also yellow underneath, also white-cheeked, but with a black top to its head, and a black bib which narrows and extends, and divides the yellow).

It is the Great Tit which has learned to peck off the tops of milk-bottles at the door.

Here are some other garden facts.

If a sturdy small bird, about robin-size, but of a very different build and character, rather like a double-ended wedge, slate-blue above and dull chestnut below, comes in to a bird-table, it will be a NUTHATCH (Plate 8). Nuthatches (i.e. hackers of nuts) like woodland, especially beech woods. They are a tree-trunk species; but that does not prevent them coming like tits to a window-sill or a bird-table after food, looping in with a low flight, and then nipping about, sideways, head up, or upside-down, with a slightly clumsy and bullying quickness.

If when most of the other spring birds have arrived, a pair of small brown neat birds, with a particularly sharp beak and particularly keen and alert movements, take up quarters in the garden, choosing perches with clear space all around, such as the posts of a tennis net, or the handle of a roller; and if you see them fluttering out from the perch with great nimbleness, and back again, they are likely to be SPOTTED FLYCATCHERS, newly arrived from overseas.

But if you live north or west of a line drawn from Northumberland to Westmorland, and then down across Wales and the Marches to Gloucestershire, your garden flycatchers may be black-and-white – i.e. PIED FLYCATCHERS. The cock bird, black-headed, has black tail and back, with a white bib and under parts, and white lines on black wings. His wife has a brownish head and upper parts, though a black tail and tell-tale white on the wings.

If a thrush-like bird, speckle-fronted, though quite a bit larger and grey-brown rather than brown, makes a harsh, rather angry sounding noise around the garden – in winter or spring – and especially around the orchard, where it is likely to have its nest, lichened outside, in the fork of an apple-tree, it will be a MISSEL-THRUSH, or Holm-scritch (which includes among its food the berries of mistletoe, and the berries of the holm, or holly). (Plate 16.)

# THE GARDEN SONGS

Can you distinguish the song of a THRUSH from the song of a BLACK-

BIRD? Not everybody can, so there could be more insulting questions. 'Bird song', ornithologists have pointed out, is very much a term devised to suit the human ear and the human liking for music. Ornithologically and scientifically, a bird song is still song if it is not musical, and has been defined as 'any performance which appears to be linked with breeding, courtship or territory holding'. I am not sure that human song could not be defined in much the same way. *God Save the Queen* or *Land of Hope and Glory* is territory holding, and *O, my luve is like a red, red rose* is courtship if not breeding (just as there are both sad and glad folk-songs which are all too much breeding rather than courtship). In any case, we ourselves like singing and being sung to; and though it may be wise to interpret the why and wherefore of bird songs in strictly functional and utilitarian terms, birds in song, conspicuously perched, in pleasant circumstance, absorbed, at least give an appearance of enjoying themselves; and that appearance may also be fact. And there are kinds of birds which certainly overhear and to some degree at times imitate the notes of birds of a different species. Whether birds enjoy song or singing or no, we enjoy the notes they make when we find them musical; and we shall always interpret that bird music as joy or as an emotive overflowing, whatever the scientific accounting may add up to.

Few bird songs can be more than suggested or labelled by an attempt to express them in words; and the best way to learn them is watching and listening, coupled with gramophone records. The garden songs to recognize are Thrush and Blackbird, Wren, Robin, Hedge-Sparrow, Greenfinch, and Chaffinch. The Wren's song is quick and voluminous, seeming to burst with astonishing abandon and cheerfulness out of so small a bird; the Robin's thin, reedy, melancholy, to my ear rather a disturbing music around the house; the Hedge-Sparrow's (nothing to match the sweetness of its sky-blue eggs) could be described as something like the Wren's song without strength or urgency or courage. The Greenfinch twitters. The Chaffinch clearly, a little brassily, pronounces a descending scale of notes ending in a three-syllabled phrase which is variously described as *tissi-ear*, or *choo-ee-o*, for instance; a song to pattern which is a little tediously characteristic of the garden in spring.

Other birds make peculiar noises in the garden, the Brown Owl, when it gets dark, does more than hoot (see page 201); the Great Tit, the Saw-Sharpener, sharpens his saws around the garden, with two notes like the forward and backward stroke of the file on the teeth of the saw; the Blue Tit monotonously sings a song of two sharp notes followed by a run. A song, though, which seems a particularly strong expression of delight is the Starling's. The April sun shines on its metallic plumage, and it outpours a nickelled sound of whistles and gurgles and clicks and snaps and hisses and chuckles – sometimes including a phrase or two imitated from other song birds. Not 'musical' or 'tuneful', perhaps, but delightful and invigorating to listen to.

Thrush and Blackbird. If there is a certain family connection between the songs of these two celebrated musicians, they are also quite distinct in structure and character. Both are bold and deliberate. The Blackbird's singing is very well described as mellow, which is the customary adjective, with the quality of a flute; a structure of sluicing sound delivered as if there were all the time in the world for singing, sliding through its full phrases, then dwindling off a little weakly.

By contrast the Thrush makes a more various run, repeating phrases, two syllabled and three syllabled – more with a liquid whistle than with a flute. In contrast to the sliding connected structure of the Blackbird's song, the thrush song is punctuated as if by distinct commas or semi-colons. The familiar verbalization of *How-d'ye-do; bo-peep; bo-peep; Judy; Judy; pretty Dick* looks a little sloppy and ridiculous in print, but it does serve quite well both as an indicator and a reminder.

Thrushes and especially Blackbirds figure a good deal in the early nature poetry of the Irish and the Welsh. Hermits in the wilderness wrote about their song. The Norman-Welsh clergyman Giraldus Cambrensis was told a blackbird story when he went to Ireland less than twenty years after the Norman Conquest. During Lent St Kevin (one of the Irish saints of the seventh century) went into retreat by himself, in a small hut or shelter in the wilderness. He was reading, praying and contemplating; and as usual he put his hand out of the shelter and lifted it towards heaven, when a Blackbird settled on it, and took it for a nest, and laid her eggs in his palm. St Kevin was so compassionate and so patient, that he did not close his hand or take it away, but held it tirelessly aloft till the Blackbird hatched its young and till the young flew away.

# THE PEACOCK

It is an odd thing that if a bird or plant is domesticated and no longer wild we become rather less interested in it as a living creature. Gilbert White did not take the Peacock in that way, but observed his neighbour's peacocks at Selborne and marked a difference between their tails and their trains. So the Peacock may well have a word even among the wild birds of this *Country Book*.

They are Indian jungle birds, by origin, which were taken to Persia, then to Greece, then to Rome, and so, by way of Rome and Byzantium (and new importations from the East) to the rest of Europe. The Peacock in a Greek or Roman – or English – garden once implied, in different ways, more than the extraordinary colour, glitter and pattern of its train. Peacocks – like Swans (page 186) – could be eaten, but they were also sacred. Rare, as well as exquisite, the Peacock in Greece, was the bird of Hera, the wife of Zeus; just as the Eagle was the bird of Zeus, the Swan the bird of Apollo, and the Dove the bird of Aphrodite. In Rome, it was the bird of Juno, counterpart of Hera. Aelian, more than seventeen hundred years ago, described how rare they had been in Athens, how they were exhibited to men of taste for a fee, and how a pair cost over £350, and he remarked – though not with contempt – on the Peacock's pride in its own beauty. Alexander the Great encountered wild peacocks glittering in a dark jungle, during his invasion of India, found them wonderful, and ordered that Peacocks should not be killed. For Christians, the Peacock emblemed both immortality and resurrection. A Peacock in Italian medieval paintings of the Adoration of the Magi, the Three Kings, often perches above the Child. The belief was that the Three Kings had brought peacocks (and apes, which are sometimes in the picture as well) from the East, in their cavalcade. Among the Three Kings, the old white-headed Melchior was held to be King of Tharshish; and from Tharshish, they remembered out of the Old Testament, Solomon's navy had brought back gold and silver and 'elephant's teeth' and apes and peacocks.

All this adds up to a good reason – if you can stand the screaming of peacocks – for keeping a pair in your garden. Not many writers have ever tried to analyse the beauty of the lights and colours and eyes and structure of a Peacock's train. 'He shivers when he first rears it and then again at intervals and when this happens the rest blurs and the eyes start forward. – I have thought it looks like a tray or green basket or fresh-cut willow hurdle set all over with Paradise fruits cut through – first through a beard of golden fibre and then through wet flesh greener than greengages or purpler than grapes.' – Gerard Manley Hopkins, 17 May, 1871.

Aelian wrote, not only of the beauty of the Peacock, but of the way the Peacock will 'raise its tail-feathers, shake them, and scream, so that the onlookers are startled as if by the clang of the armour of a hoplite'. Watching his neighbour's peacocks, Gilbert White was less poetical than Hopkins, less fanciful than Aelian: 'By a strong muscular vibration these birds can make the shafts of their long feathers clatter like the swords of a sword-dancer; they then trample very quick with their feet, and run backwards towards their females.'

The Peacock tells its history by its name, which comes (the first syllable) from Tamil, by way of Persian, Greek and Latin. In the Middle Ages, our word was 'Pecock' or 'Pocok': which explains a modern Mr or Miss Pocock.

## BIRDS WHICH ANNOUNCE THEMSELVES

There are birds whose names are what the word-expert calls 'echoic' – names echoing their own notes. *Owl* echoes the hooting of the Brown Owl; *Cuckoo* echoes the notes which everyone knows; but not so many people recognize the sounds which have given their names to the CHAFFINCH, the CHIFFCHAFF, the TURTLE DOVE, the NIGHTJAR, the CURLEW, the CORNCRAKE, the QUAIL.

The CHAFFINCH (Plate 8) ejaculates, in various renderings, *spink!* or *pink!* or *chwink!* round the gardens and hedges. This gave rise to the name 'finch' (chaffinches are also called 'Spinks' and 'Tinks'), which was then applied as well to the other similar birds we call finches. A

Finch is a *Fink* in German. So a Chaffinch is precisely a bird saying *spink, pink, chwink, tink, fink* (each time with that exclamation mark) who pecks about in the chaff – round a threshing floor for example – for seeds. All the finches are seed-eating birds.

The CHIFFCHAFF, more heard than seen, a little olive-brown warbler, arrives in April and says *chiff-chaff; chiff-chaff; chiff-chaff* . . . on and on, often from high trees, where the Chiffchaffs hunt for insects. Germans call this bird a *Zilpzalp*.

The TURTLE DOVE (Plate 14) comes at the beginning of May, the most amiable of soft-ash-coloured, soft-voiced birds, and announces itself by murmuring *tur-turr* from the green depth of hedges, gently rolling its r's. The coo of the Wood Pigeon, interpreted as *My toes are bleeding, Betty* (and so they are – its feet and legs are red) or as *Take two-o coo, Taffy!*, is quite different, musical, yet almost coarse or vulgar by comparison – not this murmur of love, as it seems, which made the Turtle Dove (in Latin *turtur*) the special bird and messenger of Venus, the goddess of love. The *tur-turring* goes on till the end of July. Turtle Doves often perch, male with female, on telegraph wires, and are often to be surprised on the road. When they fly up, they very beautifully spread a black tail edged with white.

Sometimes in the last week of April or first week of May large flocks of Turtle Doves may be seen arriving on migration. The way they fly appears the very opposite of their character, the sky above is interrupted by quick, jerky wing-beats.

> Clean birds by sevens,
> Unclean by twos,
> The dove in the heavens
> Is the one I choose.

The NIGHTJAR has other names. He is called Fern-owl (a bird of commons covered with 'fern' or bracken), Churn-owl, Eve-churr, Night-churr – the bird which 'jars' or 'churrs' out of the darkness. The noise is something like the winding up of a watch; or you can imitate it by putting your tongue up against the roof of your mouth and making it vibrate as you blow out your breath – only the Nightjar will keep the noise up a great deal longer than you can, churring three or four or even five minutes at a time.

This peculiar bird of wooded commons sucks the milk from goats according to legend; though in fact its wide mouth is adapted for the hunting of moths (Plate 17). Sometimes the headlights of a car will catch Nightjars dusting themselves on a woodland or heathland lane.

The CURLEW (Plate 9), the large bird of sea coasts and saltings, but most of all of the wet moorland; speaks its own name through a long curved beak with the most liquid melancholy. This bird is a *courlis* in France, a name which is nearer the real sound of *cour-li* than is 'curlew'. Its cry has made the curlew a bird of love poems:

> O curlew, cry no more in the air,
> Or only to the water in the West;
> Because your crying brings to my mind
> Passion-dimmed eyes and long heavy hair
> That was shaken out over my breast:
> There is enough evil in the crying of wind.
>
> W. B. Yeats

The CORNCRAKE or LANDRAIL (the cock-bird) *crakes*, not from the corn so much as from the hay, and not so commonly in our time from English hay-meadows, as from hay-meadows in Ireland, where the hay ripens and is cut later, giving the Corncrake longer to raise its young. To be exact, the Corncrake does not so much *crake* with a long a, as say *crex-crex* or *crek-crek*, harshly, with a short vowel. As the sun goes down into the Atlantic, the Corncrakes make a harsh chorus in the wet meadows along the Irish coast; but never a bird is seen until the scythe bites through the grass.

The QUAIL, now uncommon in the English countryside, and, like the Corncrake, a bird protected by special laws (see *The Law About Birds*, pages 202–5), reveals its summer presence by the three-syllable call which English countrymen used to translate as *Wet my lips*. 'Quail', though you might not think it, does come from the noise made by these little partridge-like skulkers; time has shortened it from a late Latin name: it was a *quaquila*, which in its three syllables rather resembles the *click-lik-lik* or *quic, quic-ic* which ornithologists give as their version of the Quail's cry.

The PARTRIDGE is another bird whose name echoes its cry at a linguistic remove. 'Partridge' comes to us by way of Latin and French from the Greek *Perdix*, which was how the Greeks heard its harsh, pleasant, two-syllabled cry, which bird books give as *kee'ash* (not hard enough) or as *krr-ic*. The Greeks had a tale that Perdix was an inventive nephew of the divine master-craftsman Daedalus. One thing he invented was the saw. Daedalus was jealous, and threw him off the Acropolis. But Athene saved him, caught him in mid-air, and changed him into the plump Partridge, and he still makes a noise like sharpening a saw.

The CUCKOO (Plate 12), since it contrives to get others birds to hatch and rear its young, was thought of in the Middle Ages and later as the type of the man who fathers a child on another man. So that other man whose wife deceived him, came to be called a 'cuckoo', or cuckold; and the belief was that the cuckoo flies around mocking the deceived husbands, calling out 'cuckold! cuckold!' – and often doing so in the early morning right into the bedroom window. Not everyone seems to realize that this explains Shakespeare's song in which he says

> The cuckoo then on every tree
> Mocks married men; for thus sings he,
> > 'Cuckoo;
> Cuckoo, cuckoo,' – O word of fear,
> Unpleasing to a married ear.

It is the tradition – not far out – that Cuckoos arrive or are heard for the first time on Cuckoo Day, either 14 April or 15 April.

The HOOPOE (page 176), the Yaffle, i.e. Green Woodpecker (page 176), the Golden Oriole (page 178), and the Peewit (page 180) are other birds named from the sounds they make. Also the Stonechat (page 176). In Scotland they have a rhyme about the Stonechat, or Stane-chacker. As it flits about on the gorse-sprays clattering its two pebbles, it says defiantly:

> Stane-chack!
> Deevil tak!
> They wha harry my nest
> Will never rest,
> Will meet the pest!
> De'il brack their lang back
> Wha my eggs would
> Tak, tak!

# BIRDS WITH A SPECIAL FLIGHT

Some birds (like the Eider, already mentioned, page 183, which proceeds by beats and glides, or the Gannet, page 183, dropping and diving on fish, or the Turtle Dove, page 193, which flies with a jerky movement) at once announce themselves by a peculiarity of flight.

The LARK. Of course, the obvious odd flyer is the Skylark, a bird adapted to the treeless open European prairies which succeeded the Ice Age, and so to our restricted grasslands. It is the male which soars to fifty or sixty feet, even twice as high, and hovers and sings, and sings as it descends to the grass. The necklace of song is audible when the

lark is too high almost to be seen; and the lark will sometimes be aloft
in the sun before the sunlight has touched the ground –

> Lo! here the gentle lark, weary of rest,
>   From his moist cabinet mounts up on high,
> And wakes the morning, from whose silver breast
>   The sun ariseth in his majesty.
> Shakespeare, *Venus and Adonis*.

The lark's singing is at its best and longest in March, and goes on till
July. It then begins to fizzle out, coming to an end at the beginning of
August. October is another song-month. And the lark is in full voice
again at the end of January.

The WHITETHROAT, commonest of warblers along the summer
hedges, has its noticeable peculiar song-flight early in the breeding
season. Whitethroats are easily recognized – small greyish-brown birds
– by the way they scold and flit and fidget and hide and reappear
along a low hedge. The song-flight is a delightful brief soaring or danc-
ing or leaping, as it seems, a few feet above the hedge, a few feet up
and down – in such a way that the whiteness of the throat is visible as
the bird sings in bursts of abandon.

The KESTREL (or Windhover or Standgale), neat hawk which hunts
for field-mice and voles and beetles, hovers unmistakeably; at about
fifty or sixty feet above the ground, always head to the wind (though
it bends its head down in scrutiny of its hoped-for prey). Staying aloft
or afloat for a while on its wing-beat, it will either drop, or curve, away,
regain height and hover once more (Plate 13). So the Kestrel has the
distinction of being described, or made to exist and hover, in the most
astonishing and ecstatic of all poems about a living creature – *The
Windhover*, the sonnet by Gerard Manley Hopkins, which begins:

> I caught this morning morning's minion, kingdom of daylight's
>   dauphin, dapple-dawn-drawn Falcon, in his riding
> Of the rolling level underneath him steady air . . .

The BUZZARD, a slow hawk, large, with wide blunt wings, mainly to
be seen on the west side of England, and in Wales and Scotland. Above
a valley, where they nest perhaps in an oak tree, buzzards will soar in
great gyres slowly and proudly, as if they were defining huge funnels
of air. As they turn (sometimes still in the sunlight when the valley is
already in evening shadow), you may see that the feathers along the

blunt end of their wings curve upwards. And on the wing, they call, slowly and thinly, *pee-oo*, something between a moan and a whistle. 'Buzzard' has been said most contemptuously (for instance by Shakespeare) of men who are sluggish, cruel and disgusting. Perhaps when buzzards were much commoner than they are now, everyone was aware of their taste for carrion. (Plate 13.)

The WOOD PIGEON's distinctive flight habits are firstly, that when frightened or alarmed it bundles away through the leaves and branches loudly clapping its wings; secondly, that in open glades in spring and summer, it most engagingly flies upward a few feet, as though breasting the air, and then falls, a performance as elegant as the wing clapping is clumsy.

# TWO BIRDS WITH A SPECIAL GAIT

The TREE-CREEPER is well named. It creeps and it creeps up trees, in a self-effacing spiral motion, which is strangely noticeable, all the same. It creeps and stops, creeps and stops, with a clockwork motion, a small, slight, brown-backed bird, bark-coloured, with a curved beak. The Tree-creeper seems to apologize all the while for its existence.

The PIED WAGTAIL, on the contrary, runs and walks along a wall, on a meadow, in a farmyard, across a lawn, as if remarkably pleased with itself, and as if demanding the footlights, waggling its long black and white tail; a well-groomed little bird, walking and running, with a twinkle of its dark legs, not hopping. In hilly country with quick streams and rock (for instance in Devon and Cornwall), the GREY WAGTAIL is common. It is rather more a wagtail of dells and streams, but it will frequent farmyards or gardens, if there is water at hand, running and walking in the same wagtail way, but distinguished by a much longer, still more delicately balanced black and white tail, and by a clear yellow breast in summer, when the cock bird also has a black throat. A very graceful bird, one of the most beautiful we have, but it needs a new English name to indicate that it is much more yellow than grey. 'Grey' is a bad translation of *cinerea* in its scientific name, which is Latin for ash-coloured. Its upper parts are ash or cinder-colour, a blue-grey.

The real YELLOW WAGTAIL (Plate 12), shorter tail, yellow-breasted, greenish above, is by contrast a bird of the plains, of meadows by the water.

# TO DISTINGUISH SWALLOW, MARTIN, AND SWIFT

Here are three birds often grouped together in the mind just as 'swallows', because they are rapid birds of the air and of human neighbourhood, appearing in spring as a welcome portent.

The SWALLOW. To begin with Swallow and Martin, these two are related, are both members of the Swallow family. The Swift is not related. Swallow and Martin arrive first of the three, in April, and leave last, in October. On the wing, you can see at once that the Swallow has an extremely long forked tail. A close, still view of a swallow, say on a telegraph wire outside the window, reveals its colour – especially a red throat and forehead set off and surrounded by a black which is really a very dark blue – blue-black head, back, wings, tail; blue-black above and below the red; then white underneath.

The MARTIN. On the wing or perched, you see at once that the tail is forked rather briefly. Top parts are blue-black, like the Swallow's, but the Martin has no red throat. Also when the Martin flies away it is easy to detect that his black upper parts enclose something the Swallow lacks – a patch of white feathers on the rump. Swallows fly with a cleaner thrust – watch one sweep unerringly into a shed through the narrowest opening – Martins manage a fine sweeping flight, but they are also fluttering wing-beaters.

Their nests are quite different. It is the Martin which hangs up, or sticks up, a mud cradle underneath the eaves – a cup with a hole; the Swallow which builds an open saucer or bowl of mud on a beam or a ledge, or corbel.

'Martin', by the way, is a name of affection or familiarity, simply the Christian name. The French go one better by calling the bird *Martinet*, which is Little Martin. (There are plenty more bird names of this kind such as Robin, Tomtit, Magpie (page 179). Parrot and Petrel are supposed to be diminutives of Peter – Petrel being a Little St Peter who walks on the sea. Pierrot, another Little Peter, is the French name for the chirping House Sparrow.)

The SWIFT screams, on the wing. Its screaming above the villages, towns and cities of Europe is the sound of high summer. Swifts are all black in effect – a true black; with a wide sweep of black scimitars for wings. They do not arrive till May, they are off again in August, long before Swallow and Martin; and they slip in under the slates or tiles to nest out of sight and, in that function, out of mind. As swift in their flight as their name implies. (Plate 13.)

It is an old habit of men to be kind to Swallows and Martins, and put up with any mess they make, without knocking down their nests or shutting them out.

The swallow indicates that the best time of the year has come again. And it is friendly to man, and likes to be under the same roof with him, arriving uninvited and leaving when it feels the right moment has come. We welcome the swallow according to Homer's rule of hospitality, which tells us to treat those who turn up at our houses kindly, and to give them a proper farewell when they wish to leave.

Aelian (*c.* 200).

# THE NIGHTINGALE – AND THE SWALLOW

Poems about the Nightingale singing at night (Plate 10), and about the Swallow twittering thoughtlessly by day, incline to be double Dutch without a knowledge of the stories behind them. In Greece there is a great hill below the mountain of Parnassus (the mountain of Apollo and the Muses and of poetry). This great hill is steep and grey with precipices, then it breaks into glens which give way to a wide plain. On top of the hill and the precipices are the ruins, under oaks and ivy, of ancient Daulis, supposed to have been the stronghold of King Tereus the evil-doer. Across the plain, King Pandion of Athens had two daughters, Procne and Philomela. Tereus married Procne, but then fell in love with Philomela, and ravished her in a lonely house. When Philomela declared she would tell the world of his wickedness, Tereus pulled out her tongue with pincers with one swift movement, which left the tongue writhing on the floor, and kept her prisoner in the house. But she had her revenge. Tongueless Philomela wove what she had to reveal into a tapestry, which she managed to convey to her sister Procne, the wife of Tereus. Whereupon Procne looked at her own child, her boy, and saw how like he was to his evil father. She killed him, in vengeance, cooked him on spits, and gave him to Tereus to eat, in a ritual meal.

Tereus after his meal asked for his son. Procne said he had him. Where? said Tereus. Inside you, said Procne; and at that moment the ravished, tongueless, dumb Philomela came out and flung the son's head at Tereus; and here at Daulis, where the nightingales still sing every spring and summer, Tereus leapt after the two women with a sword. The gods at once changed Tereus into a hoopoe (or a hawk), Philomela into a Swallow, making for safety under the eaves, and Procne into a Nightingale flying for safety to the wood. In our tradition, which is the tradition of the Latin and not the Greek poets, the sisters are changed about. Procne becomes the Swallow, who has blood – those red feathers – on her throat and forehead, and can only twitter, since she has no song, Philomela becomes the Nightingale, and sings and sings and throbs and sobs all night, in pain, in sorrow, in memory of rape and child murder. The change-round is a pity in some ways. Philomela is really the appropriate name for Swallow, and not Nightingale, since it means, not lover of song, but lover of flocks, the swallow in Greece, as with ourselves, liking to nest in cowsheds, or buildings in which the farm animals are collected.

There is another simpler story to explain the sorrow of the Nightingale, singing at night: that Queen Aedon of Thebes, who was jealous of her brother's wife, Niobe, for her six sons and six daughters, wanted to kill Niobe's first-born. Instead of killing her nephew, by mistake she killed her own baby son Itylus; after which Zeus, the great Father of the Gods, changed Queen Aedon into the sorrowing Nightingale. Aedon was the common Greek word for nightingale, and meant the Singing One.

It is little good listening for nightingales except in the south Midland and southern counties. Warwickshire and Northamptonshire and Surrey, for example, are good nightingale counties. There are Devonshire (but not Cornish) nightingales, some nightingales in southeastern Wales, but very few in the north Midlands or the North or East Anglia. Some listeners mistake the less rich song of the Blackcap, even the scraping song of the Sedge-warbler, for the classic singing of the Nightingale (which as a matter of fact also sings by day).

Nightingale comes from the Old English word meaning night-singer.

## TO DISTINGUISH OWLS

There are three common ones. By day, the LITTLE OWL, in twilight the BARN OWL and – though you *see* him less often – the BROWN OWL.

The LITTLE OWL is named scientifically *Athene noctua*, after Athene, the wise goddess of the Greeks, whose bird it was. It is little, short, blunt, malicious-eyed, quick in its movements, with a frowning forehead. It might very well be called the Farm Owl, since it likes fields and hedges, out of which it will call and call monotonously through the day and into the twilight its decidedly un-owlish *kiu, kiu, kiu,* which carries a long way. Often to be seen on a post or stump, or a telegraph-pole. This little creature of frown and wisdom was introduced into England at various times and in various places between 1874 and 1908. It found a gap in English wild life, and has filled it with some speed. After occupying all England and Wales, it is now spreading across Scotland.

The BARN OWL –

> Lovely are the curves of the white owl sweeping
> Wavy in the dusk lit by one large star.

The Barn Owl is pallid in such twilight – such owl-light – seeming an entirely white bird; long face and underparts are white, though else-where his soft feathers have a pinkish-yellow effect.

This owl does not hoot, it shrieks.

The BROWN OWL also shrieks, saying sharply, loudly, repeatedly, with the accent on the second syllable, ke-*wik*, ke-*wik*, ke-*wik*.

Macbeth: I have done the deed. Didst thou not hear a noise?
Lady Macbeth: I heard the owl scream and the crickets cry.

So the shrieking, screaming owl, which foretells or heralds a death in belief and poetry was either Brown Owl or Barn Owl –

> Hark! now everything is still,
> The screech-owl and the whistler shrill
> Call upon our dame aloud,
> And bid her quickly don her shroud . . .

But it is the Brown Owl alone which hoots, making a strictly *owlish*

noise (*ule*, more like the hooting, was the Old English form of Owl) –
a bird, when you do see it, as brown as dead leaves, and markedly
*blunt* about the head, in contrast to the long-seeming white face of the
Barn Owl. A noisy commotion of small birds inside an ivied tree or a
yew tree in the garden will often prove to be the mobbing of a Brown
Owl. Sometimes, as if the owl could stand it no more, he will fly out
of the tree in broad daylight.


# THE LAW ABOUT BIRDS

> The robin and the redbreast
> The robin and the wren
> If ye take out o' their nest
> Ye'll never thrive again.
>
> The robin and the redbreast
> The martin and the swallow
> If ye touch one o' their eggs
> Bad luck will surely follow.

Birds in Great Britain are most privileged creatures – a little unfairly,
other animals might consider, if they could think and talk and complain about such matters, and write letters about them to *The Times*.
The remedy – for the other living things – is no doubt to extend the
privilege, if not by law, then by educating our compassion and our
fellow-feeling for other animals (since we are animals ourselves).
Like the spontaneous growth of the soil (see page 327) and like other
wild creatures still indigenous here, wild birds *belong* to no one till
taken or killed. But the law has its restrictions on the taking and killing.
'Game birds', the object of 'the cheerful labours of the chase' (*hilares
venandi capores*), such as the pheasant and partridge and grouse and in
Scotland the ptarmigan have long had a limited legal protection
pending the day of their slaughter. And the *Protection of Birds Act*,
1954, 2 & 3. Eliz. II. c. 30, says as a principle, with exceptions, that
any person commits an offence, if he wilfully:
  (*a*) kills, injures or takes, or attempts to kill, injure, or take, any
       wild bird; or
  (*b*) takes, damages or destroys the nest of any wild bird while that
       nest is in use; or
  (*c*) takes or destroys an egg of any wild bird.
With exceptions. The Law is not so stupid that it fails to realize that

there must be exceptions – that some birds are a nuisance, that there are some we like to eat, that there are some habits of men and children, some traditions, that cannot really be forbidden – effectively – by *Thou Shalt Not, Under Penalty Of* . . .

The game birds may very justly complain that they can still be shot. So can wild ducks and wild geese of various kinds, Snipe, Woodcock, Coot and Curlew and Moorhen, and Golden Plover.

> Then silent groves denote the dying year,
> The morning frost, the noon-tide gossamer;
> And all be silent in the scene around –
> All, save the distant sea's uncertain sound,
> Or here and there the gun, whose loud report
> Proclaims to man that Death is still his sport.

Some nuisance birds which it is lawful to kill if you are an owner or an occupier, or if you are acting for an owner or occupier or for various public authorities, include Jackdaws, Jays, and Magpies, and Rooks, House Sparrows and Starlings (devils in thatch), Wood Pigeons, Cormorants and Shags, Carrion Crows and Hooded Crows, Herring Gulls, Greater Black-backed Gulls and Lesser Black-backed Gulls, and in Scotland, Red-breasted Mergansers and Goosanders and Rock-doves. For all their beauty, Bullfinches do not escape. Because of the damage they do, *The Wild Birds (Bullfinches) Order*, 1955, allows you to kill them, as owner or occupier; not everywhere, but in some of the orchard and special garden counties and districts.

Generally speaking, certain ways of killing or capturing birds are outlawed – 'any springe, trap, gin, snare, hook and line, poisoned or stupefying bait, or floating container holding explosives . . . or any net, baited board, bird-lime or substance of a like nature to bird-lime'.

There are wild birds (particularly some of the old cage favourites) which cannot be sold alive, unless they have been bred in captivity – which is a charter against the caging of Blackbirds and Thrushes and Goldfinches and Linnets and Larks and Bullfinches – birds you cannot go out and take and cage on your own account. This practically rules out – which is rather a pity – the keeping of some pet birds which were allowed a wide freedom around the house and which could be taught to speak. You cannot take and you cannot be sold a Raven, so no more Ravens will be taught to say *Nevermore*. You cannot be sold a Magpie.

Then the old, age-long tradition of bird's nesting, and collecting birds' eggs. At first, it seemed to be doomed for ever by the *Protection of Birds Act* in 1954. This allowed the taking of some eggs which are commonly eaten – Lapwings' eggs up to, but not after, 15 April in any year, and eggs of the Common Gull and the Black-headed Gull. On your own land it stated that you can still take eggs of wild geese, or wild duck or swans, if the eggs are to be hatched. But the boys of Great Britain were now limited to taking eggs of twenty 'nuisance' birds. Obviously this would not do. Bird's nesting may be dying out, but the prospect of creating little criminals by law in every country parish of Great Britain was not such a gay one. So the law was soon varied by an order, which permits the taking of the eggs of thirteen of the common birds.

As matters stand, here is the law. No policeman can interfere if child or man takes:

1. The eggs of the Common Gull, in order to eat them, or feed them to poultry or ornamental birds (though Common Gulls' eggs may not be taken in Kent and East Sussex).

2. Lapwings' eggs, up to 15 April.

3. The eggs of these 'nuisance' birds:

| | |
|---|---|
| Cormorant | Magpie |
| Carrion Crow | Rook |
| Hooded Crow | Shag |
| Domestic Pigeons gone wild | House Sparrow |
| Great Black-backed Gull | Sparrow-hawk |
| Lesser Black-backed Gull | Starling |
| Herring Gull | Stock-dove |
| Jackdaw | Wood Pigeon |
| Jay | |

And in Scotland only:

Goosander
Red-breasted Merganser
Rock-dove

And in some areas (under an Order already mentioned):

Bullfinch

4. The eggs of these other common birds:

Blackbird
Chaffinch
Coot
Greenfinch
Black-headed Gull
Hedge-sparrow
Linnet

Moorhen
Robin
Skylark
Missel-thrush
Song Thrush
Wren

Taking or smashing eggs of *any other wild birds* is an offence for which you can be fined up to five pounds; except that if you take the eggs of some of the rarer birds you incur special penalties: you can be fined up to £25, or be sent to prison for a month, for a first offence. Rarer birds protected in this more expensive way include Chough, Corncrake, Hoopoe, Golden Oriole, Kentish Plover, Quail, Black Redstart, Stone-curlew, Hen-harrier, Marsh-harrier, Merlin, Hobby, Peregrine, Dartford Warbler, and Roseate Tern.

Also no one may sell wild birds' eggs, fresh or blown, except for the eggs of the gulls, Black-headed, Greater Black-backed, Lesser Black-backed, Common, and Herring, for eating or for feeding to poultry and ornamental birds; the eggs of the Lapwing up to 15 April; and the eggs of wild duck, wild geese and swans, for hatching.

A policeman, without a warrant, may stop and search anybody who is 'found committing an offence' against the Protection of Birds Act, and he may search as well the boat, cart, motor-car, scooter, bicycle, horse, pony, donkey which the offender is using. The suspected offender can be arrested if he does not give his name and address.

## ST VALENTINE'S DAY

– is the day, still in the coldness of February, to begin to notice birds again – 14 February. Spring begins on St Valentine's Day, and the tradition is not only one of sending Valentines: it says that on this day the birds choose their mates for the year. He is a somewhat puzzling saint, this Valentinus, priest and martyr, who is said to have been done to death at Rome under the Emperor Claudius. There is nothing in his life to connect him with birds, and the idea that birds mate on his festival on 14 February has been held to have been a transference from the pre-Christian spring fertility festival of the Lupercalia, which the Romans observed on 15 February.

On 14 February, 1613, the St Valentine's Day of that year, the English Princess Elizabeth married the Prince Palatine, 'her train supported by twelve young ladies in white garments, so adorned with jewels, that her passage looked like a Milky Way'. John Donne wrote them a marriage poem, which began:

> Hail, Bishop Valentine, whose day this is,
>    All the air is thy diocese,
>    And all the chirping choristers
> And other birds are thy parishioners;
>        Thou marriest every year
> The lyric Lark, and the grave whispering Dove,
> The sparrow that neglects his life for love,
> The household bird with the red stomacher;
>        Thou mak'st the Blackbird speed as soon
> As doth the Goldfinch, or the Halcyon;
> The husband cock looks out, and straight is sped,
> And meets his wife, which brings her feather-bed.
> This day more cheerfully than ever shine,
> This day, which might enflame thyself, Old Valentine.

# Beasts, Insects and Others

Our common wild countryside beasts are not a very remarkable crew, it has to be admitted. In an island of farms, fields and villages there is no room for wild animals which are big, dangerous, and too destructive.

## BROWN BEARS

seem to have been wiped out before the English came to England – perhaps in the Roman centuries.

## BEAVERS

must still have been building cots or lodges at Bevercotes, on the river Maun, in Nottinghamshire, when the English settled there; and there were plenty more beaver streams, so place-names reveal, up and down the country from Yorkshire to Wiltshire. Beaver skeletons come to light in the fens, but all the beavers of England and Wales seem to

have been extinguished by the twelfth century, all the Scottish beavers
by the sixteenth century (see also page 115).

# WOLVES

There exist plenty of wolf place-names, in woodland districts. January used to be called the *wulfsmonath*, the wolf's month, since by that
time the wolves in English forests were getting hungry, and ready to
attack and scrounge. But the forests were cleared, and the wolves –
wolf, wolfen or she-wolf, and wolfling or cub – soon trapped and
killed. Traditionally the last English wolf was killed in Cheshire; this
would have been somewhere between 1485 and 1509. The howling of
the wolf was last heard in Scotland – in the Cairngorms – in the eighteenth century, and Scotland's last wolf seems to have been killed on the
Findhorn, in Inverness-shire, in 1743. Ireland's last wolf was killed
either in 1770, in the Knockmealdown Mountains, between Tipperary
and Waterford, or else in or about 1786, in Co. Carlow. An old Irish
poem about the Knockmealdown Mountains, written more than a
thousand years ago, runs:

> Slieve Gua, craggy and black wolf-den,
> In its clefts, wind wails;
> In its denes, wolves howl;
> Autumn on Slieve Gua,
> And the angry brown deer bells,
> And herons croak across
> Slieve Gua's crags.

– thus associating two ancient inseparables, wolf and red deer, which
were the wolf's chief prey (the deer are brown in the poem, but then
the red deer changes its coat to brown or grey in winter).

No doubt there is a strain of these extinct British wolves in the dogs
of Great Britain.

# WILD BOARS

were hunted by kings: they did great damage, they were dangerous,
but as the quarry of king and court and noblemen, they were allowed
to remain in English woodlands till the seventeenth century. The
ancient word for wild boar was *eofor*, and a number of places have
names combining boar with forest or forest features – such as Ewe-
hurst in Kent, or Eversley in Hampshire.

# WILD DEER

Not counting beasts of the sea and foxes, badgers and otters, deer are now our only sizeable wild beasts, and they too would not have lasted, if it had not been for hunting sentiment and tradition, and the picturesque socially distinctive persistence of deer parks (page 81). Unsuspected by most of us, several kinds of deer are now quite abundant in wild conditions, especially through the once forested Midlands.

Red Deer (Plate 21) and Roe Deer (Plate 21) are the two native kinds. Fallow Deer are possibly native, and at any rate have been here since the Roman era. The more recently introduced kinds, now wild in several counties, are Sika Deer from Manchuria and Japan, and Muntjacs, or Barking Deer, from India and China, and (though less abundant) Chinese Water Deer.

They do not flaunt themselves. But if you are intrigued, buy the *Field Guide to British Deer* edited by F. J. Taylor Page, for the Mammal Society of the British Isles (new edition, 1959). This tells you the clues, the tracks, droppings, voice, look, gait, habits, everything; as well as the whereabouts and the known distribution, county by county. Moreover this guide illustrates the different antlers of the male, at all stages – the branched but 'palmated' or flattened antlers of the Fallow Deer (Plate 23), the branched but unflattened antlers of the Red Deer and Sika Deer, the much shorter spiky branched antlers of the little Muntjac and the little Roe Deer. If you do not see the deer, you may at least pick up some of the shed antlers (the Chinese Water Deer, small as the Muntjac, has no antlers, and occurs, according to the *Guide*, only in Buckinghamshire, Bedfordshire and Hampshire).

# BADGERS, FOXES, OTTERS

The trouble about deer is to see them; which is equally the trouble about badgers and about the fox and the otter of rivers and riverbanks. Foxes most of us know only as the subject of hunting controversy, though we may glimpse a fox now and then streaking away from hounds or caught for a second in headlights loping along on its toes, bush held up in the air, a dog which we suddenly realize is not a dog, after all.

Here then follows a note on *seeing* badgers, foxes, and otters, by the greatest authority on badger life and history and an inveterate mammal watcher, Dr Ernest Neal:

Many mammals have some kind of refuge which they use for sleeping or breeding, and around it an area, the home ground, in which they feed. This home ground varies in extent according to the size and habits of the species. A wood mouse, for example, might use only a small corner of a copse, while a fox would have several square miles of countryside. The key to successful watching is to discover first of all a refuge which is being regularly used.

Badgers may be watched more easily than most nocturnal mammals, not only because they are widely distributed in the British Isles and in places are quite common, but because their refuges or setts are easy to find. A badger sett may be very extensive, a vast labyrinth of tunnels and chambers with many entrances scattered over a wide area, or it may be quite small with one or two entrances only. Much depends upon the type of soil and the ease of digging.

Setts are most usually found in woods or copses, especially where these are bounded by pasture, but you may come across them in hedge-rows or in quarries, on sea cliffs, on open moorland and even on rocky mountain sides. At the mouth of each entrance is a large pile of earth, in which vegetation such as bracken, leaves, hay or moss is incor-porated. This is the old bedding which has been discharged with the soil when the badgers have been digging. The tunnels are at least twice the diameter of a rabbit's, though the actual entrance may be much bigger than this, owing to continual usage.

Proof that it is a badger sett can usually be obtained by breaking up some of the lumps of earth from the heap outside the entrance; badger hairs can easily be discovered in this way. The hairs are straight and wiry, and are light at the two ends with a darker band between, nearer to the tip.

You can sometimes find badger hairs caught in the lowest strand of barbed wire round the edge of a wood where an obvious animal run comes out into the field. By following these paths back into the wood it will not be long before you find the sett.

For watching I much prefer a sett with only a few entrances. Your chances of seeing a badger are then so much greater. It is wise to make sure beforehand if the sett is occupied, since badgers move from one sett to another periodically. There are various indications of present occupation. Fresh bedding dropped near the entrance is a good sign; also the presence of flies going in and out of the entrance. Fresh dung in shallow pits near the sett is useful confirmation. A cobweb over the entrance usually indicates that the badgers are not at home.

To make quite sure which holes should be watched, place a stick vertically across each one the night before. A badger is sure to knock it over. Having found out which holes are being used, the next thing to do is to decide on the best vantage point, largely determined by the way of the wind and the amount of cover. A badger's sense of smell is very acute and it is essential to watch down wind from the sett. As local air currents are often very different from those observed by watching cloud movements, it is worth striking a match to see which way the smoke drifts.

Watching from a comfortable position in a tree is best. The badgers in their wanderings are then less likely to discover you, and if any scent does blow their way it may go over their heads. If there is no suitable tree, then sit on the ground with your back to a bush or tree trunk, choosing a place not too near to a well-worn badger run. Twenty or thirty feet away from the sett is a useful distance for watching, though with experience you can get much nearer.

Badgers may be watched at any time of the year, but it is often more interesting and pleasant to go in May or June when the cubs are about. The time of emergence varies with the season. In winter it is unpredictable, so it often means a long wait before you see one, and when a badger does come out, as often as not it will go straight off and not return for several hours. In early spring and in autumn badgers emerge more regularly, usually soon after dark, but from May to August they often come out in good light, even before sunset in secluded places.

I like to take up my position at least half an hour before the expected time of emergence. It is well to approach the sett as quietly as possible and to avoid the main paths and sett entrances, so that scent does not make the badgers suspicious. Binoculars are a great help for noticing detail. I use a pair of 7 × 50's, which combines a fair magnification with excellent visibility in poor light. When it gets too dark for binoculars, I use a strong torch fitted with red glass. Badgers take no notice of red light, but the beam is quite good enough for you to see all details quite clearly. Even without the red filter a weak torch can be used without disturbing them, but you should not focus it on the badger's eyes, as this might startle it.

WATCHING FOXES. Foxes are more difficult to watch than badgers, although chance encounters may occur more frequently since foxes are more often about in daylight. The breeding season gives the watcher his best opportunities. At that time both dog and vixen may be seen near the earth. Fox earths will be found in much the same places as badger setts, and in fact unoccupied badger setts are often used by foxes both as temporary refuges and as breeding earths. Also it is not uncommon to find badgers and foxes living together in the same sett. When this happens they use different entrances as a rule and live in separate portions of the underground system.

When making an earth, a fox often enlarges a system of rabbit holes. This is usually so when hedgerows are chosen. Unlike the badger the fox does not use bedding in its earth, so the excavated soil outside the entrance will contain no vegetation. I find I can tell an occupied earth very easily by putting my face level with the entrance and sniffing gently. The rank scent of fox is unmistakeable.

When a litter of fox cubs is present, the soil outside the earth is often flattened and bereft of all vegetation owing to the constant activity of the cubs. The remains of a rabbit or a few feathers scattered untidily about are good indications that cubs are there.

Adult foxes are most often seen in late evening and early morning; and early morning is by far the best time for watching them. To get near an adult fox is not at all easy. Foxes differ from badgers in having very good eyesight. So binoculars are even more useful and necessary. The fox's senses of smell and hearing are also acute. You must therefore take up a position down wind and keep as quiet as possible. Choose a spot where there is enough cover, get there as soon after dawn as possible, and if all goes well, you should have a good chance of seeing both dog and vixen return to the earth, and the cubs playing together before retiring below ground.

Fox cubs are much easier to watch than the adults. In isolated places I have known them show no fear when I have been within a few yards of them, but if the vixen once warns them and they associate your presence with danger they become much more difficult to approach.

Cubs may come out regularly at midday in woodland districts, but evening and early morning are undoubtedly the best times for watching. They tend to come out earlier in the evening than badger cubs.

WATCHING OTTERS. Planned otter watching is extremely difficult and needs much patience. This is due to a number of factors, one of which is the difficulty of finding a holt. Otter holts are often invisible from above, since otters often choose a den under the roots of a tree growing half in the stream, and they may enter it from under water. To make things more difficult, otters have no fixed breeding season, and can have their young during any month of the year. Outside the breeding time otters are also great travellers, seldom spending a long time in any one district.

Rivers, lakes and reservoirs are often visited periodically, and you need to be constantly on the alert for otter signs to know when they are about. Fresh tracks on the mud or sand may easily be recognized by the five toes (although the fifth toe does not always show up clearly). A good print also reveals the webbing between the toes. The presence of fish scales on the bank or on an island will show where otters have been feeding, and their sprainting places on boulders, old tree trunks near the water, or on gravel banks can be observed. Fresh spraints (spraints – a plural noun, is the huntsman's term for otter dung; from the French *espraintes* – 'out-pressings') are black and mucilaginous, but as they dry they become grey and powdery.

When these signs of recent activity are discovered, the place should be watched without delay, because the otter is likely to be about only for a few days. If you are lucky enough to find a breeding area, your chances of seeing otters are increased very greatly, and you should have a much longer time for observing them.

Otters may be seen at any time of the day or night, but they are far more active after dark. Fishermen see them most often in the late evening, and a quiet, unhurried approach to a likely stretch of river may occasionally be rewarded. Islands on lakes where food is plentiful are good places to watch, since otters often choose them for sleeping.

During night watches otters are usually heard more than they are seen. Their flute-like whistles are unmistakeable. A strong torch with a red filter may be used with success, but it is usually best to choose a moonlight night.

Of these three animals, start with badgers: they are more predictable, they can be watched from closer range. It is very thrilling in a wood as the daylight fades, to catch your first glimpse of that black and white head at the entrance to the sett. Everything else is forgotten in the intensity of the moment. And when the badgers have finished their play and gone off to their feeding grounds, a sense of wonder and very deep satisfaction accompany you on your homeward journey in the dark.

# THE BADGER

(From an Old English Riddle, in the Exeter Book)

> White is my neck, head yellow, sides
> The same. Weapons I wear, am hurried, and along
> My back as on my cheek stand hairs; two ears

Above my eyes, through the green grass
On claws I go. If in my home fierce fighter
Finds me where my children live, sorrow's
My lot, this stranger bringing doom of dying
To my door. Brave must I be then, must
Bear off my dear ones:
Here awaiting his fierceness
(On his breast crawling closer) –
That would be senseless, I
Would not dare it. But working with forefeet
A way through the steep hill, with ease I shall lead out
My dears through the down
By a tunnel in secret. I shall not fear then
A fight with the death dog, and if close behind me
He follows a pathway up on the hill top,
I shall turn, and attack, and shall viciously spear
This creature I hate
Who has harried me there.

This was written more than a thousand years ago, when the badger
was well known to our ancestors, between the green meadows and the
hill. Beginning not with black and white, but white and yellow, is both
misleading (or riddling) and true, since the badger's coarse hair has
often a yellowish tinge.

## SMALLER BEASTS

HARE and RABBIT. To distinguish, both are white-tailed, but the
hare is larger, taller, longer, with longer ears (which have black tips),
a more gaunt animal with a less rounded look. Its hindquarters, as it
jumps off fast or slow, lift up more than a rabbit's, on longer hind legs.

No one can help seeing these two, though rabbits have been greatly
reduced since 1954, when myxomatosis ran through the rabbit population. Their different history explains their quite different reputation,
or quite different popular image. Hares are indigenous, rabbits are not.
Hares have been lolloping over Britain time out of mind, rabbits were
introduced late in the twelfth century, to eke out supplies of meat.
Lords of the Manor kept rabbit warrens just as they kept dovecots, and
protected them as jealously: in the Middle Ages they called the rabbit
a coni or coning, having borrowed the word from the French ('rabbit'
we borrowed later from the Dutch), and the warren a coning-erth or

a coninger, two words which survive in place-names. So the rabbit began with us as a coddled creature. Rounded and endearing in look, we have sentimentalized him (cheerfully killing him and eating him at the same time), and turned him into woolly toys for our children, no matter how much damage the rabbit has done since he spread from his ancient warrens.

By contrast the hare is an odd, solitary animal: he goes 'mad' in March, in the rutting season (which actually lasts from early winter to mid-April), jumping, side-leaping, kicking, fighting. Men believed that the hare actually went mad: he was the most 'melancholy' of creatures, possessed not by sex but the devil, dangerous to encounter, since the hare might be the devil's servant temporarily transformed, a changeling escaped from its human home, a fairy which had stolen a dead child from a coffin, a witch who had been stealing milk (in proof of this, a wounded hare screams like a human being) – a creature of power, which appeared to pregnant women and gave hare-lips to children (if you are pregnant and meet a hare, the proper safeguard is to stoop at once and tear your petticoat).

The distrust of the hare continues, though the long tradition of per-secuting and hunting this 'evil' beast was first challenged in the eighteenth and early nineteenth century, when poets and humane people began to see it as a creature timid, wild and joyful instead of melancholic and formidable – Wordsworth, for instance:

> All things that love the sun are out of doors;
> The sky rejoices in the morning's birth;
> The grass is bright with rain-drops; – on the moors
> The hare is running races in her mirth;
> And with her feet she from the plashy earth
> Raises a mist; that, glittering in the sun,
> Runs with her all the way, wherever she doth run.
>
> *Resolution and Independence*, 1807

WEASEL and STOAT. No doubt we should also think well of these two creatures, which is not so easy. Showing themselves streaking across a road or a path or along a ditch, they are both common, they are always in a hurry, and usually on the blood hunt. But if you frighten a stoat off its kill, and then keep quiet and motionless, its desire quickly overcomes its caution, and it will reappear, and reconnect.

Size is one distinction between the two. The stoat is larger, not so low on the ground, has a longer tail, and *the tail is black-ended* (Plate

18). A weasel surprises one by its miniature size: it seems impossible that something so slight can exist – and kill – so emphatically and energetically.

If you see such a sinuous brown creature in Ireland, it will be a stoat, not a weasel, weasels not having crossed the Irish Sea. There is an Irish story that a man threw a stone at a stoat, and then went ploughing a small field enclosed between stone walls. He heard a rustling: stoats' eyes and narrow heads by the hundred looked out at him from between the stones, all round the field. In fact, stoats do occasionally hunt in packs. Also stoats (but not in Ireland, or usually not in southern England) change colour in winter, or at any rate the brown decreases and the white increases. Winter stoats in the north may be white all over, except always for the end of the tail. Such a stoat is then, strictly, an ermine, its fur and tail symbolic of justice and purity, and fit for the robes of peers of the realm and judges – though the judges, one may hope, will not be quite as savage and bloodthirsty.

HEDGEHOG. Not everyone with a garden realizes that hedgehogs are garden-haunters provided that there exists some tangled cover for them, or some old hedges into which they can retreat. They find lawns a good worm-ground, a good hunting-field, and as a token of their nocturnal presence will leave black droppings here and there. Thomas Hardy thought of dying when the hedgehog was out –

> If I pass during some nocturnal blackness, mothy and warm,
>    When the hedgehog travels furtively over the lawn.
> *Afterwards*

Gilbert White in the seventeen-sixties analysed the droppings hedgehogs made on his lawns at Selborne: 'It appears, by the dung they drop upon the turf, that beetles are no inconsiderable part of their food.' Beetles and worms and slugs are favourite food; but hedgehogs can be made, or enticed into being, associates – to use a pleasanter

word than 'pet' – particularly with the regular aid of bread and milk, or milk alone, on a saucer not too large or deep to hinder the investigation of its contents. Be warned that if they are keen-eared, they are also short-sighted. A confident hedgehog familiarized to human contact will not be vicious at all, but it may mistake a finger or thumb in front of its twitching snout for something fat and edible.

FIELD MICE, VOLES, SHREWS are smaller fry which need not detain us. The Long-tailed Field Mouse, which is the hunting cat's outdoor substitute for the House Mouse lacking in a well-conducted home, is properly mouse-like, long-eared, as well as long-tailed, rather larger than the House Mouse. The Harvest Mouse, nearly half as small as the Field Mouse and much smaller than the House Mouse, is reddish-

brown on its back and head, a bundly little object, without such prominent ears, which curls its tail around bents or wheat stalks, and may live in stacks in winter as well as in nests built around

216

wheat-stalks, in the summer. The Dormouse is less mousy, nearer in size (but not at all near in shape) to the House Mouse, but tawny yellow in fur, with a tail shortly and thickly muffled in hair of the same colour; a creature of low shrubs, as if a miniature squirrel of low life, or low altitude.

Voles, including the vegetarian, altogether harmless Water Rat, which everyone sees swimming to cover or plopping under water if the danger seems too close, are characteristically blunt about the muzzle, with rather low-set ears.

Shrews, including the Water Shrew, which enjoys the royal distinction of being eaten by kingfishers, are characterized beyond error by their pinched elongated little snouts.

MOLES – a destructive note for gardeners. If you have them in the garden and fear their advance towards the lawn, and have to trap them, remember that setting a trap across a surface run with a crumbly roof, among mole hills, will catch nothing. You need to detect the highway of the time, from home bank or mound or hedge to the feeding range. This may be betrayed by a faint ridge of broken surface or an occasional very miniature molehill. When you open it up, it will be smoothed by the passage of the mole's compact barrel of fur. Mole-trappers sometimes kill a dozen moles, one after another, in such a run. The trap needs setting so that the ring is just clear of the floor of the run, and so that nothing impedes either the snapping of the jaws or the spread of the handles. It needs to be well covered with sods and earth so that no light or draught get into the run. Moles are in fact easy to trap. If you intend to save the skins (which draw off easily so long as the feet are snipped off), note that the summer skins, marked more or less black on the inside, are thin and useless compared with the thick 'winter clears'. A skin needs to be tacked and stretched into a rectangle, fur down, against a board, and then dried simply by air, without the use of alum, etc.

SQUIRRELS. Untidy mops of sticks and twigs high up on the branches of a tree, winter or summer, unconcealed and obvious are the dreys or nests of the squirrel, either introduced Grey Squirrel, or native Red Squirrel. The case against the Grey Squirrel is in some degree emotional and unreasonable. Naturalists hold that the decrease of Red Squirrels (less general than it is supposed to be) is not due to competition with the more aggressive Grey Squirrel from North America, but may have been caused by disease. It is true that the flash of colour of a Red Squirrel is delightful to see, that grey is not red, that the Grey Squirrel

is a coarser animal, without ear-tufts, and without such delicate features. But it is a confiding animal, and a graceful one, if it is looked at
without the infection of prejudice.

BATS disturb equanimity – at least when they fly into a room at night
and go criss-cross and to and fro over the bed, as they do in the Yorkshire ballad of *The Dree Night*, in which the wicked man lies dying:

> No doves have settled on his sill, but a flittermouse to greet
> Came thrice times through the casement and flackered
> round his feet.

They do not entangle themselves in women's hair, though most women
inherit and hold this ancient belief. Add to this invasion of our sleep
that bats do not smell very pleasant, that their roosts are extra smelly,
and that they are not beauties when at rest – and the catalogue against
them finishes.

Like hedgehogs on the lawn and the Spotted Flycatcher on the pole
of a tennis net, bats – or at any rate Pipistrelle and Whiskered Bat –
speak for garden gentleness and pleasure. A Pipistrelle out over the
lawn on a mild evening early in April (they are seldom about before
the last week or so of March) is as much a spring symbol, into the
bargain, as Chiffchaff, Cuckoo, or Dove, or an emergent Brimstone
Butterfly. For one thing it means that the evening temperature is 40
degrees or more (but note that Pipistrelle and Whiskered Bat will fly
in the weak daylight of a mild winter day).

All of our kinds cannot be easily distinguished on the wing. Pipistrelle
and Whiskered Bats are the small ones. The Pipistrelle (the name
comes from the Italian, meaning little piper, little squeaker: keen ears
detect its squeaking on the wing) spans about eight inches from wing-
tip to wing-tip (i.e. if you are a man and stretch your hand to its full
extent, the span from the tip of your thumb to the tip of your little
finger): it beats to and fro overhead, a true 'flittermouse', flittering or
fluttering as it flies, a gnat eater. The Whiskered Bat (greyish on the
under side of the body, where the Pipistrelle is brown) has about the
same wing span, but is rather less of a zigzagger, is rather more slow
and deliberate, in its pursuit of beetles and moths.

Fishermen who fish the evening rise or fish at night for sea-trout,
and those who have the habit of walking or meditating by still rivers
below woods, will have observed bats flying or skimming over the
water, which they occasionally touch and dimple. These will be Water
Bats, a species more correctly burdened with the title of Daubenton's

Bat (after a French eighteenth-century naturalist), a little bigger than its near relative the Whiskered Bat, or than the Pipistrelle, with two inches more of wing span.

Large bats are the Noctule (England from Yorkshire southward), the Serotine (a few southern counties), wings spanning fourteen to fifteen inches, and a little less large, the Greater Horseshoe Bat (the horseshoe is the horseshoe-shaped extension of skin round the nostrils), found in the south-west. The Noctule flies high and quick, and only for a very brief period just before and after sunset (or before sunrise). The Serotine flies more lumpily, flutters, and often drops from high to low. The Greater Horseshoe may fly low, but is more of an aeronaut, more elegant and lighter on wings which are blunt-ended, or rounded, instead of pointed, a flutterer. These three are scrunchers of beetles and moths.

The most entrancing bat flights to observe are those of two leafage kinds. Natterer's Bat (eleven-inch span) flies away up, and rather deliberately, around trees, and will hover as it takes a moth off the leaves. The Long-eared Bat (very long-eared, with donkey's ears the length of its body, with a ten-inch wing span, and very common) flies low and quick from one tree to the next, then rises and circles the tree, not unlike a slow Humming-bird Hawk Moth, hovering, sliding on, and hovering again to pick off its food. (Plates 10 and 13.)

(Bats are described in a Field Study Book, *British Bats*, by Brian Vesey-Fitzgerald, published in 1949.)

# SEA BEASTS

> And Proteus . . . does drive his heard
> Of stinking seals and porcpisces together
> With hoary head and dewy drooping beard.
> Edmund Spenser (*Colin Clouts Come Home Againe*)

Seals, porpoises, and dolphins are the sea beasts – the sea mammals – we are most likely to encounter.

SEALS, two kinds, Grey Seal and Common Seal. The names do not help: Grey Seals are not always grey, Common Seals are not so common. Grey Seals like rough, sharp, rocky Atlantic coast with plenty of swell and rise and fall and weed, Common Seals have a liking for sandbanks and low tide rocks and estuaries and shelter.

Grey Seals are the ones you are likely to see off Cornwall or Pembrokeshire, and round the Atlantic edges of Ireland. Both Grey Seals and Common Seals live up the west coasts of Scotland, and out on the Shetlands and Orkneys. On the east coast Common Seals live around the Wash (and Grey Seals on the Farne Islands). On the west coast Common Seals frequent the Severn Sea and the twin estuaries of the Mersey and the Dee, though western Scotland is their special haunt and headquarters.

Common Seals are smaller, Grey Seals larger. Common Seals are neater, as well as shorter and smaller, Grey Seals are coarser – according to age and condition. Sideways on, adult Grey Seals have a hooked profile, gently curving outward and then down, between forehead and nose, whereas the profile of the Common Seal is indented: it curves inward, making a rounded angle.

Colour does not help very much. It varies. Common Seals are greyer as a rule than Grey Seals, the black splodges are smaller and more numerous, and mark the head as well as the body. Grey Seals are usually capped with grey on the head – 'with hoary head and dewy drooping beard' (the whiskers droop like a beard). The dark splodges on a Grey Seal often run together. When an old dog seal, for example, emerges from the water and looks benignly and inquisitively around, sleek and wet, it may appear black. Lolling on a rock, dry and warm in the sun, it would show itself brown or more obviously dappled with dark splodges.

Like man, seals have one pup at a birth, and since their shape and size (a length of seven to nine feet for a male, five to six feet for a female, of the Grey species; four and a half to six feet and three and a half to five feet for the males and females of the Common Seal) allow us to think of seal and man interchanging, there are plenty of stories of seals fathering human children (as in the famous ballad of *The Great Silkie of Sule Skerry*:

> I am a man upo the lan,
> An I am a silkie in the sea,
> And when I'm far and far frae lan,
> My dwelling is in Sule Skerry

in which the Grey Seal came to take his little son from his Shetland wife and teach him to swim the foam), of seal wives, of seals embodying humans who had drowned themselves or the souls of all who were drowned in the Flood, all the sinful people there was no room for in the Ark.

They are often sad stories, which has to do also with the sad wail or moan or keening of Grey Seal or Common Seal as it lies basking, a

sound which suggests loss of child and wife, or child and husband. As
the Great Silkie complains to his son's mother:

> An thu sall marry a proud gunner,
>     An a proud gunner I'm sure he'll be,
> An the very first schot that ere he schoots
>     He'll schoot baith my young son and me.

There were seal-wives in the Aegean: 'Eudemos says that a seal fell
in love with a man who used to dive for sponges. It would come out of
the sea and consort with him in a rocky cave. He was uglier than any
of his fellow divers, but not to the seal, who thought him extremely
handsome.' Aelian (*c.* 200).

PORPOISES and DOLPHINS are mammals no less than seals or whales,
air breathers, warm-blooded, suckling their young, sea-adapted into
fish shape. Whales, in fact, they are – in miniature, belonging to the
group of Toothed Whales. They used to be killed for their flesh, which
may explain why dolphin bones were found in a prehistorically
inhabited cave – Thor's Fissure – in North Staffordshire. Dolphins,
if you care to try, are said to be better eating than porpoises – 'the
flesh more red and well cooked of a very good taste to most palates,
and exceedeth that of porpose' (Sir Thomas Browne).

Porpoises are commoner, rolling and curving through summer seas
(they are more abundant in summer), not very big, generally four to
five feet long, black above, white below, a fin projecting from their
backs which is more or less of a triangle. The Porpoise is dumpy, a
*porcum piscem*, pig of the sea (in German a *Meer-schwein*, in French a
*marsouin*; in English also a sea hog). Rather more fish-headed or whale-
headed than a Dolphin, the Porpoise does not have a beak; which is
the distinction of the Common Dolphin, whose head extends into a

long six-inched beak (see dolphins on any mosaic pavement from a Roman villa). No one ever rode Sea Hog, Sea Pig, or Porpoise, whereas dolphins in the blue Aegean and blue Mediterranean were ridden by sea-nymphs, and were of the company of Poseidon the sea god, who sent the Dolphin to intercede for him in his courtship of Amphitrite – 'as being a fish the most active, the most endued with ingenuity and knowledge, the greatest lover of mankind, and that makes his approach to the sun upon the surface of the waters, whereas the others are stupid, lie at the bottom of the waters, and have little more to boast of than mere motion'. As a reward Poseidon elevated the Dolphin into that hump-backed group of faint stars, which is called Delphinus and shines in the summer sky near Altair (page 131) – though his presence there is also attributed to the kind way in which the Dolphin saved the great poet and musician Arion from drowning.

In addition to a beak, the Dolphin has a different back fin, not the Sea Hog's triangle, but a fin curving back to a point, like a rose thorn. The Dolphin is upwards of seven to eight feet long, in contrast to the Sea Hog's four or five feet. He is also dark above, white below, though the dark and the white are divided along the sides by lengths of yellow, white and grey. August and September are marked dolphin months: they come either side of the Isles of Scilly and Land's End, into the English Channel and into the sea space between Wales and Ireland. (Other dolphins occur in our waters, especially of three kinds, all shorter beaked but larger creatures – the White-Sided Dolphin around the Orkneys and the Shetlands, the White-Beaked Dolphin in the North Sea, and the Bottle-Nosed Dolphin along the Channel and between Wales and Ireland and just into the North Sea – see the illustrations in *Giant Fishes, Whales and Dolphins* by J. R. Norman and F. C. Fraser, 1948.) With luck one may see a school of Common Dolphins at play in calm water.

> What pleasing wonders charm the sailor's sight
> When calms the Dolphins to their sports invite!
> As jovial swains in tuneful measure tread,
> And leave their rounding pressures on the mead,
> So they in circling dance, with wanton ease
> Pursue each other round the furrow'd seas,
> With rapid force the curling streams divide,
> Add to the waves, and rive the slow-pac'd tide.
> > Diaper's translation of Oppian.

In the Isles of Scilly I have watched a school of dolphins in a high water bay racing, diving, thudding, jumping and slapping back on to the water; and I have watched them, shapes in the green water over sand, wreathing under my boat.

Stranded, decaying or decayed dolphins and porpoises, or their skulls, among the sea wrack, are easily distinguished (a pamphlet worth having is F. C. Fraser and H. W. Parker's *Guide for the Identification of Stranded Whales, Dolphins, Porpoises and Turtles on the British Coasts* published by the British Museum, Natural History). In his shorter mouth the Porpoise has two rows, top and bottom, of spade-shaped teeth, usually twenty-three on each side, which may be very much worn down, but are always quite different from the little curved, pointed teeth, forty or more on each side, which make long saws of the Dolphin's beak.

## SKULLS

If skulls do not morbidly afflict you, an animal's skull, whether dolphin's or porpoise's, fox's, badger's, stoat's, or mole's, is worth bringing home to identify; which can usually be done with the drawings and details of tooth arrangement given in a very necessary small book, Edmund Sandars' *Beast Book for the Pocket* (a book which includes Man, and the various breeds of farm animal), or with the dolphin and porpoise guide mentioned above, or with the help of T. C. S. Morrison-Scott's *List of British Mammals*, another Natural History Museum pamphlet, or with I. W. Cornwall's *Bones for the Archaeologist*. Skulls in Plate 23 show the long, sharp, interlocking canines of fox and badger skulls, for fighting, slashing, holding, killing, and the cheek-teeth of a roe deer, which wear to a grinding surface for chewing the balls of cud formed from leaves and grass and so on.

Skulls, though, weather-cleaned and dry, and shaken clear of earwigs, are structured objects of great attraction in their own right. Try setting a skull, or skulls, against an unshiny black surface.

## SNAKE AND TOAD

Some snakes are venomous, and on that account all snakes, harmful (like the Adder) or harmless, were identified with the devil. This prejudice remains. Adders, Grass Snakes, Smooth Snakes and Slow-worms or Blindworms (which are not snakes, but legless lizards) are killed without distinction. Perhaps they all bite? Anyhow they are all nasty – and down comes the stick. This is an attitude well described by Richard Jefferies in his *Wild Life in a Southern County*, in a chapter about the harmless Grass Snake.

Appreciating snakes is therefore a problem of discounting prejudice and recognizing one snake from another. Snakes are local. In your district there may be Adders, and no Grass Snakes or Slow-worms, or there may be no Adders at all and an abundance of Grass Snakes and Slow-worms. That is a first fact to ascertain, after which there are easy enough distinctions to remember and apply. Size is one of them.

ADDERS are not very long, generally short of two feet, seldom more than two feet and a few inches. A long snake three feet, three and a half feet, or four feet, is not an Adder, but a Grass Snake or Ring Neck. Certainty is made surer if you remember that Grass Snakes do have a yellow collar, a yellow 'Ring Neck', either more or less of a band of yellow against black behind their heads. The worst that a long, extremely snakish, yellow-collared Grass Snake can do to you is eject a fluid with a bad smell, and make gestures of attack. Also it is a *grass* snake, liking grassy verges and ditches and banks, and taking readily to water.

SMOOTH SNAKES – very local, on sandy heaths in a few southern counties – are more or less of adder length, demanding another look. Slow-worms are of shorter average length than Smooth Snake or Adder, anything up to sixteen or seventeen inches.

A snake of the order of eighteen inches to two feet, *with a dark zigzag down its back*, and no yellow collar, is – and no mistake – an Adder. The zigzag will not always be obvious or complete, and may be reduced to spots or splodges. There are spots or splodges along the back of the Grass Snake and the Smooth Snake, but never a zigzag. A Slow-worm bears neither zigzag nor splodges, though females (as well as young) may have a dark line down their backs.

Colour is a poor guide. Grass Snakes are frequently, but not invariably, a shade of green, Adders are frequently a shade of brown, Smooth Snakes a shade of brownish-yellow, Slow-worms a silvery brown. But colour varies too much to be trusted. Textures are different. Smooth Snakes are *smooth* and shiny compared with Adder or Grass Snake. Slow-worms do not have the larger coarser scaling of the snakes, exhibiting a high gloss on their silvery brown, as if they had used a new silicon furniture polish.

In the British Isles there are no other snakes, or slow-worms; and neither Adder, Grass Snake, Smooth Snake nor Slow-worm is found in Ireland, for which Irishmen thank that noble Briton, St Patrick.

Herpetological snobs (who can be forgiven for this particular snobbery) say there are few things so beautiful as the colours on the belly of a *live* adder – these colours disappearing the moment the adder is killed.

TOADS or PADDOCKS still suffer, like snakes, from inherited and very ancient prejudice, as another devil's creature, about at dusk and through the night. No one believes any more that toads are venomous or that they guard inside their heads a jewel which is an antidote to venom, but the legend has bequeathed so much distaste and even fear that many people will neither pick a toad up nor even touch it. And 'toad' is still – and perhaps always will be – a term of abuse.

As a matter of fact, toads – both our kinds, Common Toad and Natterjack – are venomous, slightly. Their warts supply a poison which makes them distasteful to most animals. Possibly a decoction of several toads would have an unpleasant effect. Aelian (*c.* 200) wrote of instant death from drinking wine mixed with toad's blood.

Otherwise a solitary toad is pleasant to know, agreeably coloured and textured (Plate 20), not at all unpleasant to handle, cold, since toads are cold-blooded (Herrick wrote of a child heaving up his either hand, 'Cold as paddocks though they be'), but not slimy. Moreover a toad resident in a toad hole in the garden will accustom itself to human beings, if they take the trouble.

> I have been informed also, from undoubted authority, that some ladies (ladies you will say of peculiar taste) took a fancy to a toad, which they nourished summer after summer, for many years, till he grew to a monstrous size, with the maggots which turn to flesh flies. The reptile used to come forth every evening from an hole under the garden-steps; and was taken up, after supper, on the table to be fed. But at last a tame raven, kenning him as he put forth his head, gave him such a severe stroke with his horny beak as put out one eye. After this accident the creature languished for some time and died.
>
> Gilbert White

The NATTERJACK is less common (since it likes a sandy territory) It runs instead of hopping, and can be recognized by the yellow stripe down the middle of its back – and also by a loud croaking at night, which comes from the male Natterjack in late spring and early summer, which is the mating season. The name appears to mean Poison Jack, though one would like to think of it as the Jack who natters or makes a noise, and one which carries a long way, in distinction to the feeble croaking which the Common Toad makes in the breeding season.

Toads – and frogs as well (which are smooth and wartless, though very variable in colour) – are water creatures only by origin and when it comes to breeding. They begin life in the water, but after their transformation from tadpoles they take to the land and are happy to live a considerable way from the nearest water, ditch or pond, returning to water only to mate and lay their eggs. The Grass Frog, our native species, does not provide the little chicken-tasting drumsticks (from the hind legs) of French cooking, which come from the vivid green Edible Frog. Attempts to naturalize the Edible Frog (which croaks in chorus during the night) have been made repeatedly. The colonies die out after a short or long while.

As for eggs and spawn, Adder, Smooth Snake and Slow-worm give birth to their young. If in the summer you find pale inch-long eggs in strings in an old grass heap or manure heap or garden rubbish heap, they will be eggs of the Grass Snake (which laid every summer in Gilbert White's melon beds), due to hatch out in six to eight weeks after laying. Toad spawn in spring is found in two parallel jelly strings several feet long, in ponds; frog spawn in jelly masses.

## LAND SNAILS

Men in Europe took to eating snails about 10,000 years ago, after the northern and Alpine glaciers and the Pyrenean glaciers had melted back, and the climate had turned warmer and damp. They have been eating them ever since (along with sea-shore molluscs), and not only in France. Bristol, for instance, is one of the English snail-eating centres.

The choice depends on size. In England the Common Snail of gardens and walls, etc., ('Wall-Fish'), is the kind most frequently eaten, since it is the only large snail easily found. In France, the first choice is the still larger snail we call the Roman Snail. With us, this snail, which carries a strong creamy-brown shell, is local (woods on the Cotswolds are one locality). It was *not* introduced by the Romans. The French also eat the Common Snail, and a few other kinds, some of which we have, and some of which we do not. The smaller Grove Snail can be eaten. It is very common among nettles, a snail whose shell varies much in colour and markings. The background may be yellow, white, pale brown, etc., the spiral bands differ in thickness and number, brown on yellow, brown on white, white on brown, etc., etc., although the shell always has a chocolate lip. This distinguishes it from the variable, rather less common, but also edible Garden Snail, of similar habitats, the shell of which has a whitish lip. (Plate 24.)

The collector cannot be sure that his snails have not been eating something harmless to them, but poisonous to man. So they should be starved for some time before they are cooked, or starved and then fattened again. The French like to keep a living supply of snails, which they feed, for example, on vine leaves. Snail-eating had its medicinal side, since in one form or another, from very ancient times, snails were taken against colds, coughs, and tuberculosis. But we have also admired, not only their flavour, with butter and parsley, but their looks, their timid horns, their peculiarity, their slow determination. Excellent snail poems and passages exist, by Clare, Bunyan, Walter de la Mare, and others. John Clare loved to

> . . . note on hedgerow baulks, in moisture sprent,
>     The jetty snail creep from the mossy thorn,
> With earnest heed and tremulous intent,
>     Frail brother of the morn,
> That from the tiny bents and misted leaves
>     Withdraws his timid horn,
>     And fearful vision weaves.

Slugs are nobody's friends. Nobody eats them, nobody admires them. As a test of pure sensibility, try to convince yourself of an undoubtedly true fact, that slugs – whether the Great Slug (greyish-yellow, up to six inches long), or the smaller Yellow Slug, or the long Black Slug, which is out everywhere after rain – are creatures of shapely form and exquisite markings and tones, making silver paths.

In fact slugs are more or less snails, either with a rudimentary shell (Great Slug, Yellow Slug, etc.), or no shell at all (Black Slug).

A sad note: in Victorian times London dairymen beat up snails with milk; the white frothy result they sold as cream.

# BUTTERFLIES AND MOTHS

Butterfly – a day word, which suggests a fluttering activity. Moth – a nocturnal, soft word: 'some nocturnal blackness, mothy and warm' (Thomas Hardy).

Actually flying by night is not an invariable characteristic, distinguishing moths (several thousand kinds in the British Isles) from butterflies (fifty-eight kinds). There are day moths, even if there are no night butterflies. The most easily observed distinction between moth and butterfly is one of attitude at rest, the butterfly folding its wings together vertically above its body, the moth folding them down to its back and sides. A second look shows that a moth will have more or less feathered antennae, a butterfly bare antennae, which end in a knob.

DAY MOTHS include several which frequently pass as butterflies, especially two very common kinds which are rather alike: the Cinnabar of May and June, with black fore-wings, each having a scarlet or cinnabar strip and spots, and scarlet or cinnabar hind-wings edged with black, whose yellow-barred caterpillars strip tall ragwort plants down to the rib, and the Six-Spot Burnet (i.e. brunette, or dark one) lounging about on flower-heads in June and July, looking at a glance black and crimson, though in fact the fore-wings are a dark blue-green spotted with crimson. The hind-wings are entirely crimson. (Plate 48.)

HAWK-MOTHS: some of these are the remarkable day-fliers. The Humming-bird Hawk-moth, generally about from June to September (its numbers in any year depend on migration – see below) comes into gardens, and hovers over flowers, and shifts and darts and hovers again with too rapid a wing-beat to enable one to be very clear about its colours, which are not very gay (greyish-brown and ochre). The one well-defined object, as it hovers, is the long tongue thrust into flowers: it seems as if the moth were resting on this taut, rapidly thrust in, rapidly withdrawn feeding tube.

The two Bee Hawk-moths, like bumble-bees which have lost weight and taken to aerial expertise, are about from June to August. The

Broad-bordered Bee Hawk-moth, rather more common, also likes the neighbourhood of woods. Quick movement, quick beating of their wings (which are transparent), makes them difficult to observe in their detail. Of these two, the Broad-bordered Bee Hawk-moth moved the Victorian entomologist Edward Newman to one of the oddest bits of bad poetic or exclamatory prose which ever appeared in a book:

> This sphinx is a true lover of the sun; its flight is only in his rays; he who has not seen this fairy creature pendulizing over a purple patch of the common bugle – anon descending to sip, without alighting, the sweets of each corolla; he who has not watched its porrected tube dive into cup after cup, its body the while motionless, its legs shivering and its wings invisible and undefined through rapidity of motion, he who has not seen it rise again, and again pendulize, and then dart off with immeasurable speed – he who has not witnessed these things, has a delight yet to come.

Apt enough, all the same. Both these Bee Hawk-moths like honeysuckle, and Lady's Bedstraw.

Other hawk-moths, such as the Elephant Hawk, olive-green and rosy and as neat in lines as a modern aircraft, roam after nectar as the light begins to fail. The clumsier looking, seldom seen Death's Head Hawk-moth (marked with a skull pattern, a moth which likes to enter hives and steal honey) is a night flier on its wings of a five-inch span. It can be seen from July to October.

MIGRATION. That some butterflies – and moths – migrate is a fact which not everyone yet realizes. Our butterfly immigrants include the familiar Painted Lady, and the less familiar Clouded Yellow, the very familiar Red Admiral, and the two Cabbage Whites, the Large White and the Small White. The Painted Lady migrates from North Africa (I once saw, and heard, a migratory swarm of Painted Ladies, thousands upon thousands of them, rising, rustling, settling, rustling again, over an area of mountainside in central Sardinia). The Red Admiral and the more intermittently abundant Clouded Yellow migrate from the Mediterranean area. Some immigrants of these three kinds arrive early enough for native born Painted Ladies, Red Admirals and Clouded Yellows to be on the wing before the summer ends. Some of the immigrants go south again before the summer or autumn has changed to winter. Others, immigrant and native born, are killed off by the winter cold (though a few Red Admirals survive).

Large Whites and Small Whites are all-year, life-cycle residents from caterpillar to butterfly; but huge numbers immigrate as well. Large Whites ready to light on cabbages and nasturtiums, etc., and lay their eggs neatly on the underside of the leaves, come in from the east over the North Sea, late in July, and in August. Small Whites also snow-storm a way over the Channel.

Among the immigrating moths, the Humming-bird Hawk-moth hovering at your white jasmine will have migrated from the south of France.

Note that if by a lucky chance, perhaps in Cornwall, along the Channel coast, you see a slow outsize in butterflies, wings brownish-honey, with dark veins across the honey, and with the edges dark and spotted with white, it will be a Monarch (an American species), which has crossed the Atlantic, not on a regular migration route, but on a ship, from which it will have fluttered ashore.

BUTTERFLIES INDOORS, after the summer is over, a little frayed and faded, wings closed, quiescent (but sometimes waking and fluttering around), will belong to one or other of a few species which get through the winter as developed insects and not as eggs or larvae. They like undisturbed corners by a pelmet, above a door, on a picture rail, etc. As well as a few Red Admirals, Large Tortoiseshells are found hiber-nating indoors in this way (and are sometimes confused with the much more brilliant Red Admiral). Small Tortoiseshells and Peacocks also hibernate, but generally out of doors in hollow trees. Brimstones hibernate among evergreens, which explains their early appearance on warm days in April, March, or even February, before there is a flower about.

Why 'RED ADMIRAL'? Books say because the eighteenth-century name was the Admirable or Red Admirable (in distinction to the White Admirable, or White Admiral). It is an *admirable* insect, but though the name may have begun that way, the change from 'Red Admirable' to 'Red Admiral' has a possible explanation in the Admiral of the Red, i.e. the Admiral of the Red Squadron, who flew red colours, in the old organization of the Navy.

Why a 'BUTTERFLY'? If you look into the matter, 'butterfly' itself is by origin one of the less pleasant words. It means precisely a butter fly, i.e., according to Skeat, a fly which excretes butter (in Dutch a butterfly is a *boter-schijte*). Possibly the insect originally called 'butter-fly' was the Cabbage White, large or small, or else its caterpillar, men having noticed (a) that the presence of Cabbage Whites on cabbage

230

leaves was soon followed by caterpillars, (b) that these destroying caterpillars deposited a slimy greenish-yellow excrement on the leaves.

SCENT OF BUTTERFLIES AND MOTHS. Males of a number of butterflies have scent-patches on their fore-wings, on the upper side, and the scents excite the females. The strongest scent of any British butterfly comes from the Green-veined White, of damp grassland (where its larvae feed on Lady's Smock), which smells in an expensive Parisian way of lemon verbena. Two small butterflies smell of chocolate, the Common Blue and the slightly less common or more local Brown Argus of chalk downs (where the larvae feed on the lemon-yellow-flowered Rock-rose). Males of the brown Wall also have a chocolatey aroma.

Contrariwise, caterpillars of the grey, subtly-marked Goat Moth smell goaty, so much so that they give a goaty smell to a tree whose timber they infest – ash, elm, willow, poplar. The caterpillars eat into the tree and the sap oozes out from the holes, the two-and-three-quarter to three-and-three-quarter inch moths emerging after three years.

PURPLE EMPERORS. Butterflies are emblematic of happiness and summer, they haunt flowers, they suck nectar. No doubt, but the seldom seen Purple Emperor of oak woods in the south, one of the largest and most beautiful of British butterflies, has the coarse tastes of a bluebottle or a vulture. It likes foul water and liquefying carrion. The only one I have seen sat on the decaying body of a grey squirrel, which someone had shot.

DEFOLIATED OAKS – this is moth-work, no less than an eaten dinner-jacket. An oak tree in early summer: next to no leaves remain, a million threads hang down, a million small caterpillars hang by the threads; and will develop into the Pea-green Moth (small, with green fore-wings). The oak will probably recover, and at least it can be said that the earth round the tree receives most of the digested leaf material, which goes back into the soil, and so into the oak.

WINTER MOTHS. Moths along a road, seen in car headlights in flower-less and nectarless November and December, pose a mystery. They are small, they are grey, they rise, fall, flutter; they are to be numbered in thousands, in millions, especially down a woodland road. Frost comes, and goes, and the moths are still there next time you pass in the darkness. They are males of the Winter Moth, anxious to connect with the wingless females of their kind, who have crawled up trees (including fruit trees unless they are banded), where they will lay their eggs. The larvae emerge, and attack the foliage.

These fluttering males have atrophied mouth-parts and require no food.

Gardens can be improved for moth and butterfly – of the less destructive kinds. If you want hawk-moths, especially the Humming-bird Hawk-moth, you must have, above all other shrubs, Jasmine and some of the garden honeysuckles (though Jasmine will only flower abundantly in a good year). Petunias and the long sweet-scented flowers of Tobacco attract the dusk-flying hawk-moths. Hemp Agrimony, among perennials, is not an unpleasant plant for a herbaceous border (particularly in districts where it is not too abundantly familiar along the roads): its pinkish flowers attract Red Admirals, Tortoiseshells, Peacocks, Tiger Moths, etc. The prime attractor, offering butterflies and moths a taste of Chinese Delight unknown to them in previous centuries is *Buddleia davidii*, from China, in its various garden forms, the true Butterfly Bush. Tortoiseshells, Painted Ladies, Peacocks, Red Admirals, Commas, with their curiously indented wings, and many other butterflies find it irresistible. If you dislike the mauve kinds of Buddleia, try a white-flowering buddleia.

# BEETLES AND SPIDERS

BEETLE – a hard horny word, suitable to the beetle's horny wing-cases, developed from fore-wings, though in fact 'beetle' by origin means a biter.

In our islands beetles number more than 3,600 kinds, from the large and unexpectedly suburban Stag Beetle (common in South London districts and in Surrey) to minute hard specks of life which can fly with most unwelcome effect into one's eyes. Many of these biters are harmful, some like decay and are scavengers, some stink, one is sweet-scented, one glows at night, one is a form assumed by Satan, others glitter in the purest of metallic colours.

The Cornish springs of my own childhood took me always to a deep lane where Early Purple Orchis, shiny adders, and shiny blue-black Oil Beetles appeared at the same time, the beetles defensively exuding their nasty tasting orange blood when they were picked up. In the autumn the grass banks were alive with points of glow-worm light.

A choice of beetle-biters to observe for the colour of their hard wing-cases or for their peculiarity must include common and less common species – the Stag (only the male has the stag's antlers, which are enlarged mandibles) ; the emerald-green, not very common, Rose Chafer (which feeds poetically on rose petals, contradicting the classical belief that beetles are killed by the scent of roses); the equally brilliant and more common Red-headed Cardinal Beetle, in cardinal's scarlet, often sunning itself on nettle leaves; the narrow soot-black Devil's Coach-horse, grim, smelly, a scavenger beetle which bends its tail back towards its head when provoked; the Wasp Beetle, black barred with yellow, often on decayed wooden posts; the Green Tiger, on sandy heaths; the green Musk Beetle, more than an inch long, on willow trees, sometimes announcing its presence by the perfume; and in North Wales, the Corn Chrysoline, striped green, purple and red, and reckoned the prettiest beetle in Great Britain. Also the Glow-worm and the various Ladybirds. (Plate 25.)

The DEVIL'S COACH-HORSE, sombre, not looking so much like a beetle on account of its short wing-covers, has been much killed because of the power for evil it was supposed to have, especially in Ireland. This is the beetle in which the devil hides himself; and it was the one insect which entered Christ's tomb after the Crucifixion. As a Devil's Coach-horse, the devil eats the bodies of sinful men. When it bends its tail back, it pronounces a curse. In Ireland a Devil's Coach-horse inserted in the handle of a sickle or scythe gives the devil's strength to the arm of the haymaker or harvester.

GLOW-WORM light comes from the wingless female beetles, from the underside of the two end segments of the body. The male Glow-worm has a more beetle-like appearance – 'a slender dusky *scarabaeus*', as Gilbert White described it. But since the male was not often seen, 'worm' – a worm which glowed – was apt enough for a long luminous something which crawled, even if it had legs. If you live in a glow-worm neighbourhood (glow-worms are local) and wish to see male as well as female, you might emulate Gilbert White. Living before electricity or oil lamps, he sat by candlelight in his parlour, and the male glow-worms would mistake the candle twinklings for females advertising themselves, and fly in through the window.

Car journeys at night reveal a glow-worm district. The glow of 'cold light' shows up distinctly in the headlights of a car, and can be seen as you travel.

LADYBIRDS, much liked for the way they settle on one's clothes, raise their smooth neat wing-cases and fly off, are future-tellers and weather-prophets in European belief; and were 'adopted' into Christianity as little birds of the Virgin Mary. There are many more kinds than the familiar Two-spot Ladybird (which varies: the spots are not always two, and may be red on black as well as black on red), the variable Ten-spot, or the Seven-spot, which sticks to seven. For instance, black on yellow Ladybirds, twenty-two-spot or fourteen-spot (Plate 25). Also the large uncommon Eyed Ladybird of fir trees, with yellow-circled 'eyes' of black, on red.

TREE-ENGRAVINGS, under the loose bark of a dead elm, each a pattern of furrows across the timber, radiating from a central furrow – are beetles' work, and not the indecipherable script of a lost language. Each pattern, each ideogram or hieroglyph, has been inscribed by a large Elm Bark Beetle and her larvae. The female Bark Beetle mated in the central groove, and laid her eggs there: the larvae hatched and grew and ate the radiating grooves or furrows further and further out, each furrow widening with the increasing bulk of its grub.

The beetle of Gray's *Elegy* which 'wheels his droning flight', or the beetle of the evening poem by William Collins, which 'winds his small but sullen horn' on the twilight path, 'against the pilgrim borne in heedless hum', if you pursue him into the prose of his life, turns out to be the beetle of cowpats, the Dumble-dor, Dor-beetle, or Lousy Watchman (lousy, because he is the vehicle of many small mites, obvious against the dark violet of his underparts), dung-bred, dung-fed under cowpats. Or it could be the reddish-brown, clumsy, rather unprepossessing Cockchafer, which also hums – and blunders – in a strong evening flight. (Plate 25.)

SPIDERS are small beer for the casual observer. Colours, markings, shapes, etc., vary; and in the colour plates of a spider book, one kind looks very distinct from another. But the portraits are enlarged: scale them down again to nature, to their smaller fractions of an inch, and they become more or less insignificant. As elements of our common life, we not unreasonably pass them by, so that spiders are less familiar for themselves than for their webs, if they are of the web-spinning kinds, indoors or out. A hoar-frosted web is certainly one of the attractive objects. So is a great wet field glittering in autumn with gossamer, after the dispersal flights of small Linyphiid spiders:

On September the 21st., 1741, being then on a visit, and intent on field-diversions, I rose before daybreak; when I came into the en-closures, I found the stubbles and clover-grounds matted all over with a thick coat of cobweb, in the meshes of which a copious and heavy dew hung so plentifully that the whole face of the country seemed, as it were, covered with two or three setting-nets drawn one over another. When the dogs attempted to hunt, their eyes were so blinded and hoodwinked that they could not proceed, but were obliged to lie down and scrape the incumbrances from their faces with their fore-feet. . . . As the morning advanced the sun became bright and warm, and the day turned out one of those most lovely ones which no season but the autumn produces; cloudless, calm, serene, and worthy of the South of France itself.

Gilbert White

Improbable as it may seem, 'gossamer' is derived by etymologists from 'goose-summer', the time of year when it most appears, St Martin's Summer, centering upon Martinmas (11 November), when geese were killed and eaten. Gossamer is the Goose-Summer pheno-menon, the Goose-Summer thread. Gilbert White again: 'Every day in fine weather, in autumn chiefly, do I see those spiders shooting out their webs and mounting aloft: they will go off from your finger if you will take them into your hand. Last summer one alighted on my book as I was reading in the parlour; and, running to the top of the page, and shooting out a web, took its departure from thence.' (1775.)

The GARDEN SPIDER – the Common Garden Spider or Diadem Spider – all the same, is a species everyone should know. It sticks in the memory by reason of the white cross on its brown or yellowish back, and it stretches fine orb-webs in strategic places. The cross sanctified this spider for most of Europe, 'signing' it with virtue. Like the toad, it was held to contain a stone which cured disease. Spiders were regularly used, sometimes in a locket around the neck, against malaria (ague). Elias Ashmole (whose collections were the nucleus of the world's first public museum, the Ashmolean, at Oxford), in his *Memoirs* (or diary), 11 May, 1651: 'I took early in the morning a good dose of elixir, and hung three spiders about my neck. Ague away, Deo gratias.'

# BITERS, PUNCTURERS, INFLAMERS

Apart from adders (page 224) and nettles, most of our biters, puncturers, irritators, or inflamers, are insects, a more formidable, or at any rate more numerous, platoon than we may realize. 'Biting', if we are to be pedantic and confine biting to the work of teeth and jaws, is not so much in question. Some pierce, and then suck out or pump out blood, as a necessity of their life cycle or a necessary food; others pierce, and then inject poison, or eject and squirt poison, as an act of defence.

MOSQUITOES, or GNATS, are sleek, graceful creatures, with clean lines (try a magnifying glass). They like fruit juices and nectar, the female, unfortunately – and only the female – requiring a blood meal in order that she can lay fertile eggs. Our acquaintance with most of these puncturers is *ex post facto*, a matter of swelling and itching and scratching, and even the doctor at times, after they have come and gone, unnoticed, unfelt and unswiped. This is generally so with a number of our worst biters, which do not fly indoors, or fly in for their blood meal and then out, after dark or in the evening. Some are woodland mosquitoes, attacking mostly out of doors in the early evening. There are two severe biters which breed in rot-holes in trees, especially sycamores, elms and beeches. Also there are salt marsh breeders, which can make a three-or four-mile journey to blood and back again.

The ones we get a better – or too good a  – chance of seeing are the hibernators, whose pregnant females come and winter indoors (when the males are beginning to die off).

Thousands of the common House Gnat, *Culex pipiens*, which will breed in water tanks and barrels, may enter a house during the autumn (particularly if it is not too dry), and cling to the walls, or fly around in a way that need make only birds apprehensive. This mosquito likes or requires bird's blood (for instance, from hens, canaries and budgerigars), and does not feed on man. It is not very large, has a brown hind-body banded with cream, plain brown legs, and wings without spots.

There are two common hibernators not so averse to our life-stream.

One is a slender, rather larger mosquito with *spotted wings, brown legs without rings of white, and a brown hind-body which is not boldly divided by light bands*, one of the family of *Anopheles* which is able to carry malaria (and used to carry it, when malaria or 'ague' was a common English disease). This *Anopheles maculipennis atroparvus* is mostly an insect of coast districts, since it needs salty water to breed in.

The other common hibernator is a brute, a brownish mosquito, *Theobaldia annulata*. It also has spotted wings, but it is larger than *Anopheles maculipennis*, it has white rings around its legs, and white bands around its brown hind-body. The Anopheles, like all of its family, rests with its head down and its body tilted up at an angle. The Ringed Mosquito rests more or less parallel to the wall. Beware of this *Theobaldia*: it will wake up, bite you when you are asleep – it is one of the worst of biters – and doze off again in its winter torpor, until the time comes in April to go out and deposit its now fertile eggs on a convenient surface of dung-tainted or sewage-tainted water. Very much a farmyard and farmhouse species.

All mosquitoes have two wings, and a proboscis sticking out from their head. The mosquito female keeps her piercing lancets and the tube through which she pumps up your blood, and the tube through which she injects saliva (which may be responsible for the swelling) inside this grooved proboscis or sheath, which bends up and back, as the lancets begin to enter.

MIDGES rise when the wind goes down. On the west coast of Ireland (or Scotland) a rare evening with no wind off the Atlantic brings them up from the damp moorland in clouds, and their piercing, blood-sucking, tickling attention (females only) drives every animal – man, horse, cattle, chickens – frantic. The many kinds of these tiny blood-suckers look like being an eternal pest, though modern insect repellents do repel them. Rubbing bites with sodium carbonate crystals stops the itching.

WASPS and BEES. (Plate 27.) The British Isles have nearly eighty kinds of wasp (though only seven species of true Wasp, including the Hornet), and nearly 250 kinds of bee. Most of them are 'solitary' and not social insects. Even then, if all the kinds stung fiercely and readily – i.e. pierced the skin and injected poison – this might be a parlous country to live in.

The Great Wood Horntail, rather a noble woodland insect of black and yellow with a long visible yellow 'sting', a solitary wood-boring wasp, looks frightening, but uses the sting only to cut into trees and insert its eggs; in which it is copied by the Blue Wood Horntail, which does not look so much like a wasp. A good many small solitaries, including the very attractive Ruby-tails, the more ant-like Sand Wasps and the Digger Wasps, can sting, but they do not do so very often. Of the social Paper Wasps, the Hornet (Plate 27), large – about an inch long – yellow and brown instead of yellow and black, local, and more talked about than seen, is really a most maligned insect.

> A harnet zet in a hollur tree –
> A proper spiteful twoad was he;
> And a merrily zung when he did zet
> His stinge so shearp as a baggonet –

that Wiltshire fable begins correctly, since hornets do like to nest in a hollow tree, but then goes wrong. The Hornet has a sting, but it is not at all forward in using it, at any rate on men, even if they come close up to the nest or the tree. Far from being spiteful, Hornets lack the quick vicious response of the house and jam jar invaders, i.e. the Common Wasps or German Wasps, the two kinds which nest underground, the Tree Wasps, which build paper nests around branches some way above the ground, and the Norwegian Wasps, which fashion their paper cradles nearer the ground on shrubs, particularly hawthorns and gooseberry.

Bumble-bees, such as the Buff Tail, which also form societies with queen, drones and workers, can sting, and they do – but not with the readiness either of the wasps or of the Hive Bee, that no longer properly 'wild' insect, of which our own locally developed race is the brown British Bee.

ANTS offend chiefly by ejecting formic acid, which blisters and burns, and is the acid of stinging nettles (also of some caterpillars, the larvae of the Puss Moth and the Lobster Moth, which both eject formic acid as a defence). The trouble is that ants explore, they crawl up over a shoe and march up a trouser leg or a sleeve. Or they drop down one's neck from a branch. Movement and confinement then stimulate them to squirt their ant-acid from a gland at the tail-end, with results that may be acutely painful for a short while, and irritating for a longer time. Fortunately the ant's supply is quickly exhausted. The Yellow Ant (*Acanthomyops flavus*) of fields and ant hillocks, which might well be called the Picnic Spoiler, the Small Black Ant or Garden Ant (*Acanthomyops niger*), which has a tiresome way of living indoors as well as out, and the large red and black Wood Ant (*Formica rufa*) which piles up rustling nests of dead twigs or pine-needles, are all acid flingers.

For ants' nests in the garden, the best insecticide (if boiling water does not work) is chlordane. Ants also succumb to carbon-tetra-chloride, the cleaner fluid used for clothes and typewriters.

HORSEFLIES are variously known according to district as Clegs, Dun-flies, Breezes, Stouts, Whames, Brimps, without much distinction between the related kinds, larger and smaller. The females have the greediest liking for the blood of man and other animals, extracting it especially in damp, windless, thundery, sullen midsummer weather, while the males decently occupy themselves with nectar and flowers. They will not bite in a car, or indoors, if they stray in through a window (nor will midges). The true Clegs or Dun-flies, exceedingly common, dun-coloured, silently and rather slowly flying, slyly arriv-ing creatures, will draw up blood for two or three minutes, if you do not knock them off. Sometimes, but not always, the puncture may be felt. These Clegs have rosette markings on the wing. The largest Horseflies – about as long as the first joint of one's little finger – hum as they approach like giants in a drawing by Edward Lear.

It is pleasant to be able to say something good of these insects: they are celebrated for the beauty of their large eyes – jade, verdigris, reddish-green, golden-green, greens spotted with purple, etc., accord-ing to kind; though the colours fade when they are killed.

STORM FLIES: a sudden, surprising, annoying prick on the ankle, or top of the foot, through one's sock or stocking, indoors, especially in sultry August weather, announces that Storm Flies or Stable Flies are about. These are very much farm and country irritators, breeding outdoors in dirty farmyards, in old rotting dung-trodden hay round a Dutch barn, and similar places. The Storm Fly looks like a House Fly (which is a nasty creature, but cannot 'bite'). A second look shows the weapon – a sharp proboscis sticking out from the head, a com-bination of blood tube and needle.

FLEAS, on the whole (since different animals have their own species of flea) prefer their own hosts, at any rate for keeps, and not a visit. The chicken flea, the cat flea, the dog flea, and others, may alight on you. But they will not stay, and would not even if you welcomed them.

HARVESTERS or HARVEST BUGS are not to be confused with the long-legged, frail-legged Harvestmen, quick-running creatures like tall spiders lacking a spider's waist, which are harmless. The true

Harvester is the larval stage of a mite (and mites are not insects, strictly speaking) ; they are minute, just visible, and reddish-orange. French people call the Harvester a *rouget*.

There is an insect with us, especially on chalky districts, which is very troublesome and teasing all the latter end of the summer, getting into people's skins, especially those of women and children, and raising tumours which itch intolerably. This animal (which we call an harvest bug) is very minute, scarce discernible to the naked eye; of a bright scarlet colour . . . They are to be met with in gardens on kidney beans or any legumens; but prevail only in the hot months of summer. Warreners (rabbiters), as some have assured me, are much infested by them on chalky downs; where these insects swarm sometimes to so infuriate a degree as to discolour their nets, and to give them a reddish cast, while the men are so bitten as to be thrown into fevers.

Gilbert White, from Hampshire, 1771

Late in the summer these larvae hatch out and infest the grass. If you picnic on the chalk, if you lie on grass or walk through grass, you are condemned thereafter to three days' itching and scratching. The larvae crawl on their six legs and sink their mouth-parts into your skin, under the armpits, at the back of the knee and so on – or more or less anywhere on the soft bodies of children. It is a myth that they actually bury themselves under the skin, but they are bad enough on top. Sulphur in the socks is supposed to stop them, if you can remember to put it there. But the problem is to deal with the Harvesters once they have arrived and settled in for their three-day sojourn. A dab of petrol on each spot stops the itching for a while (and kills the Harvester?). Doctors new to a Harvester district often diagnose the bites on children in their hair and over their bodies as chicken-pox, particularly since their temperature may rise a little.

TICKS – these also are mites in one stage or another; and you may find that a pale *Ixodes ricinus*, for example, which is a tick of dogs and sheep, has quietly cut its way into your knee for a blood-meal, or you may be bitten by the yellow and white tick of pigeons. Sir Arthur Shipley in *The Minor Horrors of War* wrote that this pigeon tick was once a worry to congregations in Canterbury Cathedral, the moral of which is not to allow pigeons in church. Do not pull out a tick. If you try, you only break the body from its mouth parts which remain anchored inside you, and may irritate you for months. Touch the body with petrol or surgical spirit.

# SEASIDE HAZARDS

JELLYFISH, SEA NETTLES and SCALDERS are the most feared of shore
or bathing hazards on holiday. They have stinging cells. But the commonest jellyfish in our waters, an amorphous-seeming uncoloured
jelly around a four-petalled violet-coloured shape, does no harm to
human leg or arm or skin. Nor does the jellyfish called *Rhizostoma octo-
pus*, a big greenish or grey bell, edged and frilled with purple. Beware
of others. Beware of the Compass, which is milky-white and has a
circle of brown triangles like divisions on a compass (not so common).
Beware of the Blue Hairy Jellyfish, resembling a flower imagined by
Klee, upside down in the water, with round petals or lobes, hung with
tentacles in bunches. This beautiful organism stings bathers in the
North Sea (though it occurs elsewhere), where George Crabbe of
Suffolk and the long shore line of Aldborough knew it well –

> Those living jellies which the flesh inflame,
> Fierce as a nettle, and from that its name . . .
> Soft, brilliant, tender, through the wave they glow,
> And make the moonbeam brighter where they flow.
>
> *The Borough*, Letter ix

Also Sir Thomas Browne of Norfolk: 'Urtica marina of divers kinds,
some whereof called squalders; of a burning and stinging quality if
rubbed in the hand.'

PORTUGUESE-MEN-OF-WAR sting and numb like jellyfish. They are not
so common, though the right wind will not infrequently drive them
into English waters on either side of Cornwall. Below the crested, irides-
cent, blue and pink, taut gas-bladder of the Portuguese-Man-of-War
hang long tentacles, which do the stinging. If you notice a single
Portuguese-Man-of-War bobbing on the surface, let alone a flotilla,
keep clear. Not so far south – for instance, round the Canary Islands –
Portuguese-Men-of-War can make bathing impossible.

The SEA-STRANGER. Bathers may see the Portuguese-Man-of-War or
the jellyfish which has stung them. But what are they to make of a
sudden prick, a sudden acute pain in the sole of the foot, as they stand
and enjoy themselves in the shallows off a sandy beach? It comes from
treading on the poisoned spines of a small grey fish, four to five inches
long, variously known as the Weever (its book name is the Lesser
Weever), Sting Fish, Otter Pike, or Sea-Stranger. 'A sting fish, wiver,

or kind of ophidion or *Araneus*, slender, narrowe headed, about 4 inches long with a sharpe small prickly finne along the back which often venemously pricketh the hands of fishermen' – Sir Thomas Browne.

The spines along the back are connected with poison glands, and the Weever buries itself in the sand with the spines in the black fin nearest the head sticking out. It feeds on shrimps, and is a curse to professional shrimpers. In my own experience (off a beach in Cornwall), I have found the Weever's sting the most agonizing poison-pain or puncture-pain I have ever known. But it does not last a great time, easing and ceasing – with some victims – after about twenty minutes. Weever is the same word as wyvere or wyvern, having come by way of French (the French call this fish a *vive*) from the Latin *vipera*, an adder. So the Lesser Weever is a Sea Adder, a Sea Viper, most emphatically.

SEA-ANEMONES are harmless. You will not be stung by even the snakiest tentacles of these 'flesh-flowers of the rock', though very sensitive skins have experienced a tingling from the anemone of various colour forms known as the Opelet or Snakelocks (Plates 28 and 29). The poet Gerard Manley Hopkins once did something, all the same, which we are unlikely to imitate. He fancied himself as a merman decorated with sea-anemones, eased a large anemone off the rock, and placed it on his forehead. 'It fixed itself correctly. Now one has often heard of their stinging, but I had handled them so often unharmed, and who could have imagined a creature stinging with its – base you call it in sea-anemones? But it did, loudly, and when the pain had ceased a mark remained, which is now a large red scar.' Suction, rather than stinging, must have been the trouble. Sea-anemones can even be cooked and eaten (page 264).

## SOME ASSURANCES – OR REASSURANCES

A child once clutched her father's hand as they walked through a wood in May, and said, *Do cuckoos peck?* Be assured (although traditional or irrational fears die hard) that toads are not venomous, earwigs ('ear wig' means ear beetle, ear insect) do not crawl into ears, and are harmless, and that no one will be bitten by spiders, millipedes, centipedes, Daddy Long Legs, Yellow Dung Flies from a cowpat, woodlice, sandhoppers on a beach – or Dragonflies (which for all their beauty have such collective names as Horse-Stingers, Horse-Adders and Devil's Darning Needles).

# PART FOUR

*Flowers, Fruits, Foods*

# Wild Flowers and Fruits

In the British Isles there are more than 4,000 kinds of flowering plant. Probably no man has seen them all; and they are not all worth seeing. Numbered among them, for example, are some fifty kinds of bramble, more than forty kinds of Hawkweed, more than a dozen kinds of Fumitory, and more than twenty kinds of Eyebright, which to the inexpert eye look much alike. Most of us are reasonably content to recognize an oak as an oak, without enquiring whether it is a Pedunculate Oak or a Durmast Oak: and when the May is out, we do not care if it is Common Hawthorn or Midland Hawthorn.

Which are the most beautiful plants is a matter of opinion. Among the common kinds the choice would include Lesser Celandine, Marsh Marigold, Lords and Ladies in flower and fruit, Lady's Smock, Herb Robert, Ragged Robin, Wood Anemone, Wood Sorrel, Fumitory, Primrose, Cowslip, Foxglove, Dog Rose, Bluebell, Hawthorn, Lesser Bindweed (the most detestable of all weeds), Rose-bay Willow-herb, Harebell, Water Forget-me-not, Water Crowfoot, Poppy, Purple Loosestrife, Ivy-leaved Toadflax, and the Spindle Tree in fruit.

Overlooking these common beauties, here are three lists, of Less Common, Uncommon, and Rare – all flowers it is worth getting to know or worth trying to see in a lifetime.

## *Less Common Beauties*

WILD COLUMBINE: in damp places (especially in Devon and Cornwall), tall and very blue; in spring.

BUCKBEAN: in bogs and moorland pools, leaves rather like a young broad bean, flowers pink and white, frilly, of exquisite shape and tint. Spring and early summer.

WATER AVENS: in wet shady places: drooping heads of sullen pinkish-orange. Spring and early summer. (Plate 32.)

WILD FLOWERS AND FRUITS

BISTORT: tall spikes of pink, often in hay meadows (e.g. in the mountain pastures of the West Riding).

VIPER'S BUGLOSS: a snaky sultry plant of dry places, especially chalky ones, in high summer. Spiny stems and leaves, blue and purple flowers.

SAINFOIN: near dry chalky meadows, flowers of a striped summer pink, which seem to have escaped from an Impressionist painting.

CORN MARIGOLD, or GOLD: among crops in sandy fields. No wild flower has a more pellucid and friendly yellow. It will go on flowering and yellowing a field until early winter.

MUSK MALLOW: a summer hedgerow plant, tall, with delicately cut leaves, and flowers of a warm pink (which do *not* smell of musk).

MEADOW CRANESBILL (or Blue Basons, or Loving Andrews): tall, with an abundance of large purple-blue – sometimes white – flowers. Along roads, banks, etc., (particularly in Wiltshire), but rather local. The leaves turn reddish in late summer and autumn. (Plate 34.)

OLD MAN'S BEARD: a climber, twining and looping over hedgerows, bushes and trees, making them silvery in autumn and winter with its hairy fruits. This is a chalk and limestone plant, commonest in the south. (Plate 37.)

## Uncommon Beauties

WILD DAFFODIL: most abundant as a wild plant in Gloucestershire, below the Forest of Dean, where it yellows the landscape. Preferable to most of the enlarged garden daffodils.

BIRD CHERRY. The white flowers of this small tree or shrub, a limestone lover, frequent in limestone gorges, hang down in spikes.

TRIQUETROUS GARLIC: by roads, paths, in corners, suggesting a white bluebell, to be found particularly in the Channel Islands, West Cornwall and the Isles of Scilly. A plant from the Mediterranean, flowering from April to June. The stems are triangular (triquetrous: having three edges).

BIRD'S EYE PRIMROSE: a little lilac polyanthus, greatly abundant from May to June on northern limestone.

SOLOMON'S SEAL: woodland plant, in clear spaces without under-growth. Its long stems winged with alternate leaves curve gracefully and are hung with greenish-white flowers. May to June.

GLOBE FLOWER: globes of butter-yellow, crowning tall stems, a plant growing in little squads or platoons in the mountains – West York-shire, for example – in blossom from June to August.

PARSLEY FERN: a fern with curly, crisp fronds like a fattened parsley, growing thickly on loose stones, among rocks, etc., in mountainy districts, especially the Lake District.

HENBANE: poisonous, foetid, soft-leaved, sprawling on sandy waste places by the sea. Henbane has an abundance of regularly set, almost stemless sulphur flowers, each flower streaked with purple. June to August.

BLOODY CRANESBILL: a sprawling geranium laying its wide-eyed crimson flowers on the warm sand of dunes or the warm face of lime-stone, in July and August.

MEADOW SAFFRON (or Naked Nannies): shining, very naked, pallid purple, poisonous flowers in damp autumn meadows and damp wood-land scrub. The purple lessens to white. No leaves – or rather, the leaves and fruits appear in the spring. (Plate 36.)

## Rare Beauties

PASQUE FLOWER: an Easter anemone, very surprising when its great hairy purple flowers are found on a dry chalk hill, an ancient earth-work, or the debris of a limestone quarry. Probably more abundant in Gloucestershire than any other county. (Plate 30.)

FRITILLARY: this flower probably escaped from gardens in the six-teenth and seventeenth centuries, establishing itself in water-meadows (especially of the Thames and its tributaries) where its hanging chequered purple (often white) bells darken many acres of grass, and shake in the wind in the last week of April. (Plate 30.)

LODDON LILY: like a large snowdrop (to which it is related: it is not a lily) and another flower of river-sides, particularly the Thames and its Berkshire tributary, the Loddon. You see cyclists in April and May (sometimes on the Great West Road) with great bunches tied to their handlebars, an extension of the Fritillary or the Bluebell habit.

SPRING GENTIAN: the most luminously blue of native flowers, demanding – and rewarding – a pilgrimage or journey of discovery in April or May to its limestone headquarters in Burren, above the Atlantic, in County Clare, and near High Force in Teesdale, on the Durham and Yorkshire border.

LILY OF THE VALLEY: this grows wild here and there, particularly in stony scrubby limestone woods, smelling as sweetly as the garden forms.

BASTARD BALM: a rather foetid labiate plant, which deserves a better name on account of its white flowers blotched with purple-pink. A south-western rarity, growing along high grassy earth hedges and banks in Devon and Cornwall and a few other counties, sometimes in great quantity for a mile or more. May to July.

DRYAS, or MOUNTAIN AVENS: white flowers (June, July), dark green shiny leaves, like miniature oak leaves, creeping in clumps over limestone rock, particularly in Burren, Co. Clare. After the flowers are over, the fruits are feathery, hairy, hoary and conspicuous.

SEA-BUCKTHORN: an uncommon shrub or small tree of the east coast, on dunes and across low cliffs, silvery, sharp-thorned, with yellow fruit. As beautiful as olive trees, and not unlike them in a smaller way.

PURPLE GROMWELL: as blue nearly, with as intensive a glow, as the Spring Gentian, along the scrubby edges of limestone woods, particularly on the Mendips. There is no point in picking Purple Gromwell, since it quickly dulls and shrivels in water.

FIELD COW-WHEAT. This annual is more easily seen in France, on the edge of chalky fields. There it is common and known as *Queue de Renard*, Fox's Tail, for its brilliant colour and upright bushiness. But year by year it grows in a few very similar places in England, a splendid harlequin, pink, yellow, purple and acid green.

PURPLE OXYTROPIS: silky leaves, flowers in two shades of purple clustered on short strong stems, an extraordinarily vivid plant of the pea family growing as far north as possible in dry stony fields near the sea along the north coast of Scotland (Caithness and Sutherland).

HOLLY FERN: this must be climbed or clambered for in most of its habitats, in Wales (in gullies of Snowdon, for example), in the Highlands and so on – a fern which likes crevices and damp corners. The fronds are narrow, and are made up of close-set, short, toothed, spiny segments, very intriguing in form and arrangement.

Common, less common, uncommon and rare, my own list of the most beautiful plants of Great Britain – not all of them the most lovable plants, which is another thing – would be:

| | |
|---|---|
| Early Purple Orchid | Columbine |
| Buckbean | Henbane |
| Wood Anemone | Viper's Bugloss |
| Fumitory | Guelder Rose |
| Herb Robert | Field Cow-wheat |
| Foxglove | Purple Loosestrife |
| Corn Marigold | Rest-harrow |
| Purple Oxytropis | Wood Sorrel |
| Dog Rose | Sainfoin |
| Daffodil | Sea Buckthorn |
| Bluebell | Lords and Ladies |
| Cowslip | Fritillary |
| Primrose | Solomon's Seal |
| Bird's Eye Primrose | Bindweed |
| Spring Gentian | Ivy-leaved Toadflax |
| Parsley Fern | Bistort |
| Holly Fern | Elder, in flower |

## SCENTS AND SMELLS

A proper sensual concern with our world includes appreciation of scent, and one can imagine – for those who do not smoke – a worse hobby than getting to know the more remarkably scented flowers and leaves among plants outside the garden, and attempting to analyse and describe their perfume.

Scents *en masse* are few. The two most agreeable ones are no doubt the very heady exhilarating sweetness of bean fields (Broad Beans) in spring, in the Midlands and East Anglia, and the sudden suffusion of sweetness and honey from lime trees in flower (early July), of which the best celebration I know is not English but Russian, in Pasternak's poem (translated by his sister) about July visitors to a mansion with a lime tree avenue. The trees spread their 'irresistible appeal', the visitors walk on the crunchy sand, and breathe in the 'unfathomable sweetness' –

> This gripping scent is theme and subject,
> Whereas – however well they look –
> The flowerbeds, the lawn, the garden,
> Are but the cover of a book.
>
> The clustered, wax-bespattered flowers
> On massive trees, sedate and old,
> Lit up by raindrops, burn and sparkle
> Above the mansion they enfold.

Something of this lime blossom scent is returned and given out in lime-tea (page 262). Other air-filling scents come from sun-warmed patches of Bog Myrtle (a gummy sweetness), common in the New Forest, and sun-warmed extents of Gorse and of Broom (fruity and musky). Many people dislike the stale almond sweetness flowing out from Hawthorn blossom in May, then, as the hawthorn fades, from Elder blossom in June, and from Meadowsweet in July.

Honeysuckle scent will spread itself a long way on the air, if there is enough blossom and if conditions are right – for instance, in the Lake District, a tree festooned with honeysuckle will give notice of itself in the damp air at two hundred or three hundred yards' distance.

Taking plants individually, the strongest and sweetest smelling flowers, other than Honeysuckle and the uncommon wild Lily of the Valley and the very rare Mezereon, are:

BUTTERFLY ORCHID, of woods and grass slopes on the chalk and lime-stone – ivory-white flowers (May to July) scented by day and by night and attracting moths, by which this orchid is pollinated.

FRAGRANT ORCHID, of chalk and limestone fields (July to August), a commoner orchid, with reddish flowers.

Flowers with a fainter scent, for different tastes, include:

BINDWEED, June to September, an almond (macaroon) sweetness from the sun-loving, little trumpet-flowers, yellow-throated, white, pink, or pink and white combined, of this most ineradicable weed.

GUELDER ROSE, or WATER ELDER, in June, blossoming at the same time as Elder, purest white flowers emitting a curious scent not unlike the scent which comes from fried trout, well peppered and salted. (Plate 34.)

PRIVET, in June. Not everybody's taste. Ivory flowers emit an almond-like hawthorn scent, well fitted to this now maligned shrub's ancient classical and Italian association with love and youth.

AUTUMN LADY'S TRESSES, August to September, on downs, cliff tops, etc., an orchid whose white flowers in a spiral are sweetly almond-scented by day to attract bumble-bees instead of moths.

Among plants which afford pungent leaf-smells, some scent the air, some need crushing, some develop a scent only when they are dried.

WATER MINT: very common, a menthol scent, refreshing and evoca-tive. In warm weather, particularly in the evening, the leaves scent the damp air. Crushing, treading, brings the scent out more strongly. Water Mint was planted in alleys in Tudor gardens 'to have the pleasure, when you walk or tread' (Bacon's essay, *Of Gardens*). It will grow in gardens away from water.

WORMWOOD: a not very common, tall, sturdy, bitter plant of silky, grey, furrowed stems and silky, grey, feathery leaves, highly aromatic and refreshing. Also Sea Wormwood.

TANSY: on road verges, river banks, etc., with yellow button flowers, July to September. The leaves crush to something like the Worm-wood's aroma, a little sharper and more reminiscent of eucalyptus.

FEVERFEW: a white-flowering daisy plant, with yellowish-green, cut leaves, common around old farmhouses, on walls and paths, giving a more lemony bitter leaf-scent than Tansy or Wormwood, very pleas-ant. The plant was taken against headaches.

SWEET FLAG: a shallow water plant with iris-like though crumple-edged leaves introduced into Tudor physic gardens, from which it escaped into ponds and slow rivers. Still a very common bazaar medi-cine in the East. Crush the leaves and they smell like tangerines. Sweet Flag leaves were gathered for strewing as a carpet on floors.

TUTSAN. Leaves of this shrubby St John's Wort of woods and hedges develop a rich tobacco fragrance when they are dried – for instance, in a book (they were used as Bible markers, and the plant is often called Book Leaf or Bible Leaf).

WOODRUFF. The leaves, as they dry among linen, etc., develop a hay-field scent.

A few plants possess an aromatic root. WATER AVENS (page 245) is one, the root smelling of cloves. ELECAMPANE (a garden escape) is another, the roots, which were candied as a sweet against coughs, leaving their fragrance for a long time on the fingers. The rootstocks of the ROSE-ROOT, a large yellow-flowered rather dingy stonecrop on mountains and sea-cliffs, have a delicious scent of Provence roses, if you slice them or break them.

Some of the unpleasant or less pleasant smells are too curious to disregard – HOUNDSTONGUE, in dry, especially chalky places, having a leaf-smell of mice; GLADDON, the wild dry-land iris (which exhibits a dull sultry flower, but splendid orange seeds – Plate 35 – in the autumn), a leaf-smell of raw meat; EARLY PURPLE ORCHIS (Plate 33) a flower-smell (indoors, in water) of cat urine. FRITILLARY and WOOD ANEMONE (both on Plate 30) have a somewhat similar, less aggressive flower-scent. The YELLOW WATER-LILY flower (when you get hold of one at last) has an extraordinary stale scent, attractive to flies, of the dregs of brandy.

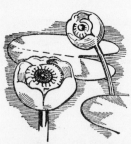

The filthiest scent of any plant in the British Isles emanates not from a flowering plant but a fungus, the Stink Horn of woods and hedges, attracting bluebottles by its far-carrying, overwhelming stench of putrefaction.

(An uncommon fascinating book, if you can find a copy, is F. A. Hampton's *The Scent of Flowers and Leaves*, 1925.)

## INVADING FLOWERS

No population of flowers is static. Species die out, species from abroad find a place, and sometimes, but not always, maintain themselves. Several 'foreign' flowers introduced into physic gardens or pleasure-gardens from which they escaped, or introduced by accident, are now as familiar or as settled and persistent as any 'native' (some have been mentioned already – Feverfew, Henbane, Greater Celandine, Corn Marigold, Triquetrous Garlic, Elecampane, Sweet Flag). A few are now landscape adornments.

## *Invaders to notice include:*

ALEXANDERS, 'Parsley of Alexandria', a happy, shining, greenish-yellow-flowered umbellifer, common near the sea on waste places, around ruins, etc. An old garden vegetable (which used to be earthed and blanched to get rid of its bitterness), anciently introduced.

SYCAMORE, from mountains across southern Europe, probably planted first in Scotland in the fifteenth century. South of the border, it was first planted late in the sixteenth century. Now wild from one end of Britain to the other.

RED VALERIAN, on walls and cliffs (such as Cheddar Gorge), introduced to gardens, probably from Italy, in the sixteenth century.

IVY-LEAVED TOADFLAX – on garden walls, etc. From southern Europe (it is often portrayed in Italian paintings of the fifteenth century); first grown in a garden in Essex before 1618.

OXFORD RAGWORT – everywhere along railways and sidings, and waste ground, cheerfully yellow in most months of the year. Native on the lavas of Etna and Vesuvius. 'Oxford' because it was planted in the Physic Garden at Oxford in the seventeenth century, from which it escaped to old walls, and eventually spread to the railways.

MONKEY FLOWER, pure yellow flowers with spots of red: a very healthy, happy-seeming plant along streams, especially in mountainy districts. Introduced from the Aleutian Islands in 1812, an escape first of all in Monmouthsire, near Abergavenny, by 1824. (Plate 34.)

HIMALAYAN BALSAM, or POLICEMAN'S HELMET, filling old canals, growing tall and robust along streams, hung with numberless pink and purple flowers. Introduced into gardens from India in 1839, escaped by 1855.

GIANT HOGWEED, immense, up to eleven or twelve feet, introduced to gardens from the Caucasus in 1893, now superb along river banks (for instance, in the Lowlands of Scotland).

MONTBRETIA. Two species of Crocosmia from South Africa were crossed by a French horticulturist, the hybrid becoming popular in gardens round about 1900. Superfluous plants or corms were thrown out into garden waste, survived, and spread. This hybrid now flourishes along rocky streams.

These are only a few introduced plants whose history is well known. Others were more anciently introduced, in Norman, Anglo-Saxon, Roman, Iron Age, Bronze Age and Neolithic centuries. The first farmers in Britain, some 6,000 years ago, were probably the accidental introducers of Fumitory and White Campion. Bronze Age settlers brought the Poppy of our cornfields. The Romans may be to blame for Ground Elder in the garden, and Corn Marigold in the fields.

## FIRST AND LAST

Emotionally and by name (page 257), if not strictly in fact, the Primrose must be counted as the first flower of the year – the favourite first flower of Easter decorations, set in bunches in damp moss.

Which is the last flower? Not always noticed, we should reckon it to be the flower – or flowers – of Ivy, autumnal, gold-green, breaking out above the gloss of the leaves in small rounded umbels in October and November, crowded with flies and with wasps, which will be dead within a few weeks.

## SOME FLOWER NAMES

If words attract you, and you begin to delve into the peculiarity of the names of flowers, you will find that they divide first of all into 'book names' more or less recently invented (by botanists chiefly), and names of ordinary speech, which are of considerable antiquity and are likely to be common, in one form or another, to most European languages, from Russian to French or Portuguese or Irish. Of course a book name may fit a plant very well, and may have graduated into one of the names of everyday speech.

The older names frequently refer to some use of the plant in medicine or magic or medicinal magic, since plants provided most of the medicine taken by our ancestors. If a plant was 'powerful' in ancient belief, the power could be for good or for evil, according to the user (like a magic wand in fairy tales, or Aladdin's lamp): the same plant might help a demon, or help to keep a demon away. Such plants (including Marsh Marigold (Plate 31) and hawthorn) were hung on doors at the right time, to keep devils away from man or his cattle. A plant thought to produce good effects if you swallowed it in any shape would often be associated with a good deity, major or minor. A plant which was poisonous and killed, or which looked poisonous, would naturally be linked with an evil or less kindly deity. When Christianity spread, 'good' plants were associated with the Virgin Mary or the saints, 'bad' – i.e. poisonous – plants with the devil, goblins, witches, etc.

Plants which were not regarded as 'useful' or active in some way or another seldom have other than a book name, unless they are very common, or remarkable – or detestable, perhaps as weeds. Plants which grow in out of the way places, especially mountains or moors (which our ancestors disliked), often have only modern book names. Many names we have inherited from Greek or Latin (particularly from medicinal or natural history treatises), a few – *poppy* is one – from languages as ancient as Assyrian or Sumerian. Some are part of our Germanic inheritance, others came into English from French in the Middle Ages, probably through monks and friars, others from German, in the sixteenth century, when the Germans led a great revival in the study of plants, publishing the first more or less scientific herbals. Plants were often named after their habitat, or because they flowered at a particular season, or from some peculiarity in form or colour. Interest in plants, though, for their 'beauty' *alone* came rather late and has named fewer plants than one would expect.

CELANDINE (Greek). The Greater Celandine, which grows on banks around villages, is named after the Greek word for a swallow, according to a legend that swallows picked it to give sight back to their blinded young. So it was grown as an eye medicine.

COMFREY (Latin): from a word meaning to grow together, since Comfrey was applied to cuts, wounds, and broken bones. (Plate 33.)

COWSLIP (English) – i.e. a cow-slop, from the Old English for a cow-pat, since it grows in pastures, in cow-pat land.

DAFFODIL (Greek), from *asphodelos*, since in the Middle Ages it was taken to be the Asphodel of the Mediterranean region, one of the spring flowers which greeted the yearly return to Earth of Persephone, Queen of Hell.

DAISY (English), the 'day's eye'. Abroad, its names connect the daisy with geese – Goose Flower, i.e. growing from goose droppings – and with the Virgin Mary – *Marienblümchen*, in explanation of the red and white, the Virgin having pricked her finger while picking daisies for the child Jesus.

DANDELION (French), 'lion's tooth', probably because the indentations of the leaf suggested the teeth in a lion's jaw and because the flower is a small golden sun, a blossom of that fire of which the golden lion was symbol (it was believed that striking a lion's bones together produced fire).

EYEBRIGHT (English) – which is signed as an 'eye plant', since the flower resembles a bruised or bloodshot eye, for which reason sixteenth-century doctors made an eye-wash of the plant.

FOXGLOVE (English) – a glove for a fox (and not for anything else), from a tale that the fox wore gloves to make his approach inaudible. (Plate 34.)

GROUNDSEL (English), from the Old English for ground swallower, since groundsel will so quickly cover a plot of farm or garden land.

FUMITORY (Latin). The medieval doctor's name was *fumus terrae*, smoke of the earth, explained partly by the bluish smoky look of Fumitory on a piece of garden ground, partly by the odd gaseous smell of the root, which made men think that the plant originated in a smoke or gas rising up through the soil.

HERB PARIS (Latin) – *herba paris*, herb of equality, because the parts are equal and harmonious in number – four leaves, twice four stamens, four inner and four outer segments to the perianth, four styles and four cells to the ovary – a harmony which commended it to early doctors. (Plate 33.)

HAREBELL (English) – the bell rung by hares – and not the bellflower which hangs on a hair stem. (Plate 36.)

HERB ROBERT (English, though from the medieval Latin *Herba Roberti*). The Robert was made out to be St Rupert of Salzburg, but is more likely to have been the house goblin called Robin Goodfellow in England and *Knecht Ruprecht* in Germany.

LADY'S BEDSTRAW (English – Our Lady's Bedstraw – borrowed from the German). According to German legends the Virgin Mary bore Jesus on a bed of bracken and Lady's Bedstraw, which was then white-flowered. Bracken then had a flower, would not acknowledge Jesus, and so lost its flower. The Lady's Bedstraw acknowledged Jesus, and its flower changed from white to gold.

LORDS AND LADIES (English): a plant symbolizing copulation by its strange form of spadix in a spathe, given names in many countries combining male and female, and believed to have powers as an aphrodisiac.

MEADOWSWEET (English): not, by origin, the sweet-looking or sweet-smelling plant of the meadow, but the mead wort, i.e. the plant used to flavour mead.

MUGWORT (English): the 'midge plant'.

MULLEIN (Latin, via French): the 'soft plant', from the Latin for soft, as in mollify.

ORCHID (Greek). In Greek, *orchis* meant testicle: the two tubers of an orchid plant, one firm and full, one shrivelled, were the testicles, so orchids were both aphrodisiac (the full testicle), and useful for restraining sex (the shrivelled testicle).

POPPY (Sumerian, by way of Latin). The Sumerian word was *pa pa*, the Latin *papaver*.

PRIMROSE (Latin): from the medieval Latin *prima rosa*, the first rose of spring. (The word rose was loosely used for flower.)

SAINFOIN (French): wholesome hay, since Sainfoin was fed to cattle.

SHEPHERD'S PURSE (English, with similar names in other languages): 'Of the likeness the seed vessel hath unto a shepherdes pouch or skrippe', according to the Tudor botanist, William Turner. The pouch, scrip, or purse was of the kind which can be seen in medieval paintings, hung from the waist by strings.

ST JOHN'S WORT (English, after the medieval Latin): the midsummer plant of St John (whose day is 24 June), a flower of the sun, brilliant yellow and so like St John whom Christ called 'a burning and shining light'. St John was beheaded, and St John's Wort has a red juice like blood. It was regarded in the Middle Ages as a plant very powerful against demons.

(Much about the names of British wild flowers – and most of the country names – will be found in *The Englishman's Flora* by Geoffrey Grigson, 1955. See also *The Naming of Wild Flowers* by G. H. Browning, 1952.)

## PICKING AND IDENTIFYING

Some puritanical persons, especially some botanists and conservationists, sternly say that wild flowers should not be picked. But to pick flowers and fruits is one of the natural pleasures of life. Experiments have proved that even heavy picking does not reduce such bulbous crop plants as Bluebell or Fritillary or Bath Asparagus or Daffodil, *so long as the leaves are not picked or too much trampled*.

'Uncommon' and 'rare' are not exact terms. Plants so described can be very abundant where they do occur, by the acre or by the district. To pick such plants in moderation does no harm. But it is a shame to interfere with plants which manage to survive only in small colonies.

The best illustrated, most complete, and most up to date amateur's handbook for identifying flowers is Collins' *Pocket Guide to Wild Flowers* (including trees, shrubs, ferns, grasses, etc.) by D. McClintock and R. S. R. Fitter, published in 1956.

For many counties in England, and some in Wales, Scotland and Ireland, there exists a Flora – a guide to the county flowers, whether common or rare. This is usually an expensive book, whether in or out of print; it is often out of date (since flower populations change), but always useful, always suggestive of places to visit and explorations to undertake.

## RECOGNIZING TREES

There are trees in and out of gardens everyone should know. Of course you may go about it as you recognize any other kind of plant, by leaves, flowers, fruit. But after a while you take in the total character of different trees at a glance – the different outlines, volumes and tints (the darker green of elms, for instance, and lighter green of ash trees), the different textures according to the shape and size of leaves, the different ways of growth, different junction and division of the branches, differences of bark – with every tree an addition sum of characteristics very difficult to draw or paint at all convincingly. Yet once you know, you know, and never forget. Begin by making sure of ash, elm, oak, beech, birch, alder, lime, sycamore, horse chestnut, sweet chestnut, Scotch fir or pine, and the large willows and poplars.

Here are some special, obvious marks of distinction:

| | |
|---|---|
| Rather naked, slender trunk, bark reddish or fox-coloured especially in evening or morning sun. Evergreen. (Plate 40.) | Scotch Fir |
| Thick, lumpy, black-massed evergreen, furrowed and fussy bark of a reddish tone also much intensified by evening or morning sun. | Yew |
| Tall, greyish, grey-barked tree, leaves turning and twisting on slack stems in the least wind, hitting each other and making a noise like rain. | Aspen (often called Women's Tongues) |
| Tall, wide tree, with darkish bark, dropping fat scarlet catkins (Plate 43) on the ground in spring. | Black Poplar |
| Huge, cylindrical, smooth, silver-grey trunk. Little or nothing growing underneath out of last year's now reddish leaves. (Plate 39.) | Beech |
| Tall, narrow, dark green, weightily branched, with a straight trunk, along field divisions, hedgerows; a few branches sometimes dead or with leaves turning yellow and brown. The dying back is caused by the fungus of Elm Disease, first | English Elm |

noticed in Britain in 1927, and much spread by the Elm Bark Beetle (page 234). (Plate 42.)

| | |
|---|---|
| Sturdy, darker, furrowed trunk grappling strongly into the ground, soon branching heavily and widely, often hung with innumerable caterpillars (page 231) which have eaten away the leaves. | Oak |
| Medium-sized tree, often with suckers, humming with bees in early July, when green flowers hang down and fill the air with sweetness, leaves sticky with the honeydew excreted by aphids. | Lime |
| Rather small tree, on chalk downs, in scrub, the leaves blowing back in the wind, and showing their silvery-white underside. | White Beam |
| Garden tree, rather slender, much branched, often with suckers. The thorny twigs and hanging white pea-like flowers frequently out of reach. | 'Acacia' or Robinia, from North America |
| Garden tree, not very large, closely covered with rosy pea-shaped flowers in May. From the Mediterranean (one of the many kinds of tree on which Judas is supposed to have hanged himself). | Judas Tree |
| Wide, thick, branchy, not very tall garden tree, magnificently hung with scented flowers, white, yellow and purple, followed by very long pods. | Catalpa or Indian Bean, from North America |
| Naked-stemmed, not very tall tree, in the west, from Scotland to Cornwall, in gardens, on railway stations, promenades, etc., with short branches, and clattering in the wind. Very foreign seeming. Not a 'palm', but a Cordyline, or Cabbage Tree, a tree of the lily family from New Zealand. | Dracaena |

# Wild Foods

The inquisitive and hungry humans of Europe in a good many thousand years have worked through the wild flora, and have quite rightly discarded the eating of plants which can be swallowed with possibly wholesome results, but no great pleasure. All the same, a few wild and semi-wild vegetables are worth the trouble of collecting and cooking, apart from the customary watercress, the aristocratic fungi (page 264) and the usual fruits (including blackberries, whortleberries and wild strawberries).

LEAF VEGETABLES – soft leaves, reducing like spinach (which had made its way north through the Middle Ages, ousting various other leaf plants, tame and wild, by the sixteenth century). Among these are Nettles, Ground Elder (which is in most gardens, willy nilly), and Red Valerian. All need to be young, and are cooked as one cooks spinach. Red Valerian leaves are a little bitter, Ground Elder leaves (which must be stripped from the stems) a little unexpectedly aromatic. Nettles should be spring tops only.

Nettles are the best of these three. They pall sooner than spinach, but come out of the saucepan most appetisingly green. They were long ago regarded as a poverty food – witness the Irish legend of St Columcille and the nettle broth: he met an old woman cutting nettles, and asked her the cause of such misery. She replied that she had nothing else to eat while she waited for the cow to calve and come into milk. Columcille promptly decided to live in hunger on nettle broth, while he waited for the kingdom of heaven – losing flesh 'till the track of his ribs used to be seen on the strand when he used to lie out there through the night time'.

SALAD LEAVES. Dandelion leaves are the best, but they must be blanched with a flower-pot over them. (Wild watercress freshly gathered from a clean rapid stream in spring, autumn or early winter, tastes much better and blander than cultivated varieties.)

LEAVES IN BATTER. Comfrey leaves, in the Bavarian mountains, and no doubt elsewhere, are washed in cold water, dipped in batter, and fried (best in olive oil). They emerge from the frying-pan viridian and gold, and tasting as well as they look. Two convenient things about this dish are that Comfrey (Plate 33) is almost universally common by streams and water-ditches, and that, once recognized, it cannot easily be mistaken for any other plant. The similarly rough leaves of Borage, self-sown in the garden, are equally good when cooked in this way (an Italian dish).

STEM VEGETABLES – forerunners of asparagus. Two of these, given enough trial, are excellent: the spring shoots of Wild Hop, or hop from the hopfield, and the flower stems (before the flowers open) of Bath Asparagus (*Ornithogalum pyrenaicum*). In either case, cook in bundles, and treat like asparagus. Bath Asparagus is a hedge and woodland plant uncommon except in certain limestone districts – as around Bath, where greengrocers sell it in June. It is sold, too, in French markets.

BLOSSOM AS FOOD. Elder flowers in June are made into two admirable dishes.

Elder pancakes: take flowerheads of Elder by the stalk, dip them in a thin pancake batter, fry them, sift them with sugar, then lift them by the stem again to your mouth. Very fragrant. Flowers of the Acacia tree (*Robinia*) – when you can reach them – may be eaten in the same way (a French practice).

Elder Milk (from Germany and Austria): two flowerheads of elder are simmered for ten minutes in two and a half pints of milk, and then removed. The milk is next thickened slightly with a dessert-spoonful of cornflour, adding sugar and salt and the yolk of one or two eggs. The Elder Milk is poured into a tureen. The egg whites are whipped with sugar, and divided into small icebergs which float on the milk, rising better if the lid is placed on the tureen for a few minutes. Best when cold. (Elder flowers will give an extraordinary spiciness and fragrance to gooseberry jam and jelly.)

Judas Tree flowers can be eaten in salad; but this is more ornamental than tasty.

Lime blossom (page 249), dried indoors, in shade, slowly, makes the best of all flower teas. If you grow Bergamot or Oswego Tea in your flower bed, try a single flowerhead, dead or fresh, in a pot of ordinary Indian tea. It works a very fragrant transformation.

FRUITS AND SEEDS. Grains of wheat (see the opening chapter of Thomas Hardy's *The Mayor of Casterbridge*) are made into frumenty, more delicious even in its simplest form than any cereal out of cardboard. You must collect ripe wheat (farmer permitting), husk it and winnow it (easier to acquire some wheat after combine-harvesting). Put the wheat in an earthenware jar, a good way short of full, top with water, let and its tand in the oven or on the stove for ten or twelve hours until the grains have all burst. Then eat hot or cold – preferably cold – with milk or cream and sugar.

Hazelnut Bread: collect *young* hazelnuts, still juicy and milky, shell them, and chop them roughly, adding two cups of self-raising flour and half a cup of sugar and a pinch of salt to a cup of hazelnuts; mix, and stir in a single egg beaten with milk. Knead into a small loaf and bake; the loaf is done (after about forty-five minutes) when it sounds hollow to a tap. These hazelnut loaves ought to be standard in English cooking. Few baked things taste so delicate.

Monkey Puzzle 'nuts': the ripe cones at the top of the Monkey Puzzle conveniently fall apart, and scatter the ripe tough-skinned seeds on the ground. These can be boiled and eaten.

RIVER FOOD. Severn elvers are good eating. They can be bought by the pint in Gloucester, the elver-fisherman's headquarters, in the market and at fishmongers, about Easter time, when the elvers crowd up the Severn on the spring tides. There are various ways of preparing them – with beaten-up eggs; dusted with flour and fried in oil or deep fat; boiled in a cloth to make elver loaf, which is then sliced and fried. Local consultations are advisable.

Crayfish, cooked or ready to cook, are more easily obtained in France (*écrevisses à pattes blanches*). But they are common in many English streams in chalky and limestone districts (for example, in the Cotswolds), and they can be taken at night by letting down into pools (especially pools by a stone bridge) small round nets or wire baskets baited with bad meat. The season is late summer or autumn.

SHORE FOOD. Our shell-fish eating is now rather limited. The Englishman needs a course in Brittany, or in the fish-restaurants of Venice, to learn that more can be eaten pleasurably than winkles, cockles, mussels, scallops and oysters among molluscs, as well as prawns, shrimps, lobsters and a single kind of crab. Or read – if you can find it – M. S. Lovell's *Edible Mollusks of Great Britain and Ireland, with recipes for cooking them*, published a century ago, full of information about eating Razor Shells, various Cockles, Ormers (in the Channel Islands), Limpets, and Squid (better, if cooked properly, than lobster).

The Common Sea-Urchin can be found in restaurants in Paris (recipes are included in Lovell's book, which also concerns itself with snails). Sea Anemones may also be tried, boiled in sea-water, or fried in olive oil.

Laver is far the best of the edible seaweeds, very common around the coast on sandy stony beaches attached to stones or rocks or washed up into the tide wrack. On the beach it is a thin membranous seaweed, red or reddish-purple. Washed and boiled and salted, it is a dark green pulp (Plate 5). Mix laver with oatmeal, make into rissoles, fry them, and eat them with bacon. Or beat laver up with olive oil, lemon juice, pepper and salt, and eat cold on bread or toast, or hot with lamb or any roast meat. People on either side of the Bristol Channel are addicts of laver: it may be bought from fishmongers in Bristol and the towns of South Wales and North Devon, travelling in tins – when you have located your fishmonger – as well as Cornish or Devonshire cream. Eighteenth-century Bath rang

– with the cries
Of fine potted laver, fresh oysters, and pies,

according to Christopher Anstey's *New Bath Guide*.

Carragheen, or Irish Moss, less of a delicacy, more of a peculiarity, is an equally common seaweed, in small flat fronds (usually stalked) like a crisp tough dark red parsley. Wash it, dry it, and bleach it in the open air, and it will keep indefinitely, turning milk into a slightly sea-tasting white jelly – a handful to a saucepan of milk, which must then be brought nearly to the boil. Be careful to strain the now slimy carragheen out of the milk, as you pour it into the jelly mould.

# Mushrooms

## THE BEST MUSHROOMS

The best for eating. And you will see I call them mushrooms, not toadstools or fungi. It is an odd thing that by tradition in England we eat only one or two kinds. In consequence we have few names, collective or individual, for these odd plants which are some of them so delicious to eat and others so beautiful or so intriguing in shape and colour. Singular or plural, fungus or fungi (from the Latin, and related to the word sponge, for something soft) has come to sound as much a word of fear and disgust as toadstool or, to exhaust our collective terms, as toad's cap, toad's hat, toad's cheese, toad's meat (as if fungi were food only for amphibians), toad's skep and toad's tump.

Since in England we are beginning to lose our fear and modify our prejudice, we obviously do need a pleasant way of talking about these plants collectively. The French call them *champignons*. Should we not talk about them all as mushrooms, instead of dividing them into mushrooms (= the Field Mushroom and the Horse Mushroom and the rather tasteless cultivated kind) and toadstools (= every other kind)? Mushroom is sometimes used only of the gill-bearing fungi, but it would be convenient (as I shall do now) to use it of all the kinds we eat or are careful to reject, indeed of all the field and woodland kinds which attract the ordinary observer. This ought not to offend sticklers for meaning and propriety, since mushroom, which we borrowed centuries ago from the French – from *mousseron* (which in modern French is used for an edible mushroom in its button stage) – meant originally something which grew in moss (*mousse*). It is French, too, which has given us names for various individual kinds, such as the Cep, the Grisette, the Morel, the Truffle. At any rate, a pleasant word will help us to exorcise what is left nowadays of our traditional disdain of almost all mushrooms except those of field and grocer. My own belief about our English fear of what I shall now call, firmly and in general, mushrooms, is that it forms part of our inherited fear of woods and forests. John Gerarde, the Tudor herbalist, wrote in 1597 'few of them are good to be eaten, and most of them do suffocate and strangle the eater. Therefore, I give my advice unto those that love such strange and new-fangled meats, to be ware of licking honey among thorns, lest the sweetness of the one do not countervail the sharpness and pricking of the other'. Such suspicion was no doubt much older. We maintain far less forest than such mushroom-eaters as the French, Poles and Russians. Thousands of years ago we cleared the downlands, hundreds of years ago we cleared most of the valleys, making ourselves into a nation of pasture-dwellers in broad daylight disliking trees and woods. So by tradition we eat only pasture mushrooms, rather cautiously adding to the Field Mushroom and the shop mushroom only the Horse Mushroom (page 272), though it does stain a little yellow on the caps and has white gills (at first) instead of pink ones, and – in some districts only – the Blewit or Blue-leg (page 270) of autumn meadows. Wood mushrooms, all the same, include some of the best eaters.

If our fear depends partly on inherited prejudice, of course it depends as well on the fact that there are poisonous kinds which do, as Gerard said, 'suffocate and strangle the eater'. *These are very few.* But since they do exist, the mushroom-eater does need to be able to identify his mushrooms with certainty. The notes which follow are pointers in the first place to good eating, in the second place to exact identification. But this is the wrong way round: identify first, cook and eat afterwards. So these notes should be supplemented, however often you refer to them, with a modern mushroom book or guide in which there are good coloured plates of the virtuous and vicious alike, together with the fullest descriptions. No one is going to die of wicked mushrooms if he acquaints himself with the plates and descriptions in, for example, two inexpensive King Penguin books, *Edible Fungi* and *Poisonous Fungi*, both by John Ramsbottom, and in the *Observer's Book of Common Fungi* by E. M. Wakefield. Having absorbed these three, the next modern book to consult (or acquire, if you can – it is now out of print) is *Common British Fungi* by E. M. Wakefield and R. W. G. Dennis, in which there are coloured likenesses by the score.

If you are abroad, you will find in German or French shops little pocket guides with coloured plates (most of which will also apply to mushrooms in Great Britain when you come home). For instance, Editions Delachaux-Niestlé, of 32 rue de Grenelle, Paris VII*e*, publish for a few francs a *Petit Atlas des Champignons*, which goes easily into the pocket.

## Time of Year and Place

Mushrooms, in colonies, in quantity, are apt to come upon us by surprise, when we have no basket. Broadly, the best time is late summer or early autumn, after the rains. There are kinds which come early in the year, though not many. I remember the surprise of finding once and once only a steep hazel copse speckled in early May with thousands of the yellowy sponges of the Morel (page 274) which is a spring mushroom. The Blewit, strong, firm, cold, continues to push itself up in meadows till Christmas, sometimes even later. On the whole mushrooms like warmth and moisture – or moist warmth – and a soft soil. A dry summer which makes the woodland soil under the leaf-mould, or the meadow soil under the turf, impenetrable and hard, is the worst prelude for a mushroomy autumn.

As for place, mushrooms are no less particular than other plants. Some are more likely to be found where the soil contains plenty of lime. Woodland kinds living in association with trees may broadly prefer, or insist upon, either conifers or deciduous trees, so that the mushroom population of a fir wood and of an oak wood or a beech wood will not be the same. And within these wide limits, a particular species may favour or require a particular kind of deciduous tree, or a particular conifer – beech, or oak, or birch for example; or larch in preference to pine. Any wood, any copse, is worth searching, if there is not too much undergrowth. Indeed an isolated tree or a single group of trees may have its mushrooms. Best of all, though, is an old forest area of glades and leaf-mould and mature or ancient timber, such as Burnham Beeches in Buckinghamshire, or Savernake Forest in Wiltshire, or the New Forest, or the old pine forests of Scotland. In much the same way pasture mushrooms are most abundant on old permanent grassland – for instance, the short grass of downs and broad hillsides and cliff tops. Sandy pastures are rewarding. Some of the best mushroom grounds I know are the sandy permanent pastures of the Isles of Scilly between the autumnal bracken and the Atlantic. Parasol mushrooms (page 269) are often splendidly gigantic and abundant in such brackeny sandy places by the sea.

## Cooking Mushrooms

This is a matter of taste, knowledge and experiment. French, German, and Italian cookery books are better informed than most English books on mushroom dishes, flavouring with mushrooms, and drying mushrooms for use out of season. Also some of these Continental books illustrate the mushrooms in colour, in a reassuring way. *Plats du Jour*, Patience Gray and Primrose Boyd's guide to foreign food (a Penguin), has an unusual chapter on cooking mushrooms of one kind and another.

The best mushrooms are not so much food as delicacies, depending upon texture and flavour. The flavour of most kinds is individual: it may be pronounced, it may be subtle and easily destroyed. As a rule, mushroom species should not be mixed. One dish, one kind.

Stewing under a lid with butter, pepper, salt and parsley is a good basic recipe for mushrooms which do not contain too much water. But frying in olive oil or butter or grilling – no matter what some books say – is not to be despised. Boletuses fry well. So do the Parasols; and I doubt if many mushroom dishes are really better than Field Mushrooms or Horse Mushrooms fried in butter and served on buttered toast. Obviously, though, some of the solider kinds do not lend themselves to frying.

Time is wasted by peeling mushrooms, which is not at all necessary. The tubes of the Boletus kinds harbour concealed livestock and need scraping away. It is not always worth cooking the legs. They should be discarded whenever they are dry or stringy.

Comparative tastiness is roughly indicated or suggested in the following selection by the number of stars affixed to the name of each kind. The highest award, of six stars, goes to the Shaggy Cap. In my opinion, the best half dozen are:

Shaggy Cap
Parasol
Common or Field Mushroom
Oyster Mushroom
Cèpe de Bordeaux (and the Netted Cep)
Morel

But there can be no absolutes in a choice depending on individual peculiarities of palate.

\* \* \* \*

The GRISETTE (*Amanitopsis vaginata*) – i.e. the little grey one, the girl in the grey dress, is a woodland species which some mushroom-eaters are shy of collecting since they are afraid of confusing it with one or other of the poisoners of the genus *Amanita* (described on page 279). For that reason alone it is worth studying and knowing, as an introduction. First of all, the Grisette is a mushroom of shady places in late summer and autumn, neatly shaped and rather elegant, six inches or so high with a grey cap which comes to a boss in the middle. It does resemble the poisonous (though more robust) *Amanitae* in several characteristics.

1. Some mushrooms are at first, when they are small and young, contained in a seamless wrapper or 'universal veil'. The mushroom expands, and the Universal Veil breaks. What is left of this Universal Veil remains in the ground, like a broken-edged cup, around the bottom of the leg of some species, *including poisonous Amanitae and the Grisette*. This cup-like remnant is the volva.

2. As the mushrooms burst out of the Universal Veil, scraps of the membrane of this veil may adhere in a dry way to the cap, like patches or more substantially like warts. The grey cap of a Grisette is usually smooth, but it *may* carry a few grey patches in this way. Likewise the cap (greenish or white) of the deadliest of the *Amanita* mushrooms is

generally smooth, though it may also be patched with a few scraps of
the Universal Veil. Other *Amanitae* which are poisonous, though they
do not murder, have their cap surfaces quite rough with thicker wart-
like fragments.

3. The cap of the Grisette is regularly indented with short lines or
furrows around the circumference. But so are some of the poisonous
*Amanitae*.

4. An aid to identifying mushrooms is the colour of the spores which
fall from the gills (or tubes). If you lay the cap of a mushroom, gills or
tubes downward, on a piece of grey paper and leave it for some time
(say overnight) the spores fall, making an engaging pattern as they
do so. But the spores of both *Amanita* mushrooms and the Grisette are
white.

There is one particular in which the Grisette does immediately differ
from an *Amanita*. Some mushrooms have a ring around the stem. It
comes about in this way. In many species, vicious or virtuous, the
young unexpanded cap is joined to the stem by a wrapper or veil,
called the Partial Veil (in distinction to the Universal Veil). The cap
lifts and spreads, this Partial Veil breaks all the way round, leaving a
ring of its own membranous substance around the stem. The poisonous
*Amanitae* have such a ring. The stem of a Grisette is naked, without
such a ring.

The true Grisette is this little grey one. Colour apart, the description
applies also to the *Tawny Grisette*, which is a form (just as good to eat)
with brown instead of grey tints. The cap is a cheerful, slightly pale
chestnut.

The flavour of either one is delicate and good.

*Of the edible mushrooms described in this book only the Grisette and Tawny
Grisette grow out of a volva* (though see the note on page 280 describing
the Blusher).

If you wish to learn at once more of the poisonous *Amanitae* before
going on to the other edible mushrooms, turn to page 278.

The *Parasol* or *Lepiota Mushrooms* have rings, and no volva. The two
described are among the best of all edible mushrooms, and are not
difficult to identify, first of all from the brown scales on the cap. The
spores (see above) are white.

\* \* \* \* \*

The PARASOL (*Lepiota procera*) could be called a mushroom on a stilt. The leg may be a foot high, or taller still, towering out of the grass or among the dying bracken. As the Parasol matures, the cap opens like a parasol or an umbrella which rises to a boss in the middle. The cap is shaggy with brown scales. The long leg is also scaly and brown, and the gills are white. The rather strong ring below the gills can be moved up and down. These shaggy, grey-brown, very obvious and oddly endearing Parasols usually grow in a colony, so if you find one you are likely to find a basketful. But very tall, foot-high, fully opened Parasols are apt to have leathery caps and gills, in which case they are not worth cooking. Young ones are altogether delicious, especially fried, or cooked in the oven in butter and their own juice, under a lid.

\* \* \* \* \*

The WOOD PARASOL or RAGGED PARASOL (*Lepiota rachodes*) is no less tasty. It does not grow so tall. The scaly cap is flat and does not rise to a boss in the middle, the leg is smooth, and the white flesh blushes to red when it is broken. Woods, compost heaps, etc. Late summer to autumn.

*The Tricholoma Mushrooms.* Woodland and pasture dwellers. Rather large, squat, sturdy and substantial, with flavours to match. No rings on the stem. No volva.

\* \*

BLEWIT or BLUE-LEG (*Tricholoma personatum*). A field mushroom, solid, sturdy, naked-seeming; cap grey to brown, with a tinge of violet, blunt edged, standing firmly on a violet leg. Gills more or less white. An autumn mushroom growing in rings in coarse damp meadows, still to be found in early winter, even when there have been considerable frosts. Not a first-class eater. It makes rather too solid a meal in

itself, and is to be preferred for soup and flavouring. Still, it is always tempting to cook Blewits after the surprise of finding them so late in the year, growing so unconcernedly in the cold crumpled grass. This is one of the few kinds with an authentic English name, neither borrowed in modern times from the French nor invented by botanists. It is particularly common in pastures in the Midlands, where Blewits are sold in the markets and by grocers (for instance, in Derby). The spores (page 269) are pink.

* * *

ST GEORGE'S MUSHROOM (*Tricholoma gambosum*). Not so common. It may be found in meadows in chalk or limestone districts, in April (about the time of St George's Day, 23 April), in May, June or July, having something of the look of a Blewit out of season, though it tends to white and faintly yellow, instead of grey and violet. The cap is white tinged with yellow, so is the sturdy leg. The gills are whitish, the spores are white, and the flesh is white, with a smell of meal or bran.

* * *

WOOD-BLEWIT (*Tricholoma nudum*). More violet than the Blewit of the fields – violet cap, violet gills, violet leg – and also slighter and more elegant (see page 284, for a species with which it might be confused). The violet gills are exceedingly pretty in tone. Late autumn, fir woods or deciduous woods. Cooked with butter and parsley in their own juice, these Wood-Blewits have a pleasant, less meaty or solid taste.


*The True Agaric Mushrooms.* The first three included grow in pastures; of these the Field Mushroom is everybody's idea of a mushroom. There are as well woodland species of Agaric which do not differ much in form and are good eating (though one should reject the Yellow-staining Mushroom, *Agaricus xanthoderma*, the skin of which changes at once from white to brilliant yellow when it is touched).

Note that these mushrooms do have a ring around the leg, in common with the poisonous *Amanita* mushrooms described on pages 279 and 280. Unlike the *Amanita* kinds, they do not exhibit a volva (page 268), and their spores (page 269) are purple, and not white.

* * * * *

COMMON or FIELD MUSHROOM (*Agaricus campestris*). When all is said and done, the most delightful mushroom to eat *in any quantity*, and the best for flavouring. But the cultivated mushroom, *Agaricus hortensis*, has only just enough flavour to be worth eating, and should never be bought when the full flavoured Field Mushrooms are about. For the most part, their season is late summer or autumn, according to the degree of warmth and moisture.

\* \* \* \* \*

HORSE MUSHROOM (*Agaricus arvensis*). Horse Mushrooms do not smell quite so appetizing. The leg and the cap often have a touch or stain of yellow. The gills when they are still white (i.e. when the mushrooms are at their best), are not as attractive to the eye as the exquisitely pink gills of the young Field Mushroom which may be growing along-side. But I doubt if many people could tell the difference between Field Mushroom and Horse Mushroom when they are cooked. (Not to be confused with the woodland Yellow-staining Mushroom, mentioned above.)

\* \* \*

OX MUSHROOM (*Agaricus villatica*). The very big mushrooms of the meadow or the downs are Ox Mushrooms, with a brownish scaly cap, pallid gills, and white flesh which stains red when broken. A tasty mushroom when it is not too old or too big. Summer and autumn.

\* \* \* \*

BROWN WOOD MUSHROOM (*Agaricus silvaticus*). This has the appear-ance of a slightly small Field Mushroom parodied in brown, growing in the wrong place, i.e. in woods. It has reddish-brown scales on the rusty cap, gills which are at first white, then rather red or pink, and last of all brown, and whitish flesh which turns reluctantly to red – in young specimens – when broken or cut. Summer and autumn.

\* \* \* \*

BLOODY WOOD MUSHROOM (*Agaricus haemorrhoidaria*). Good to eat like the last kind, but less common. Also with a reddish-brown cap abundantly covered with darker reddish-brown scales. When broken or cut, the white or cream flesh immediately goes a bright red. This woodlander of summer and autumn is rather taller and has a slightly wider cap than the Field Mushroom. It has a liking for conifers.

\* \*

The PUFFBALLS. Various kinds commonly grow along with the meadow, downland or cliff-top mushrooms described above. All these meadow puffballs can be eaten with pleasure when they are young and white. They are best cut in slices, and may be cooked separately or with Field or Horse or Ox Mushrooms. Puffballs are also called Bunts (perhaps the same word as bun or bunt for a hare's tail or rab-bit's tail). Less politely they were connected with Pucks or goblins.

The smoking puffball (emitting its ripe spores) gave rise to the impolite name of Puckfist, which means goblin's fart. Young puffballs are very pure objects all the same.

\* \*

FAIRY RING MUSHROOM or CHAMPIGNON (*Marasmius oreades*). Tiny, two to three inches high, pale yellow or yellowish-brown, will grow in rings marked by the darker green of the turf in the same pasture with puffballs and Field Mushrooms. The caps are small cones, which flatten out, preserving a boss in the middle. Last of all, the edges often turn up showing the pale rather widely spaced gills. In my opinion these little summer to autumn mushrooms are rather overrated, either cooked on their own or as a flavouring (for which they are best used). They can very easily be dried and kept for the winter.

\* \*

The MILLER (*Clitopilus prunulus*). Recipes for the Champignon, above, apply well to this common woodlander, which dries easily and is good for flavouring. It is a good deal eaten abroad, the Frenchman's *Meunier* (i.e. miller, since it is white and a little floury, like the miller at his mill door), the German's *Mehlpilz* (i.e. meal mushroom) or *Moosling* (i.e. little moss one). The white cap, three inches across, and at times a little slimy, has a frosty bloom. The edges roll inwards, and eventually the cap deepens in the middle. The gills – white, then pink after a while – run down on to the short leg, which is cottony at the base. The flesh is white, the smell is positive and mealy. The Miller grows in woodland grass very abundantly, from early summer to autumn. The spores (see page 269) are pink.

\* \* \* \* \* \*

SHAGGY CAP, INKY CAP, or LAWYER'S WIG (*Coprinus comatus*). Shaggy Caps, very beautiful and quite unmistakeable objects, need to be gathered before the soft, scaly, brilliantly white and pure cap begins to fray at the edges and to dissolve, or auto-digest, into ink. The gills should still be in the white or pink stage. This is a late summer and autumn mushroom, often in populous colonies, in hedges, on banks, on rubbish heaps, usually near houses. The flavour is exceptionally piquant and delicate. Excellent (cap only) when baked across an egg. It is said to be unwise to partake of Inky Caps and alcohol at the same meal. (Plate 38.)

\* \*

HORN OF PLENTY, DEAD MAN'S TRUMPET (*Craterellus cornucopioides*) is often to be found by the hundred in woods crouching among the damp autumn leaves and sticks. When perfect, each is a small wavy horn or funnel, ebony touched with brown on the outside, inside a blue ashy colour. They are better eating than books allow, and may be stewed slowly with butter, parsley, and onion, or a touch of garlic.

\* \*

PIG'S TROTTER, RUBBER BRUSH (*Hydnum repandum*). Always a pleasure to see and pick in autumn woods. Few mushrooms appear so clean. Its wavy cap is yellowish, suffused with pink. Underneath there hang down, instead of gills or tubes, innumerable soft spines like the spines of a rubber brush, except that they are unequal in length. These again are a pale blush-yellow, highly tender and agreeable in tone. The leg is white. The French call this mushroom by equivalents of Pig's Trotter or Cow's Beard. The flavour is slight and pleasant, the texture is delicately attractive. Stew in butter, with parsley.

\* \*

EGG MUSHROOM, or CHANTERELLE (*Cantharellus cibarius*). A horn-shaped mushroom of the woods, from late summer to late autumn. The horn is vivid egg yolk in colour, and is wider and more lax than in the last species. Few mushrooms appear so clean and wholesome, or smell – the smell is of dried apricots or ripe greengages – so attractive. They are a little tough, so before they are cooked they need to be put for a short while into boiling water.

\*

ORANGE MILKER, SAFFRON MILK CAP (*Lactarius deliciosus*). There are many Lactarius kinds, mostly in woods. When you break them drops of 'milk' exude, generally white, though exposure changes it, according to species, to lilac or violet or yellow or grey or green. A few kinds have a red milk. This Saffron Milk Cap has a saffron (i.e. reddish-yellow) milk, which turns green, and a cap ringed in pale and darker orange, shaped like a funnel. It will be found only in fir woods. Not so very delicious. A French mushroom book says loftily that the Saffron Milk Cap is liked by foreigners – 'et surtout des Allemandes, qui en font de grosses provisions'. It is eaten through all the forest areas of Europe.

\* \* \* \*

MOREL (*Morchella esculenta*). Like St George's Mushrooms, Morels are to be found in the spring when mushrooms and mushroom eating are the last things one has in mind. But they are not very common, and a locality where they occur cannot be depended upon. They like open woods and disturbed ground. The ordinary Morel has a yellow-ochre cap, not smooth but haphazardly ribbed and pitted. The cap is more or less globular, is hollow, and fits close to the short hollow stem. These peculiar caps can be detached and stuffed. Usually the rib-spaces will have collected earth, grit, scraps of leaf-mould, etc., which will need washing out.

MITRE MUSHROOM (*Helvella crispa*). An autumn mushroom of grassy woodland glades, which has some of the virtues of the Morel. The cap is divided into three thin, wavy, untidy lobes, curling downwards. On the upper side these lobes are yellowish-white or pinkish-white. Underneath they are dirty yellow. The stem is white and irregularly grooved (exhibiting a pretty pattern, if you cut a section across with a razor-blade) – and tough. The taste of these Mitre Mushrooms is much more agreeable than some books allow, *but they must not be eaten raw*. In Germany, they are first of all heated in a saucepan in salted water, which is then thrown away. This removes an acid they contain which affects the blood. The stems are useless.

*The Boletus Mushrooms*. These are wood-dwellers, easily recognized because they have thick bun-like caps, vertical tubes underneath instead of gills (so the German name for a Boletus is a *Röhrling*, i.e. tubeling), and legs which are either sturdy or swollen. Most kinds are good eating, and they go to waste by the ton every autumn in English woods. Some exhibit rather bizarre and startling changes of colour when the flesh is broken or bruised, but that does not mean they are poisonous.

In deciduous woods you find:

\* \* \* \* \*

CEP, or CÈPE DE BORDEAUX (*Boletus edulis*). We have no authentically English name for any Boletus, including this one, the most famous of them all, which nowadays is imported from the Continent and is sold dried and divided in cellophane packets in grocers' shops. In the woods (beech woods in particular) the living Cèpe de Bordeaux has a light yellow-brown cap which is smooth and moist and darkens in colour in the centre. This is firmly set on a stem which is bulbous and plump, white or yellow-brown, and marked at the top with a raised net-work of white lines. The tubes begin by being more or less white, and turn more or less green. The flesh is white, though it may be pink under the skin. Summer to autumn. The trouble always is to find specimens which slugs have not already begun to eat.

\* \* \* \* \*

NETTED CEP (*Boletus reticulatus*) is very similar in taste and appearance.

The cap is downy and the whole stem, instead of the top only, is netted with white lines. Summer to autumn.

\* \* \*

BIRCH BOLETUS (*Boletus scaber*), well thought of in France as a second string to the Cèpe de Bordeaux. It has a slimy grey cap – which may incline to brown – and a very different stem, not bulbous, but tapering, not marked with a net-pattern in white, but covered, on a white ground, with grey to black fibres. The tubes are white, or very soon dirty white. The flesh is white, and stays white (though it may go a little pink). Summer to autumn, favouring birch woods.

\* \* \* \*

RED CAP, or ORANGE CAP (*Boletus versipellis*), which differs from the Birch Boletus by displaying in the woods a strikingly reddish-orange cap, dry and downy, and often fringed with scraps of the Partial Veil (page 269). It has dirty white tubes, and the stem, on a white ground, is rough with grey to black fibres or scales. The white flesh changes to drab pink or violet. Late summer and autumn.

\* \* \*

RED FOOT, or RED-CRACKING BOLETUS (*Boletus chrysanteron*). Easy to recognize from the cap which is dingily felted in greyish-yellow on a plum-brown skin, and from the way the cap cracks open (especially in dry weather) to reveal little troughs of reddish-pink. The tubes are yellow or greenish-yellow, and the flesh goes blue. The leg is yellow streaked with blood-colour. In woodland grass, from early summer to autumn.

Under fir trees of various kinds are to be found:

\* \* \*

BUTTER BOLETUS, or YELLOW BOLETUS (*Boletus luteus*), which gives a first impression, not of yellow or butter colour, but of brown. The cap, which is slimy, is brown or pale brown. The tubes are yellow. There is a creamy or later bluish-black ring around the stem (so the Germans distinguish this favourite kind as *Ringpilz*, though the commoner name is *Butter-Röhrling*). The leg is white inclined to yellow, and is marked with grains, above the ring. Below the ring it is dusky white. The flesh is white or slightly yellow. Summer to late autumn.

\* \* \*

GOLDEN BOLETUS (*Boletus elegans*), a species which looks too lurid and feels too slimy on top to be edible, though it makes a good dish. It favours the close neighbourhood of larch trees, and below its very slimy golden cap it has yellow tubes, close packed, and stands on a golden leg netted with grains around the top. There is a ring round the leg. The yellow flesh, when damaged, blushes to red, or changes to pale violet. The Golden Boletus has a strong, rather encouraging, fragrance. Summer to late autumn.

\* \* \*

GRAINED BOLETUS (*Boletus granulatus*). This resembles the Butter Boletus, but has no ring. The cap is slimy, begins by being reddish-brown, and turns yellowish. Yellowish flesh, tubes and leg. At the top the leg is marked with darkish grains. Milky drops come from the tubes in young specimens. Early summer to late autumn.

\* \* \* \* \*

OYSTER MUSHROOM (*Pleurotus ostreatus*). There is no rule that to be edible a mushroom must grow out of the soil. Edible kinds grow on trees, above all this Oyster Mushroom colonizing tree trunks when the

tree is dead or dying. This Oyster Mushroom does not have much of a stem. Under a cap which is velvety and smooth, at first blackish-brown, then blue-grey or pale violet, the very purest white gills run more or less together, from the rim to a stem which is more like a narrowing of the cap than a proper leg. Commonest in autumn. In taste, clean and uncommonly and delicately piquant.

\* \*

VEGETABLE BEEFSTEAK (*Fistulina hepatica*). Another tree-trunk mushroom, growing horizontally out of living trees, often out of reach. It is commonest in oaks. The structure is raw-flesh-coloured when broken or cut. Pressure makes it bleed. In growth it looks not unlike a piece of liver, and the Germans call it by names meaning liver-sponge or blood-sponge. Sideways on, it may also seem like a tongue protruding and slightly curling up at the end, which accounts for other foreign names such as the ones which mean Ox Tongue or Hart's Tongue.

The surprise is to find a soft texture and a soft inside to something which, from the ground, looks so wooden and solid. Scrape away the tubes before cutting up and stewing with parsley and butter, or frying in slices. The French would probably say that it is only food for gross-eating foreigners, like the Saffron Milk Cap.

\* \* \*

FIR SPONGE, FIR CAULIFLOWER (*Sparassis crispa*) forms a considerable 'head' of yellowish-white or creamy lobes, weighing several pounds, on the stump of a conifer or on the ground underneath fir trees. Sponge or cauliflower is an apt description, though from a way off in a wood one of these rounded objects looks rather like an outsize in brains. It is crisp, curly, pleasant smelling, and with us not very common, appearing in late summer or early autumn. Much cooked for its nutty flavour in the Black Forest. It can be dried.

THE ENGLISH TRUFFLE (*Tuber aestivum*) is best looked for in beech plantations on chalky soil (particularly on Salisbury Plain and the chalk downs of the southern counties). Those who want to go truffling, should read the detailed chapter in John Ramsbottom's *Mushrooms and Toadstools* (1953), absorb the clues, and then get to work in the autumn and winter months – more perhaps in hope than expectation, since the blackish, warty, irregular potato shapes grow a finger's depth underground. But they can be found without dogs. The two species most valued by chefs do not occur in Great Britain, where the collection of the 'English' Truffle spread first of all in the eighteenth century. Gilbert White was familiar with truffles on the Hampshire chalk at Selborne.

## THE FATAL MUSHROOMS

Read again the remarks above (pages 268–9) on the Grisette and the Tawny Grisette. Except for the Blusher, mentioned below, they are the only mushrooms in our selection of edible kinds which at all closely resemble the fatally poisonous, and the poisonous, mushrooms of the genus *Amanita*.

The Grisette and the Tawny Grisette are also, remember, the only mushrooms in this selection which grow, like the *Amanita* kinds, out of a *volva* (page 268) – this membranous volva remaining like a sheath or a cup (either with an untidy broken fringe or with a tidy edge or ridge) around the foot of the stem, partly or mostly in the soil.

Only some of the *Amanita* mushrooms kill. Of these killers one only is very common in England. This is:

(*a*) The DEATH CAP (*Amanita phalloides*)

1. It is a mushroom of deciduous woods (but it may be found in grassland near a wood or trees), appearing from spring to autumn.
2. The cap is dirty white to olive, greenish-white, generally the latter. It is convex, and from the centre of the cap outwards it is marked with blackish little fibres. In dry weather the cap will be satiny in texture, in damp weather a little sticky. Generally the cap is altogether smooth, but sometimes it carries white patches of the volva.
3. A white or greenish-white ring surrounds the white or greenish-white leg. The ring usually hangs back towards the ground; it may have disappeared.
4. The gills are white, or greenish-white.
5. The volva, too, like a cup or sheath round the swollen bottom of the leg, is white or greenish-white.

Two other pallid *Amanita* mushrooms occur, exceedingly poisonous, not greatly dissimilar, but fortunately rare. Like the Death Cap, each has a cup-like volva, and a downward drooping ring, and grows in deciduous woodland. These two are:

(*b*) The FOOL'S MUSHROOM (*Amanita verna*), which is white instead of greenish-white. The cap dimples in the centre. Early summer to autumn, particularly under beech trees.

(*c*) The DESTROYING ANGEL (*Amanita virosa*), also white, as an angel should be. Sometimes it lacks its ring, and scraps of the Partial Veil (of which the ring is a detached portion—see page 269) may hang from the cap. The cap is sticky, and in expanded specimens has something of a boss in the middle. The stem is scaly. Summer to autumn.

Two more *Amanita* mushrooms – common ones – are poisonous:

(*d*) The PANTHER (*Amanita pantherina*), parading a very pretty brown or brown-grey cap, which is warty (rather than patched) with scraps of the Universal Veil. The white stem swells to a bulbous foot inside the volva. The gills are white, and the ring may disappear. Deciduous or fir woods. Summer to autumn.

(*e*) FLY AGARIC (*Amanita muscaria*), which no one is likely to confuse with an edible mushroom. Notable for its orange-red cap beautifully 'warted' with white or yellow oddments of the Universal Veil. Gills and stem are white. This is the painted toadstool of bric-à-brac shops and sentimental pictures of elves, described by the poet James Woodhouse as

> All deeply dyed in sanguine gore,
> With brazen bosses studded o'er.

Late summer to autumn, under birches; less often under pines.

A sixth *Amanita* is usually avoided, though harmless:

(*f*) The FALSE DEATH CAP (*Amanita citrina*). Summer to autumn, in deciduous woods, sometimes under conifers. White or usually pale lemon cap, patched with pieces of the Universal Veil. White (or yellow-white) gills. Around the swollen foot of the white leg there is a yellowish volva neatly bordered, without loose edges. Smells of raw potato.

A seventh *Amanita* it is perhaps just as well to avoid, although it has modest virtues of edibility, is:

(*g*) The BLUSHER (*Amanita rubescens*). Summer to autumn, under deciduous trees or conifers. Cap red-brown or red-grey, warted with grey scraps of the Universal Veil (these may be washed off). A large, white, hanging ring on the pinkish stem. Scales left from the volva make ridges around the swollen base of the stem. The white flesh blushes – reluctantly at times – when broken.

The particular rule is: Suspect and reject mushrooms which have both a ring around the stem and a volva around the base of the stem.

The general rule is: be sure of what you are collecting and eating. Learn your mushrooms. Acquaint yourself with the look and character of the poisoners, at first-hand, from these notes, and from books (e.g. from John Ramsbottom's King Penguin booklet, *Poisonous Fungi*). Check your suspicions every time against pictures and the decisive distinguishing marks of an *Amanita*.

Also be careful – especially careful – about mushrooms which are still in the unbroken button stage, and so hard to identify.

The *Amanita* kinds apart, there are of course other mushrooms which prove disagreeable, or indigestible to a greater or lesser degree, so deserving the label of poisonous. There are mushrooms which disagree with some digestions, but not with others. And obviously ageing or decomposing mushrooms may cause an upset. So might a rotten cabbage or a decomposing pork chop.

## CURIOUS MUSHROOMS

EARTH STARS have – or some of them have – an oddly artificial look. They are not very common, and they are quite useless. Finding Earth Stars is one of the rarest pleasures of searching woods in the autumn – beech woods in particular.

(a) FRINGED EARTH STAR (*Geaster fimbriatus*) may be discovered among dead beech leaves and twigs. About two inches across, each individual in a colony consists of a roundish ball nestling in a 'star' of five or more rays or triangular sections. The prevailing colour is a pretty buff. Between colour and shape it is rather as if a medlar lay rooted in the leaf-mould. A pale-edged mouth opens in the ball, and 'smoke' (the spores) emerges strongly as if from a volcano when the ball is pressed.

(b) THREEFOLD EARTH STAR (*Geaster triplex*) is bigger, opening to a star of six, seven or eight rays. The roundish ball sits comfortably between the rays on a yellowish-brown collar. More bizarre than these two kinds, but less frequent, is the –

(c) VAULTED EARTH STAR (*Geaster fornicatus*), which is less like a star than a little brown parody of a human being carved or conceived by Henry Moore. It stands up six inches or so in woodland grass, seeming to hold a skirt, and presenting to view a head without features. It is 'vaulted' because, on a closer look, the organism appears divided into two shapes in reverse, a cup in the ground (the skirt) with four lobes pointing upwards, and the 'arms' which are four lobes pointing downward and then joined to the upward lobes. The 'arms' bend down from shoulders, on which there stands a 'neck' supporting the 'head', the spore-body.

STINKHORN (*Phallus impudicus*). Very common in damp woods, copses hedges, wooded corners, where there is plenty of decay, though by most people it is perhaps more often smelt than seen. This smell, which comes from the leather-green slime on the cap, is corruption, like the smell of a dead rat, or something bigger – dead cat, dead badger; and on the damp air of a September or October evening it carries a long way. In shape, no fungus is so much one of nature's dubious jokes. Books have the courage to say 'edible when unexpanded' – which is true. If they are fried, the unexpanded 'eggs' (called by the Germans in the Black Forest Witches' Eggs or Devil's Eggs) from which the Stinkhorns emerge, do have a pleasant, crisp, earthy taste, though one should first remove the top gelatinous layer, which peels off without trouble. Stinkhorns have been used abroad (if not in England) to make love philtres and as a medicine against gout. The German name is *Gichtmorchel*, Gout-morel. If you take an 'egg' home and leave it on a saucer in a damp cloth, a Stinkhorn will sooner or later emerge, almost suddenly. But it will not make you popular.

DOG STINKHORN (*Mutinus caninus*). This kind does not smell so badly, is much shorter and more slender, appearing in woods and on tree stumps from summer to autumn. Under the green slime, the cap is red instead of white, as in the Stinkhorn.

JEW'S EAR (*Hirneola auricula-Judae*). Everyone who has ever played in a shrubbery as a child knows the velvety, clammy, convoluted 'ears' of this fungus, which owes its name, not to antisemitism so much as to the medieval legend that Judas, after betraying Christ, hanged himself on an Elder. So Elders are weak and hollow-hearted, and soon decay, and break out with the ears of Judas.

BIRD'S NEST, CUP AND EGGS (*Cyathus striatus*). Look for these little oddities on rotten stumps in autumn, in colonies – each little cup or beaker less than an inch across, rusty coloured and hairy outside, inside shining, grey-blue and fluted. The cups contain white, circular, flattened spore-bodies, each on a thread. These are splashed out of the cup by drops of rain, the essential agent in dispersing the spores.

## ORNAMENTAL FUNGI

There are hard and lasting fungi, specimens of which are well worth taking home for their subtle beauties of pattern or tone, or for their brave colour.

RED CUP, MOSS CUP, SCARLET ELF-CUP (*Sarcoscypha coccinea*) grows in spring and winter out of dead sticks in the shape of little stalked cups, superbly scarlet inside. The colour lasts well. The first of these Elf-cups I ever saw were growing by a ride in a Wiltshire hazel copse, scarlet against the snow.

CORAL SPOT (*Nectria cinnabarina*). Hazel sticks left in the garden after the autumn clearance commonly develop an exquisite hard growth of Coral Spot. The clear pink spots look even more beautiful on the naked twigs and dead branches of Sycamore. They will keep their colour indoors for a long while.

OAK MAZE (*Daedalea quercina*), by contrast, is a bracket fungus on dead oaks, very corky and tough, on top and below a study in tones. On top the bracket is zoned in brown, on the underside it is an extraordinary maze of dark openings edged in silvery-grey.

## BEAUTIFUL AND USELESS MUSHROOMS

All in all, mushroom tints are some of the most vivid, the most subtle, and the least expected. Often the attraction is one of tones in combination or contrast (brown and grey, for example, or brown and yellow, or brown and pink) which are not at all easy to describe. Often the tints are brilliantly and outstandingly sensational, though even then they are little noticed, though fungi could be an art library of suggestion for any enquiring designer of fabrics. A poet who noticed mushroom colours was the cobbler James Woodhouse, in Surrey in the eighteenth century. He wrote that mushrooms (i.e. Field Mushrooms), 'shooting after show'rs', were 'lovelier far than vernal flowers',

> They fear no more the fatal scythe,
> But proudly spread their bonnets blythe,
> With coverings form'd of silk and snow,
> And lin'd with brightening pink below.

Even more this sensible man liked

>          ... the later Fungus race
> Begot by Phebus' warm embrace,
> In Summer's months, on procreant Earth,
> By damp September brought to birth;
> That, just like Jove, produce their seed,
> From teeming brain, for future breed:
> Their forms and hues some solace yield,
> In wood, or wild, or hurried field;
> Whose tapering stems, robust, or light,
> Like columns catch the searching sight,
> To claim remark where e'er I roam,
> Supporting each a shapely dome;
> Like fair umbrellas, furl'd, or spread,
> Display their many-colour'd head;
> Grey, purple, yellow, white, or brown,

Shap'd like War's shield, or Prelate's crown –
Like Freedom's cap, or Friar's cowl,
Or China's bright inverted bowl –
And while their broadening disks unfold
Gay silvery gills, or nets of gold,
Beneath their shady, curtain'd cove,
Perform all offices of love.

(from *Autumn and the Redbreast*, written in 1787).

The most brilliant mushrooms are not, most of them, very local or very uncommon, surprising as they may be when observed for the first time.

VIOLET. There are two species more remarkably violet than either the Blewit or the Wood-Blewit which have already been mentioned under the edible mushrooms (pages 270, 271). One is the violet form of the sticky Lac Mushroom (*Laccaria laccata* var. *amethystina*), only two or three inches high, carrying a little violet cap (with a boss in the middle), with violet flesh, violet gills, and violet stem. This is very common in the autumn woods. Brilliant green moss or dead rufous beech leaves often pull away with the violet stem. On such a damp foundation specimens can be kept awhile indoors, on a saucer.

A larger, firmer, fleshier species which looks particularly brilliant under its favoured birches and beeches in autumn is the Violet Veil-Mushroom (*Cortinarius violaceus*). It is violet throughout, cap, gills and stem, though the gills look brown when the spores begin to fall. This shining mushroom might be taken for a Wood-Blewit (page 271). One difference is that these Cortinarius mushrooms, when they are young, have a special kind of Partial Veil (page 269) joining cap to stem – a 'cortina', like stretched spider's web. This 'cortina' soon vanishes, but other differences are that the spores are brown, whereas the spores of the Wood-Blewit are pink, and that the foot of the purple stem is extremely bulbous, compared to the straighter stem of the Wood-Blewit. The Violet Veil can be eaten, so a mistake would hardly matter.

VERDIGRIS – i.e. bluish copper-green, an unexpectedly mineral colour to find in a plant, distinguishes the very common little Verdigris Mushroom (*Stropharia aeruginosa*), in woods and fields in the autumn. The copper-green cap is sticky, edged with a few white scales. Turn the cap over, and the gills will be almost black (though they are white at first). The rain sadly washes the colour of this probably poisonous mushroom to an unexciting yellow.

GREEN. In the wet autumn grass of meadows and downs look for the tropical combination of translucent colours which announce the Parrot Mushroom (*Hygrophorus psittacinus*). Basically its two-inch cap, which rises to a boss, is bright yellow, but this yellow is varied with green – a brilliant green glue. The green glue also covers the stem. The gills are yellow.

ORANGE. A common colour, already noted in some of the edible mushrooms. I shall mention two special and very different orange beauties. Orange Cup (*Peziza aurantia*), each wavy cup three to four inches across, grows commonly on bare woodland ground in the autumn; and can be cooked and eaten. Contrariwise, the Sulphur Bracket (*Polyporus sulphureus*), on trunks of trees from spring to autumn, is a most unvirtuous species which will attack and ruin ship's timbers. But it strikes the eye with surprise and wonderment, and deserves a better name. On top, as one often sees them first, the brackets are not sulphur but reddish-orange like a sunset. Underneath, the tubes display a sulphur-yellow which looks curiously sophisticated and not at all natural. The yellow flesh (of young specimens) will weep a yellow liquor.

SCARLET. Besides the astonishing Fly Agaric (page 279) and the little stabs of blood of the Scarlet Elf-Cup (page 282), everyone must have noticed in the damp autumnal grass (especially of the downs) that mushroom which for the want of a more vivid name may be called the Sticky Top (*Hygrophorus coccineus*). The slimy translucent caps are scarlet to begin with, changing, from the centre to the circumference, to an equally bright golden yellow. A beauty which is lurid, but harmless, even edible, in a dull way, like the related Parrot Mushroom (above).

Woods have their broad scarlet caps – not only Fly Agaric, but in beech woods, very commonly, the Sickener (*Russula emetica*), with white gills and a white leg. Though it attracts attention at once, the Sickener is not a very shapely mushroom, and the scarlet all too quickly washes out to a most unlovely purple, even to a drab white. More pleasure of form and colour is to be had from another of the Cortinarius species (see page 284) the Bloody Veil-Mushroom (*Cortinarius sanguineus*), a shaggy little mushroom growing in colonies in fir woods, half the size of the Violet Veil-Mushroom or the Sickener, with blood-red cap and gills and leg and juice, and a smell of radishes.

WHITE. If mushrooms are associated with devils, goblins, witches, toads, they can also be white; not merely a dirty white or a dull white of various tones, but a white which is shining, pearly and infinitely pure – in the darkness of the woods.

Beech woods nourish three particular kinds. One is the Beech Tuft (*Armillaria mucida*), admittedly owing its pure appearance to the glistening slime on the caps. It colonizes the dead branches and the dead and dying trunks of beech trees with tuft upon tuft of destroying purity. Caps, gills, and stem are snow-white.

The Coral Fungus (*Hydnum coralloides*) colonizes beech logs, hanging them with short, snowy, glistening spines. The Hedgehog (*Hydnum Erinaceus*) hangs much longer spines of snow on the trunks of beech trees. Both these species of *Hydnum* recall delicate stalactites of the purest white in limestone caves. (For another *Hydnum*, see page 274).

# Paper from Plants

Nearly all paper, even common newsprint, is made from some form of vegetation. The commercial kind made from wood may be cheap, may be good for its purpose, but in itself it is of very little interest, whereas the look, feel, and even smell of hand-made paper are unique and very special. Only three small mills in this country, one in Somerset, one in Devon, one in Kent, continue to produce hand-made paper, but if you have the patience, and are deft handed, you can excitingly make sheets of paper from *any plants which have fibrous leaves or stems* – nettle, cow parsley, iris, bulrush, gladiolus, montbretia, aloe, etc., wild plants and garden plants. This home craft has been inventively developed by John Mason, who has written this note:

Since we require only the skeleton fibres, the fleshy parts have first to be removed. It is most profitable to harvest your plants (of which you will need a considerable bulk) in late summer or in autumn when the fibres are toughened and mature. Throw the plants in a heap upon a stone floor and keep them wet until they start to rot or 'ret'. This will ease the work of beating and pulping, which is the most difficult task.

Meanwhile I suggest a simple experiment which will demonstrate the process of sheet forming. From a hardware store obtain an ordinary nylon kitchen sieve about eight to ten inches in diameter and also a pound of caustic soda. Half fill an enamelled saucepan with ordinary grass from the hedgerows, cut to short lengths with scissors, cover with water, and add half a cupful of caustic soda. Stir the mixture with a wooden spoon, bring to the boil and allow to simmer for half an hour. Strain off the liquor and wash under a running tap. The caustic will have loosened the unwanted fleshy parts of the grass and these will wash away, leaving behind only the true fibres. Place two handfuls of grass fibre in the sieve and float it in a bucket of warm water. Push the sieve an inch or two down into the water so that the fibre is awash and, with the hand, distribute it evenly. Lift the sieve, let the water drain away, and then place it outside or in a warm room to dry. To remove the sheet, first run the point of a nail file round the edge to sever contact with the wooden sides, then gently peel away.

You will have made your first sheet of paper.

The amount of useful fibre in ordinary grass is very small, so we must turn back to our more fibrous heap for our real papermaking material.

When sufficiently decomposed, place some of the material in a large saucepan, cover with water, add a liberal helping of caustic soda and boil for as long as possible, for at least three hours. There should be sufficient soda to give the water a greasy feel when rubbed between the fingers. The longer the boiling process the easier will be the operation of beating to pulp. If an old pressure cooker is available, this will be better than an ordinary saucepan and will not boil dry.

Place the boiled mass in a bucket, and wash thoroughly in several waters. Pound and squeeze with the hands until all the fleshy matter is removed and the water is clear and colourless. Next the fibres need bleaching. Put some bleaching powder into an earthenware jar, fill up with cold water, stir and allow to settle. The supernatant bleaching liquid is poured over the fibre and left as long as possible, overnight at least, and given an occasional stir with a stick. Do not attempt to bleach quite white, since this would injure the fibres. A light biscuit colour is as far as the bleaching process should be taken. If you have time and patience, it is a good plan to tip the heap outside for final bleaching in the sun.

Again you must thoroughly wash the fibres, and wring out the surplus water. With a large pair of tailor's scissors or shears cut them up into short lengths of not more than half an inch. This operation is tedious, and perhaps it could be done by a chaff-cutter or some other farm implement. Some day I hope to look into this possibility. The next process is beating into pulp, and its object is to pound the fibres so that they split lengthwise, like a bamboo cane, into the finest fibrils. The longer you beat, the finer will be your pulp, the smoother the paper made from it. The simplest method, rather rough and ready, is beating with a mallet on a stone slab. The resulting paper will have a coarse, uneven, but nevertheless very interesting texture. A large pestle and mortar will enable this operation to be somewhat speeded up. For the larger quantities I use a hollowed out tree trunk as a mortar and have made a large pestle from lignum vitae. Later on you may decide to have a small mechanical beater made. (This and other devices I have described in my book *Paper Making as an Artistic Craft*.) A large stone jar or a plastic bin may be used for storing your pulp. If a little preservative such as Santobrite is added, it will keep sweet and in good condition for many months.

Place a few cupfuls of the pulp into a small tank of some sort and fill up with warm water. Make a trial sheet or two as I have already described. Stir in more pulp if the paper is too thin (and constantly add more to replace the pulp which is removed in the paper-making). A rectangular wooden frame with a piece of fabric nailed across it makes a good mould of more useful shape. The great drawback is that you cannot peel off the paper until mould and sheet are quite dry. If, in place of fabric, you nail a piece of perforated zinc to the frame, it will be rigid enough to allow you to turn the frame upside down and press it upon a well wetted blanket. By this means the 'waterleaf' sheet is transferred for drying, and the mould is released for continuous work. A wet stack of alternate felts and paper forms what is termed a 'post'. If the water is then squeezed out by means of heavy weights or in a press, the quality of the paper is much improved. At first it is best to separate each sheet after pressing and lay it out together with its blanket to dry. Later, when experience has been gained, it is possible to peel off the wet paper and dry it apart from the blanket. There is great risk of tearing and of forming cockles, however, which are avoided when sheet and blanket are dried together.

Only quite thin paper may be made by the method just described. For thicker, more professional looking paper it is necessary to retain more pulp upon the mould. This is achieved by placing a second loose fitting frame upon it forming a temporary rim. This outer frame is called the deckle, and gives its name to the familiar rough edges associated with hand made paper. The mould is much more rigid and satisfactory if a few thin wooden intermediate supports are fitted to prevent the zinc from bending. Later on, woven rustless wire may be used in place of the perforated zinc. This gives quicker drainage and imparts better surface texture. A piece of expandomet metal to serve

33 Flowers of early summer, including Early Purple Orchis and Comfrey

34　Monkey Flower, and other summer flowers

35 Autumn: Gladdon in fruit, Sea Aster, and magenta flowers of Orpine

36  (*left*) Harebell, Cross-leaved Heath, and Autumn Crocus
37  Old Man's Beard

38   Hedgehog and Dormouse in winter sleep

39   Trees and bark

40   Trees in January

41    Fossils (including ammonites) in a Dorset landscape, with lobster, and Blue Vinney cheese

42   Trees in February

43    March trees and catkins

44  Purple Emperors

45    Oystercatchers and the tide-line

46   Sea shells

47  Various fossils

48   Moths, common and less common

as support is tacked to the frame before fitting the wire. Most professional moulds have bronze or brass wire, sometimes woven and nailed to the frame. Paper made from this type is known as 'wove' and has no watermark. Moulds for the familiar 'laid' paper, used for high-class stationery, are composed of parallel wires spaced at twenty-two to the inch and finally stitched to supports about one inch apart. This special construction produces the 'laid' watermark. Decorative devices also may be made in wire and stitched to the upper surface of the mould. Since the watermark is in relief less pulp lies on it than on the rest of the mould and so the paper there is thinner, and when it is held to the light a transparency of the design is clearly visible. But only paper made from finely beaten pulp carries clear watermark impressions.

To the left of your tank or vat place a dish to catch water and in it a wooden board a little larger than your mould. At the back of the dish should be a pile of well wetted blankets or couching felts. Two of the felts are laid ready on the board. Fit the deckle over the mould, grip together firmly at each side and hold vertically over the far side of the vat. Lower mould and deckle into the pulp, still in the upright position, and then gradually level out. This should be a slow rhythmic and continuous movement, bringing the mould – quite horizontal – an inch or two below the surface of the pulp. The mould is then lifted to the surface and given a slight sideways and forward shake in order to felt the fibres. Tilt the mould to one corner and allow to drain, and remove the deckle. Turn the mould upside down and press to the upper side of the wet felt. Raise the mould, and the sheet will remain transferred to the felt. Cover with another felt, and repeat the process. Add a few cupfuls of pulp every few sheets to maintain a constant strength. When sufficient sheets are made, place a wooden board on top of the pile and press out as much of the water as possible.

You must now separate the sheets, each one on its blanket, and lay them out to dry. In fine weather they may be dried out of doors. Light open slatted racking is best for indoor drying, and an electric convector fire will speed the operation. When quite dry peel the sheets from the blankets, place in a pile and press for a short time. Sheets made as already described are slightly absorbent, but quite suitable for any kind of printing. If you wish to use writing ink or watercolour on them, they will need to be sized. If your vat is copper-lined and fitted with an electric heating plate, the pulp may be kept at blood heat and animal gelatine added. This obviates making the sizing a separate operation in itself. If heavy sizing is required, you must wait until the sheets have matured for a week or two and then pass them through a bath of size and dry them out a second time. But it is a tricky process and should be avoided if possible.

The electric mixers, liquidizers and mincers of the kitchen are invaluable aids in making pulp. I should not be surprised if in the dairy, too, there are not some other appliances which would help if they could be borrowed. There certainly are some useful machines in most canteen kitchens but their custodians usually have no sympathies with papermakers.

*The arch enemy is rust*, and so all things of naked iron must be kept away from pulp and paper.

# PART FIVE

*Man Again*

# Objects for the Fancy

Any object is worth contemplating – worth taking home and contemplating – if its shape, colour, texture, or peculiarity intrigues the finder. That is the degree of its 'value', which has nothing to do with common opinion or record bids at Sotheby's.

The object may be mineral, vegetable, animal, anything peculiarly shaped by natural forces, anything from shell to skull, anything crystalline with a faceted, sparkling surface, or it may be an artifact, a fragment shaped by human fingers, with an extra attraction on that account. Museums originated in the cabinet of curiosities, in the sense of delight and wonder, which is worth preserving in our own age of organized knowledge and shrivelled imagination. At any rate painters and sculptors know a good 'curio' when they see it. Sight and sense of form are their strength, and their studios are frequently the most engaging of to-day's curiosity cabinets.

FOSSILS come high in this category for attraction of form and for the pleasures of discovery, and have intrigued men for thousands of years. About a hundred fossil sea-urchins enclosed the remains of a woman and child under a Bronze Age barrow in Bedfordshire, and the builders of the Somerset long barrow at Stony Littleton seem to have chosen a portal stone because it showed an ammonite, or rather the print of an ammonite.

Sea-urchins of various kinds (Shepherd's Crowns, Pound-stones, Fairy Loaves, in common speech), large coiling ammonites (Snakestones) in the floor of a limestone quarry or small ones transformed to iron pyrites and washed clean on Dorset beaches, belemnites (Elfbolts, Thunderbolts, Stone Bullets), which were part of the internal shells of extinct sea creatures resembling cuttle-fish, fossilized corals from old coral reefs, St Cuthbert's Beads, to be found, for example, along the edges of St Cuthbert's island off Lindisfarne or Holy Island, where they sell them in the shops (discs from the 'stem' of an animal known as a crinoid or sea lily) – these are a few of the fossils likely to pull the trigger of interest. Fossils, though, is a small word covering such an immensity of life in death, the casts, the prints or the remains of so many species of plant, insect, fish, mammal, reptile, mollusc, bird, etc., even in the fossiliferous strata of Great Britain, that the fossils of a single country cannot be reduced to a collector's handbook. All the same, there are books which introduce British fossils. In addition, the Palaeontological Society in 1954 published a *Directory of British Fossiliferous Localities*, arranged by counties; district 'memoirs' of the Geological Survey – which are not expensive – indicate and illustrate the fossils you are likely to encounter in your home neighbourhood (though you may of course live in an irritatingly unfossiliferous countryside) ; and the British Museum (Natural History) has begun to publish a very crisply drawn series of British fossils, era by era, starting with *British Caenozoic Fossils* (1959), which costs only six shillings.

There are fossils to be found not only in cliffs and quarries and on beaches, but along road and railway cuttings, in debris from old coal mines, among flints on a field, or along the cut-away banks of small streams. (Plates 41 and 47.)

FLINTS: there are flint and flints, the shining stuff and the things shaped from it by fingers most anciently dead. Flint nodules, differing in colour and often intriguingly shaped, are often worth bringing home and mounting like the *objets trouvés* of the surrealists. In any case each nodule is a kind of natural sculpture, or a natural casting, formed under pressure. A sea some 900 feet deep was surrounded by desert, and the water of it was hot enough to precipitate its calcium carbonate. This chalk sea withdrew, the deposit of calcium carbonate – of chalk – was left bare, warm rains brought a covering of vegetation, and the rain carried carbonic acid down into the chalk: the acid attacked the chalk and the spicules of sponges which the chalk contained, and so became charged with calcium carbonate and colloidal silica, forming nodules of flint in bands, or layers, through the chalk.

Recognizing flints which have been deliberately shaped, pointed and chipped to an edge, and turned into tools or weapons 3,000, 4,000, 5,000, or 25,000 years ago by men of the Old and New Stone Ages and the Bronze Age, is more a matter of experience than difficulty. *Flint Implements* (1950) published by the British Museum, describes how flint was broken and worked by ancient tool-makers and armourers, and has good illustrations which help to distinguish

294

artificial from natural or accidental shapings. You need to be sure, not to wish – and so believe – that the weapon or tool-shaped flint you have picked up was actually worked; and making sure is a nice exercise in observation and intellectual discipline.

Finding 'flints' and knowing where to look for them is another matter. Where flint occurs naturally and in great abundance on the ground, the search for worked flints demands a very quick discerning eye. Where flint does not occur by nature, every chip or scrap or core lying about must have been brought there by man, and will be worth picking up to examine.

Bronze Age people seem to have lived alongside their barrow groups (page 53), near which you can sometimes discover a chipping floor, or at least an area where broken flints abound after ploughing, and are very easily detected in sunshine after rain. Such floors are worth searching for scrapers, awls, knife blades and small barbed arrowheads.

POTSHERDS. Fossils serve as indicators for the geologist, flint implements and sherds of pottery (first made in Britain about 5,000 years ago, or 5,000 years after the invention of potting) serve as indicators for the archaeologist; but to the rest of us a sherd, whether neolithic, Bronze Age, Iron Age, Romano-British, Anglo-Saxon, Norman, or Tudor or Early Victorian, may be fascinating and treasurable in its own right, for its look, or its evocation of ancientness, or its evidence of human activity. And very few of us live far from some ancient habitation site which is frequently ploughed or where moles burrow and scuffle oddments to the surface.

On the chalk downs lynchets and field outlines mark Bronze Age or Iron Age farm sites which may be rich in pottery. Roman villa sites (page 74) provide more sophisticated wares – for instance, red glossy Samian – as well as ornamented roof tiles. Or there may have been kilns somewhere near, Romano-British or medieval. Places where potting took place are at times obvious by name. Potters or 'crockers' worked at Crockerton in Wiltshire, at Potterton in Yorkshire, at Pottersbury in Northamptonshire.

The best place for getting to know the look, the feel and the characteristics of the different kinds of ancient pottery, historic or prehistoric, is the local museum – museum first, books second. Scraps dug up in the garden or picked up from ploughed fields (which were fertilized with house refuse) or found on the site of a ruined cottage indicate the kinds of 'antique' earthenware which our more recent ancestors used to buy at fairs and in market towns. Different districts had their different preferences according to the nearest pottery towns. If you keep an eye on local antique shops, fragments you have found from old cottages, etc., can usually be matched sooner or later with whole mugs, jugs, salts, bowls, or tea pots, which have been brought in by people in the neighbourhood.

CLAY PIPES and BOTTLE SEALS – seals off wine bottles – are common objects of the past often to be found, which have their own literature. The clay pipe of the sixteenth century, after the introduction of tobacco, followed the Indian shape, and was described in Queen Elizabeth's day as an 'instrument formed like a little ladell': the bowl, that is to say, was not much wider than the stem, and was bent up and pushed forward at a wide angle. Before very long the bowl was made larger, and was often given a flat base, so that the pipe would stand. On the flat base pipe-makers had room to impress their name or their initials and often, very obligingly, the date.

If you find a clay pipe bowl in which the plane of the rim of the bowl is *not* parallel with the line of the stem, or as much of the stem as remains, then it will be a pipe of the seventeenth century, or earlier.

People who thought well of themselves, from the late seventeenth century into the nineteenth century, used dark coloured wine bottles made specially for themselves and each marked on the side with a glass circle, a little raised circle of glass impressed with their name or their initials, their crest or their coat of arms, and frequently the year. They bought their wine in cask and then bottled it, or else they took their bottles to the wine merchant. Bottle seals often survive the breaking of the bottle and turn up in old rubbish heaps, or in ploughed fields. Pepys had such bottles blown for him: 'October 23rd, 1683 . . . saw some of my new bottles, made with my crest upon them, filled with wine, about five or six dozen.' A bottle of the kind (according to Sheelah Ruggles-Brise's *Sealed Bottles*, 1949) which was made in 1727 for Jonathan Swift, exists in the National Museum of Ireland. And there exists a sealed bottle made in 1836 for Robert Stephen Hawker, the Cornish poet, who liked a glass of wine in his famous vicarage at Morwenstow. Bottle seals frequently come to light in the gardens of old vicarages or old rectories, or manor-houses.

COINS are dropped – and were dropped in the past, especially gold ones – with a most disappointing infrequency. It should be remembered, though, that the chance find of a very small, unimportant looking coin is always worth reporting to a museum. You dig up such a coin, you cannot decipher the legend and image (can it be a figure of Victory holding a spear and dragging a captive, or Victory with a wreath in one hand and a palm in another?); send it off to the museum (*without* attempting to clean it first): it may be the commonest of Roman coins, or you may have found a valuable piece of evidence, perhaps a Roman *denarius*, with Victory on one side, from that obscure fifth century when Roman power came to an end in Britain.

SHELLS – and OTHER BEACH OBJECTS. Collecting shells may be a kind of false natural history. A marine biologist prefers his shells to be tenanted, to contain the living creature, cockle, mussel, scallop, etc.; in which case tenant and shell have a double fascination. But that does not prevent the rest of us behaving like men for many thousands of years past, and enjoying the single, easier fascination of shells without their tenants. They are the best of all objects of the beach – of the right beach, sandy, not too steep, and on a lee shore. Long open sand beaches are often disappointingly but inevitably devoid of shells or exceedingly thin in shells, in contrast, for example, with the low-tide sands of the north coast of Norfolk, an excellent extent for tiny scallops or queens of all shades from orange to deepest claret, or the low-tide lagoon of the Isles of Scilly, an area for seaweed species and sand species, where you find abundance of pink cowries, wentletraps, top-shells, dog-whelks, cockles, tellins, queens, and a most colourful miscellany of periwinkles washed out of the seaweed. At low tide on the Scillonian cockle bars you crush shells as you go – violet, white, pink, yellow, the colours of the sunsets away across Tresco and Bryher. But this – like others – is rather a dangerous shelling area, where as you walk and search you have to remember the swiftness and depth of the returning tide.

It is true that shells around the British coast are not spectacular in form or tint. There is no kind, for instance, as shimmering, as opaline and oriental on a large scale as the shell of the Ormer, with its row of holes, from the Channel Isles. Yet even limpets of different kinds are less dull in their iridesence *inside*, when they are fresh, than one would think from old tide-line specimens. The cowries, auger shells, tops, periwinkles, queens and scallops offer an education in tint and form, especially the queens and scallops (see page 36 for the scallop as the badge of medieval pilgrims), which have been an ancient motif in the arts of Europe and the arts of Mexican and South American Indians. Also there is variation around the coasts, some shells being local – such as the Wide-mouthed Whelk of the north-east, a larger relative of the Buckie or Common Whelk, or the Spiny Cockle, the Red Nose of the Devonshire beaches, in contrast to the smooth ridged shells of the Common Cockle. Some are uncommon, particularly shells of the Violet Sea-Snail, stranded now and again on ocean beaches around Land's End or along the south-west of Ireland – shells of a mollusc which lives on the Atlantic upheld by a float of its own mucus, eating miniature jelly-fish. These violet shells, though, are frail and easily broken. (Plate 46.)

Scallops have an extraordinary book to themselves, with learned and exquisite illustrations, *The Scallop: Studies of a Shell and its influences on Humankind* edited by Ian Cox, and published in 1957 to mark the diamond jubilee of the Shell Company. In general the best book for identifying shells and those objects of the beach among which the oystercatchers run and peer and peck in their search for food is Collins' *Pocket Guide to the Sea Shore*, by John Barrett and C. M. Yonge. It deals with shells, stranded jelly-fish, sea-urchins, starfish, with the soft 'bones' of cuttlefish (which used to be made into tooth powder), with seaweeds, with the blackish horny egg capsules – or 'Witches' Purses' or 'Mermaids' Purses' – of dog-fish and Common Skate and other kinds of ray (dog-fish purses have curly tendrils, instead of points or horns), with the egg capsules of the whelk, which blow around like hardened froth (Plate 45). It deals with everything, I nearly wrote, forgetting those other *objets trouvés* of the tide line, *objets involontaires* or *perturbés* which a scientific handbook has to overlook – from the glass balls or floats from a trawler net to every object washed ashore and rolled back and forth and moulded and transformed by sea-action, the sea being a sculptor bizarrely gifted. Sea-moulded and blunted shapes of bottle glass of every colour, of ornamental earthenware, or red brick and tile, sea pebbles, sea-moulded pieces of branch or wood, can all prove objects of valid fantasy. To be mentioned among them are the lumps of amber occasionally washed ashore on the beaches and shingle bars of North Norfolk and elsewhere along the east coast – not yellow translucent bits like necklace beads, but little knobs battered, scratched, and dulled (but still amber) in a long transit across the North Sea; also – I do not know that they have a name, though they are among the oddest objects of natural sculpture – the fish-shaped lengths or rolls of clay to be found where the sand of very active open beaches is backed by fine shingle and by cliffs of glacial mud (e.g. in North Wales). These are embedded with shingle in a coloured mosaic, blue, yellow, purple, white, orange, red, on a pottery background, Assyrian clay tablets of the shore.

Along western beaches from Orkney to Cornwall, beach debris may contain the beans of two climbers of the pea family, which currents have floated across the Atlantic – shiny, flattish, hard beans up to two inches across, brown, of the West Indian *Entada gigas*; and much prettier, the beans of the tropical climber *Mucuna urens*, smaller brownish-purple except for a rim marking of café au lait and black which nearly encircles the bean.

I have always found that a few of these various beach objects consort very well with human products – with china, earthenware, silver, etc., the miscellaneous decoration of table, shelf and mantelpiece.

For beach pebbles, in their mineral variety, see a curious recent book, Clarence Ellis' *Pebbles on the Beach*.

# Country Writers and Painters

Which writers and painters of Great Britain have most felt and given body and meaning to things of the countryside? It is not the job of artists to be nature-mirrors, to copy nature, to be 'accurate' or realistic in their details and effects. Yet many of them experience and record nature, and by the newness, quickness, purity, honesty, strength, tenderness and individuality of the way they have seen and known, and of the way they have recorded their acts of sensation, in words, rhythms, colour, etc., they open our own senses, making us less automatic, more responsive, more alive.

## COUNTRY WRITERS

This visionary quality is uncommon, and is rather scattered in the life-work of writers, in brief passages so intense that we recognize in them a singing or delightful essence of all life, helping us each to our 'reasonable share of the beauty of earth'. The best of such country writing is in poetry, our particular art – in Chaucer, Shakespeare, Milton, Wordsworth, John Clare and Hopkins. It begins with wonderful purity in the nature verse of Irishmen and Welshmen writing in the Dark Ages and early Middle Ages, translated well in two books, Kenneth Jackson's *Early Celtic Nature Poetry* (1935) and *A Celtic Miscellany* (1951). Then as the centuries go by, my choice of other poets extra-specially concerned with nature would be:

Dafydd ap Gwilym (fourteenth century). The best translations of his love poetry are Nigel Heseltine's *Selected Poems*, 1944. (Cardiganshire.) See page 312.

Alexander Hume (1560?–1609). *Poems*, 1902, for his long poem *Of the Day Estival*. (Berwickshire.)

Michael Drayton (1563–1631), especially for his immense *Poly-Olbion*, a travel poem of all England and Wales. (Warwickshire.) See pages 16, 315–16.

John Donne (1573–1631), a Londoner whose intellectually realistic poems have much more of 'nature' or 'country' in them than is often admitted. See pages 206, 313.

Robert Herrick (1591–1674). A London man in roughest Devonshire. *Poetical Works*. See page 305.

George Herbert (1593–1633), for the direct and often 'country' realism of his poems, especially 'The Flower'. (Montgomeryshire.) See pages 307, 313.

Henry Vaughan (c. 1622–95), *Works*, 1957. (Breconshire.) See pages 304, 311.

Andrew Marvell (1621–78). *Poems*, Muses Library, 1958. (East Riding.) See pages 173, 177, 322.

Charles Cotton (1630–87). *Poems*, Muses Library, 1958. (Peak District.) See pages 316–17.

James Thomson (1700–48). *The Seasons*. (Roxburghshire.) Once the most famous of the world's nature poets.

John Dyer (1700?–58). *Grongar Hill*. (Carmarthenshire.) See page 312.

Alexander MacDonald (1700?–80?), for 'The Song of Summer', published with his other Gaelic poems, 1751. Stanzas in translation in Kenneth Jackson's *Celtic Miscellany*. (The Highlands.)

Thomas Gray (1716–71), for the 'Elegy in a Country Churchyard'. (Buckinghamshire.) See page 304.

Duncan Bàn MacIntyre (1724–1812), for 'The Misty Corrie', in Gaelic – often, though badly, translated. (Argyllshire.) See page 324.

George Crabbe (1754–1832). *Poems*, especially 'The Borough'. (Suffolk.) Well described as 'nature's sternest painter'. See pages 160, 241, 319.

S. T. Coleridge (1772–1834). *Poems*. (Devon, Somerset and the Lake District.) See pages 114, 116, 154, 159, 163, 185, 306, 323.

William Barnes (1801–86). *Selected Poems*, Muses Library. (Dorset.) See page 306.

Alfred Tennyson (1809–92). *Poems*. (Lincolnshire.) See pages 141, 143, 305, 318, 319, 320.

Matthew Arnold (1822–88). For 'Thyrsis' and 'The Scholar Gipsy'. (Berkshire. Middlesex.) See pages 309, 310.

William Morris (1834–96), especially for *The Defence of Guenevere and Other Poems* and *Poems by the Way*. (Essex and Oxfordshire. The banks of the Thames.) See pages 310, 318.

Thomas Hardy (1840–1928). *Collected Poems*, 1932. (Dorset.) See pages 147, 215, 304, 306, 307.

Walter de la Mare (1873–1956). *Collected Poems*, 1934 – after they have been sifted from the whimsical and the sentimental. (Buckinghamshire.) See page 227.

Edward Thomas (1878–1917). *Collected Poems*. (Wiltshire especially.)

Andrew Young (b. 1885). *Collected Poems*, 1960. (Scotland and England.)

Louis MacNeice (b. 1907). *Collected Poems*, 1949. (Ireland and England.)

In prose, while country mirror-writing and sentimentality are very common, visionary, hard, pure writing is very uncommon. My selection will be:

Sir Thomas Browne (1605–82), particularly for *Urne-buriall* and *Miscellaneous Writings*, 1931. (Norfolk.) See pages 51, 58, 221, 241.

Thomas Traherne (1637?–74). *Centuries*, new edition 1960. (Herefordshire.) See page 310.

Gilbert White (1720–93). *Natural History of Selborne*, records, observations, comments put down with the severity and economy and authority of a prose poetry. (Hampshire.) See pages 192, 215, 225, 233, 235, 240, 307.

Dorothy Wordsworth (1771–1855). *Journals.* (Somerset and the Lake District.) See pages 153, 163, 306.

Francis Kilvert (1840–79). *Diary.* (Wiltshire and Radnorshire.) See page 311.

Gerard Manley Hopkins (1844–89). Journals, in *The Journals and Papers of Gerard Manley Hopkins*, 1956. A Londoner who wrote many of his best poems in and about North Wales. See especially page 315.

# COUNTRY PAINTERS

There are individual country pictures, English and Welsh, which everyone should know, among them Richard Wilson's *Cader Idris*, in the National Gallery, and his *Northop, Flintshire*, at Corsham Court in Wiltshire; Gainsborough's *Robert Andrews and His Wife*, Turner's *Evening Star*, and Constable's *Weymouth Bay*, all three in the National Gallery; James Ward's *Gordale Scar*, G. R. Lewis' *View in Herefordshire – Harvest*, John Crome's *Slate Quarries*, all in the Tate Gallery; Cotman's *Ploughed Field* (Leeds); Samuel Palmer's *Magic Apple Tree* (Cambridge) and *In a Shoreham Garden* (Victoria and Albert Museum), and William Dyce's *Pegwell Bay* (National Gallery).

The country painters of my own choice are:

For calm, serenity, and stillness:

Richard Wilson (1714–82) – particularly in his Welsh landscapes, National Gallery; National Gallery of Wales, Cardiff, etc. (Montgomeryshire.) See pages 313, 315.

George Stubbs (1725–1806), a steady light surrounding the landscape and the detail of his horse portraits, in the National Gallery; Tate Gallery; Walker Gallery, Liverpool; Lady Lever Gallery, Port Sunlight, etc. See page 322.

Thomas Gainsborough (1727–88) – his early portraits of figures surrounded by landscape, in the National Gallery; Fitzwilliam Museum, Cambridge, etc. (Suffolk.) See page 319.

For water, rock, bird, beast and miniature landscape:

Thomas Bewick (1753–1828) – his wood-engraved books. (Northumberland.) See endpapers of this book.

For calm light and clear colour and picturesqueness of corner, hill, valley:

Thomas Rowlandson (1756–1827) – an eye open on landscape, on villages and gardens, especially in watercolours he painted in Cornwall. To be seen in the British Museum, etc.

For drama of sky, light, colour, rock, sea:

J. M. W. Turner (1775–1851), mostly in the Tate Gallery.

For sparkle, wetness, freshness, with agitation and repose:

John Constable (1776–1837), in the National Gallery; Victoria and Albert Museum, etc. (Suffolk). See pages 167, 168, 306, 319.

For the breadth and clarity of mountains (Wales):

Cornelius Varley (1781–1873) – watercolours in the British Museum; Victoria and Albert Museum; Birmingham and Hereford Art Galleries.

For vegetation in valleys, landscape openness and width and vertical pattern, and the contrast in surface between old buildings and living landscape:

John Sell Cotman (1782–1842) – Norfolk (though he painted some of his best watercolours in Yorkshire). See pages 322, 323. There are Cotmans in the British Museum; Tate Gallery; Victoria and Albert Museum; the art galleries at Ipswich and Norwich, etc.

For intensities of twilight, stars, moonlight, fullness of fertile shapes, and landscape textures:

> Samuel Palmer (1805–81), in his best compositions painted from the now built-over hill scenery around Dulwich, and from scenery around Shoreham. Ashmolean Museum; Victoria and Albert Museum; Tate Gallery; Fitzwilliam Museum; British Museum.

For light-filled etchings and drawings akin to Impressionism:

> Charles Keene (1823–91), notably in drawings and etchings of the Suffolk coast around Dunwich and Walberswick. See page 319.

For the simplest and purest forms of landscape:

> Ben Nicholson (b. 1894), particularly in his landscapes of Cumberland and the Cornish coast.

# ASSOCIATIONS

Country writers can be 'visited' as well as read. Henry Vaughan wrote in a poem about the Usk in Wales, which he loved more than any other river, that

> Poets – like angels – where they once appear
> Hallow the place, and each succeeding year
> Adds rev'rence to't, such as at length doth give
> This aged faith, that there their genii live.

It is this feeling which takes us to Stratford on account of Shakespeare, Chalfont St Giles on account of Milton, Stoke Poges churchyard on account of Gray and Gray's Elegy, Dove Cottage and Grasmere for the Wordsworths, or Haworth for the Brontës.

So by counties here are some less frequented shrines or possible pilgrimage places (if you care to be that kind of pilgrim), to do mostly with country poets, but also with other poets, novelists, etc., as well as country painters – places where they were born, lived, worked, or died, which may be imagined to retain something of their spirit.

## In Cornwall

St Juliot, near Boscastle, the cliff scene of Thomas Hardy's best love poems. He came to restore the church in 1870, when the rectory

304

door was opened to him by his future wife. After this first journey he wrote 'When I set out for Lyonesse'. More than forty years later he wrote love poems about St Juliot in her memory:

> . . . A ghost-girl-rider. And though, toil-tried
> > He withers daily,
> > Time touches her not,
> > But she still rides gaily
> > In his rapt thought
> > On that shagged and shaly
> > Atlantic spot,
> > And as when first eyed
> Draws rein and sings to the swing of the tide.

Polperro. Tennyson came in a boat from Fowey to Polperro on 20 June, 1848, enquiring for traditions about King Arthur. In Couch's House he called on Jonathan Couch, the Polperro doctor, who did not admire his slouch, his slovenly dress, or some verses he read about King Arthur, which he thought 'prolix and modern'.

Zennor, near Land's End. D. H. Lawrence lived here in 1916 and 1917, until forced to leave Cornwall under suspicion of being a spy. 'At Zennor one sees infinite Atlantic, all peacock-mingled colours, and the gorse is sunshine itself.'

## In Devonshire

East Budleigh, in rich country north-east of Exmouth. Near this village one of the most proud of English poets, Sir Walter Ralegh, was born in 1552, in the thatched Tudor mansion of Hayes Barton –

> But true love is a durable fire
> > In the mind ever burning;
> Never sick, never old, never dead,
> > From itself never turning.

In the red church in which he was christened, one of the oak pews (1537) is carved with the Ralegh arms.

Dean Prior, near Ashburton, below Dartmoor. Robert Herrick was the vicar, lonely and unmarried, from 1629 to 1648 and 1662 to 1674. Hating exile in Devon, he wrote a hate poem about the stream, the village and the villagers –

> Rocky thou art; and rocky we discover
> Thy men; and rocky are thy ways all over

– yet he owed to his Devonshire life here many of his loveliest perceptions. He is buried (without a stone) in the churchyard.

Ottery St Mary. In this small town Coleridge was born, about 11 a.m., on 21 October, 1772. In the remarkable church a black and white tablet in memory of his father, the vicar, mentions him together with his brothers – without an inkling of course that he was to be one of the most famous of Englishmen.

## In Somerset

Nether Stowey, under the Quantocks. Coleridge Cottage (National Trust) was the home of Coleridge and his wife from 1797 to 1800. Here he wrote *The Ancient Mariner*, and saw the moonlight glittering on his child's tears.

Holford, near by. In 1797 Dorothy and William Wordsworth lived in this parish at Alfoxden House (now a hotel) directly under the Quantocks, Dorothy writing in her journal of the snow, the hollies, the great trees in the park, of walking on the Quantocks, of the 'union of earth, sky, and sea'.

Culbone, near Porlock. No village, only a miniature church in a narrow pit under Exmoor. Loved and painted by the visionary artist Samuel Palmer. Coleridge dreamed and wrote down 'Kubla Khan' in a farmhouse (perhaps Ash Farm) above the church, overlooking the Severn Sea.

East Coker, near Yeovil. The home of the forebears of T. S. Eliot. In the church, reached through curious deep lanes, there is an Eliot family window, from New York.

## In Dorset

Osmington, near Weymouth. Two couples spent their honeymoons together in Osmington vicarage, in November 1816 – the vicar and his wife and John Constable and his wife. Then, or later, Constable painted from the Osmington shore his cloudy, breezy, sunny, tawny, happy picture *Weymouth Bay* (in the National Gallery).

Winterborne Came, near Dorchester. William Barnes the poet (1801– 1886) was carried from his thatched rectory to the churchyard on 11 October, 1886. Thomas Hardy walked to the funeral, and was greeted by the sun flashing from the old poet's coffin – a farewell he described in his poem 'The Last Signal'. A Celtic cross stands over Barnes' grave.

Higher Bockhampton, Stinsford, near Dorchester. Thomas Hardy was born in a thatched cottage (National Trust) in this hamlet below a brown swell of heath land, in 1840. Here his mother found an adder asleep on him in his cradle. His heart was buried in his first wife's grave under the yew tree in Stinsford churchyard, in 1928.

## In Wiltshire

Bemerton, near Salisbury. George Herbert was the rector. Here, says Izaak Walton, 'his chiefest recreation was music, in which heavenly art he was a most excellent master, and did himself compose many divine hymns and anthems, which he set and sang to his lute or viol'. He also says that 'some of the meaner sort of his parish did so love and reverence Mr Herbert, that they would let their plough rest' when they heard him ring the sanctus bell from the church – so that 'they might also offer their devotions to God with him; and would then return back to their plough'. This great poet died in 1633, in the rectory opposite the small church, and was buried by the altar under a stone which says only 'G. H. 1633'.

Liddington, near Swindon. The green unfrequented Iron Age hill-camp of Liddington Castle, above Swindon and the Vale of the White Horse, was much frequented by the nature writer Richard Jefferies. A small uncommon pretty bright yellow flower, the Field Flea-wort, grows there as if in his memory. The canal reservoir at Coate Farm, where he was born nearer Swindon in 1848, is now a public lido and the farmhouse is a Jefferies museum.

## In Hampshire

Winchester. In the cathedral look for the tombstone of Jane Austen, who died in the city in 1817. The fact that she wrote novels was not thought to be worth mentioning in the inscription.

Selborne, south of Alton (and not far from Chawton, where the house in which Jane Austen wrote *Persuasion* and *Emma* is preserved) seems completely protected by the investing spirit of Gilbert White, the naturalist. In the church a stone saying 'G. W. 1793' shows where he was buried. The yew tree in the churchyard which Gilbert White described – 'This is a male tree, which in the spring sheds

clouds of dust and fills the atmosphere around with its farina' – still
continues strong, healthy, and productive.

## In the Isle of Wight

Bonchurch. In the rather suburban churchyard, the grave and gravestone of Algernon Charles Swinburne, who died in 1909. For much
of his childhood he lived in a house along the sheltered Undercliff
between Ventnor and Niton.

## In Sussex

In this county it is said you cannot throw a stone without hitting a
novelist, but Sussex has encountered poets as well, from Shelley to
Kipling.

Felpham, near Bognor Regis. William Blake lived in a smaller and
simpler Felpham from 1800 to 1803. 'Felpham is a sweet place for
study, because it is more spiritual than London. Heaven opens here
on all sides her golden gates; her windows are not obstructed by
vapours; voices of celestial inhabitants are more distinctly heard.'
On the shore below his cottage (the thatched Blake's Cottage, in
Blake's Road) he had a vision at sunrise –

> To my friend Butts I write
> My first Vision of Light,
> On the yellow sands sitting

– seeing every particle of light, every grain of sand, and all the
phenomena of nature as human creatures.

Chichester. In the medieval Guildhall (once the chapel of a house of
the Grey Friars) William Blake was tried for high treason, at
Chichester Quarter Sessions, on 11 January, 1804, and acquitted.
A charge of seditious talk had been brought against him by an angry
dragoon whom he had turned out of his garden at Felpham.

In the cloisters, in mid eighteenth century, shocked citizens of
Chichester saw and heard a 'pock-fretted man with small keen black
eyes' moaning and howling 'in horrible accordance with the choir'.
This was the poet William Collins, who was born in Chichester in
1721 and died there, in madness, in 1759. Look for the white
memorial of him in the cathedral, by Flaxman (though his grave is
in St Andrew's church).

Petworth House, near Midhurst (National Trust). Entertained by Lord Leconfield, who was in some ways as eccentric as himself, J. M. W. Turner painted some of his happiest designs at Petworth during the eighteen-thirties – especially watercolours (in the British Museum) in which his host, his fellow guests (including the parson), and the furniture are lyrically dissolved into the purest colour.

## In Middlesex

Laleham, on the Thames, near Staines. Matthew Arnold (for those who like 'Thyrsis' and 'The Scholar Gipsy') was born at Laleham in 1822, and is buried in Laleham churchyard.

## In Kent

Penshurst, near Tunbridge Wells. If your favourite poems include 'With how sad steps, O moon' by Sir Philip Sidney, then visit the great house of the Sidneys, Penshurst Place (open several days a week), where Sidney was born in 1554.

Allington Castle, outside Maidstone, on the Medway. If your favourite love poems include Sir Thomas Wyatt's 'They flee from me who sometime did me seek', then visit this squat moated castle of the thirteenth century, in which Wyatt, handsomest of Tudor poets, was born in 1503 (it is open daily, and belongs now to the Order of Carmelites).

Shipborne, north of Tonbridge. If your favourite poems include Christopher Smart's nature paean, *A Song to David*, visit the wooded country around Shipborne. In this parish Christopher Smart was born in 1722, at Fairlawn, where he delighted in the golden carp in the ponds.

Shoreham, five miles from Sevenoaks. If your favourite visions of the English country include the black and white designs and the pictures of Samuel Palmer, then visit Shoreham village, in the valley of the Darenth. Here he lived from 1825 to 1832, here he painted, as he called them, 'glimpses of the perfumed and enchanted twilight', here Palmer and his friends declaimed *Macbeth* in deserted chalkpits at midnight. His house stands on the edge of the river, by Shoreham bridge.

All four of these places of pilgrimage are within a pastoral rectangle, about ten miles by sixteen, of some of the most intimate hill and valley and field and woodland scenery of Great Britain, though some of it (but not Shoreham) is now a little suburbanized.

Eastwell, near Ashford. Not a great way to the east, in this special county of poets, is Eastwell Park, where Anne Finch, Countess of Winchilsea (1661–1720) listened to nightingales, looked for 'Something too high for syllables to speak', and wrote nature poems.

## In Oxfordshire

At Bablock Hythe, near Oxford, the ferry described in Matthew Arnold's 'Scholar Gipsy' still plies by wired punt across the Thames between Oxfordshire and Berkshire, from lane to lane, under grey-leaved coral-rooted willows –

> Thee, at the ferry, Oxford riders blithe,
> Returning home on summer nights, have met
> Crossing the stripling Thames at Bablock-hithe
> Trailing in the cool stream thy fingers wet,
> As the slow punt swings round.

Stanton Harcourt. Two miles down the lane from Bablock Hythe the small slight hunchbacked figure of a very different poet, Alexander Pope, frequented the now vanished and then ruinating manor-house of Stanton Harcourt. In the top room of 'Pope's Tower', which was part of the house, Pope worked in 1717 and 1718 on his version of Homer's *Iliad*. He wrote an epitaph for Lord Harcourt (in the church) and one for two lovers who were struck by lightning (outside the church, on the south wall).

Kelmscott, further up the Thames. William Morris' books and tapestries and furniture are preserved in his light-filled Jacobean manor-house near the river, in which he thought about socialism and human dignity, about England, its past, its future, its preservation, and the protection of ancient buildings. Here also he wrote poems and grieved over his wife's preference for Rossetti. He was carried out to his grave in Kelmscott churchyard in 1896, on a flower-decorated cart.

## In Herefordshire

Hereford and Credenhill, four miles away. In the fields outside Hereford, where he was born in 1637, Thomas Traherne in his childish vision saw the standing corn as 'orient and immortal wheat which never should be reaped, nor was ever sown'. He was parson of Credenhill, a beautiful parish, from 1657 to 1674.

Bredwardine (near Hay), remote village between the Wye and a steep long ridge, was for a little while the home of the Rev. Francis Kilvert, the diarist with a Pre-Raphaelite eye for the life and scenery of Wiltshire, Herefordshire, and Radnorshire where he had been curate at Clyro. In 1879, soon after becoming vicar of Bredwardine he died here of tuberculosis, and is buried in the churchyard.

## In Monmouthshire

Abergavenny. Henry James, unlikely as it may seem, climbed the hill of Little Skirrid in April 1878, admiring the primroses, 'of as pale and tender a yellow as if their gold had been diluted with silver', and the wood anemones.

Llanthony Priory, near Abergavenny, in the Black Mountains. The Priory ruins on a green hill flank belonged to Walter Savage Landor who quarrelled in his usual way with his tenants and neighbours and had to leave. An exquisite place, as serene as the quarrelsome old poet's improbable summary of his own life:

> I strove with none, for none was worth my strife:
> Nature I loved, and, next to Nature, Art:
> I warm'd both hands before the fire of Life;
> It sinks; and I am ready to depart.

## In Breconshire

Llansantffraed, near Brecon, in the Vale of Usk. Henry Vaughan, visionary poet and the Swan of Usk, was born at Newton in this parish in 1621 or 1622. There he lived, there he died on 23 April, 1695, and was buried in Llansantffraed churchyard, beside the big main road from Abergavenny to the west (Newton, where the house is not the one Vaughan knew, will be found a little nearer Scethrog, along the same road, between the road and the railway). The superlative mixed scenery around Newton, vale, mountain, river, lake, helped Vaughan to feel

> through all this fleshly dress
> Bright shoots of everlastingness.

A ridge separates Newton from Llangorse Lake. Wide, shallow and misty and surrounded by church towers, this lake must have suggested the poem by Vaughan about an evening shower, which begins:

> 'Twas so, I saw thy birth: that drowsy lake
> From her faint bosom breath'd thee, the disease
> Of her sick waters, and infectious ease.
> > But now, at even,
> > Too gross for heaven,
> Thou fall'st in tears, and weep'st for thy mistake.

Look in the churchyard for his very worn flat gravestone, which says in Latin the few words he wanted to say – 'Unprofitable servant, greatest of sinners, here I lie. Glory. Have mercy.'

## In Carmarthenshire

Llangathen, near Llandilo (further along A 40, the highway from Abergavenny to Carmarthen) is the unsullied home ground of John Dyer, painter and poet, and author of *Grongar Hill*, which he published in 1726. A lane goes up past the white mansion of Aberglasney, in which the Dyers lived, towards the fortified green summit of Grongar Hill, which gives long views of the Vale of Tywi, the looping river, the last scraps of Dryslwyn Castle, the woods, the field-quilted slopes, and the low mountains; a vale especially beautiful in the evening light of Dyer's poem.

## In Cardiganshire

Llanbadarn Fawr, outside Aberystwyth. Dafydd ap Gwilym, greatest of Welsh poets and one of the great poets of Europe, was born here in the fourteenth century. The large medieval church is the actual one he attended, in which – so he says in his poem to the Llanbadarn girls who will have nothing to do with him – he stood Sunday after Sunday

> With my face to a fine girl,
> With my back to the good God,

a pale boy with long hair under a feathered cap.

Strata Florida, near Tregaron. Though he wrote about frequenting the love chapel among the leaves, about the religion of green birches and love and the cuckoo, in due time the white monks of the Cistercian abbey of Strata Florida buried Dafydd ap Gwilym in their graveyard, under a yew. A few lovely odds and ends of this abbey of the 'Valley of Flowers' remain by the head-waters of the Teifi, among brown moorlands. (See page 105.)

## In Montgomeryshire

Montgomery, little, forgotten eighteenth-century town, is situated between a big church and a (very) ruined castle: in the castle George Herbert was born (on 3 April, 1593), in the church coloured effigies of this poet's father and mother lie on a huge canopied tomb, under golden stars on a white ground. The mother was Magdalen Herbert. John Donne stayed in the castle, and wrote poems to her, including 'The Primrose, being at Montgomery Castle, upon the hill, on which it is situate', which begins:

> Upon this primrose hill,
> Where, if Heav'n would distill
> A shower of rain, each several drop might go
> To his own primrose, and grow manna so;
> And where their form, and their infinity
> Make a terrestrial galaxy,
> As the small stars do in the sky,
> I walk to find a true love . . .

The primroses continue to grow large and thick on the castle hill, as they did in 1600. A place of double pilgrimage.

Penegoes, near Machynlleth, on the main road down the Vale of the Dyfi. Independent, prickly, indifferent to criticism or neglect, a true painter of serene landscape, Richard Wilson was born in the rectory (not the existing one) at Penegoes in 1714, in just the right scenery for the first great interpreter of the illuminated skies, the blue mountains and valleys of Wales. Penegoes has Plynlimmon at its back, Cader Idris in front. English romantic painters knew the lake folded under the precipices of Cader Idris as 'Wilson's Pool', so much did they admire his great *Llyn-y-Cau, Cader Idris*, which is now in the National Gallery. He painted Cader Idris also from the northern side, in his *Valley of the Mawddach* (now in the Walker Art Gallery, Liverpool).

## In Shropshire

Ludlow. A poet's country town long before A. E. Housman, partly because Ludlow Castle was something of a viceregal lodge, as the official dwelling of the Lords President of Wales. Philip Sidney as a boy knew Ludlow and the castle and the woods when his father was Lord President. In his twenties John Milton wrote *Comus* to be sung and acted at Ludlow Castle, on Michaelmas night, 1634, in the castle hall, before a new Lord President, the Earl of Bridgewater. The Miltonic way to come into Ludlow is by the hill roads from Richards Castle or Aston, skirting the tall woods and wooded parks, the 'wild wood' discovered in the first scene of *Comus*, in which the virgin is lost, and in which she sings

> strains that might create a soul
> Under the rib of Death.

Ludlow churchyard. Ludlow and the long blue hills folded up by the pressure of Welsh mountains were the Shropshire of A. E. Housman. So a tablet to him on the church wall (though hardly mentioning that he was a poet) appropriately faces north to the blue of Wenlock Edge and the Long Mynd –

> Into my heart an air that kills
> From yon far country blows:
> What are those blue remembered hills,
> What spires, what farms are those?

In his poem Housman had the acutest sense of Shropshire as a border county and the scene of ancient fighting.

Wistanstow. To the north of Ludlow, along A 49, and past Craven Arms, a signpost to the left says Wistanstow. This is the stow or holy place of St Wigstan or Wystan, the royal Mercian saint martyred there in 849 by a sword blow on the head. For thirty days a pillar of light rose from the ground on which he had been killed, and every year the hairs cut from his head by the sword grew out of the same ground like grass. The poet Wystan Hugh Auden, whose antiquarian uncle was once the rector of Wistanstow, is named after this Shropshire saint (page 97).

Among Shropshire poets are William Langland, who wrote *Piers Plowman* (by which the young Auden was much influenced), born about 1332, probably at Cleobury Mortimer under the Clee Hills, a few miles east of Ludlow (there is a window to him in the church), and Wilfred Owen, born in north-west Shropshire at Oswestry, on 18 March, 1893.

## In Denbighshire

The Vale of Clwyd. Gerard Manley Hopkins (then at St Beuno's College, near St Asaph) wrote many of his greatest and happiest poems in 1876 and 1877, when he was raised to ecstasy by the scenes of the Vale of Clywd and the valley of the Elwy. From the college he looked westward across the Vale into Denbighshire and to the Welsh mountains –

> Lovely the woods, waters, meadows, combes, vales,
> All the air things wear that build this world of Wales.

## In Flintshire

Mold. As a child Richard Wilson lived less at Penegoes in Montgomeryshire, his birthplace, than at Mold, where like Gerard Manley Hopkins he loved all the good scenery of the Vale of Clwyd and the Clwydian Hills. He came back to Flintshire as an old man, died in 1782 at Plas Colomendy, in the Alwyn valley, and was buried in the churchyard at Mold.

## In Worcestershire

The Malvern Hills should be visited for an essential experience of England, since looking down from this unique crow's nest of ancient rock can make one feel, like William Langland in the fourteenth century, that one is surveying all of England – even of the world. Nowhere else would have done for William Langland's vision 'concerning Piers the Plowman'. In the poem, 'In a somer seson whan soft was the sonne' – to be exact, 'On a May mornynge on Malverne hulles' – Langland rested on a broad bank by a bourne, and was lulled asleep by the sound of the water, and then saw in his dream, as if he had been looking downward to the plain and the Severn,

> A faire felde ful of folke . . .
> Of alle manner of men, the mene and the riche,
> Worching and wandryng as the worlde asketh.

## In Warwickshire

The county of Shakespeare, of Michael Drayton ('Since there's no help, come let us kiss and part', and *Poly-Olbion*), and of George Eliot. On a summer evening, when the Stratford theatre is performing *Romeo and Juliet*, there will be as many nightingales performing in their turn in thickets and on 'banks' of the surrounding country as anywhere in England. 'Bank' for a small hillside or slope (as in the opening of *Twelfth Night*) is pure Warwickshire.

Pure Warwickshire also is the landscape of the novels of George Eliot, born 22 November, 1819, at Arbury Farm, in the parish of Chilvers Coton, outside Nuneaton, at the north end of the county. Her father was agent for the Newdegate family, whose gothicized house, Arbury Hall, is now opened in the summer. Drayton's village (where he was born in 1563) was Hartshill, a few miles away on the north-western side of Nuneaton. He was also a celebrant of Warwickshire nightingales, already writing against the 'lothsome ayres of smoky cittied towns'.

## In Staffordshire

Chartley Castle, near Weston on Trent. The place of a first fatal view, or interview. In this castle (of which only scraps are left) Queen Elizabeth was entertained by Walter Devereux, Earl of Essex, in July 1575, on one of her progresses. Philip Sidney, aged twenty-one, was in her train, and here he met Lady Penelope Devereux, a child still, though a beautiful and lively one with golden hair and black eyes. She was the Stella of his poems, and six years later, when she was eighteen, she was married against her inclination to Lord Rich –

> Ring out your bells, let mourning shows be spread;
> For Love is dead:
>   All Love is dead, infected
> With plague of deep disdain:
>   Worth, as nought worth, rejected
> And Faith fair scorn doth gain.
>
>   From so ungrateful fancy,
>   From such a female franzy,
>   From them that use men thus,
>   Good Lord, deliver us!

So the Chartley meeting occasioned some of the best of love poems.

Beresford Dale, south of Buxton. On the Staffordshire side of the limestone dale (which is threaded by the Dove) Charles Cotton the poet lived a happy-go-lucky life in his 'harbour of delight', Beresford Hall (site marked by Cotton's re-erected beacon tower), in which he was born and in which he died in 1687. The Fishing House he built by the Dove in 1674, and in which he sat with Izaak Walton,

is still there. After a journey which left him

> Just the same sot I was e'er I removed,
> Nor by my travel, nor the Court improved,
> The same old fashioned Squire, no whit refined,
> And shall be wiser when the Devil's blind,

Cotton wrote:

> My river still through the same channel glides,
> Clear from the tumult, salt and dirt of tides,
> And my poor Fishing-house, my seat's best grace,
> Stands firm and faithful in the self-same place
> I left it four months since, and ten to one
> I go a fishing e'er two days are gone.

## *In Derbyshire*

Edlastone, south of Ashbourne. In Wootton Lodge Jean-Jacques
Rousseau, philosopher and grand expositor of man's feelings vis-à-
vis nature, lived in exile with Thérèse le Vasseur, in 1766 and 1767,
writing his *Confessions*, but in no state of mind to enjoy the felicities
of Dove Dale, a few miles to the north, and of the Peak. In the
National Gallery a portrait of one of his Derbyshire friends Sir
Brooke Boothby (by Wright of Derby) shows the baronet reclining
and communing with nature, and holding a book marked 'Rousseau', the great man having given him the manuscript of his
*Dialogues*, when he was in Derbyshire.

## In Essex

Epping Forest. Much loved by poets for its glades, its solitudes, its fine-textured pollarded hornbeams, for its far views of a London so very different to itself. At High Beech John Clare spent just over four years in a private asylum (1836–41), walking among the trees and the bracken, writing poems –

> Tie all my cares up in thy arms, O Sleep,
> And give my weary spirits peace and rest,

and catching glimpses of London –

> Thus London, like a shrub among the hills,
> Lies hid and lower than the bushes here.

Tennyson also came to live in a house (now destroyed) at High Beech in 1837, when he was twenty-eight. Here he lived until 1840, reading and writing poems among the glades, skating in a long blue

cloak on the pond where Clare admired the water-lilies, and observing

> ... in heaven the light of London flaring
> like a dreary dawn.

Since Tennyson knew the doctor who looked after Clare, the sane poet and the mad poet probably met.

William Morris was born on one side of the Forest at Waltham-stow, in 1834, and grew up on the other side at Woodford. He used to ride among the hornbeams in a toy suit of armour, and he peopled the chequered gloom of Epping Forest with medieval incident and adventure – for instance, in his poem 'Shameful Death', in which brave Lord Hugh was killed among the trees:

> He did not strike one blow,
> For the recreants came behind,

In a place where the hornbeams grow,
A path right hard to find,
For the hornbeam boughs swing so,
That the twilight makes it blind.

## In Suffolk

Suffolk guidebooks – and most books on East Anglia – are eloquent
about Gainsborough's Sudbury and Constable's East Bergholt
(where Constable was born in 1776, on 11 June, and where the
National Trust preserves his father's Flatford Mill). There are two
places such books say less about: these are Dunwich – if Dunwich,
where a whole town has been washed away since the Middle Ages,
can be named a place, instead of an absence – and Aldeburgh.

Dunwich. The crumbling cliff top, livened by snowdrops, then by
wild roses of particular charm, delighted the Suffolk poet Edward
Fitzgerald (1809–83), and also his friend Charles Keene (1823–91),
one of the few artists of Victorian England who never falsified his
vision. Keene made air-filled drawings and etchings of the loneliness of Dunwich. He liked to walk up and down the brown shingle
below the cliff, playing bagpipes at midnight to the North Sea.
Henry James was another devotee of Dunwich melancholy.

Aldeburgh. The two great melancholic poets of the North Sea are
Tennyson of Lincolnshire and George Crabbe of Suffolk, born in
1754 at Aldeburgh where he viewed the waters of the North Sea and
the sluggish Alde in all the forms which 'The calm and storm, the
day and moonlight make'. The Suffolk heathland, the low coasts,
wild sands, incoming tides, glistening mudbanks, and huge skies
were always active in Crabbe's imagination:

With ceaseless motion comes and goes the tide,
Flowing, it fills the channel vast and wide;
Then back to sea, with strong majestic sweep
It rolls, in ebb yet terrible and deep;
Here samphire-banks and salt-wort bound the flood;
There stakes and sea-weeds, withering on the mud;
And, higher up, a ridge of all things base,
Which some strong tide has roll'd upon the place.

## In Northamptonshire

Helpston, a village of grey cottages in Barnack stone, between

Peterborough and Stamford, on the edge of the fens. In one of these grey cottages (still to be seen) John Clare was born on 13 July, 1793, to a farm labourer and his wife –

> A silent man in life's affairs,
> A thinker from a boy,
> A peasant in his daily cares,
> A poet in his joy.

His body was brought back from Northampton Asylum in 1864, and buried in the churchyard: 'I wish to lye on the North side of the churchyard, about the middle of the ground, where the Morning and Evening sun can linger the longest on my Grave. I wish to have a rough unhewn stone, something in the form of a mile stone, so that the playing boys may not break it in their heedless pastimes, with nothing more on it than this Inscription "Here rest the hopes and ashes of John Clare." I desire that no date be inserted thereon, as I wish it to live or dye with my poems and other writings, which if they have merit with posterity, it will, and if they have not it is not worth preserving.'

Burghley House, outside Stamford. Through all the centuries this great Tudor mansion of the Marquesses of Exeter never bred a sensibility half so exquisite as Clare's in his cottage. In 1806 Clare, aged thirteen, walked from Helpston to Stamford, bought a copy of Thomson's *Seasons* for a shilling, and on the way home wrote down his first poem among the lime trees in Burghley Park.

## In Lincolnshire

Somersby, near Horncastle, east of Lincoln, in the wolds. Alfred Tennyson was born in the rectory on 6 August, 1809, fourth child

among eight sons and four daughters. Living here till 1837, Tennyson was delighted by the wolds, the springs, the sheepcotes, the woodland and wild snowdrops, and the North Sea not many miles away. On the day when he heard of Byron's death, when he was a boy of fourteen, he carved 'Byron is dead' in grief on a sandstone rock. The stream below the rectory 'haunted Tennyson through life', making him write the poem 'A Farewell', beginning:

> Flow down, cold rivulet, to sea,
>     Thy tribute wave deliver:
> No more by thee my steps shall be,
>     For ever and for ever.

He was describing Somersby, the rectory, the cold rivulet, when he wrote (in 'Ode to Memory') about

> . . . the woods that belt the gray hill-side,
> The seven elms, the poplars four
> That stand beside my father's door,
> . . . . . . . . . . . . . . the brook that loves
> To purl o'er matted cress and ribbed sand
> Or dimple in the dark of rushy coves
>                 . . . the livelong bleat
> Of the thick-fleeced sheep from wattled folds,
>     Upon the ridged wolds.

Mablethorpe, near Louth, north-east of Somersby. Like Crabbe in Suffolk, Tennyson in Lincolnshire was a North Sea poet, and Mablethorpe, fourteen miles from Somersby across the marshes, was the favourite wild shore of the young Tennysons. When the Tennysons gave up their home in 1837, Tennyson wrote of coming to Mablethorpe and finding of the 'fair strand and free' he had delighted in, only

> The drain-cut level of the marshy lea,
> Gray sand-banks, and pale sunsets, dreary wind,
>     Dim shores, dense rain, and heavy-clouded seas.

Nowadays Tennyson's Mablethorpe can be felt best at night, in the winter, out of season, when

>                 . . . the great waters break
> Whitening for half a league, and thin themselves
> Far over sands marbled with moon and cloud.

Horkstow, near Barton-upon-Humber. Scene of a most unlyrical proceeding which led to some of the noblest English country pictures.
At an isolated farmhouse in this parish, which runs between the
wolds and the dismal Humber, the painter George Stubbs spent
eighteen months in 1758 and 1759 dissecting horses, with only his
mistress for company. First he bled each horse to death, then rigged
it to a long iron bar, and cut away skin, flesh, etc., and made drawings, and cut down towards the skeleton, until what was left of the
horse became unendurable (though Stubbs was a farmer's son, and
used to decaying animals). From the drawings he engraved his
*Anatomy of the Horse*, and the knowledge he gained went into his great
equestrian pictures.

## In Yorkshire – the West Riding

Bolton Percy, south-east of Tadcaster. Here the gardens and meadows
of Nun Appleton Hall, on the banks of the Wharfe, provoked from
Andrew Marvell some of the most curious and intense of English
nature poetry – particularly in his long poem 'Upon Appleton
House, to My Lord Fairfax'. Marvell (who was born in the rectory
at Winestead, near Hull, in 1621) was tutor to the great Lord Fairfax's daughter Mary at Nun Appleton, where the flower gardens
went down to the Wharfe. See this neighbourhood in May or June –

> The tawny mowers enter next;
> Who seem like Israelites to be
> Walking on foot through a green sea.

Marvell celebrates the quails in the hay, the green woodpecker, the
kingfisher (a 'sapphire-winged mist'), and the salmon-fishermen of
the Wharfe who have 'shod their heads in their canoes' – i.e. hoisted
their coracles on to their shoulders.

After the ripe hay has been scythed and cleared, the aftermath

> . . . with moister colour dasht
> Seems as green silks but newly washt.

## In Yorkshire – the North Riding

Duncombe Park, near Helmsley. Hereabouts the hanging woods, the
river, and the ruins of Rievaulx Abbey in the depth of Rye Dale
helped to make John Sell Cotman one of the most original masters
of English landscape. He first came to this part of Yorkshire when
he was twenty-one, in the high summer of 1803, the protégé of a

family living a few miles to the south at Brandsby Hall. He came again in 1804 and 1805. Duncombe Park gave him the subject of a famous watercolour *The Drop Gate* (in the British Museum), and there is a record that with his hosts on 5 September, 1803, he enjoyed an autumn picnic on the Great Terrace in the Park, above Rievaulx, between the Greek temples, one of the most extraordinary prospect places of England. His name, affectionately abbreviated to 'Cottey' was carved – and is still visible – on a hornbeam at Brandsby Hall.

Rokeby, near Barnard Castle. On 30 July, 1805, Cotman left Brandsby for Rokeby Park between the Greta and the Tees, on the limestone edge of the North Riding. For six weeks he found himself in extra-ordinary communion with the woods, the rivers, and the limestone rocks which enclose them and over which they run, in this very peculiar part of England; and he evolved an autumn fullness in the most individual patterns, in watercolours now in the British Museum (*Greta Bridge, The Scotchman's Stone*), the Tate Gallery (*Distant View of Greta Bridge*), the Norwich Museum (*The Devil's Elbow, Rokeby*) and the National Gallery, Edinburgh (*The Meeting of the Tees and Greta*). Coleridge was another devotee of Rokeby and the meeting of the waters. So was Scott, who first stayed at Rokeby Park some years after Cotman's visit, and who peppered his long romance poem *Rokeby* with landscape descriptions generally as banal as Cotman's watercolours are fresh and strong.

## In Co. Durham

Raby Castle, between Barnard Castle and Bishop Auckland. When he was still a boy Christopher Smart left the pastoral landscape of Kent, in 1733, and came to live in Durham. He spent school holi-days at Raby Castle, on the edge of the limestone uplands of Tees-dale, and in his great poem, *A Song to David*, he remembered the Bird's Eye Primrose of the northern limestone (which would have been strange to him) growing by one of the innumerable little waterfalls of highly polished limestone:

> The grass the polyanthus cheques;
> And polish'd porphyry reflects,
> By the descending rill.

Staindrop, near Raby Castle. At the castle, Christopher Smart fell in love with Lady Anne Vane, daughter of his patron Lord Barnard.

The two children tried to elope. Years after (in his partly mad, partly lucid poem 'Jubilate Agno') he describes the moment he had never forgotten inside the celebrated church at Staindrop, when he looked at Anne Vane during the service:

> For I saw a blush in Staindrop Church, which was of God's own colouring.
> For it was the benevolence of a virgin shewn to me before the whole congregation.

## In Northumberland

Capheaton, north-east of Hexham, and north of Hadrian's Wall. Algernon Charles Swinburne as a child lived partly in the Victorian hothouse of the Undercliff in the Isle of Wight, among the myrtles, partly at Capheaton, among splendid trees, above a splendid lake, in a remarkable house, Capheaton Hall, between moorland and greener lowland. His family had ruled Capheaton since the thirteenth century.

Two most different spirits encounter each other at Capheaton. A few miles away, at Kirkhale, 'Capability' Brown was born in 1715. He planted the trees and made 'Sir Edward's Lake', when the feudal Swinburnes redesigned their house, their park, their village. Perhaps 'Capability' Brown in designing so many landscape gardens in England and contriving so many winding lakes had at the back of his mind the dark green stateliness of trees – sycamores especially – in Northumberland glades and along Northumberland burns, in contrast to the bare and brown Northumberland moors below the Cheviot. There are other lakes and gardens by him in Northumberland, especially the Rothley Lake (1776), below the wonderful moorland road from Hexham to Rothbury, a blue extent under crags in a bracken-brown place. Along the crags stretches a parapet of rough romantic fortification.

## In Argyllshire

Glenorchy. On 20 March, 1724, Duncan Bàn MacIntyre was born in a croft on a spur called Druimliaghart, near Loch Tulla, in the mountain theatre of Glenorchy. As Coleridge said of himself, this Gaelic poet of the eighteenth century was 'full of love and joy towards hills and rocks and steep waters' – which led him to write his *Coire a' Cheathaich*, or 'The Misty Corrie', a long rushing exclamatory poem about deer and fawns and white-bellied salmon, about fast water and moss and watercress and rowan and cloud-berries. It is said of him that as a young forester at the head of Glenorchy, or by the Corrie which was further east in the Forest of Mamlorn, he lay in bed on a wet day making poems, when the roof began to leak. He called out to his wife: 'Fair young Mary, go out and thatch the roof. The rain's coming in'. Duncan Bàn MacIntyre has an odd, more or less classical, monument on a hill at the Glen-orchy end of Loch Awe.

# The Law and the Countryside

## RIGHTS OF PASSAGE

There are many legal questions incident to your passage over the countryside. The metalled road you drive along is a public highway, available for the passage of all Her Majesty's subjects. Public foot-paths are also highways. You observe a signpost inviting you to such and such a place along a footpath, over private land. No doubt assails you about using such a path.

But here there is private land. A minatory notice tells you as much. Yet a path lies across it, with no signpost. Is it another public high-way? Footpaths are marked on the one-inch ordnance survey map you have in your pocket. But that is not proof. However – though it will not help you to a quick decision here and now on a walk – most county councils have by this time fulfilled the duty put upon them by the *National Parks and Access to the Countryside Act*, 1949, and have their maps which show all public ways in their area. These dispel doubts.

The Act, too, which created the National Parks Commission, en-joined the Commission – and gave it power – to improve public paths in the National Parks, and to link them by providing new paths, thus giving the public access, for open air recreation, to mountain, moor-land, heath or foreshore. These paths will also be on the county council maps. Some of them will depend on an 'access agreement' which the local planning authority has made with the landowner, or else upon an 'access order' obtained (when such agreement could not be reached) from the Minister of Housing and Local Government. Follow the path and enter upon such land without damaging wall, fence, gate, etc., and you will not be a trespasser. But a trespasser you will become if

you ignore the restrictions provided in the Act to safeguard the landowner: there is to be no driving of vehicles on the land, no lighting of
fires, no wilful damage. The path is for passage, on foot or on horse-
back; use it, or the land to which it gives access, unreasonably, and
you change from a licensed visitor into a trespasser.

## NO DRIVING ON NATIONAL PARK LAND

The right of access to the now vast extent of National Park land is for
'air and recreation' (the nearest of the parks to London is that stretch
of the Sussex and Hampshire downs designated in 1961 as one of the
'areas of outstanding natural beauty'). But the recreation does not
include organized games, or any despoiling of the land. Though driving is forbidden (as it is over the common land you can reach in your
car), there is an exception: that you may, without offending, park
your car on the common within fifteen yards of the road.

## TRESPASS

Across private land runs a stream, a spring, which would give us the
kettleful of water we want to boil for our open-air meal. May we
enter? The occupier can give a right of entry. Without his sanction an
entry is a trespass; and a trespass is a wrong for which the occupier
can sue for such damage as the trespass occasions. He can also order the
trespasser out and, if necessary, expel him by force. But the threat on
the notice board 'Trespassers Will Be Prosecuted' is a wooden lie; for
a trespass is not a crime. He that commits a crime is liable to prosecu-
tion and may have to pay a penalty, he that commits a civil wrong is
liable to be sued and may have to pay damages. A trespass becomes a
crime only when an offence attends upon it, when for instance the
unsanctioned entry is in search of game, or when there is malicious
damage to crops.

## FOXHUNTING AND TRESPASS

For good reasons trespass is justifiable. But the hunting of the fox is
not one of these good reasons. In Paul v. Summerhayes, 1878, the
suggestion was that to rid the land of these pillagers of poultry houses,
these scamps that kill for delight more than to satisfy hunger, is laud-
able and allowable. Disregarding his express prohibition hunters had
persisted in riding over a farmer's land, and the Lord Chief Justice
said: 'It was suggested that foxhunting as a sport can be carried on

over the land of a person and against his will. No such right exists. The
sport of foxhunting must be carried on in subordination to the ordinary
rights of property. Questions such as the present fortunately do not
often arise; because foxhunters only go upon the lands of those whose
consent is expressly, or may be assumed to be tacitly, given.'

## WHOSE MUSHROOMS ARE THEY?

The occupier notes, and his wrath kindles, that the trespasser has
gathered a goodly amount of mushrooms or blackberries or primroses.
These, the natural products of the soil, had no owner till the trespasser gathered them; the gathering made the trespasser the owner
(as the hare belongs to the hunter though he caught it on another's
land). The occupier cannot demand the mushrooms, nor can the
trespasser be prosecuted for stealing them: 'It is', said one judgment,
'no offence to take mushrooms, blackberries, or wild plants of any

kind, or to trespass to find them; and "Trespassers Will Be Prosecuted"
is a threat as empty as ever it was unless actual damage is maliciously
committed'. It would be otherwise if the trespasser pulled up a turnip,
one item of a cultivated crop; that would be stealing, and stealing
does not transfer ownership. An astute farmer, indeed, may spend a
little on mushroom-spawn and put up a notice 'Cultivated Mushrooms'; in which case even the mushrooms that grow of themselves
may come under the umbrella so that the taking would be theft.

And if your children, weary of sitting still, ignore a prohibition to
enter, are you, as the parents, liable for the trespass or for what added
wrong the children do? Not unless you have countenanced the wrong-
doing; in general no father or mother is, so far as legal liability goes,
answerable for a child's wrong-doing. A father could be answerable,

if he were culpably negligent in respect of the particular wrong-doing: thus, a father allowed his fifteen-year-old son to retain an air-gun after the smashing of a neighbour's window, and he was held liable for the son's injury to another boy's eye with the gun (Bebec v. Salus, 1916).

## WHO MAINTAINS THE FOOTPATHS?

The footpaths marked on the county maps are highways. More often than other highways they have been dedicated by the owners of the land, or are deemed to have been dedicated, subject to some reserved rights of the owner. Thus for the better managing of his farm he requires stiles and gates or needs to plough periodically. At times, the path is not, therefore, propitious to progress. Here, for example, is a decrepit stile and here a gate tottering to its fall. They prompt your comment and question: who should repair these? Probably the parish council, which has power to spend on the maintenance of public footpaths, though for his own sake it is the occupier who usually does the repairs. If a path is dedicated subject to the continuance of impediments upon it, the public in accepting it accept also the liability of gates and stiles to wear and decay.

## PROTECTING THE PATHS

A farmer may wish, when as he often does, he sees town people (or country people, who are often just as bad in offence) careless of his crops, careless of closing gates, careless in leaving litter, that his predecessor far back had been less complacent and had not allowed the path across the fields to become a public path. But he may not now impede its use. He has a right to maintain the existing stiles and 'squeeze-bellies' and the swing-gates – the 'kissing-gates' – across it; the district council, however, has the duty of seeing that this use of a footpath by the public is not hindered by the erection of stiles or gates a good deal less convenient than in the past. The farmer's ploughing over the path, when he does retain the right to do so, is to be only a transitory obstacle to progress. Indeed, the *National Parks and Access to the Countryside Act* makes it an offence penalized by a fine for an occupier to plough agricultural land crossed by a public path without giving at least seven days' notice to the highway authority, or for failing to make good the surface after ploughing.

## BEWARE OF THE BULL

Nor may the occupier discourage use by a 'Beware of the Bull' notice or its like. As for the bull, in fact, most county councils have their bye-laws to protect the users of the paths. To the common law the bull is a gentle creature not to be reft of freedom till he has shown himself to be savage. A timid pedestrian does not agree with the common law and approves of the bye-law curtailing the bull's freedom where the public path lies. The type is this: 'No person, being the occupier of any field or enclosure through which there is a public path, may permit any bull exceeding the age of twelve months to be at large.' He must be tethered. Some counties add: 'This Bye-Law shall not apply to any bull which is at large in any field or enclosure in which cows or heifers are also at large.' It is to be assumed that female society and discipline are bars to truculence, so that the walker passes unscathed.

## THE GRASS VERGE

You reach a still subsisting stretch of Roman road grass-covered, or a green lane which tempts exploration, or you come to a length of ordinary road with wide grass verges. The 'green road', the 'green lane', is still a public highway, the wide grass verges are still part of a highway. There is nothing – in the law – to prevent your leisurely way along them if you are tired of metalled surfaces. But you will not use this supplementary highway for purposes alien from passage; you will not camp or light fires upon them. Using a highway unreasonably turns you from a licensed user into a trespasser, as it did one unlucky Newmarket tipster, who had walked to and fro over about fifteen yards of the highway for over an hour to watch and take notes of race-horse trials on the plaintiff's land adjoining the highway (Hickman v. Maisey, 1900, Queen's Bench).

## ABOUT TAKING PHOTOGRAPHS

I am on the highway; must I get permission to take photographs of that lovely Palladian mansion?

You will need to get permission if, to get a good picture, you wish to enter on private land. However, you are free to photograph from the highway just as you are free to photograph the landscape of which the house, or the other building you want a memento of, forms a part.

And does that freedom also apply to my taking, without his

knowledge, a photograph of that country worker or that red-faced retired general who owns the Palladian mansion?

It does. English law does not recognize a right to privacy. 'No one', one judgment ran, 'possesses a right of preventing another person from photographing him; any more than he has a right of preventing another from giving a description of him.'

## ON THE SEASHORE

You reach the sea; and the foreshore, the beach which is covered and then left dry by the tide, invites you. May you go upon it? So far as the Crown has not assigned stretches to another owner or is not using it for Crown purposes, the beach is yours for 'air and recreation': you

are also probably welcome upon it when part has been assigned to a seaside resort. Restrictions upon you there are while enjoying the beach. In particular you are not entitled to appropriate such goods as the waves deposit on the beach; those beachcombers you see prowling are most likely in search of what belongs to another. For the Crown will have granted to someone the royal privilege which is called a 'franchise of wreck'. He it is that, when a ship becomes a wreck cast within the limits of his franchise, can appropriate it, and the goods it carried. He must, however, give the owner of the ship or goods a year and a day in which to establish claim to them. An old statute, probably adopting the customary law, says that a vessel must not be adjudged a wreck when there survives upon it a man or a dog or a cat.

The goods from the wreck are such as have floated away ('flotsam'), or have been thrown overboard to lighten the ship ('jetsam'), or have been thrown overboard and marked by a buoy or cork ('ligan'). The owner of the franchise may sue one that seizes goods before he himself can take them. In Bailiffs of Dunwich v. Sterry, the plaintiffs had the franchise of wreck at Dunwich. The defendant took a cask of whisky from a wreck before the plaintiffs could get it; and the Court said that the defendant was liable for trespass to goods, because 'the right to the possession draws after it a constructive possession, which is sufficient to support the action'.

Other restrictions, too, in most seaside resorts where the local authority owns the foreshore, exist upon your freedom to behave as you would. There will be bye-laws imposing rules conducive to the enjoyment of visitors, conducive also to the profit of the owning authority – regulations about dress, about pitching tents, about itinerant vending of ice-creams, and the like. This bye-law, for instance, tells you to hire a deck chair and prohibits your own. You go upon the shore under your implied promise to have due regard to the regulations.

## THE LAW ABOUT BIRDS (see pages 202–5).

## A LITTLE ABOUT FISHING RIGHTS

We know that the angler over there with his rod cannot fish wherever he likes. Long ago the owners of land over which a river runs established their right to take the fish, even to take the salmon or sea-trout on its way up from the sea. The riparian owner, that is, may exclude others from fishing, or, for a consideration, may assign his right.

Anyone who wishes, however, may fish in the sea or in the river *so far as sea-water comes with the inflowing tide*. Even long usage, usage 'whereof the memory of man runneth not to the contrary', cannot elsewhere than in tidal waters give rise to a public right of fishing.

When, therefore, a public right is asserted the question to be answered is, 'Does the tide reach the contested spot?' And it seems that we must taste the water for our answer. In Reece v. Miller (Queen's Bench, 1882) public fishing in the Wye was in debate. When the eagre or bore rushes up the Severn it acts as a dam to the Wye:

> There twice a day the Severn fills;
> The salt sea-water passes by,
> And hushes half the babbling Wye,
> And makes a silence in the hills.

The pressure, that is, of sea-water forces even the fresh water to rise with the tides, but the place where the public claimed a right to fish was not one of tidal water; for sea-water did not reach it.

## YOUR STAY AT THE INN

When journeying over the countryside, you look for temporary lodging at an inn. You expect comfort and convenience there, board and lodging at a reasonable price. The law requires, in addition, that the innkeeper shall be answerable for the safety of his guests and of their goods. It does not constrain the innkeeper beyond reason. If there is no room in the inn, you must seek a place of rest elsewhere; and he is not obliged to entertain an obviously undesirable guest. If he does exclude, though, he has the heavy burden of satisfying the Court that he could not be expected to receive such a guest. His reason for exclusion must be much more than whim or caprice. By exhibiting a conspicuous notice, he is allowed to limit his liability in respect of your goods. But there must be no repetition of Falstaff's experience, 'Shall I not take mine ease in mine inn but I shall have my pocket picked?', and his obligation remains an exacting one. One House of Lords judgment put it this way: 'It signifies not that the goods are stolen by burglars, or by the servants of the inn, or by another guest. He is liable for not keeping them safely unless they are lost by the fault of the traveller himself. That is a tremendous liability. It is a liability fixed upon the innkeeper by the fact that he has taken the goods in.'

The liability is illustrated by the case of Gee v. Friary Hotel, decided by the Court of Appeal in 1950. The traveller, intending to stay the night, parked his car on the forecourt of the hotel; he locked the car and took away the ignition key, but while he was dining a thief stole the car. Was the innkeeper liable? 'Yes,' the three members of the Court agreed, 'the defendants have not discharged the onus that lies on them of showing that the loss of the car was due to the failure of the guest to take that degree of care of it which would be shown by an ordinary prudent car owner.'

## THOSE COWS ON THE ROAD

You are crossing the moor, the road is unfenced, which is another hazard calling for the motorist's vigilance. You may expect to meet cattle astray on the road – real cattle, cows or sheep or pigs or fowls – in addition to the irresponsible driver you now and again vituperate. Driving though you are with added care, you cannot always avoid accident owing to the unwelcome meeting. All the same you are unable to hold the owner of the cattle, sheep, pigs, fowls, etc., liable for accident or damage. And you still could not hold him liable if you had been driving down a road with high field hedges or wire fences. The House of Lords has ruled that it would be harsh to impose upon cattle owners in rural areas an obligation to maintain effective fences along the highway so as to prevent the strayings.

'Mutual respect and forbearance', said one Law Lord, 'are called for; the motorist must put up with the farmer's cattle; the farmer must endure the motorist.' The strange result emerges that to leave an inanimate object so that it obstructs the highway and causes an accident, may entail liability; but no liability arises for letting an animal, a sow for instance, stray and go to sleep on the highway, thereby causing an accident.

This rule of no liability applies to animals at large: it does not apply when the animal has been brought upon or is being driven along the highway, for then there arises a legal duty to control the animal. The driver or his employer may be judged negligent in fulfilling that duty and be obliged to compensate an injured motorist.

Motor traffic has in fact raised a problem that could not have troubled our forefathers. Driving a horse and cart, they could avoid collision with a straying cow; the motorist at forty miles an hour will have difficulty in dodging. The Committee on the Law of Civil Liability for Damage done by Animals, reporting in 1953, recommended that liability should depend on negligence; and that an occupier should be under a duty to take reasonable care that cattle and poultry do not escape on to the highway, other than parts of the highway passing over common, waste, or unenclosed ground. But the motorist must still await legislation that will give him some little comfort.

# Necessary Maps and Guides and Identification Books

We have the best and most variously informative of all maps, the Ordnance Survey maps (called by that name because the mapping of Britain, when it was first planned for military purposes at the end of the eighteenth century, was made the duty of the Board of Ordnance). For walking and taking to footpaths the best of these are the familiar maps of 1 inch to the mile, and the less familiar maps of $2\frac{1}{2}$ inches to the mile (which show field boundaries). The $2\frac{1}{2}$-inch is really to be preferred, since the larger scale gives more room for the exact pinpointing of some object or some antiquity. For the closer detail of your own neighbourhood or holiday surroundings, the maps to use – but these are not always to be bought from a local stationer – are the sheets on the scale of 6 inches to the mile, each covering one quarter of every $2\frac{1}{2}$-inch sheet. Or you can buy your whereabouts on the scale of 25 inches to the mile.

For exploring extensively by car, away from the main roads, the choice is between the 1-inch sheets of the Ordnance Survey, and the blue-covered sheets (rather easier to use) of Bartholomew's $\frac{1}{2}$-inch maps.

If you really want to know your neighbourhood in time as well as space, then the thing is to acquire older maps for comparison, and for clues to all manner of objects – cottages, mills, farmhouses, kilns, etc., etc. – which have disappeared. Old issues of the 1-inch Ordnance maps are frequently to be found in second-hand bookshops (or there may have been a fairly large-scale, eighteenth-century, pre-Ordnance map of your county, with rather more accurate and liberal detail than you can expect from the still older county maps of the Elizabethan period.

For many counties the drawings made by the first Ordnance surveyors still exist, a few of them on a larger scale than 1 inch to the mile. Most of these originals include detail which was left out when the first Ordnance Survey maps were engraved and printed. The Map Room at the British Museum supplies photostats from these drawings inexpensively.

That does not exhaust the maps of the Ordnance Survey. The surveyors have made a number of special 'time machines' for travel back into the lost centuries – inexpensive maps of Roman Britain, Britain in the Dark Ages, Monastic Britain, and Ancient Britain – as well as publishing a pamphlet, *Field Archaeology*, which is a guide to the kinds of monument, prehistoric, Roman, post-Roman, medieval and more recent, to be encountered from one end of Britain to the other.

If you are going to explore the counties, the necessary guides, county by county, are the old red-covered Murray's *Handbooks for Travellers*, out of date, especially when it comes to explaining something prehistoric, but never surpassed for variousness of information; also the *Little Guides*, some new and revised, some good, some atrocious, many out of print, though few of these are hard to find.

*Murray* and the *Little Guides* need supplementing by the *Buildings of England*, the county architectural guides by Nikolaus Pevsner, coming out one by one, wonderful books, and the first to measure English houses, churches, ruins, monuments, by a sophisticated European standard. The old large Kelly's *County Directories*, no longer published, are always worth acquiring.

The Stationery Office publishes guides of many kinds and remarkable quality, which are seldom to be found or examined in bookshops – Ministry of Works guides, individual and regional, to the ancient monuments looked after by the state, guides to the National Parks, and guides to the greater forests – 'National Forest Parks' – controlled by the Forestry Commission.

There are a number of entertaining *Shell Guides* to counties; also one to Mid Wales (excellent), and one to the West Coast of Scotland.

Wales and Scotland each have a modern *Blue Guide*. Nicholas Thomas' *Guide to Prehistoric England* (1960) guides the reader, county by county, to all the major visible antiquities.

## IDENTIFICATION BOOKS

For quick reference (though many of them have been mentioned), here is a list of books for identifying living things. Not all of them are in print:

*A Beast Book for the Pocket* by E. Sandars, Oxford University Press, 1937.

*List of British Mammals* by T. C. S. Morrison-Scott, British Museum (Natural History), 1952.

*British Animal Tracks* by J. S. R. Chard, Pearson, 1936.

*British Bats* by Brian Vesey-Fitzgerald, Methuen, 1949.

*Field Guide to British Deer* by F. J. Taylor Page, Mammal Society of the British Isles, 1959.

*British Reptiles and Amphibia* by Malcolm Smith, Penguin, 1949. (A King Penguin: very good colour plates.)

*The British Amphibians and Reptiles* by Malcolm Smith, Collins, 1951.

*Guide for the Identification and Reporting of Stranded Whales, Dolphins, Porpoises and Turtles on the British Coasts* by F. C. Fraser and H. W. Parker, British Museum (Natural History), 1953.

*Giant Fishes, Whales and Dolphins* by J. R. Norman and F. C. Fraser, Putnam, 1948.

*Fishes of the British Isles* by J. T. Jenkins, Warne, 1936.

*The Pocket Guide to the Sea Shore* by J. Barrett and C. M. Yonge, Collins, 1958.

*Shell Life* by Edward Step, Warne, 1927.

*British Snails* by A. E. Ellis, Oxford University Press, 1926.

*A Field Guide to the Birds of Britain and Europe* by R. Peterson, G. Mountfort and P. A. D. Hollom, Collins, 1958.

*A Practical Handbook of British Beetles* by N. H. Joy, Witherby, 1932.

*Flies of the British Isles* by C. N. Colyer and C. O. Hammond, Warne, 1951.

*British Ants* by H. Donisthorpe, Routledge, 1927.

*The Dragonflies of the British Isles* by C. E. Longfield, Warne, 1949.

*The British Mosquitoes* by J. F. Marshall, British Museum (Natural History), 1938.

*British Blood-sucking Flies* by F. W. Edwards, H. Oldroyd and J. Smart, Oxford University Press, 1939.

*The Spiders and Allied Orders of the British Isles* by T. H. Savory, Warne, 1945.

*A Butterfly Book for the Pocket* by E. Sandars, Oxford University Press, 1939.

*The Caterpillars of the British Butterflies* by W. J. Stokoe and G. H. T. Stovin, Warne, 1944.

*The Moths of the British Isles* by R. South, 1961.

*The Caterpillars of British Moths* by W. J. Stokoe, Warne, 1949.

*The Pocket Guide to Wild Flowers* by D. McClintock and R. S. R. Fitter, Collins, 1956.

*Identification of Trees and Shrubs* by F. K. Makins, Dent, 1948.

*Welsh Ferns* by H. A. Hyde and A. E. Wade, National Museum of Wales, 1954.

*Common British Fungi* by E. M. Wakefield and R. W. G. Dennis, Gawthorn, 1950.

*The Observer's Book of Common Fungi* by E. M. Wakefield, Warne, 1954.

*Edible Fungi* by J. Ramsbottom, Penguin, 1948.

*Poisonous Fungi* by J. Ramsbottom, Penguin, 1945.

(These two are King Penguin books, with good colour plates.)

# KEY

*to the Colour Plates*

*Plate 1*

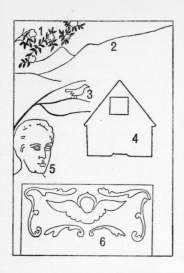

1 Dog Roses
2 Skirrid Fawr
3 Redstart
4 Seventeenth-century Welsh inscription on the porch of an old manor-house in Monmouthshire
5 Walter Savage Landor
6 Eighteenth-century coloured tombstone at Llanvetherine

*Plate 2*

White Horse, cut on a Wiltshire hillside

# KEY TO THE COLOUR PLATES

*Plate 3*

1   Open fields at Laxton
2   Oaks
3   Norman font from Holy Trinity church, Lenton
4   The Flawford Madonna, in alabaster
5   Green Man from the early fourteenth-century Chapter House of Southwell Minster

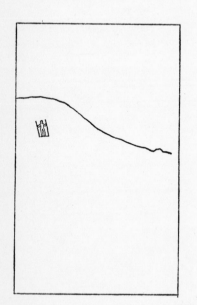

*Plate 4*

The Long Man of Wilmington

### Plate 5

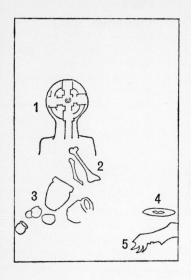

1 The Great Cross of Conbeline, a carved wheel cross (eighth–twelfth centuries)
2 Old Stone Age human bones
3 Urns and cups from Bronze Age barrows
4 Cakes of laver and oatmeal
5 Laver seaweed

### Plate 6

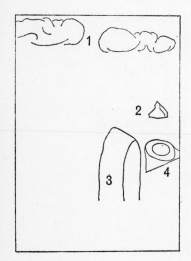

1 Cumulus clouds
2 Mwnt church, Cardiganshire
3 The Corbelanus Stone, a standing stone of the Dark Ages
4 Limekiln

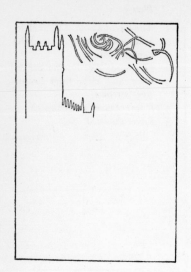

*Plate 7*

Vapour trails

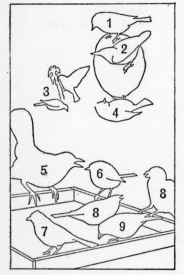

*Plate 8*

1  Coal Tit
2  Nuthatch
3  Wood Pigeons
4  Blue Tit
5  Blackbird
6  Robin
7  Cock Chaffinch
8  House Sparrows
9  Hedge Sparrow

344

*Plate 9*

1  Curlew
2  Swallow
3  Whimbrel

*Plate 10*

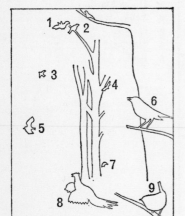

1  Long-eared Bat
2  Wood Pigeons
3  Skylark
4  Pipistrelle
5  Lapwing
6  Nightingale
7  Natterer's Bat
8  Cock Pheasant
9  Wren

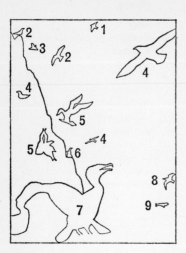

*Plate 11*

1 Peregrine
2 Great Blacked-backed Gulls
3 Raven
4 Fulmars
5 Gannets
6 Guillemots
7 Cormorants
8 Kittiwake
9 Grey Seal

*Plate 12*

1 House Martin
2 Yellow Wagtail
3 Cuckoo
4 Shelducks
5 Ruff

### Plate 13

1 Swift
2 Kestrel (or Windhover or Standgale)
3 Buzzard
4 Skylark
5 House Martins
6 Mounting Cumulus clouds
7 Vapour trail
8 Swallow
9 Long-eared Bat
10 Greater Horseshoe Bat
11 Rose-bay Willow-herb seeds
12 Dandelion seeds

### Plate 14
Turtle Dove

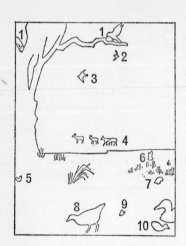

*Plate 15*

1  Jackdaws
2  Swifts
3  Hobby
4  Fallow Deer
5  Painted Lady butterfly
6  Whiskered Bat
7  Daubenton's Bat
8  Moorhens
9  Large White butterfly
10 Mallard duck and duckling

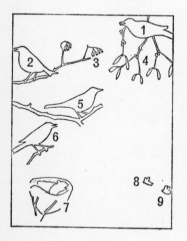

*Plate 16*

1  Missel-thrush (or Storm-cock)
2  Song-thrush
3  Haws
4  Mistletoe
5  Fieldfare
6  Redwing
7  Long-tailed Field Mouse
8  Chaffinch
9  Yellowhammer

*Plate 17*

1   Cock Nightjar
2   Badger and cubs

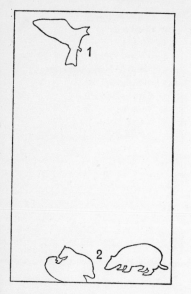

*Plate 18*

1   Yellowhammer
2   Sparrow-hawk
3   Greenfinch
4   House Sparrow
5   Stoat

349

*Plate 19*

Grey Squirrel

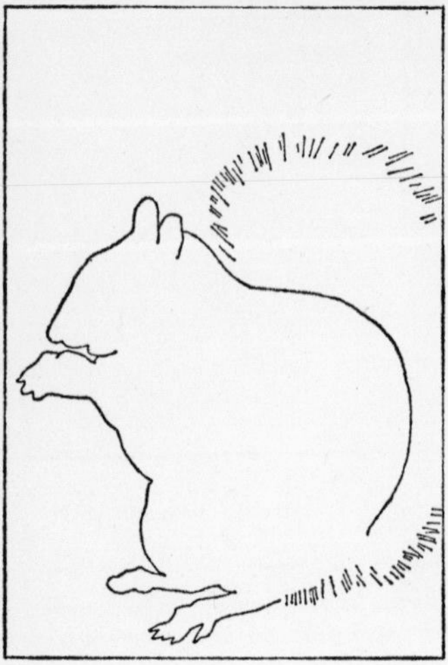

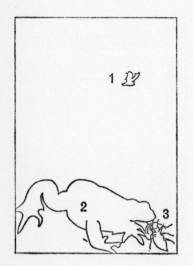

*Plate 20*

1  Lesser Horseshoe Bat
2  Common Toad
3  Violet Ground-beetle

### Plate 21

1 Scotch Firs
2 Buzzard
3 Spruces
4 Red Deer
5 Roe Deer

### Plate 22

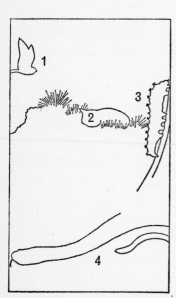

1 Short-eared Owl
2 Wild Cat
3 Emperor Moth caterpillar
4 Adder and young

*Plate 23*

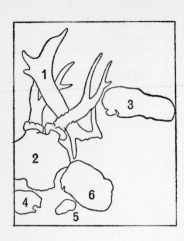

1  Fallow Deer
2  Roe Deer
3  Fox
4  Hedgehog
5  Mole
6  Badger

*Plate 24*

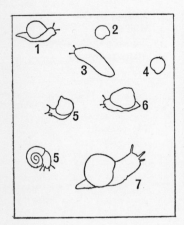

1  Garden Snail
2  Kentish Snail
3  Black Slug
4  Heath Snail
5  Grove Snails
6  Common Snail
7  Roman Snail

### Plate 25

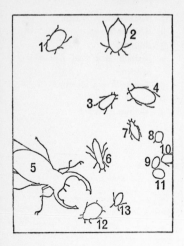

| | |
|---|---|
| 1 | Dumble-dor |
| 2 | Cockchafer |
| 3 | Red-headed Cardinal |
| 4 | Rose Chafer |
| 5 | Stag Beetle |
| 6 | Devil's Coach-horse |
| 7 | Wasp Beetle |
| 8 | Seven-spot Ladybird |
| 9 | Twenty-two-spot Ladybird |
| 10 | Two-spot Ladybird |
| 11 | Fourteen-spot Ladybird |
| 12 | Corn Chrysoline |
| 13 | Green Tiger |

### Plate 26

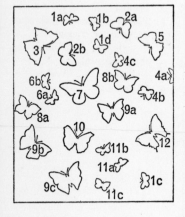

1 Common Blue (1*a*, male, upper side; 1*b*, male, under side; 1*c*, female, upper side; 1*d*, female, under side)

2 Marbled White (2*a*, male; 2*b*, female)

3 Camberwell Beauty

4 Chalk-hill Blue (4*a*, male, upper side; 4*b*, male, under side; 4*c*, female)

5 Red Admiral

6 Green Hairstreak (6*a*, upper side; 6*b*, under side)

7 Monarch

8 Brimstone (8*a*, male; 8*b*, female)

9 Purple Emperor (9*a*, male; 9*b*, female, upper side; 9*c*, female, under side)

10 Peacock

11 Adonis Blue (11*a*, male, upper side; 11*b*, male, under side; 11*c*, female, under side)

12 Swallow-tail

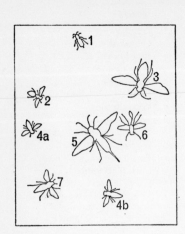

*Plate 27*

1   Ruby-tailed Wasp
2   Digger Wasp
3   Hornet
4   British Bee (4a, worker; 4b, queen)
5   Great Wood Horntail
6   Sand Wasp
7   Common Wasp

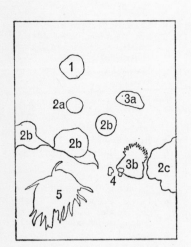

*Plate 28*

1   Beadlet
2   Plumose Anemones (2a, shut; 2b, open; 2c, colony)
3   Strawberry Anemones (3a, shut; 3b, open)
4   Devonshire Cup Coral
5   Opelet

354

*Plate 29*

1 Opelet
2 Plumose Anemone colony

*Plate 30*

1 Fritillaries
2 Woodrush
3 Greater Stitchwort
4 Primroses
5 Wood Anemones
6 Pasque Flowers

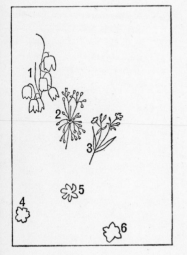

# KEY TO THE COLOUR PLATES

*Plate 31*

1. Blackthorn
2. Butcher's Broom
3. Ivy
4. Marsh Marigolds or Kingcups
5. Dandelions
6. Daisies
7. Ground Ivy
8. Lesser Periwinkles
9. Lesser Celandines
10. Butterbur

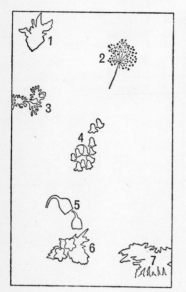

*Plate 32*

1. Green Alkanet
2. Cow Parsley
3. Ragged Robin
4. Bluebells
5. Water Avens
6. Heartsease
7. Ferns

*Plate 33*

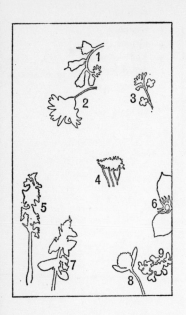

1  Comfrey
2  Ox-eye Daisy
3  Cuckoo Flowers
4  Woodruff
5  Early Purple Orchis
6  Herb Paris
7  Bugle
8  Red Clover
9  Birdsfoot Trefoil

*Plate 34*

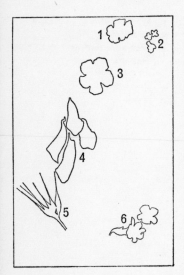

1  Dog Rose
2  Guelder Rose
3  Meadow Cranesbill or Loving
   Andrews
4  Foxgloves
5  Shepherd's Needle
6  Monkey Flowers

# KEY TO THE COLOUR PLATES

*Plate 35*

1 Gladdon
2 Orpine
3 Yellow Bartsia
4 Sea Asters

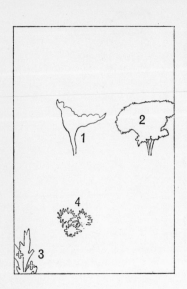

*Plate 36*

1 Harebells
2 Cross-leaved Heath
3 Meadow Saffron or Naked Nannies

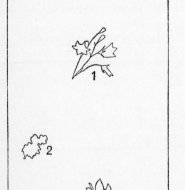

*Plate 37*

Old Man's Beard

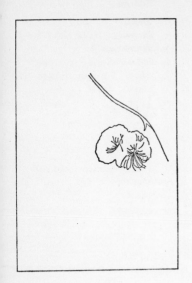

*Plate 38*

1  Wood Pigeons
2  Tree-creeper
3  Red Squirrel
4  Wren
5  Shaggy Cap mushroom
6  Bracket fungi
7  Dormouse
8  Hedgehog

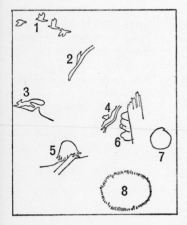

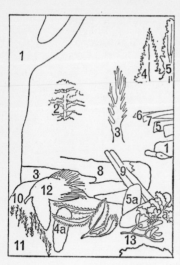

### Plate 39

1 Beech
2 Holly (2a, leaves and berries)
3 Hornbeam
4 Norway Spruce (4a, cone)
5 Silver Fir (5a, foliage and cones)
6 Lime
7 Scotch Fir
8 Oak
9 Larch
10 Sycamore
11 Juniper branches and cones
12 Maritime Pine cone and needles
13 Mistletoe

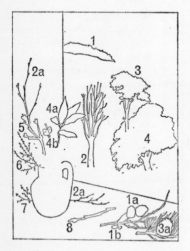

### Plate 40

1 Larch plantation (1a, cones and twigs; 1b, seeds)
2 Lime (2a, twigs)
3 Scotch Fir (3a, cones and needles)
4 Ilex (4a, leaves; 4b, acorns)
5 Oak buds
6 Blackthorn or Sloe twigs
7 Bullace twigs
8 Rowan or Mountain Ash buds

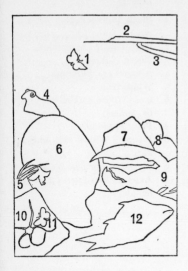

*Plate 41*

1 Lulworth Skipper
2 Isle of Portland
3 Chesil Bank
4 Dorset Horned Sheep
5 Gladdon
6 Ammonite
7 Blue Vinney Cheese
8 Dorset 'knobs'
9 Lobster
10 Fossil Starfish
11 Silver-Studded Blue
12 Fossil fish

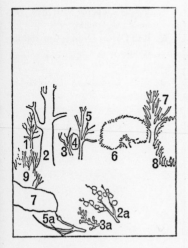

*Plate 42*

1 Cornish Elm
2 English Elm (2a, blossom)
3 Field Maple (3a, buds)
4 Irish Yew
5 Sycamore (5a, twigs)
6 Yew
7 Wych Elm
8 Box
9 Hazel

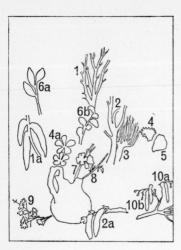

### Plate 43

1 Black Italian Poplar (1*a*, catkins)
2 Grey Poplar (2*a*, catkins)
3 Crack Willow
4 Almond (4*a*, blossom)
5 White Willow
6 Goat Willow catkins (6*a*, male; 6*b*, female)
7 Plum blossom
8 Weeping Willow twig and catkins
9 Blackthorn or Sloe blossom
10 Alder catkins (10*a*, male; 10*b*, female)

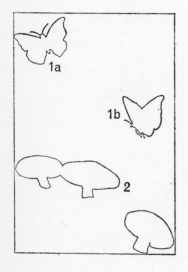

### Plate 44

1 Purple Emperor butterflies (1*a*, male; 1*b*, female)
2 Red Cap or Orange Cap mushroom

362

*Plate 45*

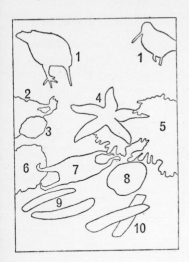

1  Oystercatchers
2  Sugar Laminaria seaweed
3  Whelk egg capsules
4  Common Starfish
5  Bladderwrack seaweed
6  Purple Laver seaweed
7  Skate egg capsules or 'Witches' Purses'
8  Heart Urchin or Sea Potato
9  Sword Razor shells
10 Pod Razor shells

*Plate 46*

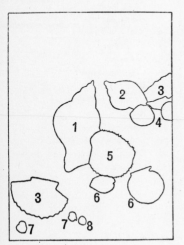

1  Wide-mouthed Whelk
2  Common Whelk or Buckie
3  Scallops
4  Limpets
5  Spiny Cockle
6  Queens
7  Cowries
8  Periwinkle

# KEY TO THE COLOUR PLATES

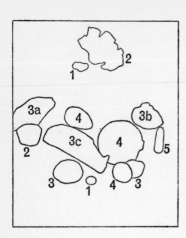

*Plate 47*

1 Ammonites transformed to Iron Pyrites
2 Corals
3 Sea-urchins (3*a*, Pound Stone; 3*b*, *Cidaris florigemma* or the 'flower-gemmed tiara of the Persian kings'; 3*c*, spines)
4 Ammonites
5 Belemnite

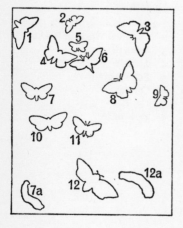

*Plate 48*

1 Goat Moth
2 Black Arches
3 Red Underwing
4 Emperor
5 Cinnabar
6 Elephant Hawk
7 Puss Moth (7*a*, caterpillar)
8 Clifden Nonpareil
9 Magpie
10 Garden Tiger
11 Cream-spot Tiger
12 Death's Head Hawk-moth (12*a*, caterpillar)

# Acknowledgements

The colour plates are details from a series of country pictures commissioned by Shell-Mex and B.P. Ltd.

Plates 39, 40, 42, 43 and the cover picture are by S. R. Badmin
Plate 5 is by John Elwyn
Plate 3 is by David Gentleman
Plates 2 and 6 are by Keith Grant
Plate 4 is by Rowland Hilder
Plates 30, 31, 32, 33, 34, 35, 36 and 37 are by Edith and Rowland Hilder
Plates 23, 24, 25, 26, 27, 28, 29, 46, 47 and 48 are by Tristram Hillier
Plate 1 is by Walter Hoyle
Plates 13, 44 and 45 are by John Leigh-Pemberton
Plate 41 is by John Nash
Plate 7 is by John O'Connor
Plate 21 is by Maurice Wilson
Plates 8, 9, 10, 11, 12, 14, 15, 16, 17, 18, 19, 20, 22 and 38 are by Maurice Wilson, in collaboration with Rowland Hilder

The drawings in the text and on the half-titles are by Frederick Huntley.

# Index

366

381